CASE CLOSED™

VOLUME

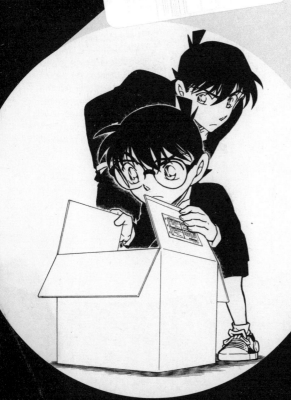

Gosho Aoyama

Case Briefing:

Subject:
Occupation:
Special Skills:
Equipment:

Jimmy Kudo, a.k.a. Conan Edogawa
High School Student/Detective
Analytical thinking and deductive reasoning, Soccer
Bow Tie Voice Transmitter, Super Sneakers,
Homing Glasses, Stretchy Suspenders

The subject is hot on the trail of a pair of suspicious men in black when he is attacked from behind and administered a strange substance which physically transforms him into a first grader. When the subject confides in the eccentric inventor Dr. Agasa, they decide to keep the subject's true identity a secret for the safety of everyone around him. Assuming the new identity of first-grader Conan Edogawa, the subject continues to assist the police force on their most baffling cases. The only problem is that most crime-solving professionals won't take a little kid's advice!

Table of Contents

CASE CLOSED

Volume 67
Shonen Sunday Edition

Story and Art by GOSHO AOYAMA

MEITANTEI CONAN Vol. 67
by Gosho AOYAMA
© 1994 Gosho AOYAMA
All rights reserved.
Original Japanese edition published by SHOGAKUKAN.
English translation rights in the United States of America, Canada,
the United Kingdom and Ireland arranged with SHOGAKUKAN.

Translation
Tetsuichiro Miyaki

Touch-up & Lettering
Freeman Wong

Cover & Graphic Design
Andrea Rice

Editor
Shaenon K. Garrity

Printed in the U.S.A.

Published by VIZ Media, LLC
P.O. Box 77010
San Francisco, CA 94107

10 9 8 7 6 5 4 3 2 1
First printing, July 2018

PARENTAL ADVISORY
CASE CLOSED is rated T+ for Older Teen
and is recommended for ages 16 and up.
This volume contains realistic and graphic
violence.
ratings.viz.com

viz.com

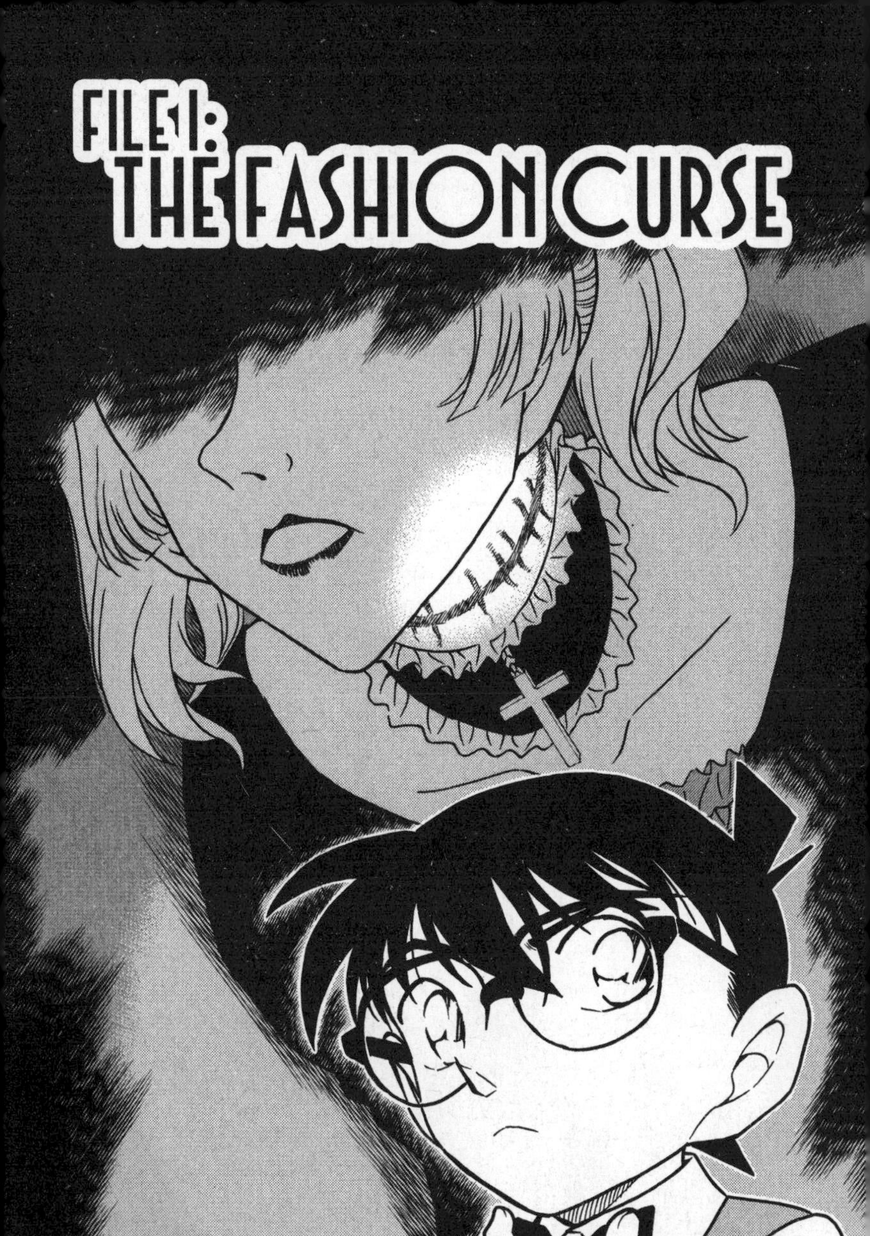
FILE 1:
THE FASHION CURSE

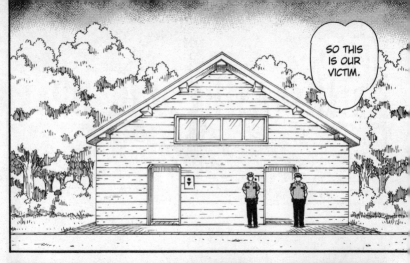

SO THIS IS OUR VICTIM.
QUITE A SIGHT.
IS THIS WHAT THE YOUNG FOLKS ARE WEARING THESE DAYS?
UM, IT'S CALLED GOTHIC LOLITA.
IT'S BEEN AROUND FOR A WHILE NOW.
SORRY THIS OLD MAN'S NOT UP ON FASHION.
HEH...
DO WE HAVE A NAME?
ACCORDING TO HER DRIVER'S LICENSE...

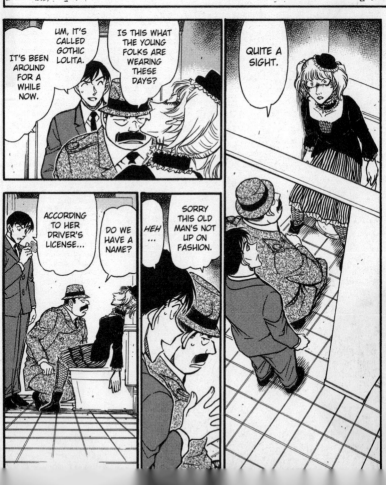

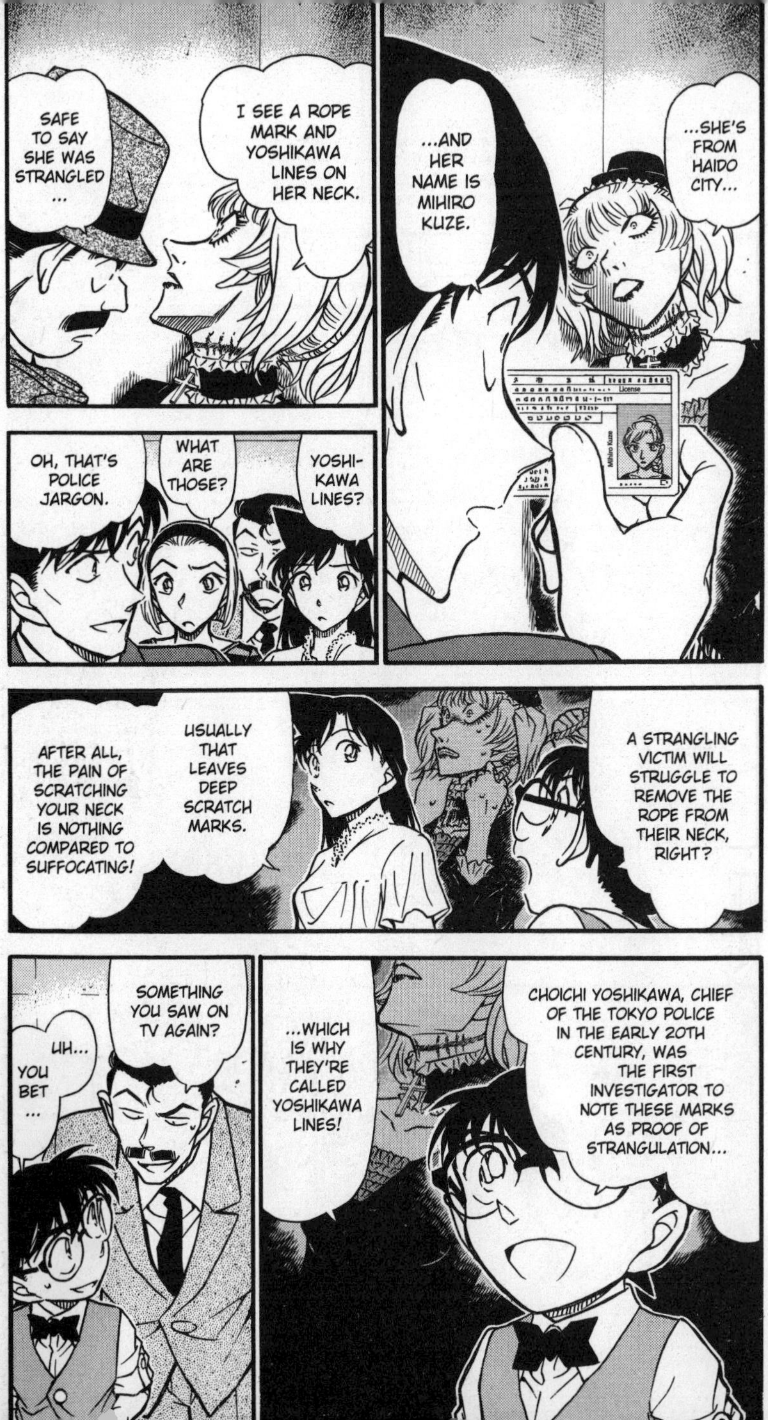
...SHE'S FROM HAIDO CITY...
...AND HER NAME IS MIHIRO KUZE.
License
Mihiro Kuze
I SEE A ROPE MARK AND YOSHIKAWA LINES ON HER NECK.
SAFE TO SAY SHE WAS STRANGLED ...
YOSHI-KAWA LINES?
WHAT ARE THOSE?
OH, THAT'S POLICE JARGON.
A STRANGLING VICTIM WILL STRUGGLE TO REMOVE THE ROPE FROM THEIR NECK, RIGHT?
USUALLY THAT LEAVES DEEP SCRATCH MARKS.
AFTER ALL, THE PAIN OF SCRATCHING YOUR NECK IS NOTHING COMPARED TO SUFFOCATING!
CHOICHI YOSHIKAWA, CHIEF OF THE TOKYO POLICE IN THE EARLY 20TH CENTURY, WAS THE FIRST INVESTIGATOR TO NOTE THESE MARKS AS PROOF OF STRANGULATION...
...WHICH IS WHY THEY'RE CALLED YOSHIKAWA LINES!
SOMETHING YOU SAW ON TV AGAIN?
UH... YOU BET ...

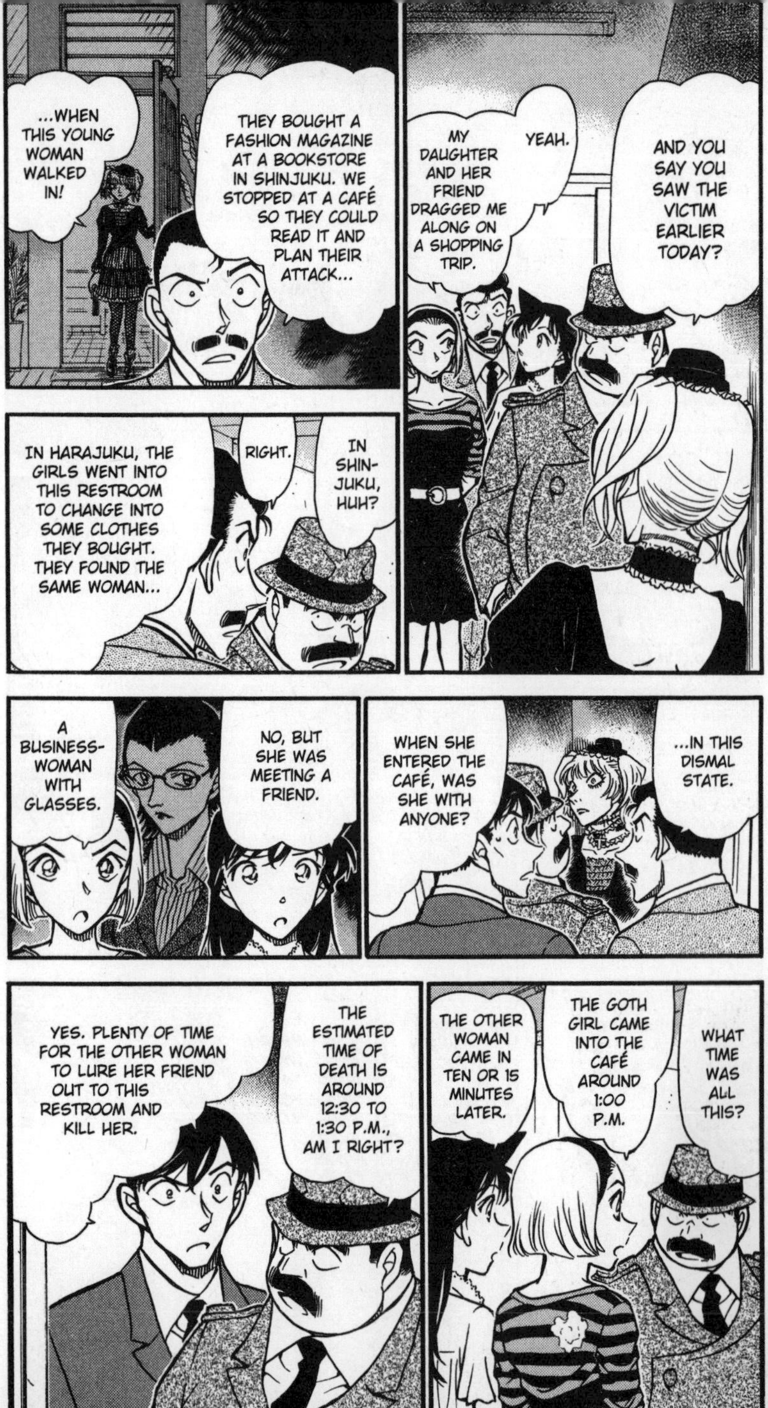
AND YOU SAY YOU SAW THE VICTIM EARLIER TODAY?
YEAH.
MY DAUGHTER AND HER FRIEND DRAGGED ME ALONG ON A SHOPPING TRIP.
THEY BOUGHT A FASHION MAGAZINE AT A BOOKSTORE IN SHINJUKU. WE STOPPED AT A CAFÉ SO THEY COULD READ IT AND PLAN THEIR ATTACK...
...WHEN THIS YOUNG WOMAN WALKED IN!
IN SHIN-JUKU, HUH?
RIGHT.
IN HARAJUKU, THE GIRLS WENT INTO THIS RESTROOM TO CHANGE INTO SOME CLOTHES THEY BOUGHT. THEY FOUND THE SAME WOMAN...
...IN THIS DISMAL STATE.
WHEN SHE ENTERED THE CAFÉ, WAS SHE WITH ANYONE?
NO, BUT SHE WAS MEETING A FRIEND.
A BUSINESS-WOMAN WITH GLASSES.
WHAT TIME WAS ALL THIS?
THE GOTH GIRL CAME INTO THE CAFÉ AROUND 1:00 P.M.
THE OTHER WOMAN CAME IN TEN OR 15 MINUTES LATER.
THE ESTIMATED TIME OF DEATH IS AROUND 12:30 TO 1:30 P.M., AM I RIGHT?
YES. PLENTY OF TIME FOR THE OTHER WOMAN TO LURE HER FRIEND OUT TO THIS RESTROOM AND KILL HER.

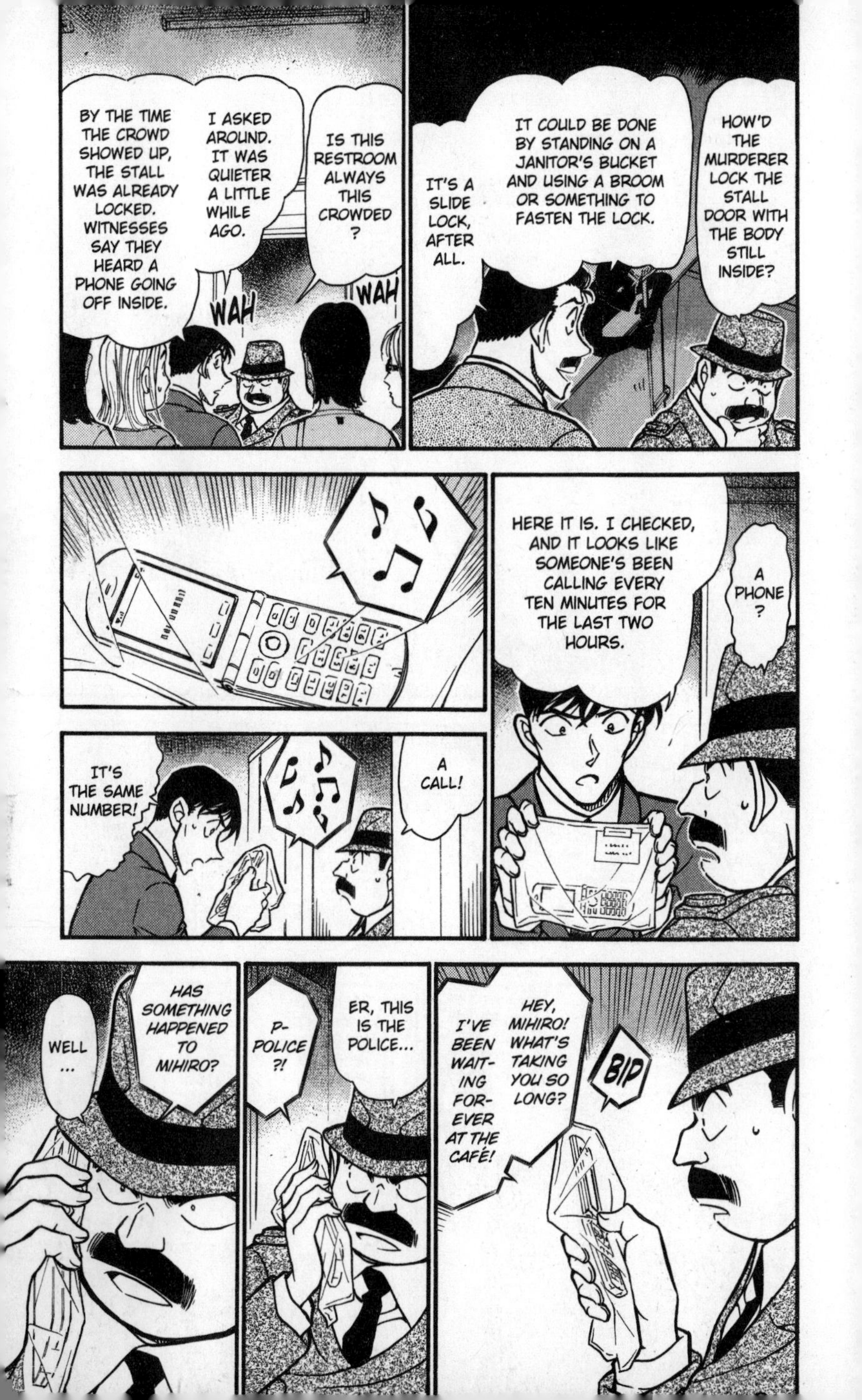
HOW'D THE MURDERER LOCK THE STALL DOOR WITH THE BODY STILL INSIDE?
IT COULD BE DONE BY STANDING ON A JANITOR'S BUCKET AND USING A BROOM OR SOMETHING TO FASTEN THE LOCK.
IT'S A SLIDE LOCK, AFTER ALL.
WAH
IS THIS RESTROOM ALWAYS THIS CROWDED?
I ASKED AROUND. IT WAS QUIETER A LITTLE WHILE AGO.
BY THE TIME THE CROWD SHOWED UP, THE STALL WAS ALREADY LOCKED. WITNESSES SAY THEY HEARD A PHONE GOING OFF INSIDE.
WAH
A PHONE?
HERE IT IS. I CHECKED, AND IT LOOKS LIKE SOMEONE'S BEEN CALLING EVERY TEN MINUTES FOR THE LAST TWO HOURS.
A CALL!
IT'S THE SAME NUMBER!
BIP
HEY, MIHIRO! WHAT'S TAKING YOU SO LONG?
I'VE BEEN WAIT-ING FOR-EVER AT THE CAFÉ!
ER, THIS IS THE POLICE...
P-POLICE?!
HAS SOMETHING HAPPENED TO MIHIRO?
WELL...

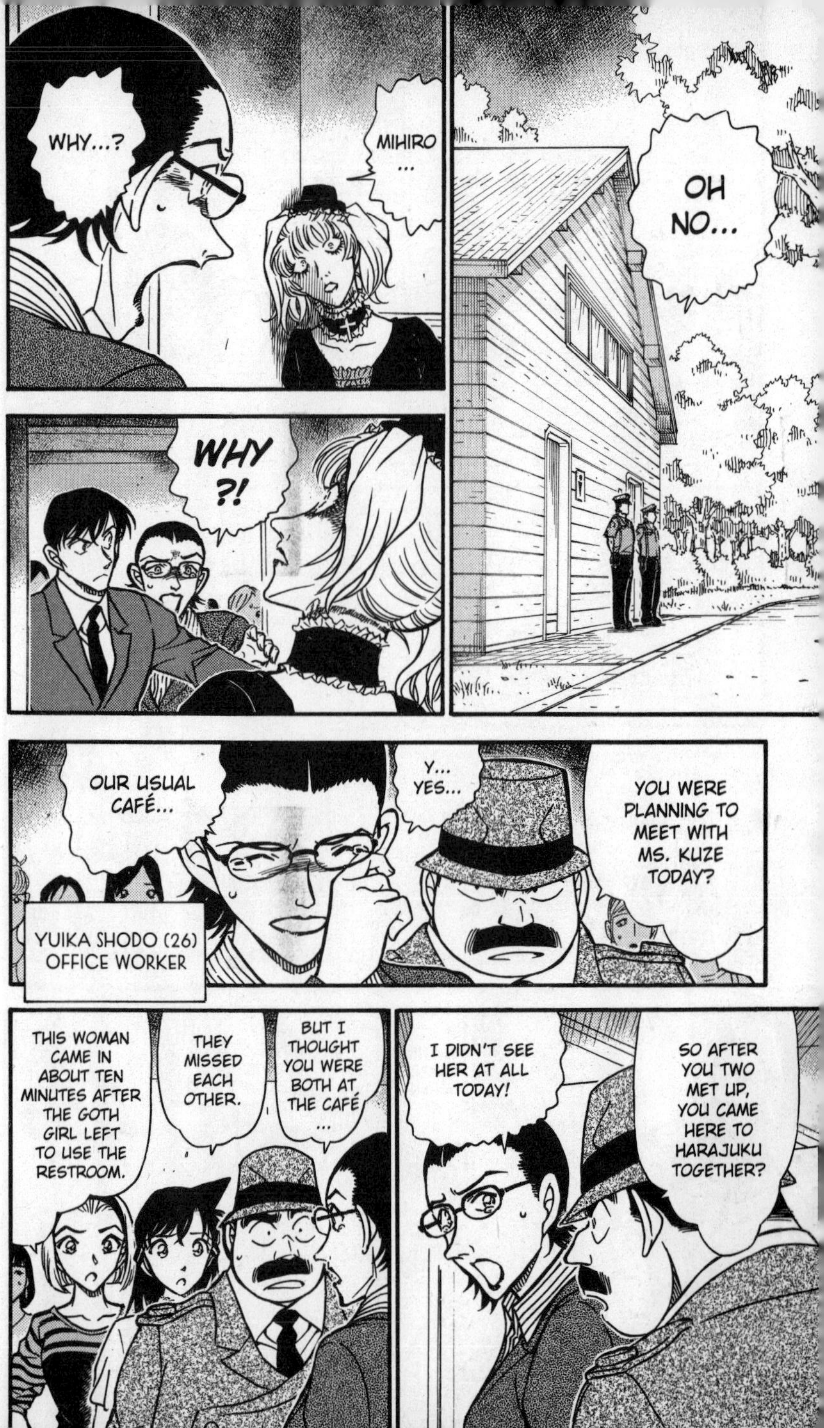
OH NO...
MIHIRO ...
WHY...?
WHY ?!
YOU WERE PLANNING TO MEET WITH MS. KUZE TODAY?
Y... YES...
OUR USUAL CAFÉ...
YUIKA SHODO (26) OFFICE WORKER
SO AFTER YOU TWO MET UP, YOU CAME HERE TO HARAJUKU TOGETHER?
I DIDN'T SEE HER AT ALL TODAY!
BUT I THOUGHT YOU WERE BOTH AT THE CAFÉ ...
THEY MISSED EACH OTHER.
THIS WOMAN CAME IN ABOUT TEN MINUTES AFTER THE GOTH GIRL LEFT TO USE THE RESTROOM.

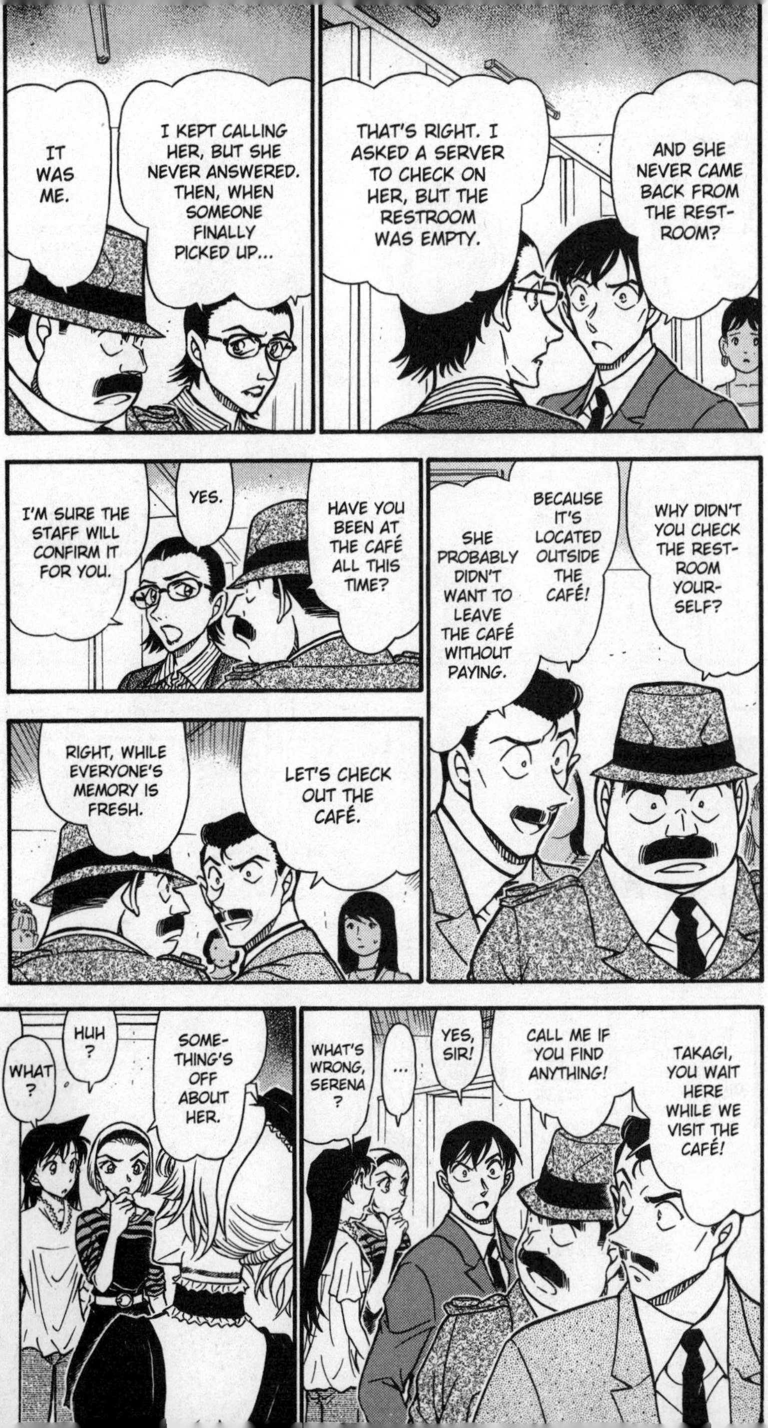
AND SHE NEVER CAME BACK FROM THE REST-ROOM?
THAT'S RIGHT. I ASKED A SERVER TO CHECK ON HER, BUT THE RESTROOM WAS EMPTY.
I KEPT CALLING HER, BUT SHE NEVER ANSWERED. THEN, WHEN SOMEONE FINALLY PICKED UP...
IT WAS ME.
WHY DIDN'T YOU CHECK THE REST-ROOM YOUR-SELF?
BECAUSE IT'S LOCATED OUTSIDE THE CAFÉ!
SHE PROBABLY DIDN'T WANT TO LEAVE THE CAFÉ WITHOUT PAYING.
HAVE YOU BEEN AT THE CAFÉ ALL THIS TIME?
YES.
I'M SURE THE STAFF WILL CONFIRM IT FOR YOU.
LET'S CHECK OUT THE CAFÉ.
RIGHT, WHILE EVERYONE'S MEMORY IS FRESH.
TAKAGI, YOU WAIT HERE WHILE WE VISIT THE CAFÉ!
CALL ME IF YOU FIND ANYTHING!
YES, SIR!
...
WHAT'S WRONG, SERENA?
SOME-THING'S OFF ABOUT HER.
HUH?
WHAT?

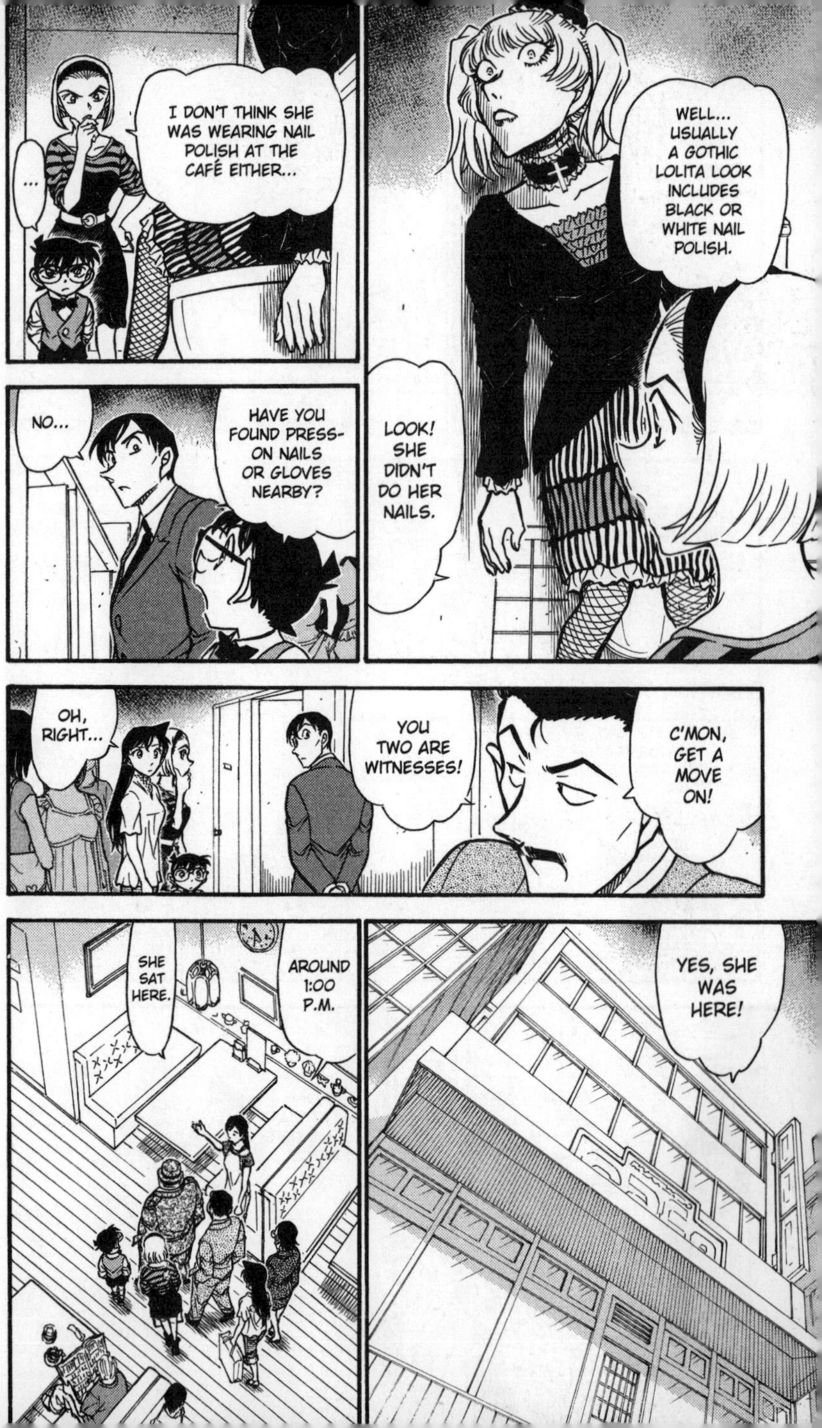
WELL... USUALLY A GOTHIC LOLITA LOOK INCLUDES BLACK OR WHITE NAIL POLISH.
LOOK! SHE DIDN'T DO HER NAILS.
I DON'T THINK SHE WAS WEARING NAIL POLISH AT THE CAFÉ EITHER...
...
HAVE YOU FOUND PRESS-ON NAILS OR GLOVES NEARBY?
NO...
C'MON, GET A MOVE ON!
YOU TWO ARE WITNESSES!
OH, RIGHT...
YES, SHE WAS HERE!
AROUND 1:00 P.M.
SHE SAT HERE.

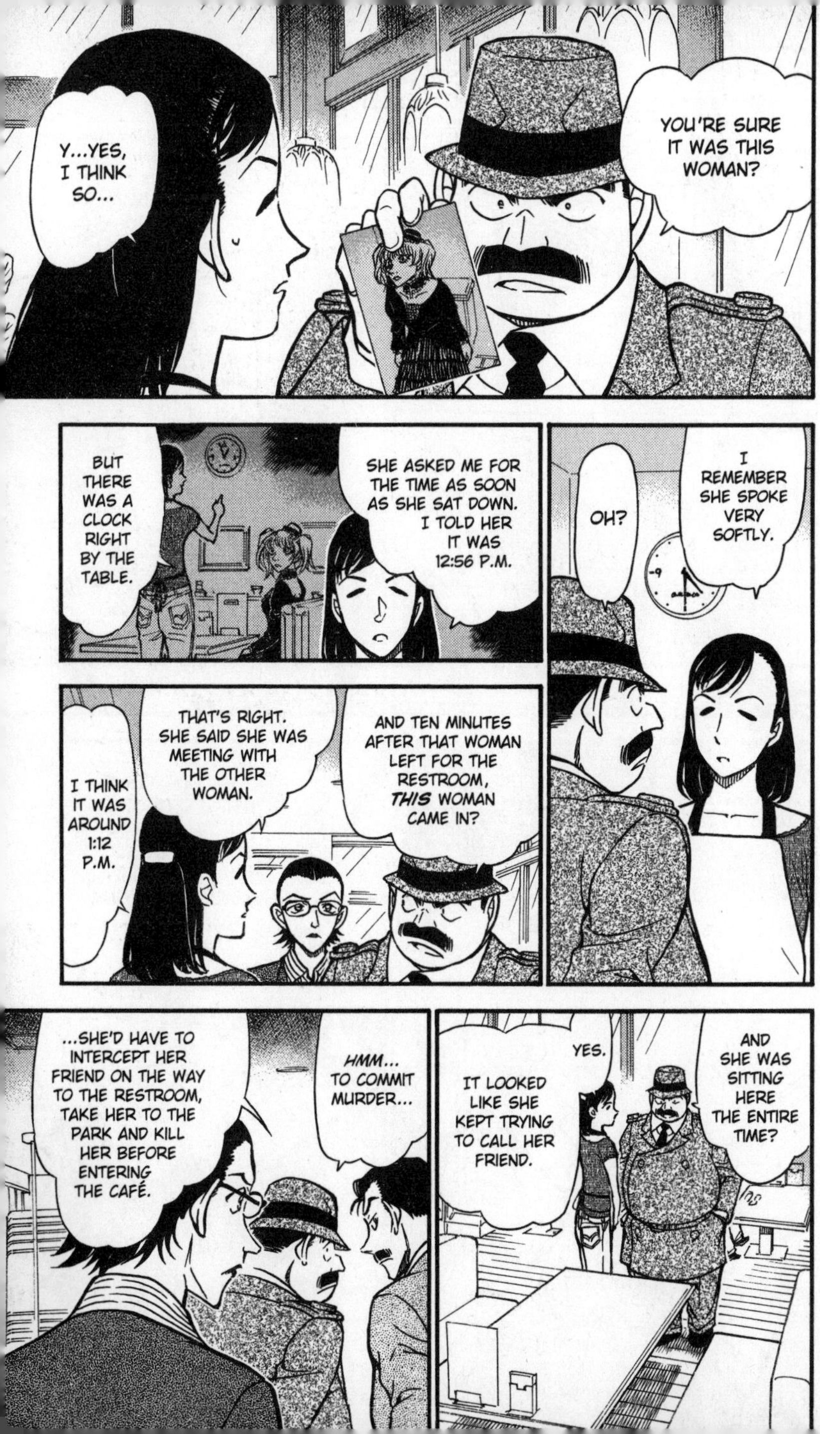
YOU'RE SURE IT WAS THIS WOMAN?
Y...YES, I THINK SO...
I REMEMBER SHE SPOKE VERY SOFTLY.
OH?
SHE ASKED ME FOR THE TIME AS SOON AS SHE SAT DOWN. I TOLD HER IT WAS 12:56 P.M.
BUT THERE WAS A CLOCK RIGHT BY THE TABLE.
AND TEN MINUTES AFTER THAT WOMAN LEFT FOR THE RESTROOM, *THIS* WOMAN CAME IN?
THAT'S RIGHT. SHE SAID SHE WAS MEETING WITH THE OTHER WOMAN.
I THINK IT WAS AROUND 1:12 P.M.
AND SHE WAS SITTING HERE THE ENTIRE TIME?
YES.
IT LOOKED LIKE SHE KEPT TRYING TO CALL HER FRIEND.
HMM... TO COMMIT MURDER...
...SHE'D HAVE TO INTERCEPT HER FRIEND ON THE WAY TO THE RESTROOM, TAKE HER TO THE PARK AND KILL HER BEFORE ENTERING THE CAFÉ.

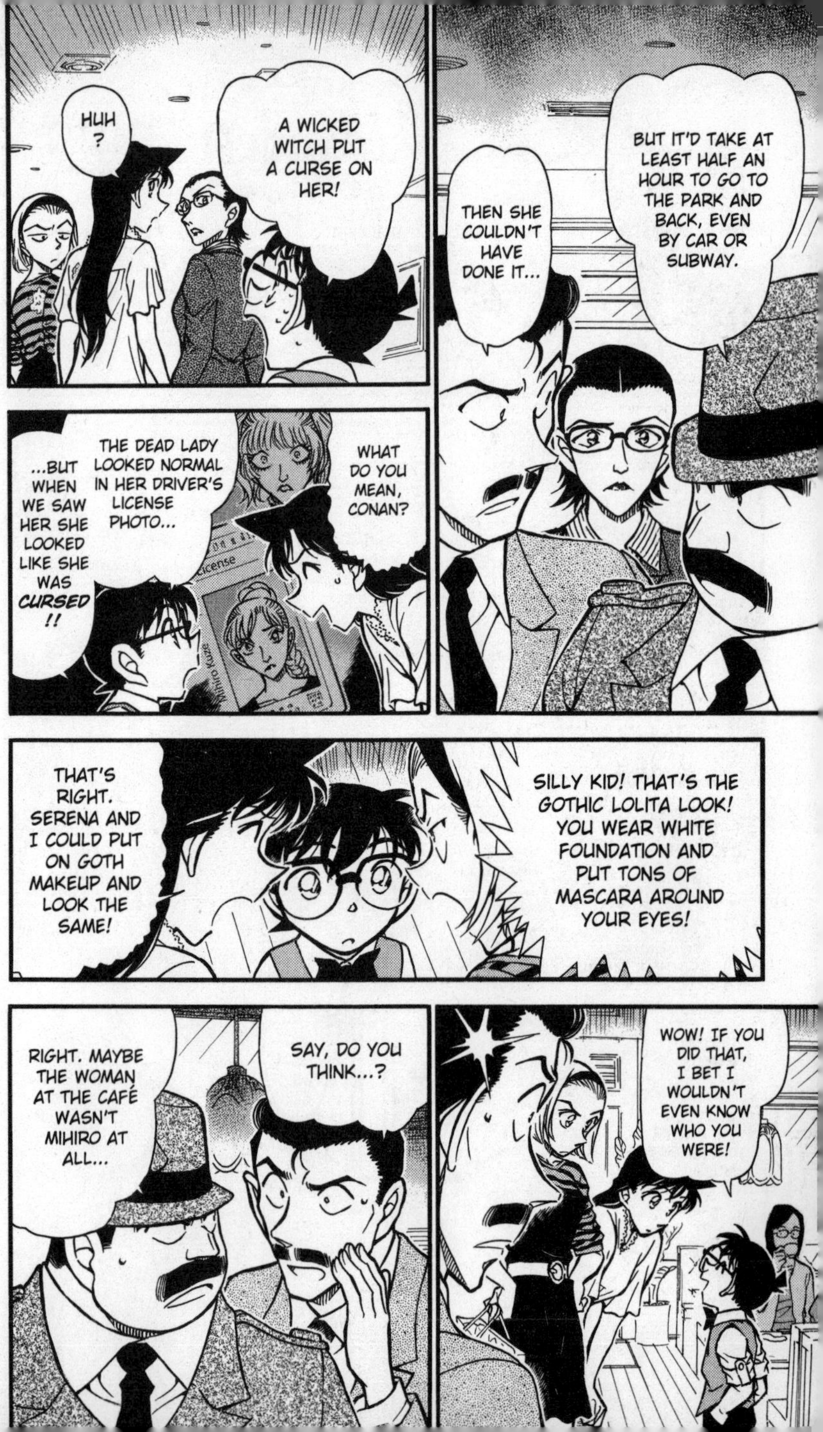
BUT IT'D TAKE AT LEAST HALF AN HOUR TO GO TO THE PARK AND BACK, EVEN BY CAR OR SUBWAY.
THEN SHE COULDN'T HAVE DONE IT...
A WICKED WITCH PUT A CURSE ON HER!
HUH ?
WHAT DO YOU MEAN, CONAN?
THE DEAD LADY LOOKED NORMAL IN HER DRIVER'S LICENSE PHOTO...
...BUT WHEN WE SAW HER SHE LOOKED LIKE SHE WAS *CURSED* !!
SILLY KID! THAT'S THE GOTHIC LOLITA LOOK! YOU WEAR WHITE FOUNDATION AND PUT TONS OF MASCARA AROUND YOUR EYES!
THAT'S RIGHT. SERENA AND I COULD PUT ON GOTH MAKEUP AND LOOK THE SAME!
WOW! IF YOU DID THAT, I BET I WOULDN'T EVEN KNOW WHO YOU WERE!
SAY, DO YOU THINK...?
RIGHT. MAYBE THE WOMAN AT THE CAFÉ WASN'T MIHIRO AT ALL...

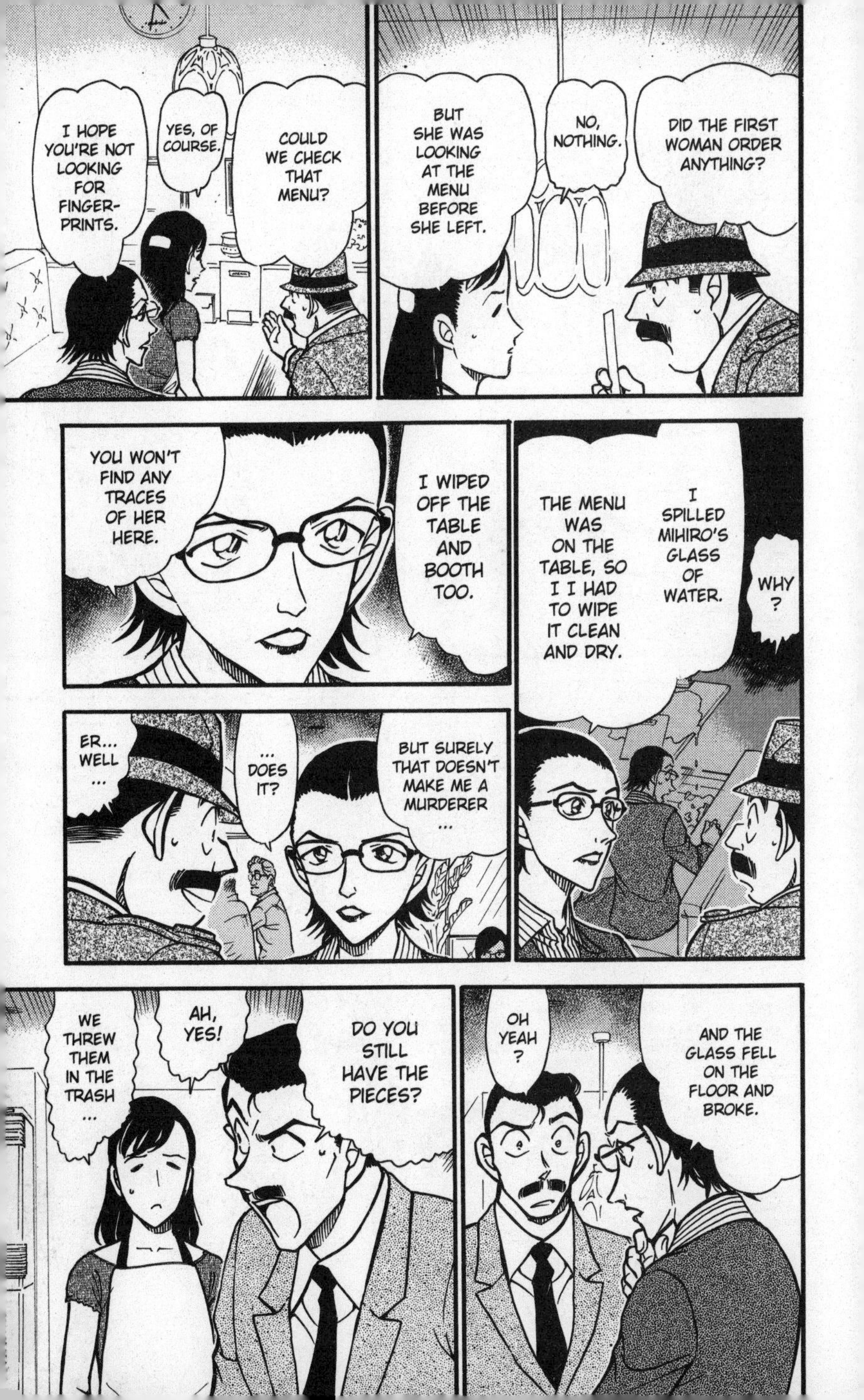
DID THE FIRST WOMAN ORDER ANYTHING?
NO, NOTHING.
BUT SHE WAS LOOKING AT THE MENU BEFORE SHE LEFT.
COULD WE CHECK THAT MENU?
YES, OF COURSE.
I HOPE YOU'RE NOT LOOKING FOR FINGER-PRINTS.
WHY?
I SPILLED MIHIRO'S GLASS OF WATER.
THE MENU WAS ON THE TABLE, SO I I HAD TO WIPE IT CLEAN AND DRY.
I WIPED OFF THE TABLE AND BOOTH TOO.
YOU WON'T FIND ANY TRACES OF HER HERE.
BUT SURELY THAT DOESN'T MAKE ME A MURDERER ...
... DOES IT?
ER... WELL ...
AND THE GLASS FELL ON THE FLOOR AND BROKE.
OH YEAH?
DO YOU STILL HAVE THE PIECES?
AH, YES!
WE THREW THEM IN THE TRASH ...

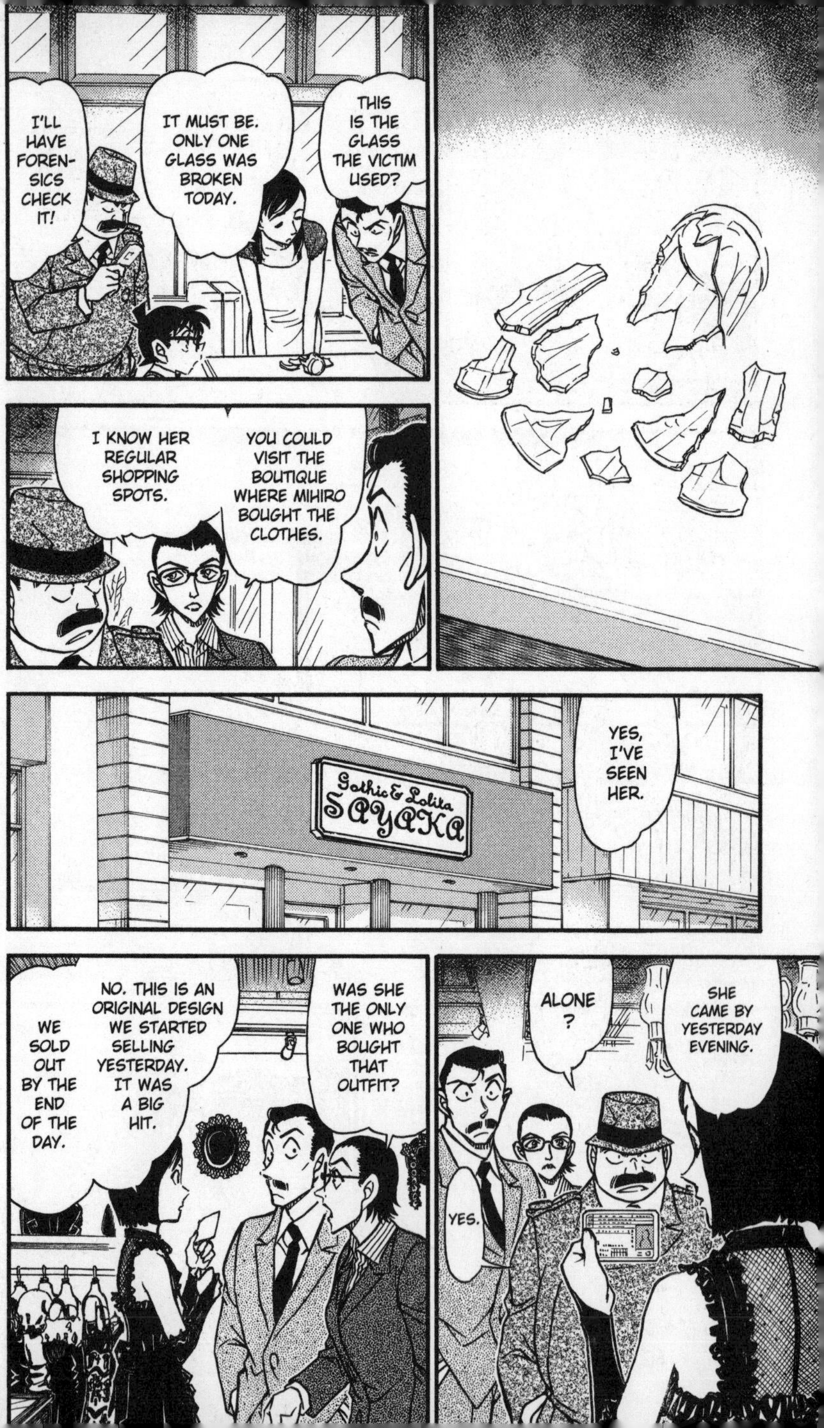
THIS IS THE GLASS THE VICTIM USED?
IT MUST BE. ONLY ONE GLASS WAS BROKEN TODAY.
I'LL HAVE FORENSICS CHECK IT!
YOU COULD VISIT THE BOUTIQUE WHERE MIHIRO BOUGHT THE CLOTHES.
I KNOW HER REGULAR SHOPPING SPOTS.
Gothic & Lolita SAYAKA
YES, I'VE SEEN HER.
SHE CAME BY YESTERDAY EVENING.
ALONE?
YES.
WAS SHE THE ONLY ONE WHO BOUGHT THAT OUTFIT?
NO. THIS IS AN ORIGINAL DESIGN WE STARTED SELLING YESTERDAY. IT WAS A BIG HIT.
WE SOLD OUT BY THE END OF THE DAY.

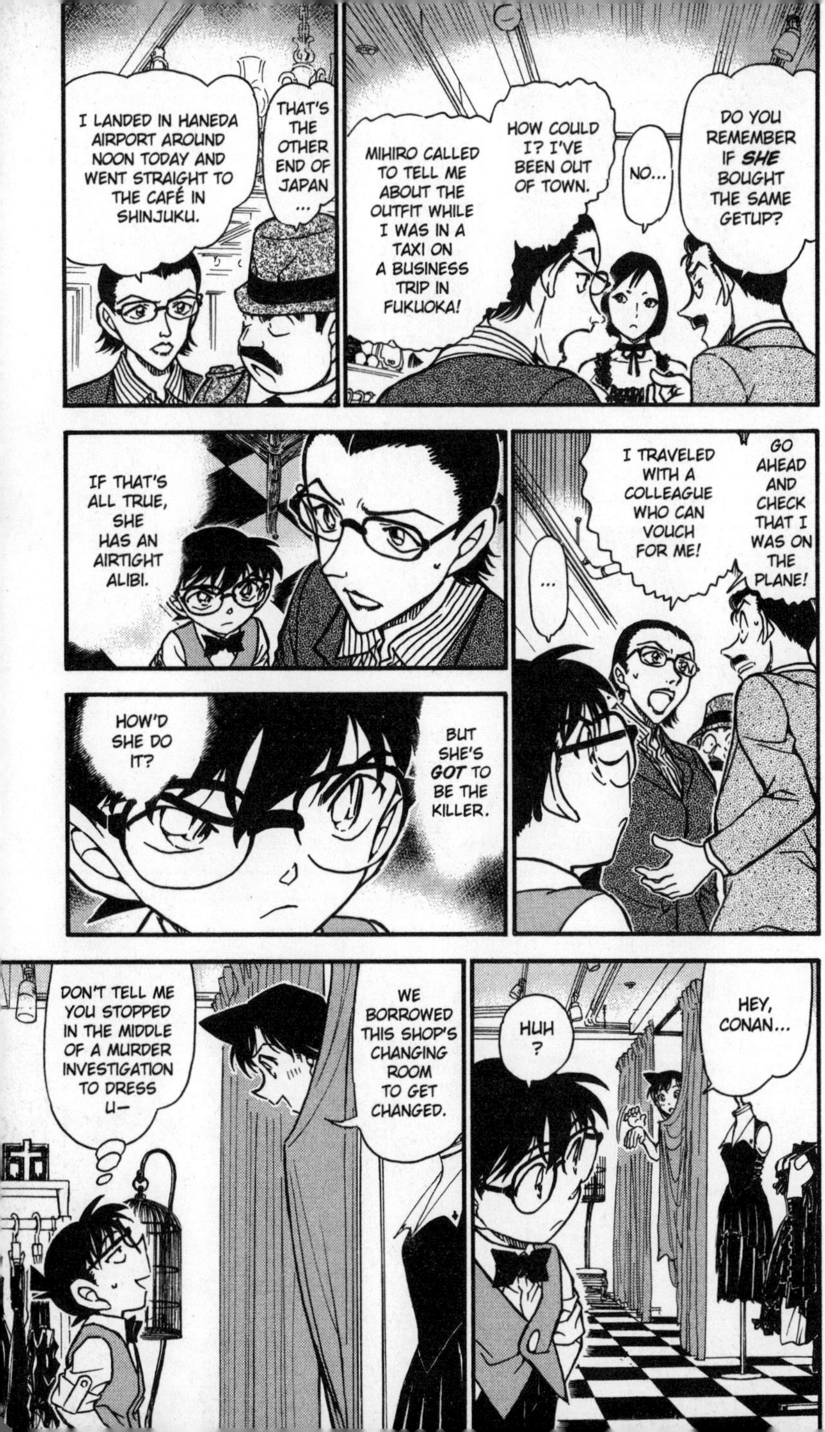
DO YOU REMEMBER IF *SHE* BOUGHT THE SAME GETUP?
NO...
HOW COULD I? I'VE BEEN OUT OF TOWN.
MIHIRO CALLED TO TELL ME ABOUT THE OUTFIT WHILE I WAS IN A TAXI ON A BUSINESS TRIP IN FUKUOKA!
THAT'S THE OTHER END OF JAPAN ...
I LANDED IN HANEDA AIRPORT AROUND NOON TODAY AND WENT STRAIGHT TO THE CAFÉ IN SHINJUKU.
GO AHEAD AND CHECK THAT I WAS ON THE PLANE!
I TRAVELED WITH A COLLEAGUE WHO CAN VOUCH FOR ME!
...
IF THAT'S ALL TRUE, SHE HAS AN AIRTIGHT ALIBI.
BUT SHE'S *GOT* TO BE THE KILLER.
HOW'D SHE DO IT?
HEY, CONAN...
HUH ?
WE BORROWED THIS SHOP'S CHANGING ROOM TO GET CHANGED.
DON'T TELL ME YOU STOPPED IN THE MIDDLE OF A MURDER INVESTIGATION TO DRESS U—

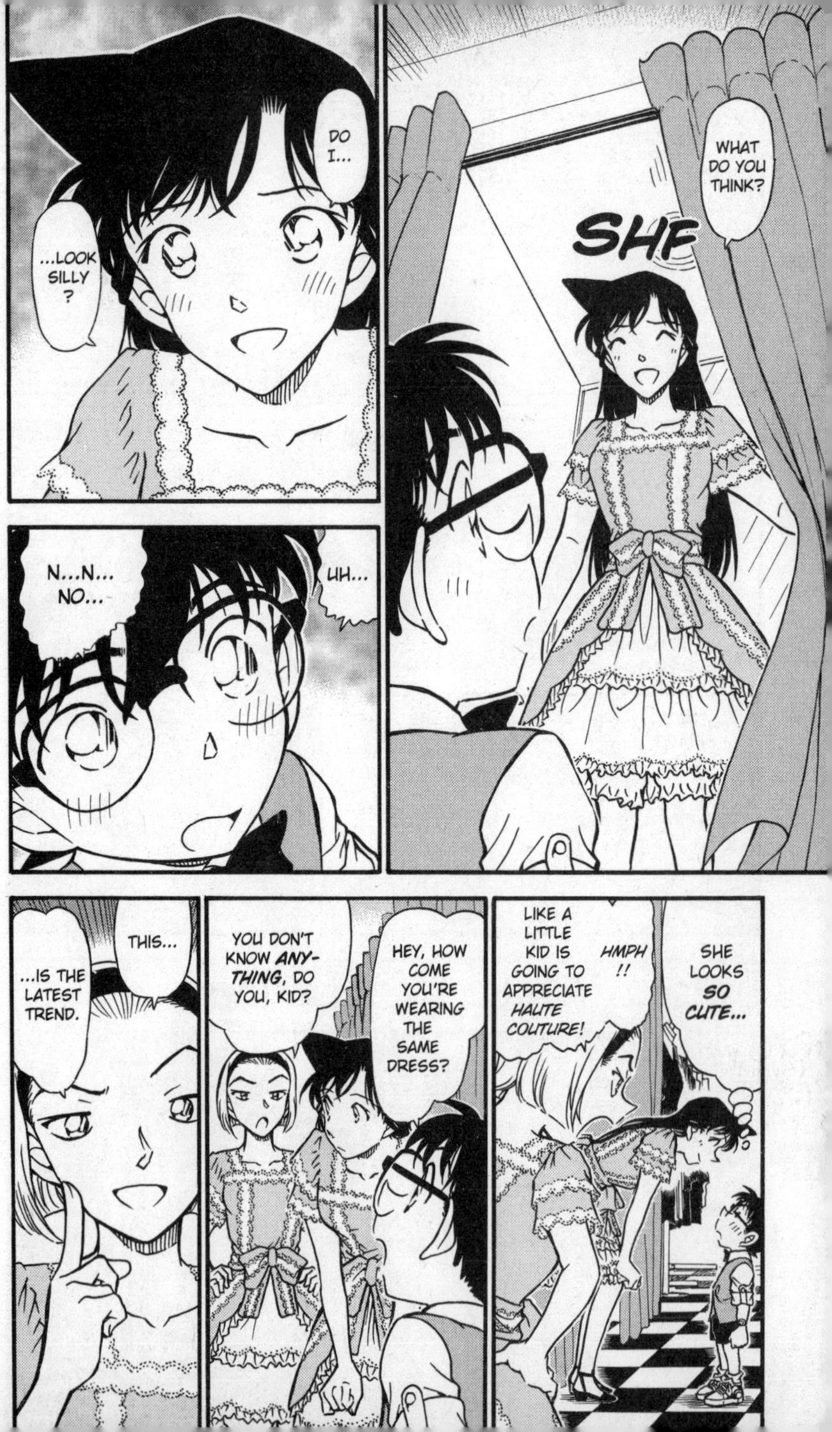
WHAT DO YOU THINK?
SHF
DO I...
...LOOK SILLY?
UH...
N...N... NO...
SHE LOOKS *SO CUTE...*
HMPH !!
LIKE A LITTLE KID IS GOING TO APPRECIATE *HAUTE COUTURE!*
HEY, HOW COME YOU'RE WEARING THE SAME DRESS?
YOU DON'T KNOW ***ANYTHING***, DO YOU, KID?
THIS...
...IS THE LATEST TREND.

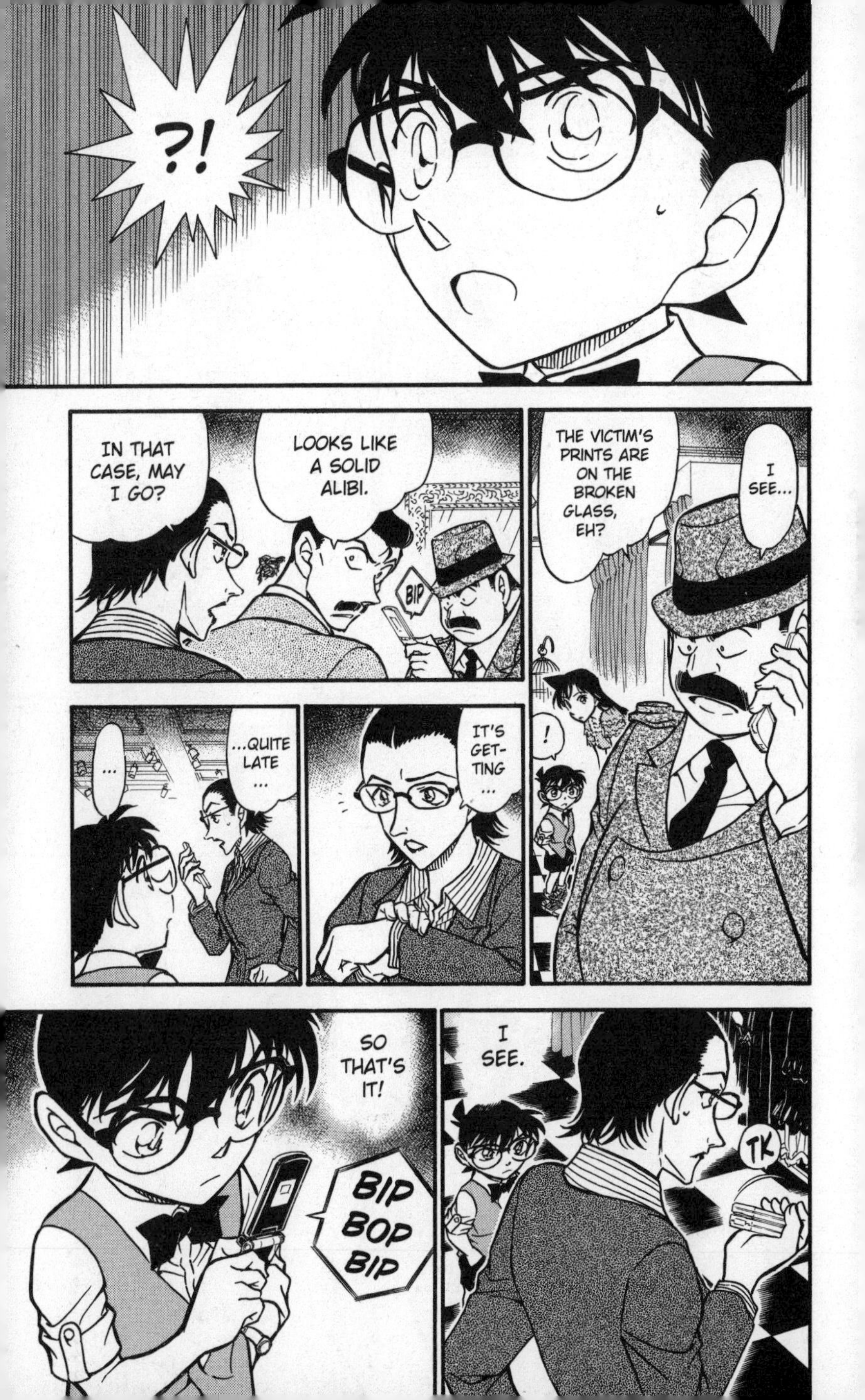
?!
I SEE...
THE VICTIM'S PRINTS ARE ON THE BROKEN GLASS, EH?
!
LOOKS LIKE A SOLID ALIBI.
BIP
IN THAT CASE, MAY I GO?
IT'S GET-TING...
...QUITE LATE...
...
I SEE.
TK
SO THAT'S IT!
BIP BOP BIP

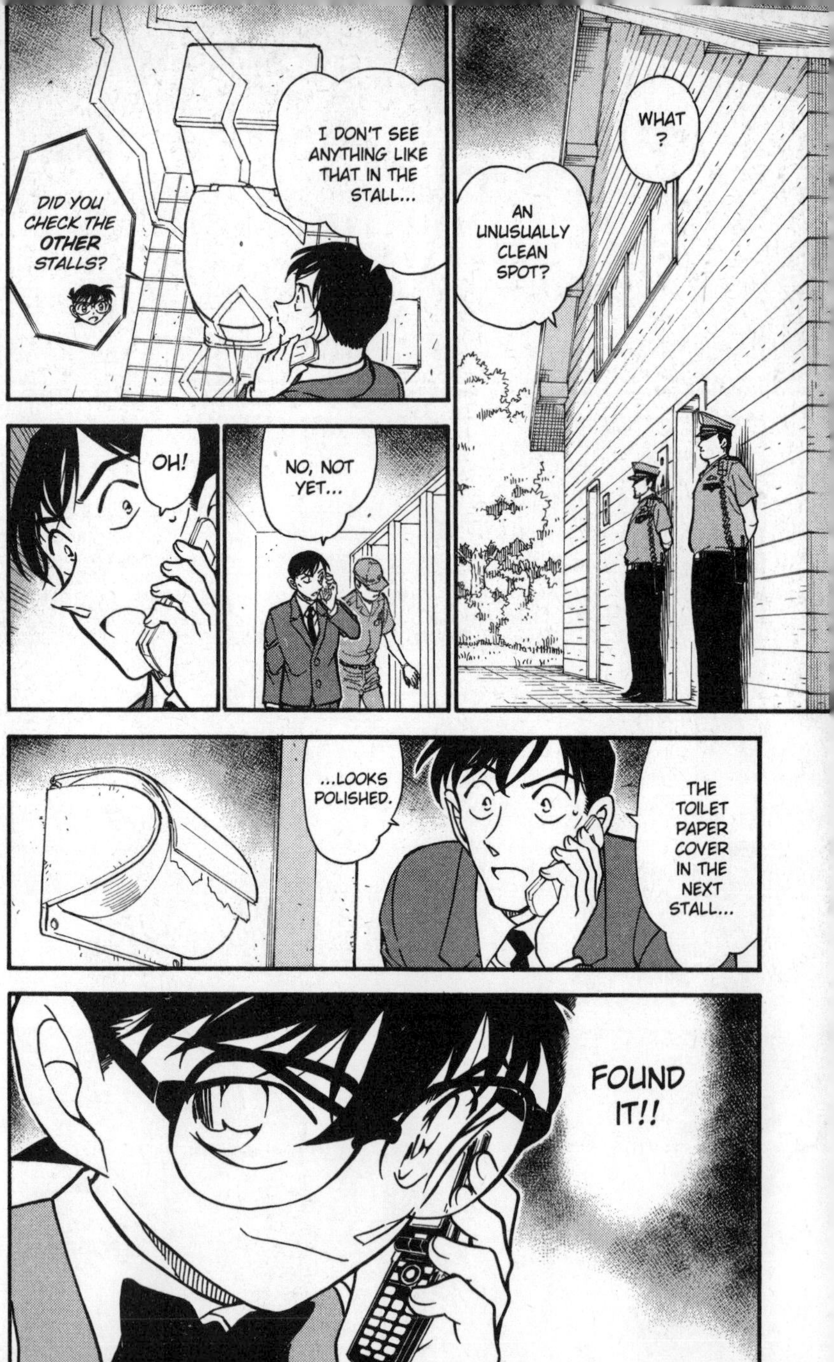
WHAT?
AN UNUSUALLY CLEAN SPOT?
I DON'T SEE ANYTHING LIKE THAT IN THE STALL...
DID YOU CHECK THE OTHER STALLS?
NO, NOT YET...
OH!
THE TOILET PAPER COVER IN THE NEXT STALL...
...LOOKS POLISHED.
FOUND IT!!

FILE 2: SOMETHING FRAGILE AND UNSURE

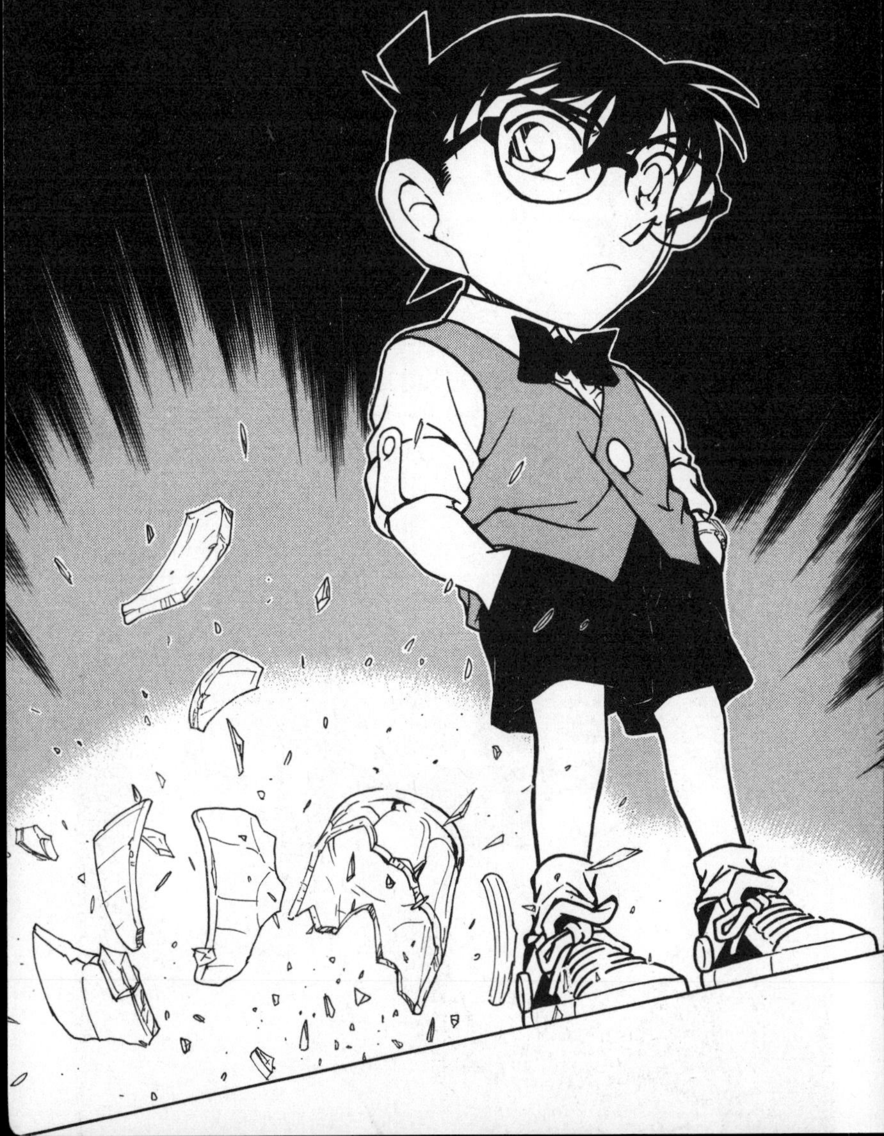

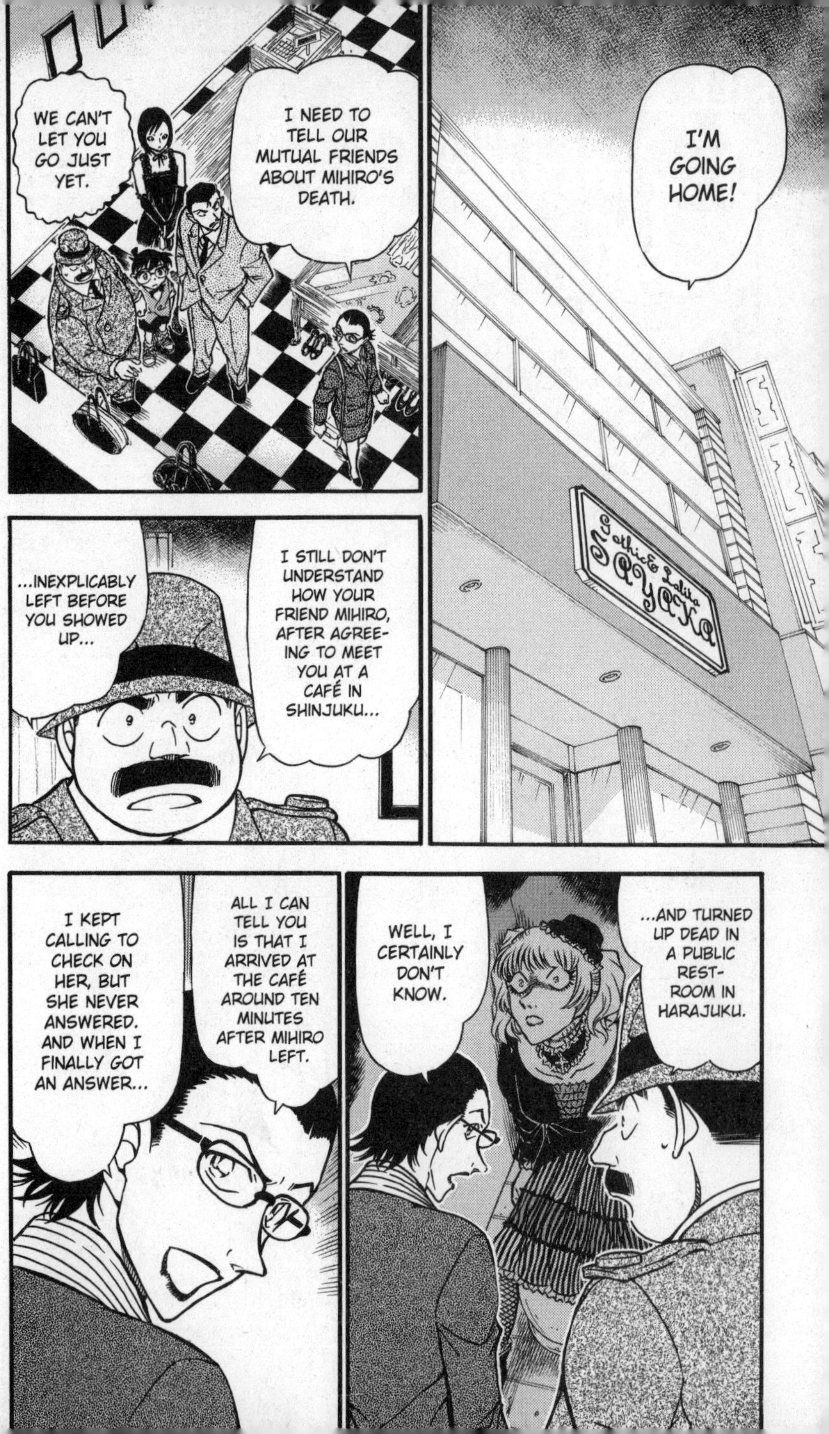
I'M GOING HOME!
WE CAN'T LET YOU GO JUST YET.
I NEED TO TELL OUR MUTUAL FRIENDS ABOUT MIHIRO'S DEATH.
I STILL DON'T UNDERSTAND HOW YOUR FRIEND MIHIRO, AFTER AGREEING TO MEET YOU AT A CAFÉ IN SHINJUKU...
...INEXPLICABLY LEFT BEFORE YOU SHOWED UP...
...AND TURNED UP DEAD IN A PUBLIC REST-ROOM IN HARAJUKU.
WELL, I CERTAINLY DON'T KNOW.
ALL I CAN TELL YOU IS THAT I ARRIVED AT THE CAFÉ AROUND TEN MINUTES AFTER MIHIRO LEFT.
I KEPT CALLING TO CHECK ON HER, BUT SHE NEVER ANSWERED. AND WHEN I FINALLY GOT AN ANSWER...

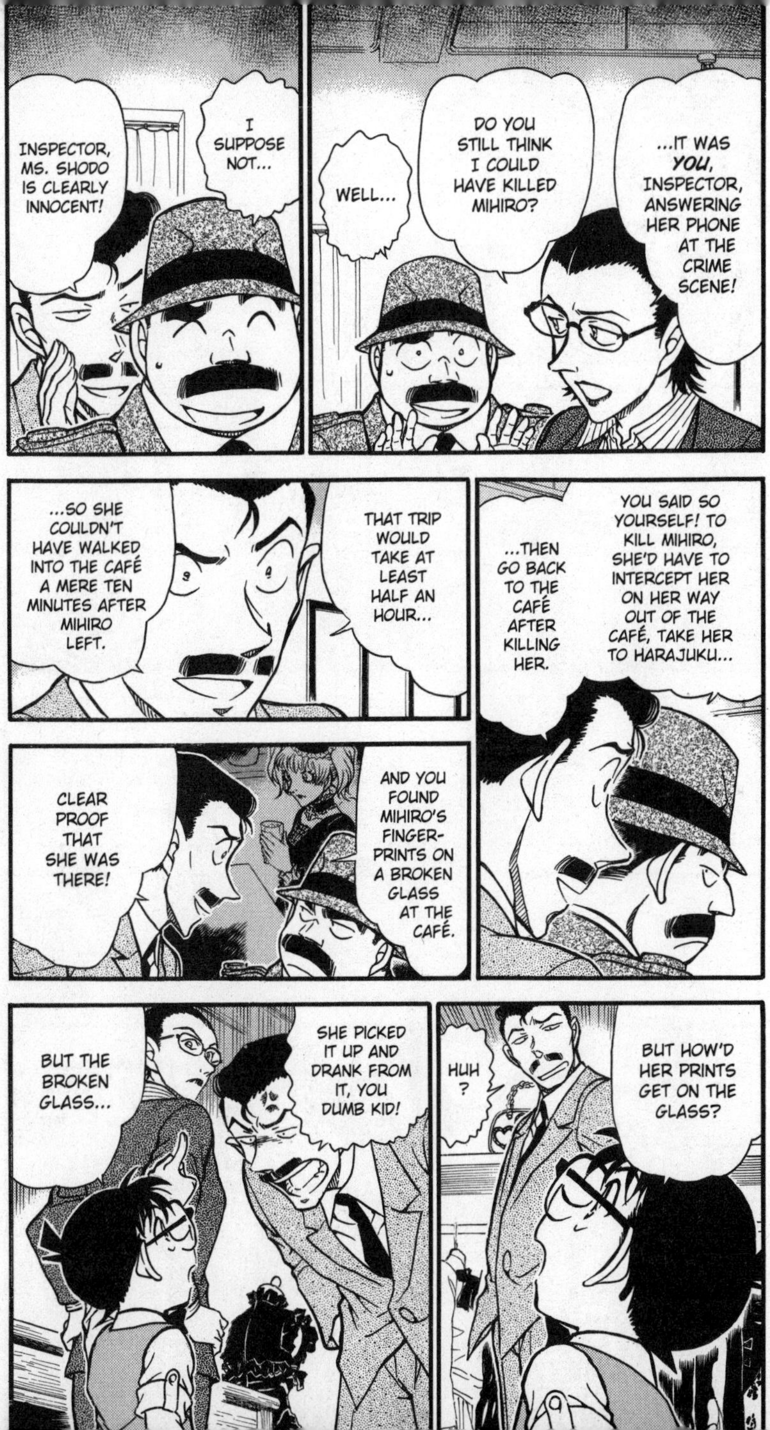
...IT WAS YOU, INSPECTOR, ANSWERING HER PHONE AT THE CRIME SCENE!
DO YOU STILL THINK I COULD HAVE KILLED MIHIRO?
WELL...
I SUPPOSE NOT...
INSPECTOR, MS. SHODO IS CLEARLY INNOCENT!
YOU SAID SO YOURSELF! TO KILL MIHIRO, SHE'D HAVE TO INTERCEPT HER ON HER WAY OUT OF THE CAFÉ, TAKE HER TO HARAJUKU...
...THEN GO BACK TO THE CAFÉ AFTER KILLING HER.
THAT TRIP WOULD TAKE AT LEAST HALF AN HOUR...
...SO SHE COULDN'T HAVE WALKED INTO THE CAFÉ A MERE TEN MINUTES AFTER MIHIRO LEFT.
AND YOU FOUND MIHIRO'S FINGER-PRINTS ON A BROKEN GLASS AT THE CAFÉ.
CLEAR PROOF THAT SHE WAS THERE!
BUT HOW'D HER PRINTS GET ON THE GLASS?
HUH?
SHE PICKED IT UP AND DRANK FROM IT, YOU DUMB KID!
BUT THE BROKEN GLASS...

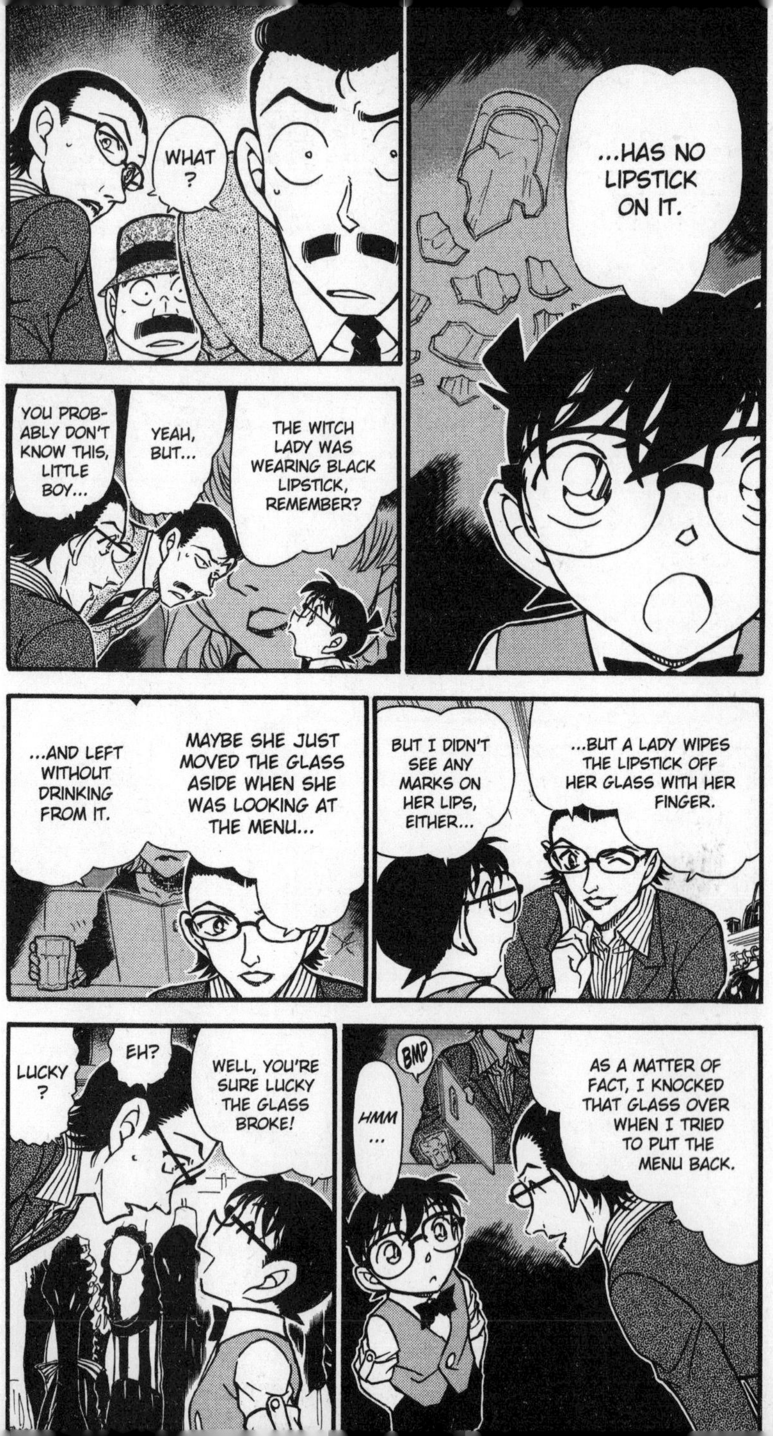
...HAS NO LIPSTICK ON IT.
WHAT ?
THE WITCH LADY WAS WEARING BLACK LIPSTICK, REMEMBER?
YEAH, BUT...
YOU PROB-ABLY DON'T KNOW THIS, LITTLE BOY...
...BUT A LADY WIPES THE LIPSTICK OFF HER GLASS WITH HER FINGER.
BUT I DIDN'T SEE ANY MARKS ON HER LIPS, EITHER...
MAYBE SHE JUST MOVED THE GLASS ASIDE WHEN SHE WAS LOOKING AT THE MENU...
...AND LEFT WITHOUT DRINKING FROM IT.
AS A MATTER OF FACT, I KNOCKED THAT GLASS OVER WHEN I TRIED TO PUT THE MENU BACK.
BMP
HMM ...
WELL, YOU'RE SURE LUCKY THE GLASS BROKE!
EH?
LUCKY ?

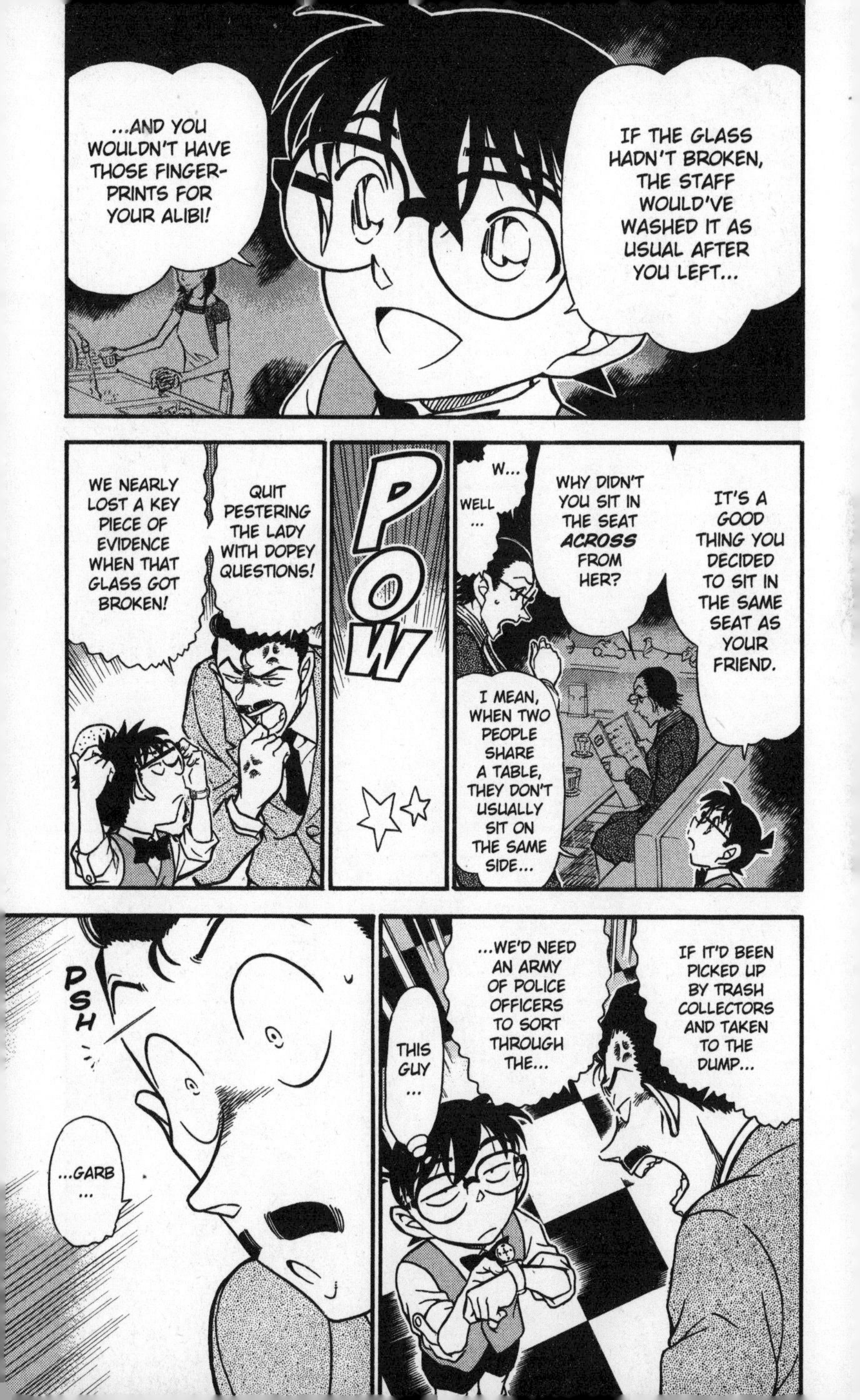
IF THE GLASS HADN'T BROKEN, THE STAFF WOULD'VE WASHED IT AS USUAL AFTER YOU LEFT...
...AND YOU WOULDN'T HAVE THOSE FINGER-PRINTS FOR YOUR ALIBI!
IT'S A GOOD THING YOU DECIDED TO SIT IN THE SAME SEAT AS YOUR FRIEND.
WHY DIDN'T YOU SIT IN THE SEAT ACROSS FROM HER?
W... WELL...
I MEAN, WHEN TWO PEOPLE SHARE A TABLE, THEY DON'T USUALLY SIT ON THE SAME SIDE...
POW
QUIT PESTERING THE LADY WITH DOPEY QUESTIONS!
WE NEARLY LOST A KEY PIECE OF EVIDENCE WHEN THAT GLASS GOT BROKEN!
IF IT'D BEEN PICKED UP BY TRASH COLLECTORS AND TAKEN TO THE DUMP...
...WE'D NEED AN ARMY OF POLICE OFFICERS TO SORT THROUGH THE...
THIS GUY...
PSH
...GARB...

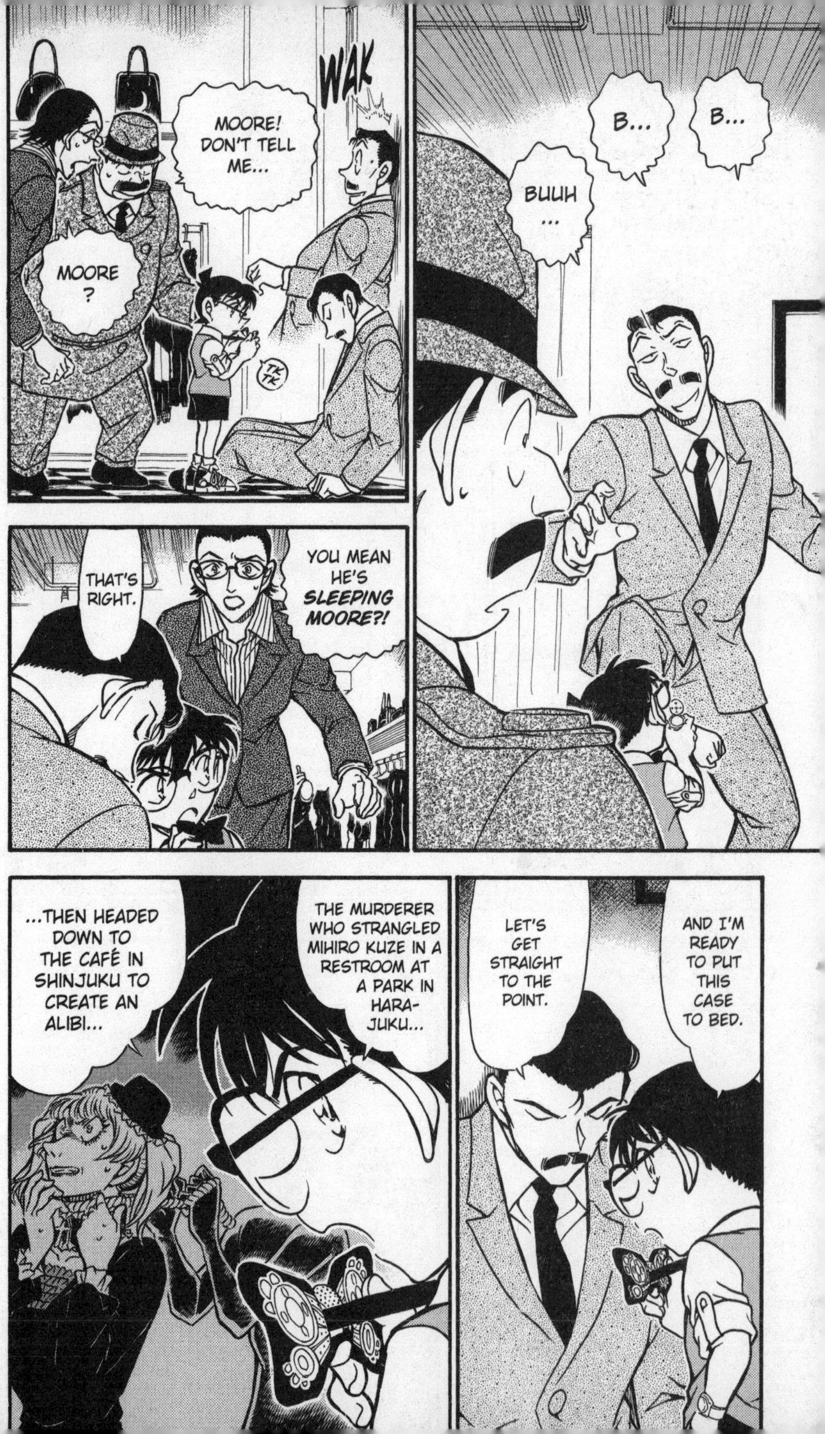
B...
B...
BUUH ...
WAK
MOORE! DON'T TELL ME...
MOORE ?
TK TK
YOU MEAN HE'S *SLEEPING MOORE?!*
THAT'S RIGHT.
AND I'M READY TO PUT THIS CASE TO BED.
LET'S GET STRAIGHT TO THE POINT.
THE MURDERER WHO STRANGLED MIHIRO KUZE IN A RESTROOM AT A PARK IN HARA-JUKU...
...THEN HEADED DOWN TO THE CAFÉ IN SHINJUKU TO CREATE AN ALIBI...

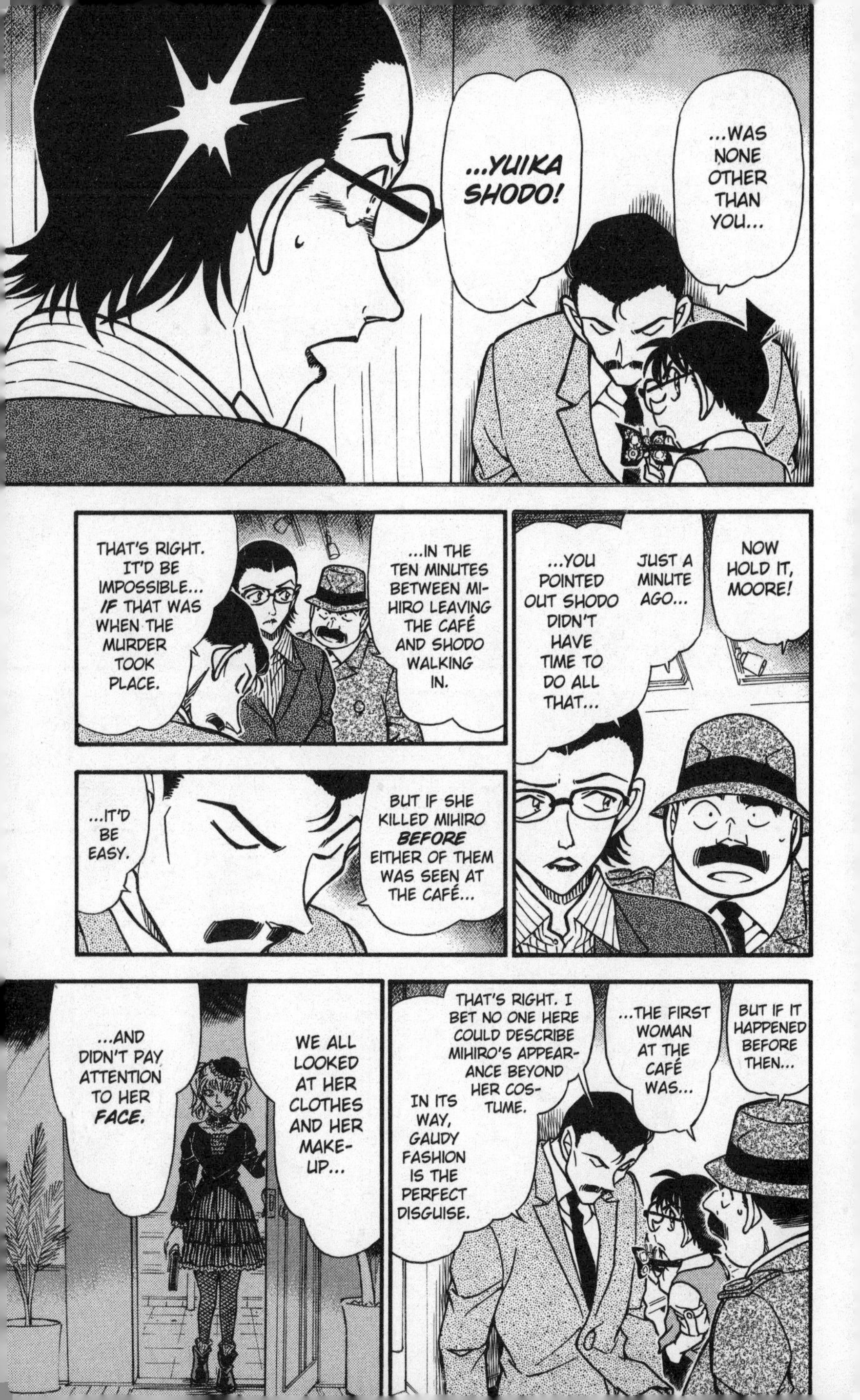
...WAS NONE OTHER THAN YOU...
...YUIKA SHODO!
NOW HOLD IT, MOORE!
JUST A MINUTE AGO...
...YOU POINTED OUT SHODO DIDN'T HAVE TIME TO DO ALL THAT...
...IN THE TEN MINUTES BETWEEN MIHIRO LEAVING THE CAFÉ AND SHODO WALKING IN.
THAT'S RIGHT. IT'D BE IMPOSSIBLE... *IF* THAT WAS WHEN THE MURDER TOOK PLACE.
BUT IF SHE KILLED MIHIRO ***BEFORE*** EITHER OF THEM WAS SEEN AT THE CAFÉ...
...IT'D BE EASY.
BUT IF IT HAPPENED BEFORE THEN...
...THE FIRST WOMAN AT THE CAFÉ WAS...
THAT'S RIGHT. I BET NO ONE HERE COULD DESCRIBE MIHIRO'S APPEARANCE BEYOND HER COSTUME.
IN ITS WAY, GAUDY FASHION IS THE PERFECT DISGUISE.
WE ALL LOOKED AT HER CLOTHES AND HER MAKE-UP...
...AND DIDN'T PAY ATTENTION TO HER ***FACE.***

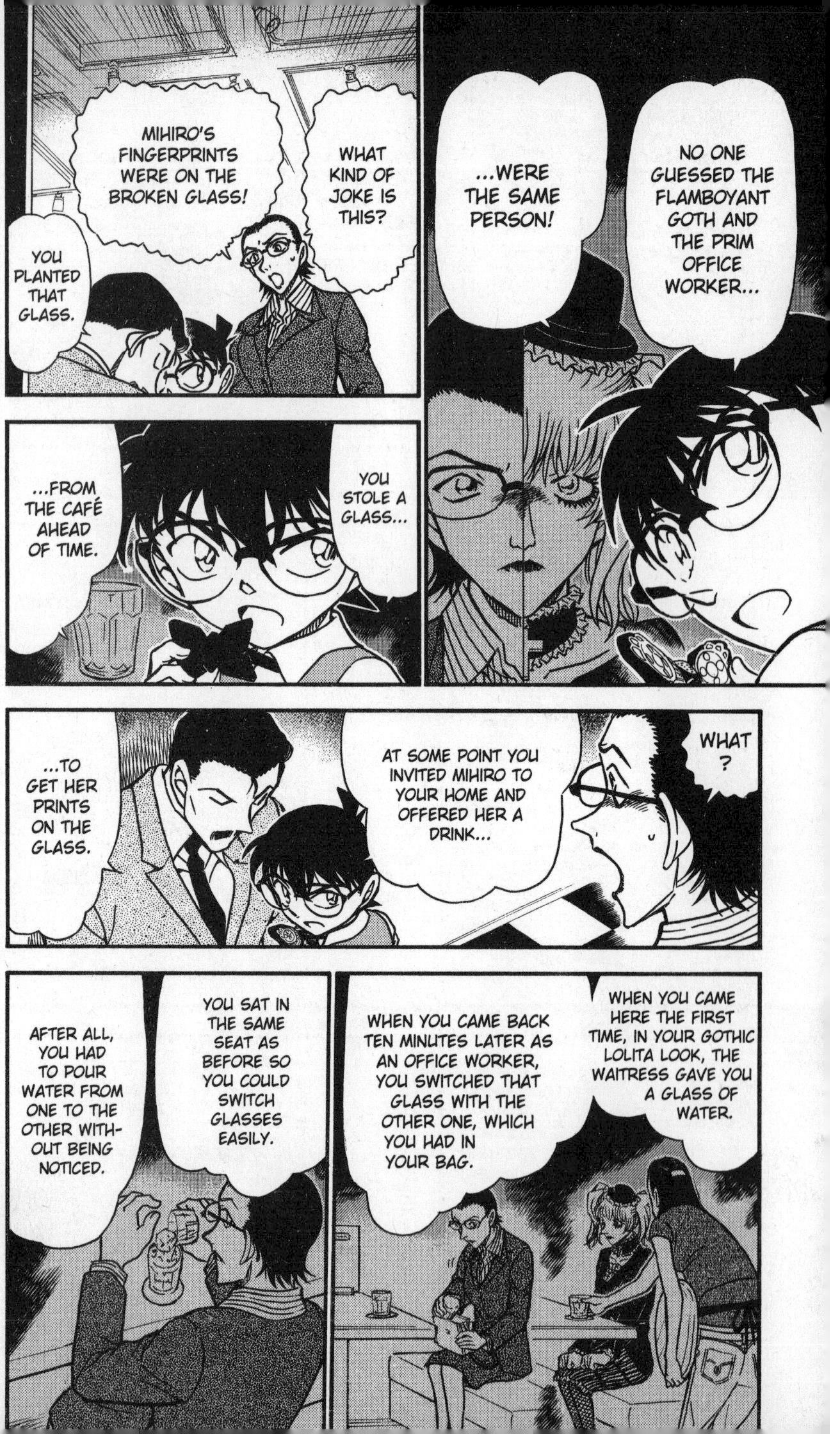
NO ONE GUESSED THE FLAMBOYANT GOTH AND THE PRIM OFFICE WORKER...
...WERE THE SAME PERSON!
WHAT KIND OF JOKE IS THIS?
MIHIRO'S FINGERPRINTS WERE ON THE BROKEN GLASS!
YOU PLANTED THAT GLASS.
YOU STOLE A GLASS...
...FROM THE CAFÉ AHEAD OF TIME.
WHAT?
AT SOME POINT YOU INVITED MIHIRO TO YOUR HOME AND OFFERED HER A DRINK...
...TO GET HER PRINTS ON THE GLASS.
WHEN YOU CAME HERE THE FIRST TIME, IN YOUR GOTHIC LOLITA LOOK, THE WAITRESS GAVE YOU A GLASS OF WATER.
WHEN YOU CAME BACK TEN MINUTES LATER AS AN OFFICE WORKER, YOU SWITCHED THAT GLASS WITH THE OTHER ONE, WHICH YOU HAD IN YOUR BAG.
YOU SAT IN THE SAME SEAT AS BEFORE SO YOU COULD SWITCH GLASSES EASILY.
AFTER ALL, YOU HAD TO POUR WATER FROM ONE TO THE OTHER WITH-OUT BEING NOTICED.

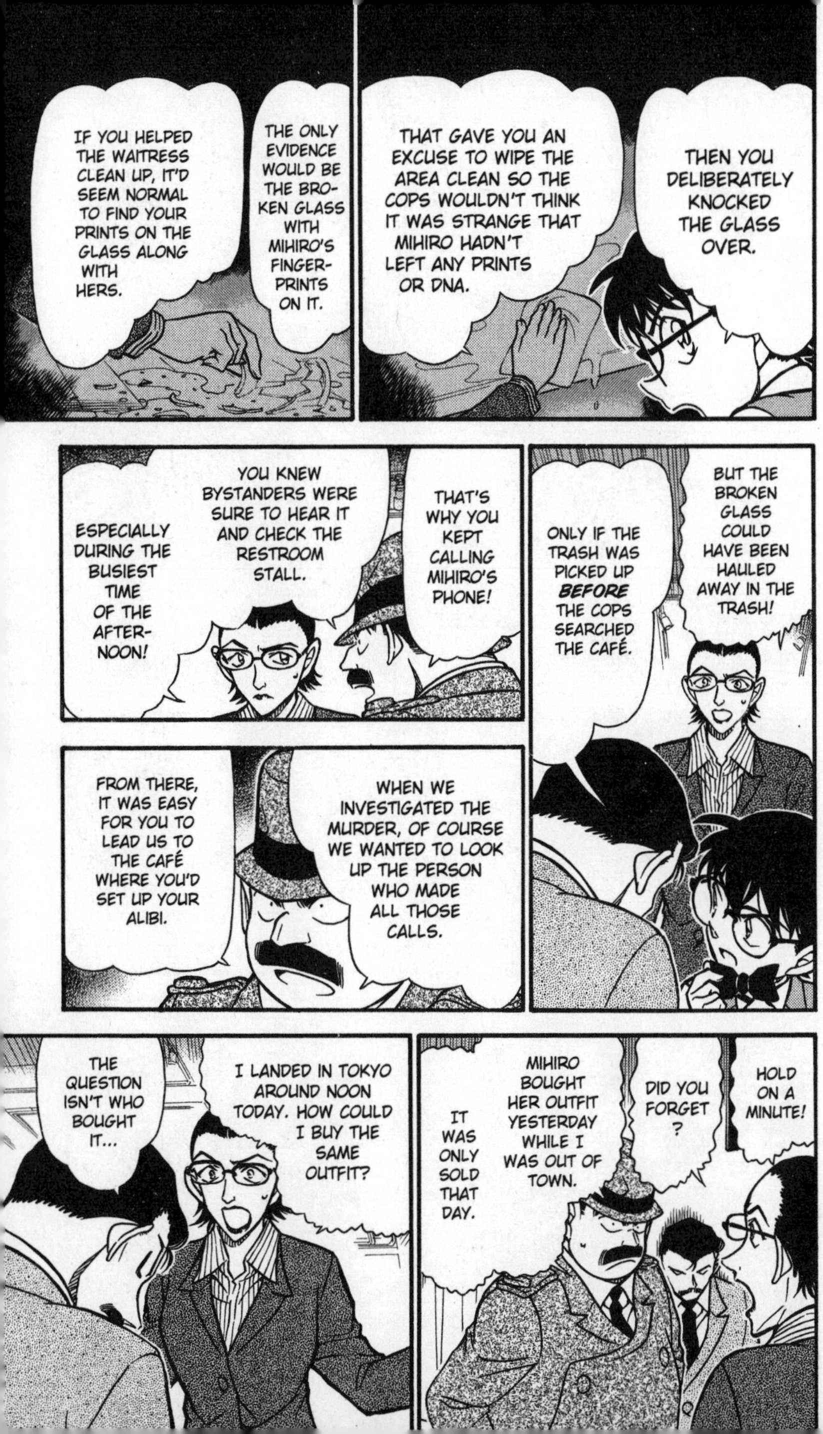
THEN YOU DELIBERATELY KNOCKED THE GLASS OVER.
THAT GAVE YOU AN EXCUSE TO WIPE THE AREA CLEAN SO THE COPS WOULDN'T THINK IT WAS STRANGE THAT MIHIRO HADN'T LEFT ANY PRINTS OR DNA.
THE ONLY EVIDENCE WOULD BE THE BRO-KEN GLASS WITH MIHIRO'S FINGER-PRINTS ON IT.
IF YOU HELPED THE WAITRESS CLEAN UP, IT'D SEEM NORMAL TO FIND YOUR PRINTS ON THE GLASS ALONG WITH HERS.
BUT THE BROKEN GLASS COULD HAVE BEEN HAULED AWAY IN THE TRASH!
ONLY IF THE TRASH WAS PICKED UP *BEFORE* THE COPS SEARCHED THE CAFÉ.
THAT'S WHY YOU KEPT CALLING MIHIRO'S PHONE!
YOU KNEW BYSTANDERS WERE SURE TO HEAR IT AND CHECK THE RESTROOM STALL.
ESPECIALLY DURING THE BUSIEST TIME OF THE AFTER-NOON!
WHEN WE INVESTIGATED THE MURDER, OF COURSE WE WANTED TO LOOK UP THE PERSON WHO MADE ALL THOSE CALLS.
FROM THERE, IT WAS EASY FOR YOU TO LEAD US TO THE CAFÉ WHERE YOU'D SET UP YOUR ALIBI.
HOLD ON A MINUTE!
DID YOU FORGET?
MIHIRO BOUGHT HER OUTFIT YESTERDAY WHILE I WAS OUT OF TOWN.
IT WAS ONLY SOLD THAT DAY.
I LANDED IN TOKYO AROUND NOON TODAY. HOW COULD I BUY THE SAME OUTFIT?
THE QUESTION ISN'T WHO BOUGHT IT...

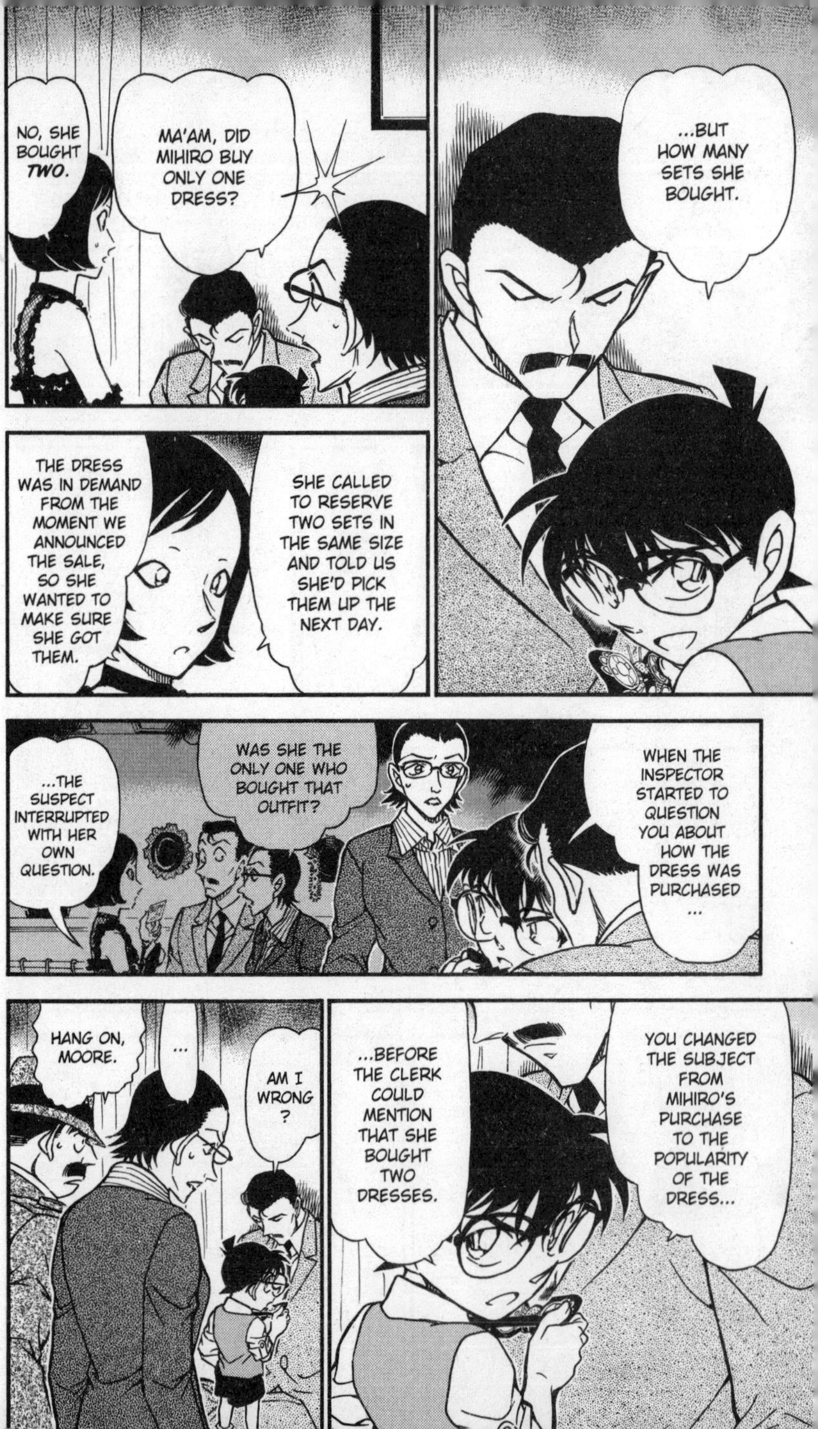
...BUT HOW MANY SETS SHE BOUGHT.
MA'AM, DID MIHIRO BUY ONLY ONE DRESS?
NO, SHE BOUGHT *TWO*.
SHE CALLED TO RESERVE TWO SETS IN THE SAME SIZE AND TOLD US SHE'D PICK THEM UP THE NEXT DAY.
THE DRESS WAS IN DEMAND FROM THE MOMENT WE ANNOUNCED THE SALE, SO SHE WANTED TO MAKE SURE SHE GOT THEM.
WHEN THE INSPECTOR STARTED TO QUESTION YOU ABOUT HOW THE DRESS WAS PURCHASED...
WAS SHE THE ONLY ONE WHO BOUGHT THAT OUTFIT?
...THE SUSPECT INTERRUPTED WITH HER OWN QUESTION.
YOU CHANGED THE SUBJECT FROM MIHIRO'S PURCHASE TO THE POPULARITY OF THE DRESS...
...BEFORE THE CLERK COULD MENTION THAT SHE BOUGHT TWO DRESSES.
AM I WRONG?
...
HANG ON, MOORE.

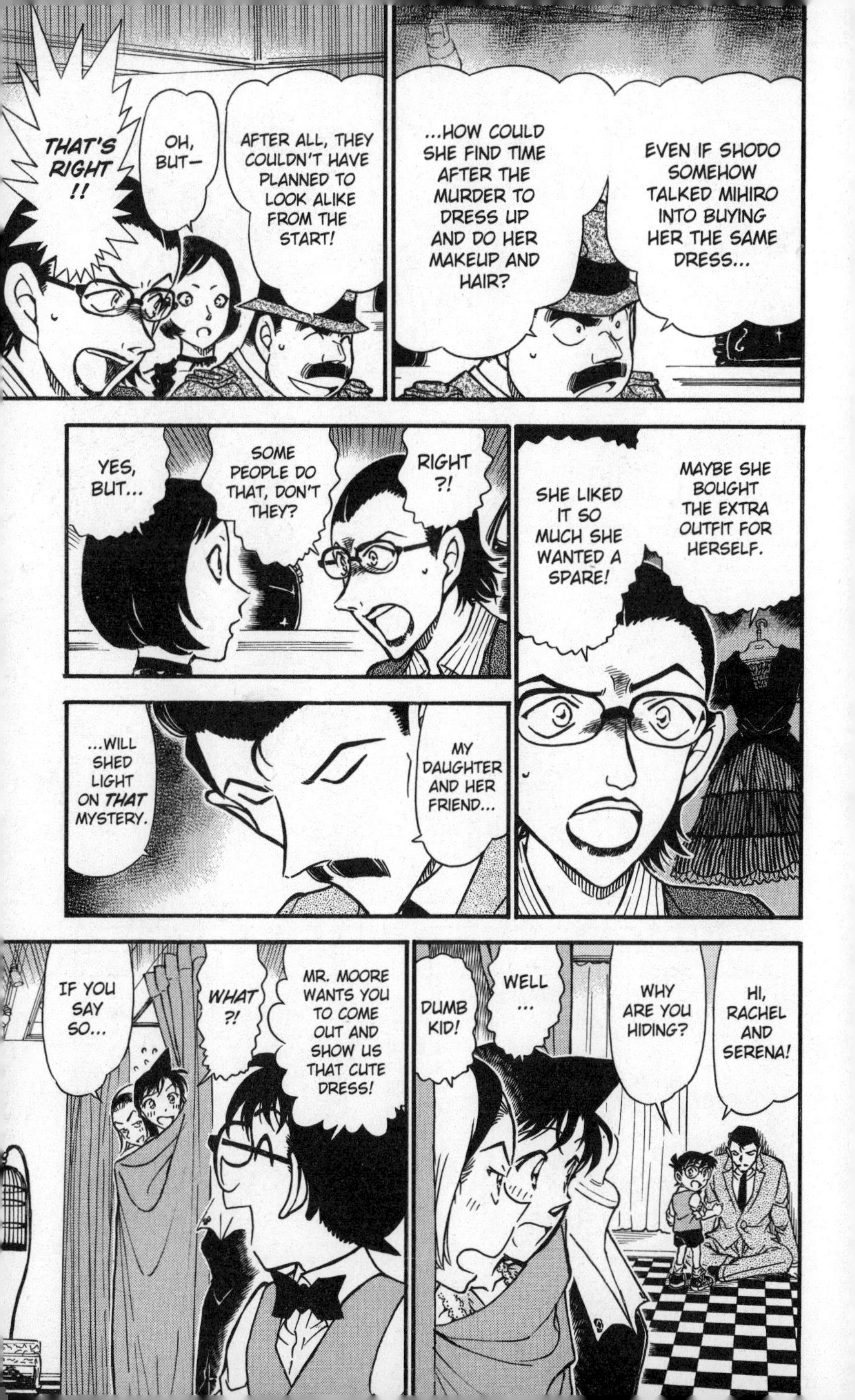
EVEN IF SHODO SOMEHOW TALKED MIHIRO INTO BUYING HER THE SAME DRESS...
...HOW COULD SHE FIND TIME AFTER THE MURDER TO DRESS UP AND DO HER MAKEUP AND HAIR?
AFTER ALL, THEY COULDN'T HAVE PLANNED TO LOOK ALIKE FROM THE START!
OH, BUT—
THAT'S RIGHT !!
MAYBE SHE BOUGHT THE EXTRA OUTFIT FOR HERSELF.
SHE LIKED IT SO MUCH SHE WANTED A SPARE!
RIGHT ?!
SOME PEOPLE DO THAT, DON'T THEY?
YES, BUT...
MY DAUGHTER AND HER FRIEND...
...WILL SHED LIGHT ON THAT MYSTERY.
HI, RACHEL AND SERENA!
WHY ARE YOU HIDING?
WELL ...
DUMB KID!
MR. MOORE WANTS YOU TO COME OUT AND SHOW US THAT CUTE DRESS!
WHAT ?!
IF YOU SAY SO...

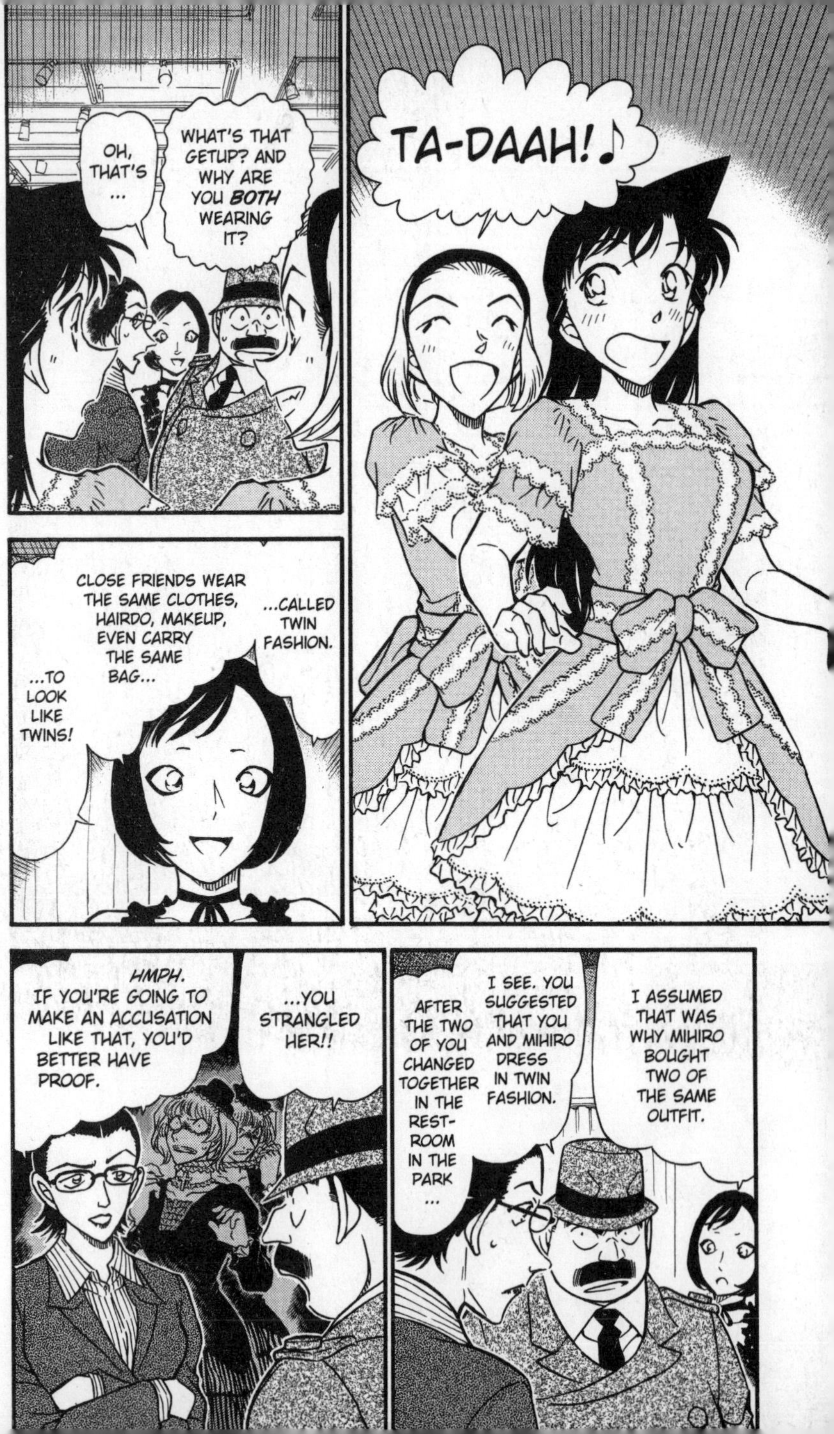
TA-DAAH!♪
WHAT'S THAT GETUP? AND WHY ARE YOU *BOTH* WEARING IT?
OH, THAT'S ...
...CALLED TWIN FASHION.
CLOSE FRIENDS WEAR THE SAME CLOTHES, HAIRDO, MAKEUP, EVEN CARRY THE SAME BAG...
...TO LOOK LIKE TWINS!
I ASSUMED THAT WAS WHY MIHIRO BOUGHT TWO OF THE SAME OUTFIT.
I SEE. YOU SUGGESTED THAT YOU AND MIHIRO DRESS IN TWIN FASHION.
AFTER THE TWO OF YOU CHANGED TOGETHER IN THE REST-ROOM IN THE PARK ...
...YOU STRANGLED HER!!
HMPH. IF YOU'RE GOING TO MAKE AN ACCUSATION LIKE THAT, YOU'D BETTER HAVE PROOF.

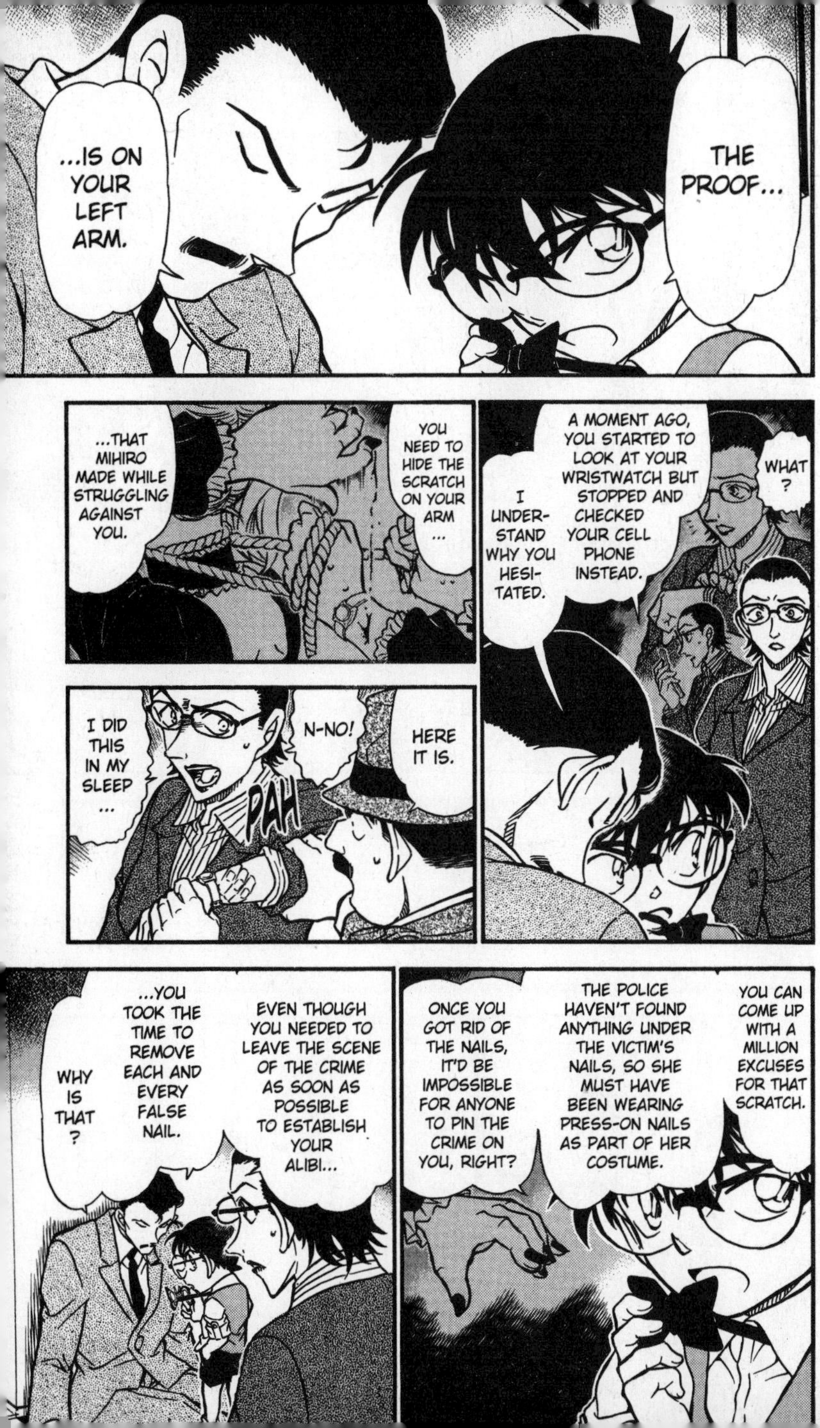
THE PROOF...
...IS ON YOUR LEFT ARM.
WHAT?
A MOMENT AGO, YOU STARTED TO LOOK AT YOUR WRISTWATCH BUT STOPPED AND CHECKED YOUR CELL PHONE INSTEAD.
I UNDER-STAND WHY YOU HESI-TATED.
YOU NEED TO HIDE THE SCRATCH ON YOUR ARM...
...THAT MIHIRO MADE WHILE STRUGGLING AGAINST YOU.
HERE IT IS.
N-NO!
PAH
I DID THIS IN MY SLEEP...
YOU CAN COME UP WITH A MILLION EXCUSES FOR THAT SCRATCH.
THE POLICE HAVEN'T FOUND ANYTHING UNDER THE VICTIM'S NAILS, SO SHE MUST HAVE BEEN WEARING PRESS-ON NAILS AS PART OF HER COSTUME.
ONCE YOU GOT RID OF THE NAILS, IT'D BE IMPOSSIBLE FOR ANYONE TO PIN THE CRIME ON YOU, RIGHT?
EVEN THOUGH YOU NEEDED TO LEAVE THE SCENE OF THE CRIME AS SOON AS POSSIBLE TO ESTABLISH YOUR ALIBI...
...YOU TOOK THE TIME TO REMOVE EACH AND EVERY FALSE NAIL.
WHY IS THAT?

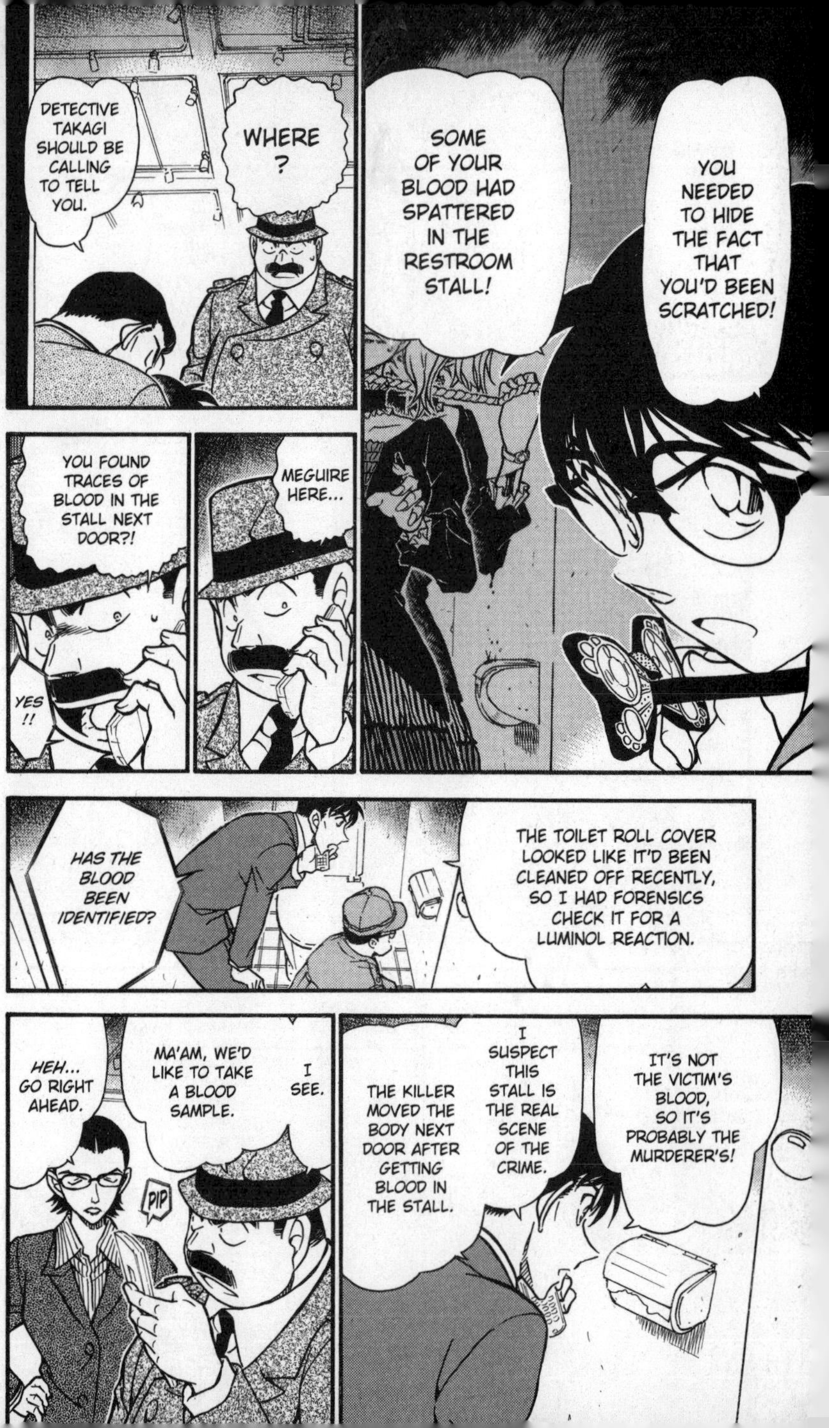
YOU NEEDED TO HIDE THE FACT THAT YOU'D BEEN SCRATCHED!
SOME OF YOUR BLOOD HAD SPATTERED IN THE RESTROOM STALL!
WHERE ?
DETECTIVE TAKAGI SHOULD BE CALLING TO TELL YOU.
MEGUIRE HERE...
YOU FOUND TRACES OF BLOOD IN THE STALL NEXT DOOR?!
YES !!
THE TOILET ROLL COVER LOOKED LIKE IT'D BEEN CLEANED OFF RECENTLY, SO I HAD FORENSICS CHECK IT FOR A LUMINOL REACTION.
HAS THE BLOOD BEEN IDENTIFIED?
IT'S NOT THE VICTIM'S BLOOD, SO IT'S PROBABLY THE MURDERER'S!
I SUSPECT THIS STALL IS THE REAL SCENE OF THE CRIME.
THE KILLER MOVED THE BODY NEXT DOOR AFTER GETTING BLOOD IN THE STALL.
I SEE.
MA'AM, WE'D LIKE TO TAKE A BLOOD SAMPLE.
PIP
HEH... GO RIGHT AHEAD.

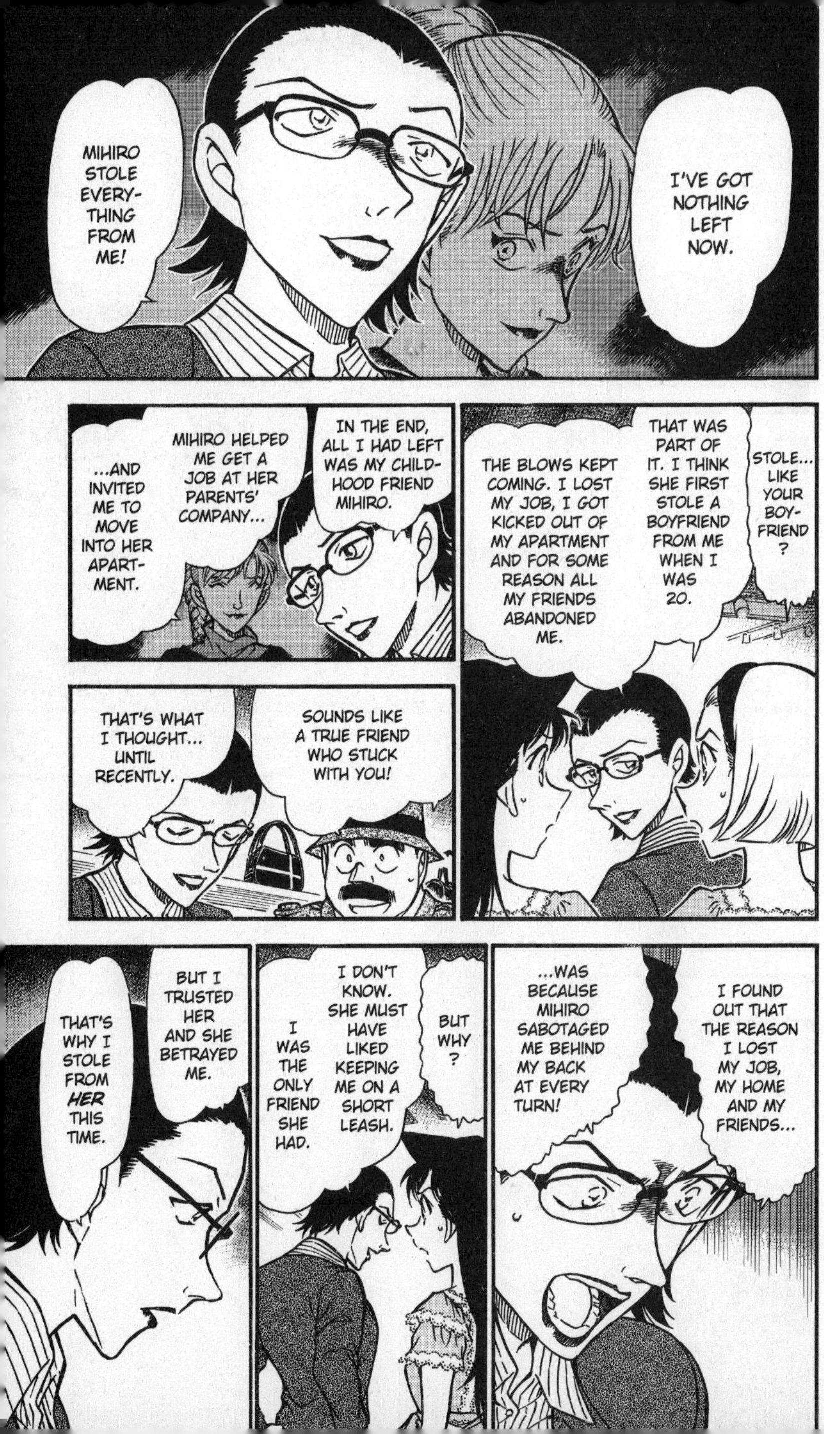
I'VE GOT NOTHING LEFT NOW.
MIHIRO STOLE EVERYTHING FROM ME!
STOLE... LIKE YOUR BOYFRIEND?
THAT WAS PART OF IT. I THINK SHE FIRST STOLE A BOYFRIEND FROM ME WHEN I WAS 20.
THE BLOWS KEPT COMING. I LOST MY JOB, I GOT KICKED OUT OF MY APARTMENT AND FOR SOME REASON ALL MY FRIENDS ABANDONED ME.
IN THE END, ALL I HAD LEFT WAS MY CHILDHOOD FRIEND MIHIRO.
MIHIRO HELPED ME GET A JOB AT HER PARENTS' COMPANY...
...AND INVITED ME TO MOVE INTO HER APARTMENT.
SOUNDS LIKE A TRUE FRIEND WHO STUCK WITH YOU!
THAT'S WHAT I THOUGHT... UNTIL RECENTLY.
I FOUND OUT THAT THE REASON I LOST MY JOB, MY HOME AND MY FRIENDS...
...WAS BECAUSE MIHIRO SABOTAGED ME BEHIND MY BACK AT EVERY TURN!
BUT WHY?
I DON'T KNOW. SHE MUST HAVE LIKED KEEPING ME ON A SHORT LEASH.
I WAS THE ONLY FRIEND SHE HAD.
BUT I TRUSTED HER AND SHE BETRAYED ME.
THAT'S WHY I STOLE FROM *HER* THIS TIME.

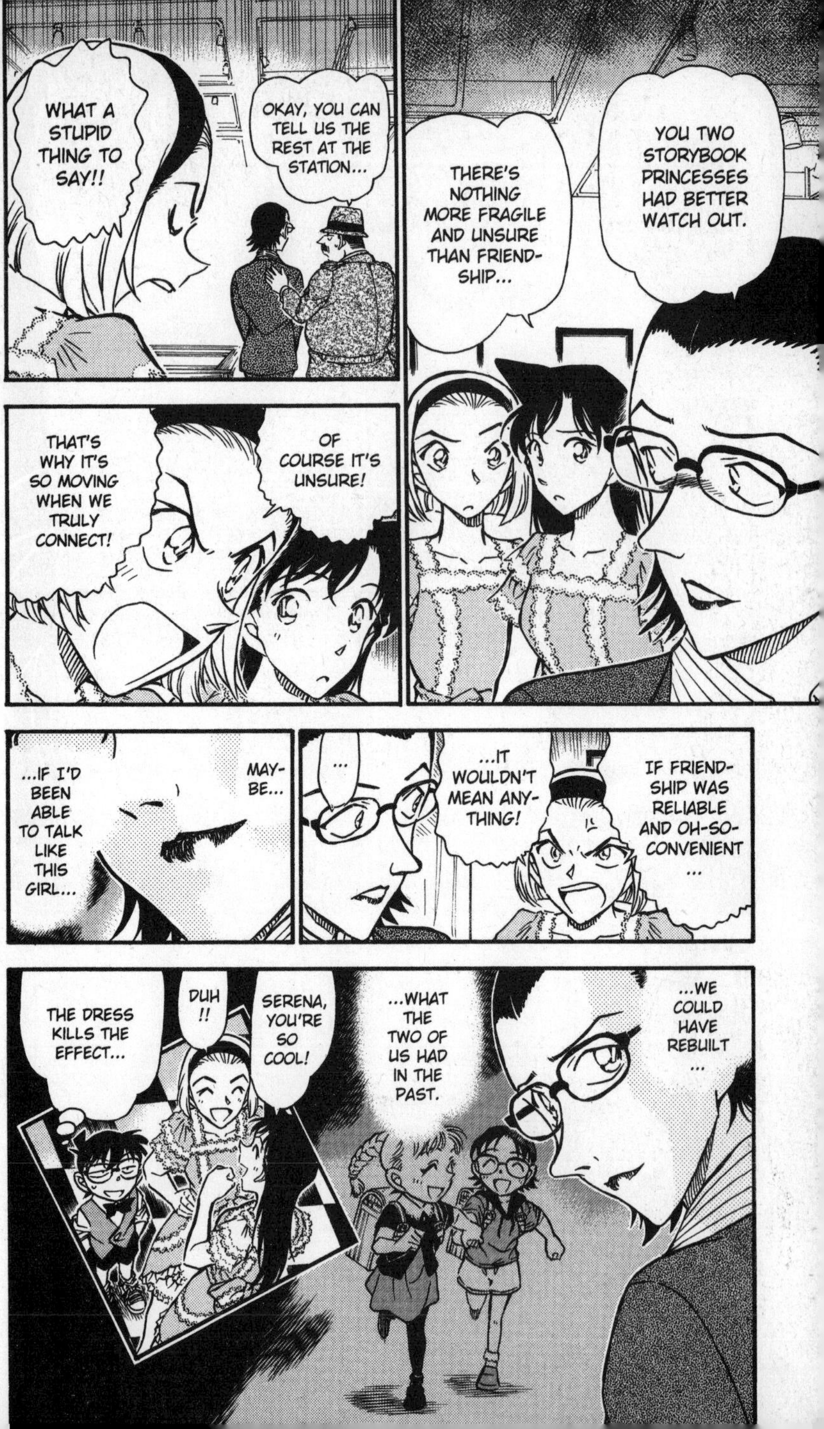
YOU TWO STORYBOOK PRINCESSES HAD BETTER WATCH OUT.
THERE'S NOTHING MORE FRAGILE AND UNSURE THAN FRIEND-SHIP...
OKAY, YOU CAN TELL US THE REST AT THE STATION...
WHAT A STUPID THING TO SAY!!
OF COURSE IT'S UNSURE!
THAT'S WHY IT'S SO MOVING WHEN WE TRULY CONNECT!
IF FRIEND-SHIP WAS RELIABLE AND OH-SO-CONVENIENT ...
...IT WOULDN'T MEAN ANY-THING!
...
MAY-BE...
...IF I'D BEEN ABLE TO TALK LIKE THIS GIRL...
...WE COULD HAVE REBUILT ...
...WHAT THE TWO OF US HAD IN THE PAST.
SERENA, YOU'RE SO COOL!
DUH !!
THE DRESS KILLS THE EFFECT...

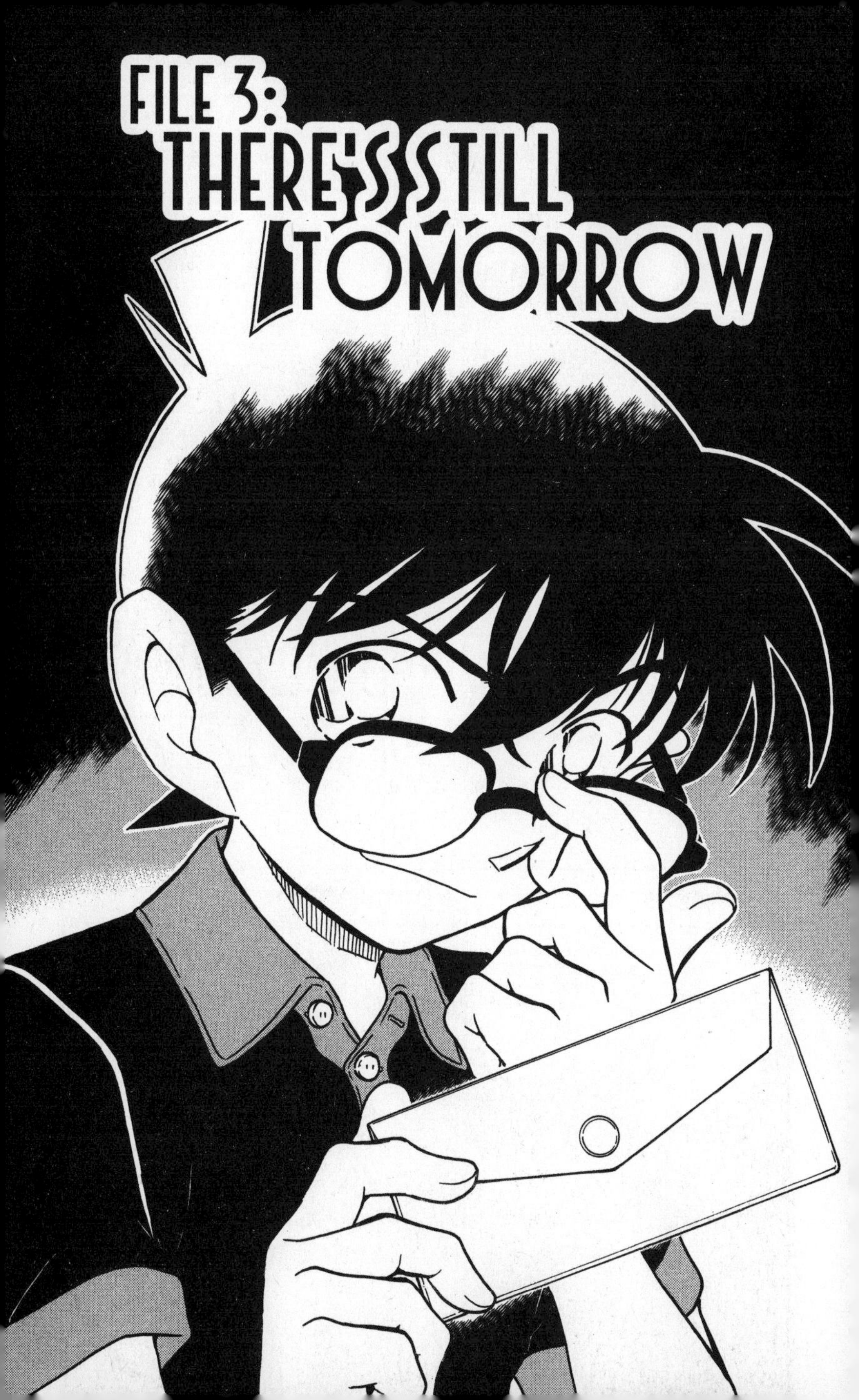
FILE 3:
THERE'S STILL
TOMORROW

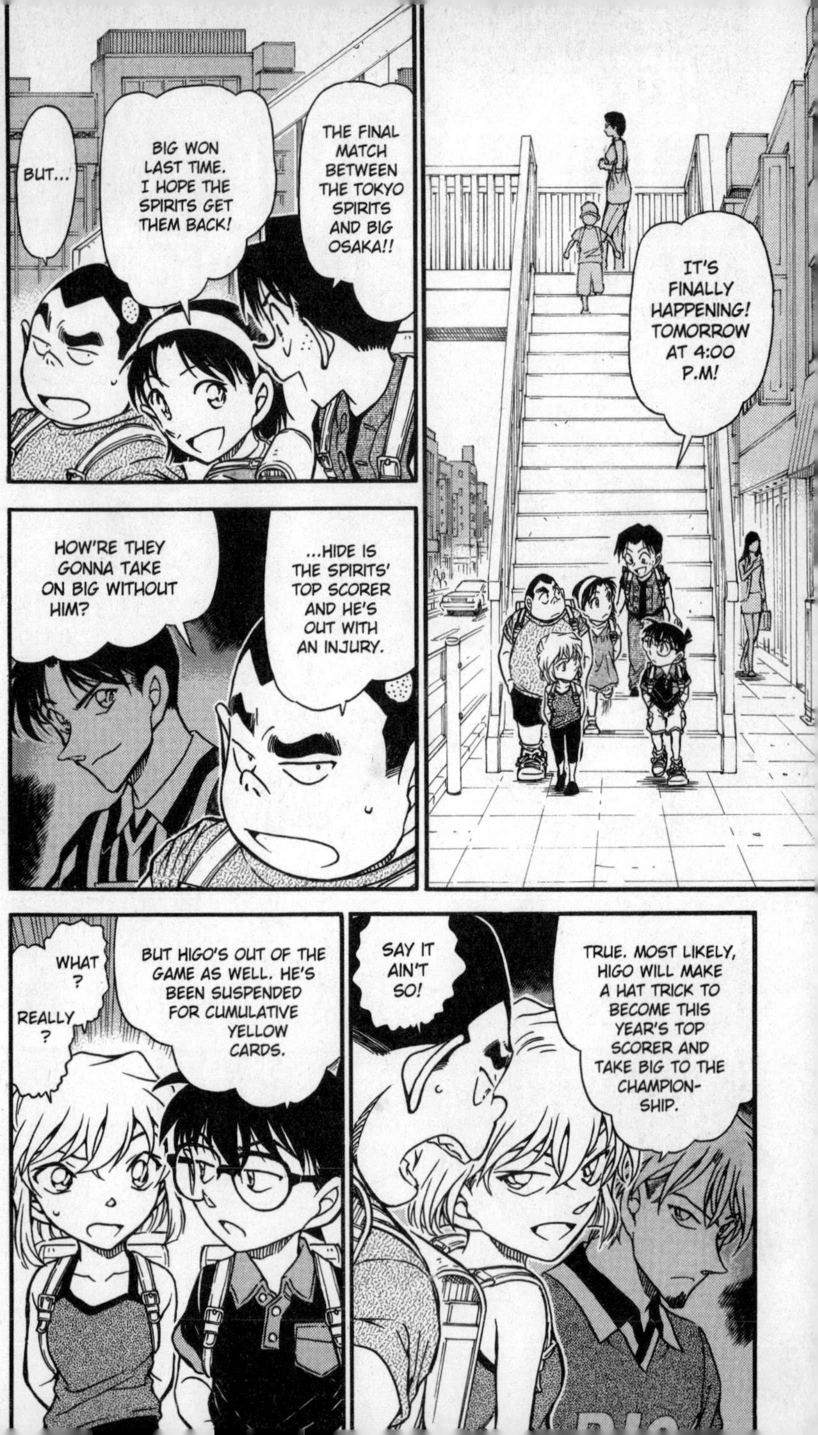
IT'S FINALLY HAPPENING! TOMORROW AT 4:00 P.M!
THE FINAL MATCH BETWEEN THE TOKYO SPIRITS AND BIG OSAKA!!
BIG WON LAST TIME. I HOPE THE SPIRITS GET THEM BACK!
BUT...
...HIDE IS THE SPIRITS' TOP SCORER AND HE'S OUT WITH AN INJURY.
HOW'RE THEY GONNA TAKE ON BIG WITHOUT HIM?
TRUE. MOST LIKELY, HIGO WILL MAKE A HAT TRICK TO BECOME THIS YEAR'S TOP SCORER AND TAKE BIG TO THE CHAMPIONSHIP.
SAY IT AIN'T SO!
BUT HIGO'S OUT OF THE GAME AS WELL. HE'S BEEN SUSPENDED FOR CUMULATIVE YELLOW CARDS.
WHAT?
REALLY?

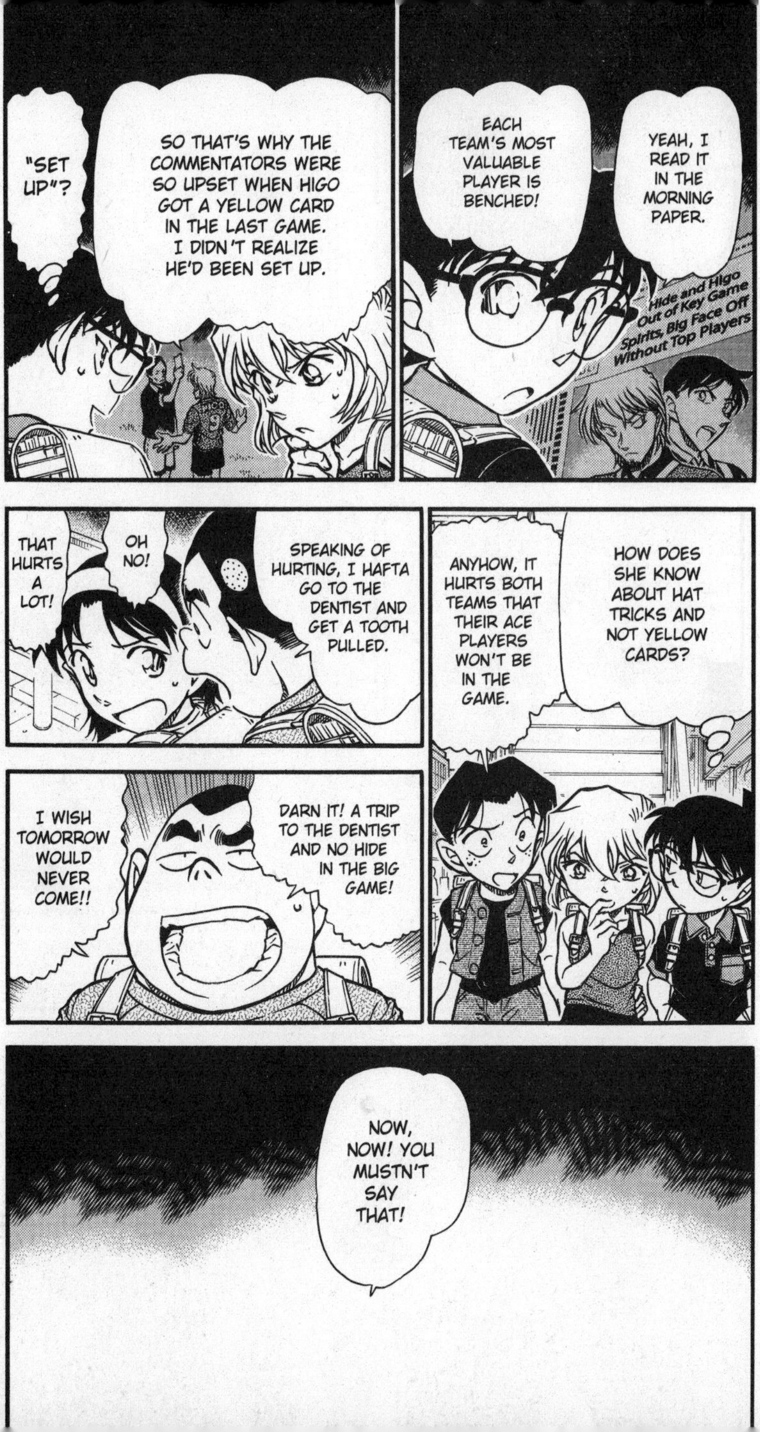
YEAH, I READ IT IN THE MORNING PAPER.
EACH TEAM'S MOST VALUABLE PLAYER IS BENCHED!
Hide and Higo Out of Key Game
Spirits, Big Face Off Without Top Players
SO THAT'S WHY THE COMMENTATORS WERE SO UPSET WHEN HIGO GOT A YELLOW CARD IN THE LAST GAME. I DIDN'T REALIZE HE'D BEEN SET UP.
"SET UP"?
ANYHOW, IT HURTS BOTH TEAMS THAT THEIR ACE PLAYERS WON'T BE IN THE GAME.
HOW DOES SHE KNOW ABOUT HAT TRICKS AND NOT YELLOW CARDS?
SPEAKING OF HURTING, I HAFTA GO TO THE DENTIST AND GET A TOOTH PULLED.
OH NO!
THAT HURTS A LOT!
DARN IT! A TRIP TO THE DENTIST AND NO HIDE IN THE BIG GAME!
I WISH TOMORROW WOULD NEVER COME!!
NOW, NOW! YOU MUSTN'T SAY THAT!

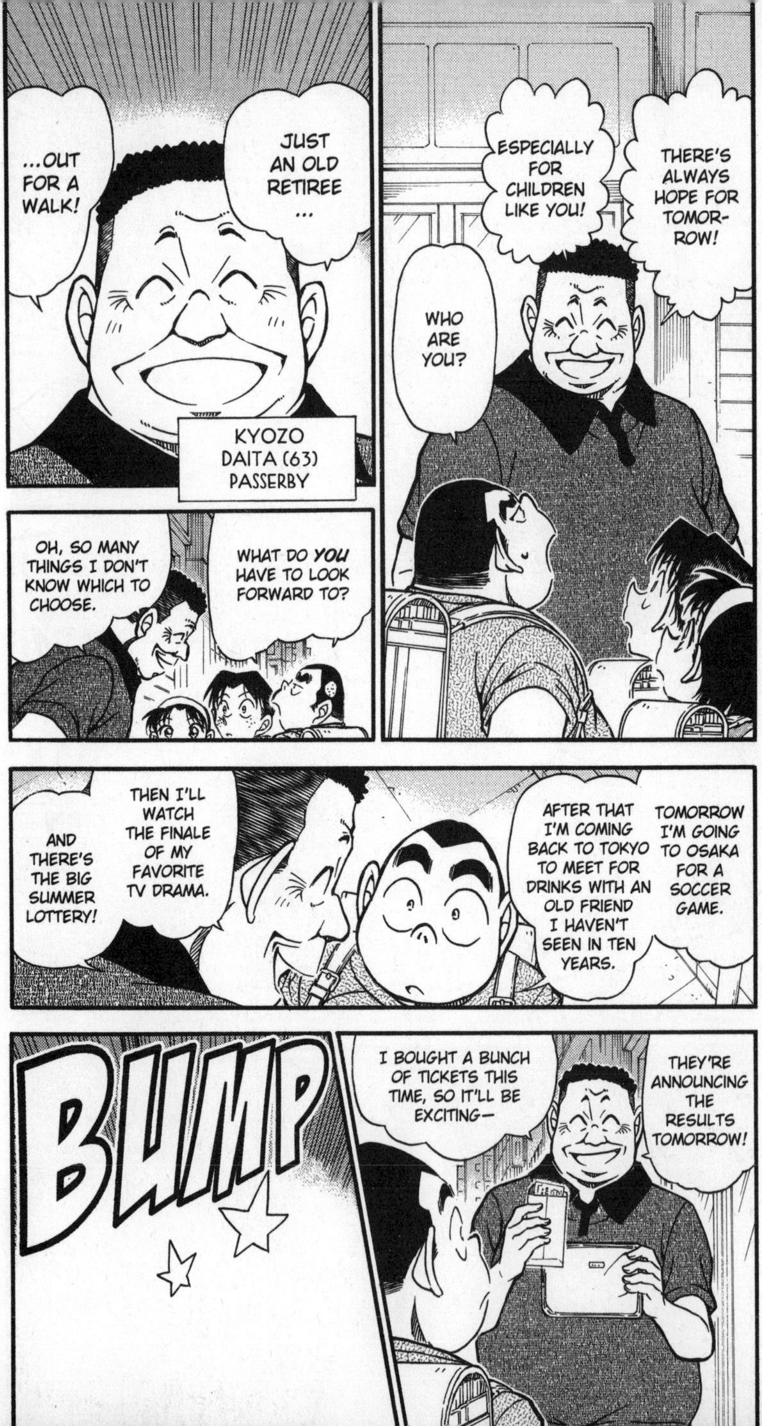
THERE'S ALWAYS HOPE FOR TOMORROW!
ESPECIALLY FOR CHILDREN LIKE YOU!
WHO ARE YOU?
JUST AN OLD RETIREE ...
...OUT FOR A WALK!
KYOZO DAITA (63) PASSERBY
WHAT DO *YOU* HAVE TO LOOK FORWARD TO?
OH, SO MANY THINGS I DON'T KNOW WHICH TO CHOOSE.
TOMORROW I'M GOING TO OSAKA FOR A SOCCER GAME.
AFTER THAT I'M COMING BACK TO TOKYO TO MEET FOR DRINKS WITH AN OLD FRIEND I HAVEN'T SEEN IN TEN YEARS.
THEN I'LL WATCH THE FINALE OF MY FAVORITE TV DRAMA.
AND THERE'S THE BIG SUMMER LOTTERY!
THEY'RE ANNOUNCING THE RESULTS TOMORROW!
I BOUGHT A BUNCH OF TICKETS THIS TIME, SO IT'LL BE EXCITING—
BUMP

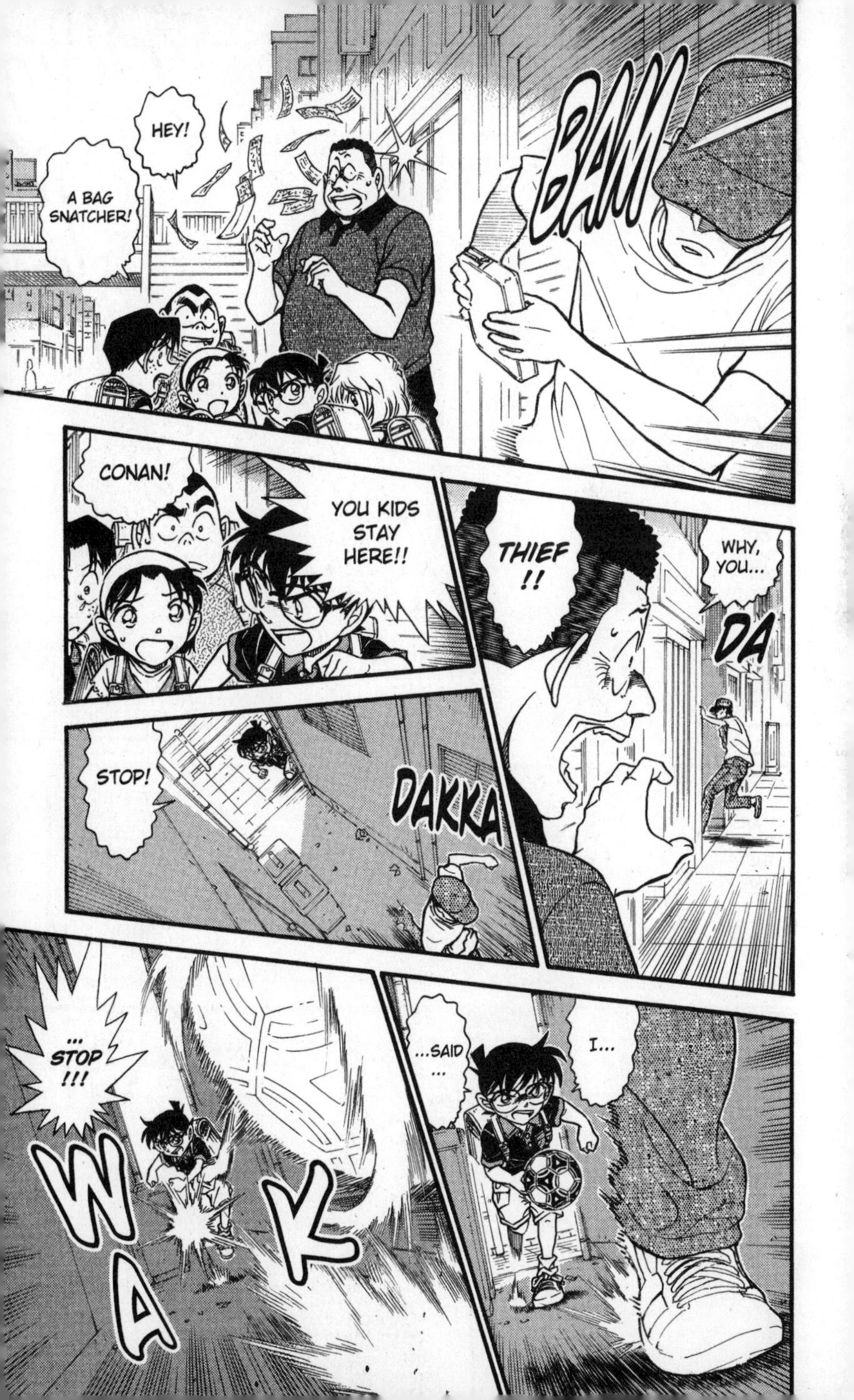
BAM
HEY!
A BAG SNATCHER!
WHY, YOU...
THIEF !!
DA
CONAN!
YOU KIDS STAY HERE!!
DAKKA
STOP!
I...
...SAID ...
... STOP !!!
WAK

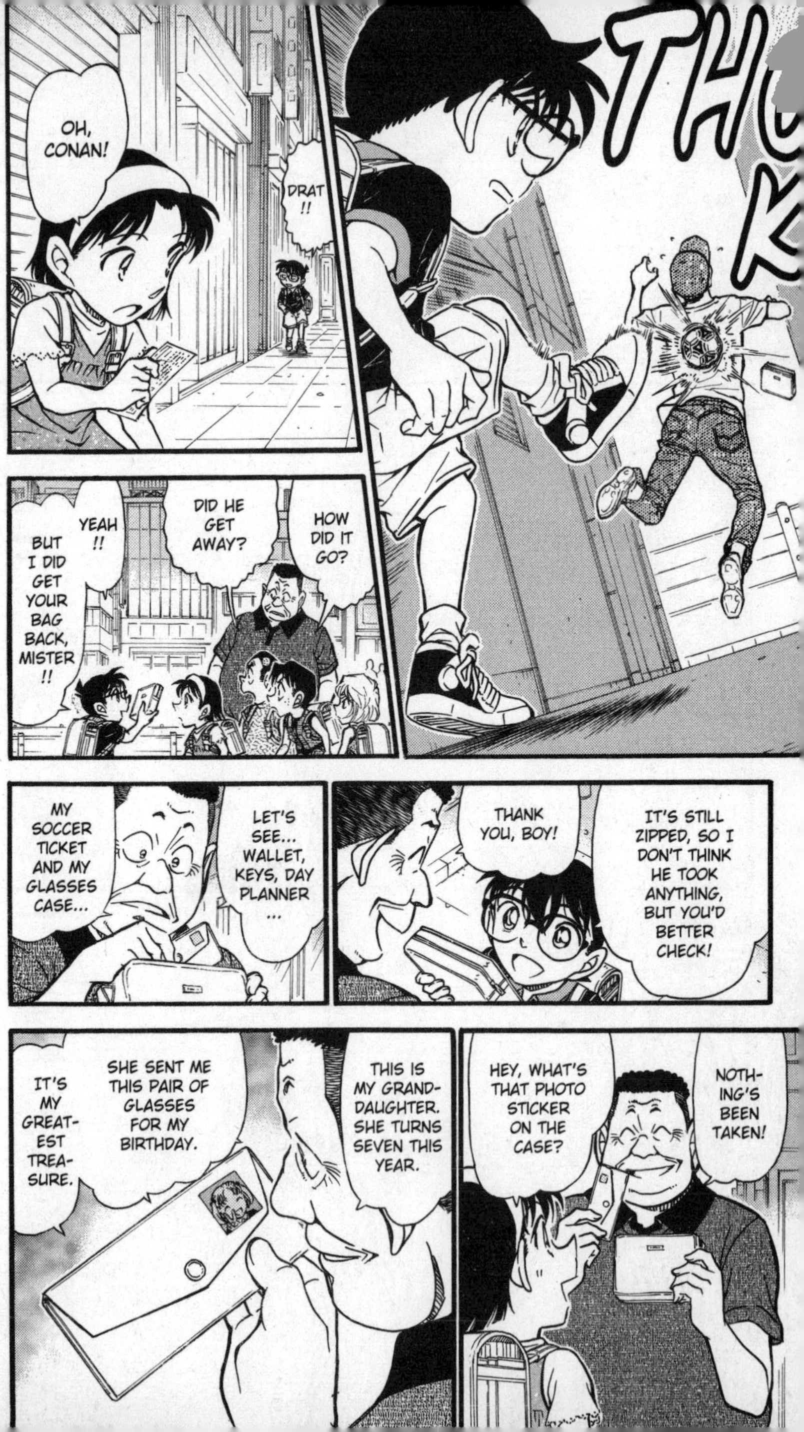
OH, CONAN!
DRAT!!
HOW DID IT GO?
DID HE GET AWAY?
YEAH!!
BUT I DID GET YOUR BAG BACK, MISTER!!
IT'S STILL ZIPPED, SO I DON'T THINK HE TOOK ANYTHING, BUT YOU'D BETTER CHECK!
THANK YOU, BOY!
LET'S SEE... WALLET, KEYS, DAY PLANNER...
MY SOCCER TICKET AND MY GLASSES CASE...
NOTH-ING'S BEEN TAKEN!
HEY, WHAT'S THAT PHOTO STICKER ON THE CASE?
THIS IS MY GRAND-DAUGHTER. SHE TURNS SEVEN THIS YEAR.
SHE SENT ME THIS PAIR OF GLASSES FOR MY BIRTHDAY.
IT'S MY GREAT-EST TREA-SURE.

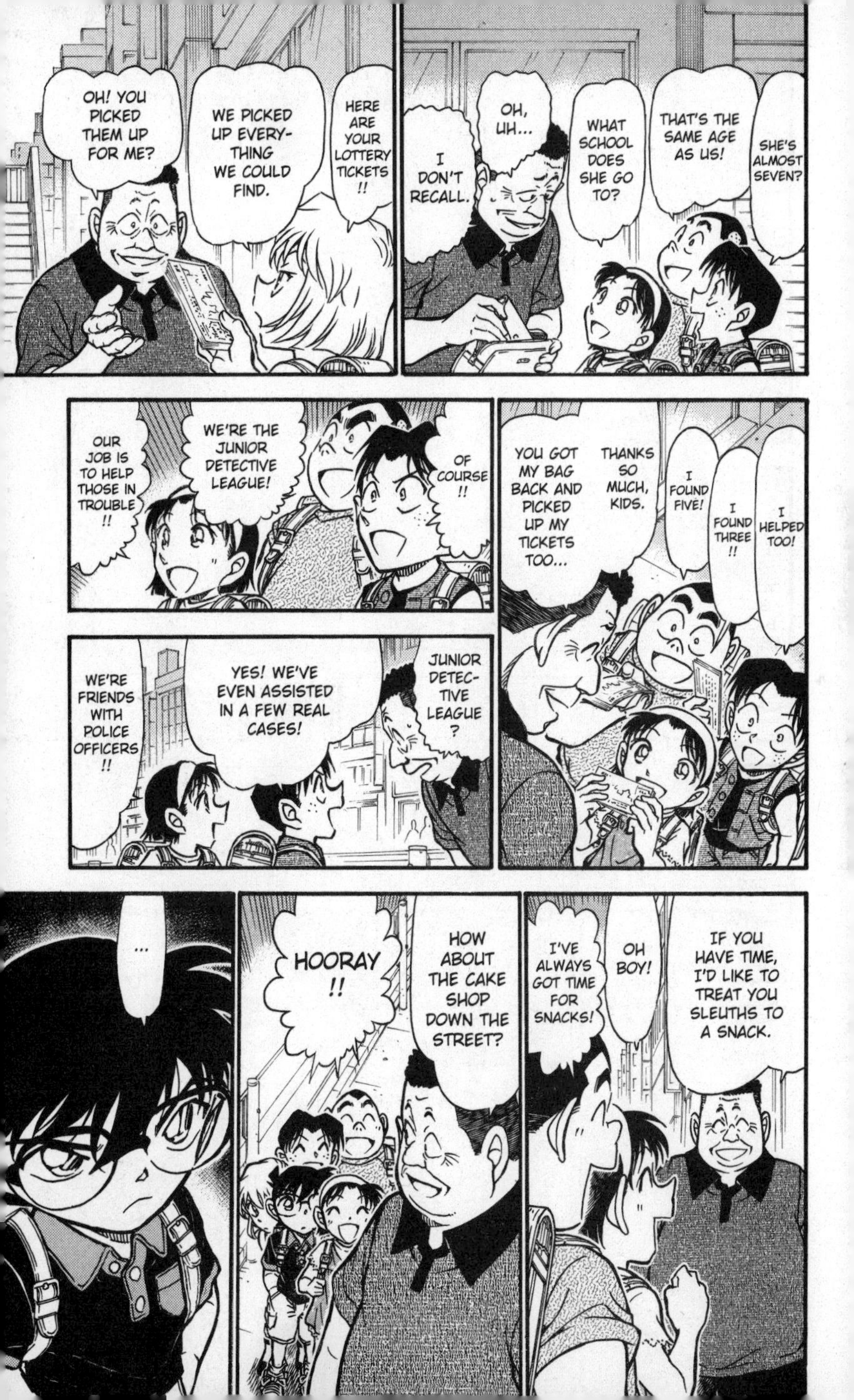
SHE'S ALMOST SEVEN?
THAT'S THE SAME AGE AS US!
WHAT SCHOOL DOES SHE GO TO?
OH, UH...
I DON'T RECALL.
HERE ARE YOUR LOTTERY TICKETS !!
WE PICKED UP EVERYTHING WE COULD FIND.
OH! YOU PICKED THEM UP FOR ME?
I HELPED TOO!
I FOUND THREE !!
I FOUND FIVE!
THANKS SO MUCH, KIDS.
YOU GOT MY BAG BACK AND PICKED UP MY TICKETS TOO...
OF COURSE !!
WE'RE THE JUNIOR DETECTIVE LEAGUE!
OUR JOB IS TO HELP THOSE IN TROUBLE !!
JUNIOR DETECTIVE LEAGUE ?
YES! WE'VE EVEN ASSISTED IN A FEW REAL CASES!
WE'RE FRIENDS WITH POLICE OFFICERS !!
IF YOU HAVE TIME, I'D LIKE TO TREAT YOU SLEUTHS TO A SNACK.
OH BOY!
I'VE ALWAYS GOT TIME FOR SNACKS!
HOW ABOUT THE CAKE SHOP DOWN THE STREET?
HOORAY !!
...

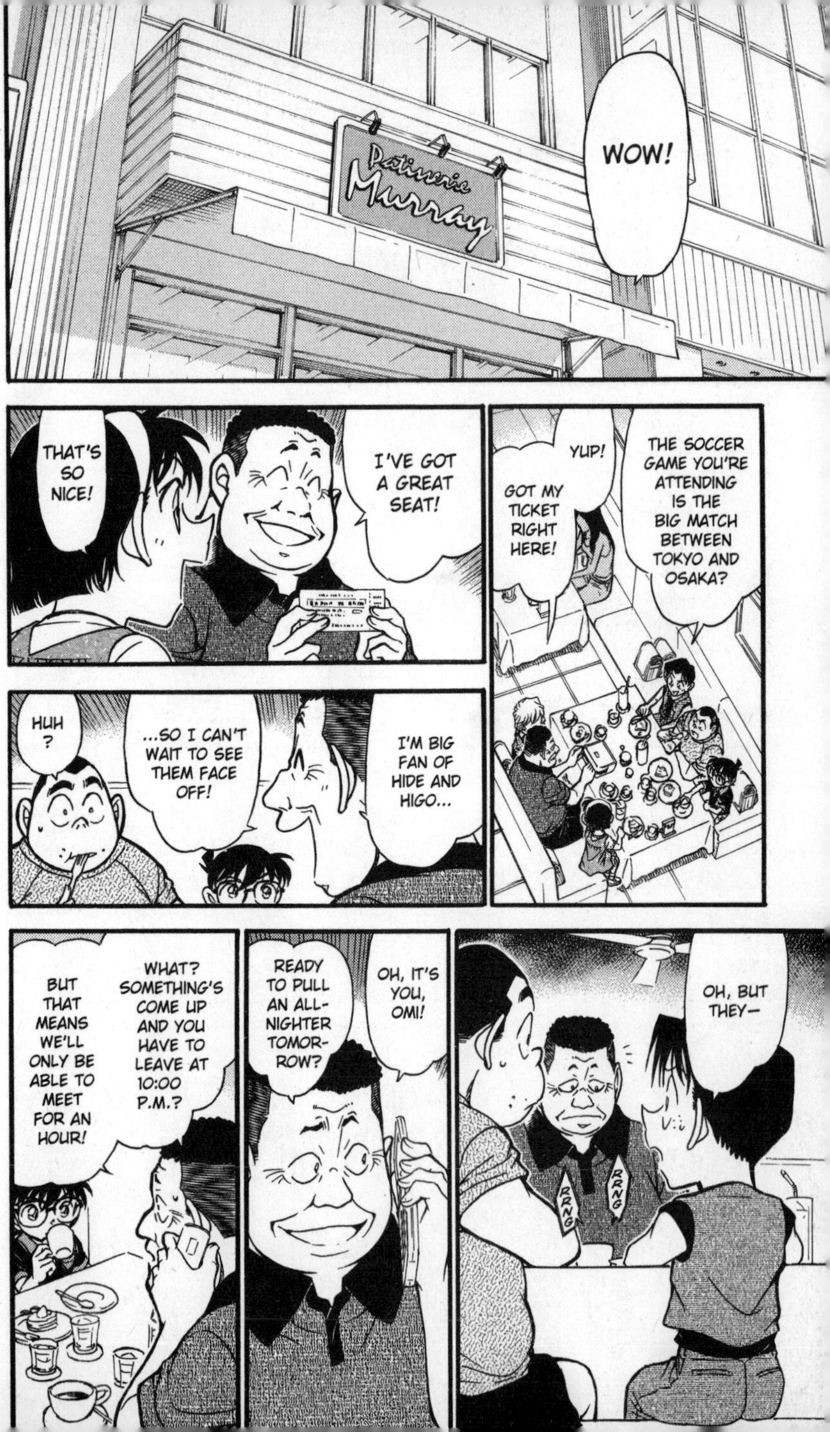
Patisserie Murray
WOW!
THE SOCCER GAME YOU'RE ATTENDING IS THE BIG MATCH BETWEEN TOKYO AND OSAKA?
YUP!
GOT MY TICKET RIGHT HERE!
I'VE GOT A GREAT SEAT!
THAT'S SO NICE!
I'M BIG FAN OF HIDE AND HIGO...
...SO I CAN'T WAIT TO SEE THEM FACE OFF!
HUH?
OH, BUT THEY—
RRNG
RRNG
OH, IT'S YOU, OMI!
READY TO PULL AN ALL-NIGHTER TOMORROW?
WHAT? SOMETHING'S COME UP AND YOU HAVE TO LEAVE AT 10:00 P.M.?
BUT THAT MEANS WE'LL ONLY BE ABLE TO MEET FOR AN HOUR!

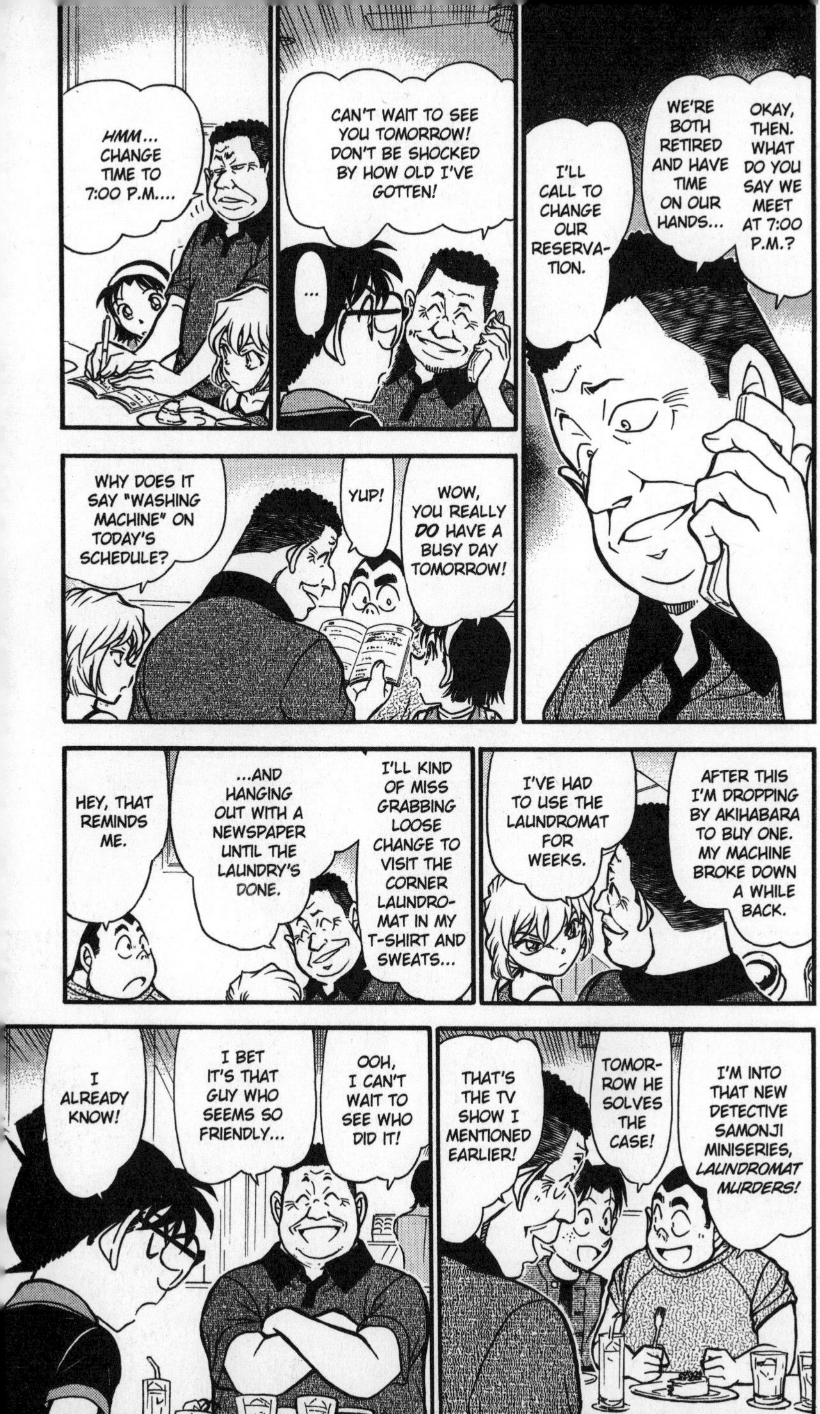
OKAY, THEN. WHAT DO YOU SAY WE MEET AT 7:00 P.M.?
WE'RE BOTH RETIRED AND HAVE TIME ON OUR HANDS...
I'LL CALL TO CHANGE OUR RESERVATION.
CAN'T WAIT TO SEE YOU TOMORROW! DON'T BE SHOCKED BY HOW OLD I'VE GOTTEN!
...
HMM... CHANGE TIME TO 7:00 P.M....
WOW, YOU REALLY *DO* HAVE A BUSY DAY TOMORROW!
YUP!
WHY DOES IT SAY "WASHING MACHINE" ON TODAY'S SCHEDULE?
AFTER THIS I'M DROPPING BY AKIHABARA TO BUY ONE. MY MACHINE BROKE DOWN A WHILE BACK.
I'VE HAD TO USE THE LAUNDROMAT FOR WEEKS.
I'LL KIND OF MISS GRABBING LOOSE CHANGE TO VISIT THE CORNER LAUNDROMAT IN MY T-SHIRT AND SWEATS...
...AND HANGING OUT WITH A NEWSPAPER UNTIL THE LAUNDRY'S DONE.
HEY, THAT REMINDS ME.
I'M INTO THAT NEW DETECTIVE SAMONJI MINISERIES, *LAUNDROMAT MURDERS!*
TOMORROW HE SOLVES THE CASE!
THAT'S THE TV SHOW I MENTIONED EARLIER!
OOH, I CAN'T WAIT TO SEE WHO DID IT!
I BET IT'S THAT GUY WHO SEEMS SO FRIENDLY...
I ALREADY KNOW!

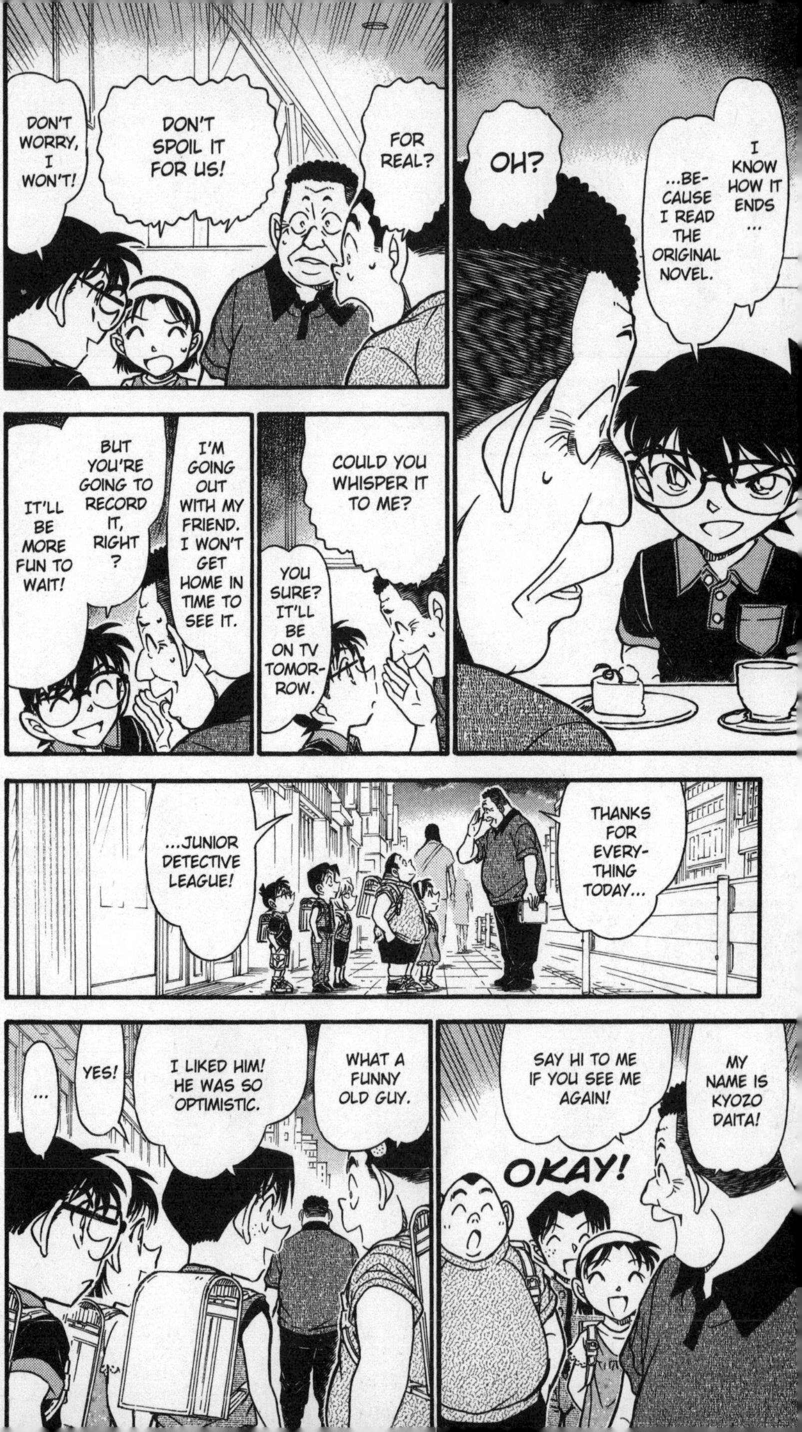
I KNOW HOW IT ENDS...
...BECAUSE I READ THE ORIGINAL NOVEL.
OH?
FOR REAL?
DON'T SPOIL IT FOR US!
DON'T WORRY, I WON'T!
COULD YOU WHISPER IT TO ME?
YOU SURE? IT'LL BE ON TV TOMORROW.
I'M GOING OUT WITH MY FRIEND. I WON'T GET HOME IN TIME TO SEE IT.
BUT YOU'RE GOING TO RECORD IT, RIGHT?
IT'LL BE MORE FUN TO WAIT!
THANKS FOR EVERYTHING TODAY...
...JUNIOR DETECTIVE LEAGUE!
MY NAME IS KYOZO DAITA!
SAY HI TO ME IF YOU SEE ME AGAIN!
OKAY!
WHAT A FUNNY OLD GUY.
I LIKED HIM! HE WAS SO OPTIMISTIC.
YES!
...

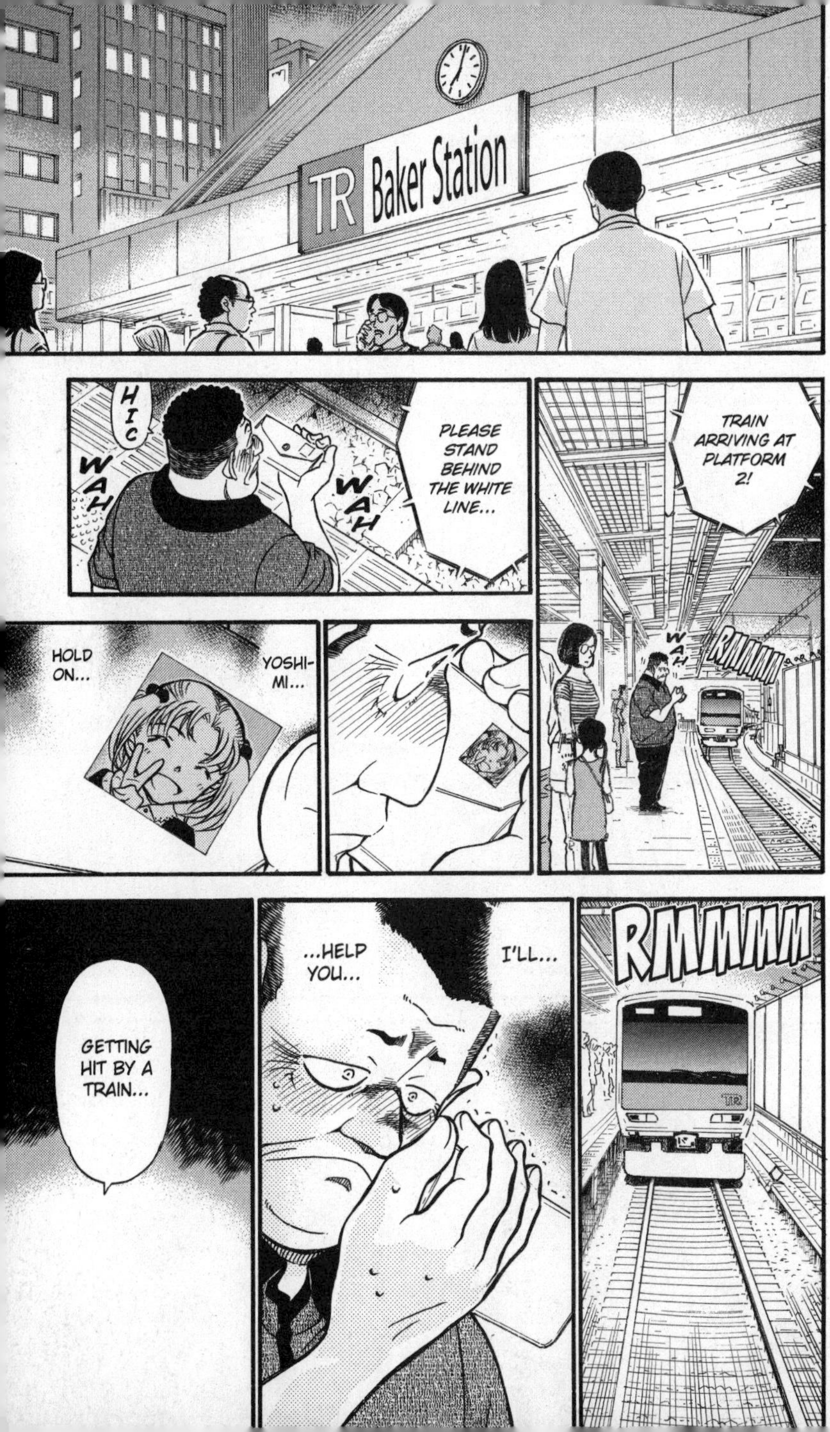
TR Baker Station
TRAIN ARRIVING AT PLATFORM 2!
WAH
RMMMM
PLEASE STAND BEHIND THE WHITE LINE...
WAH
HIC
WAH
YOSHI-MI...
HOLD ON...
RMMMMM
I'LL...
...HELP YOU...
GETTING HIT BY A TRAIN...

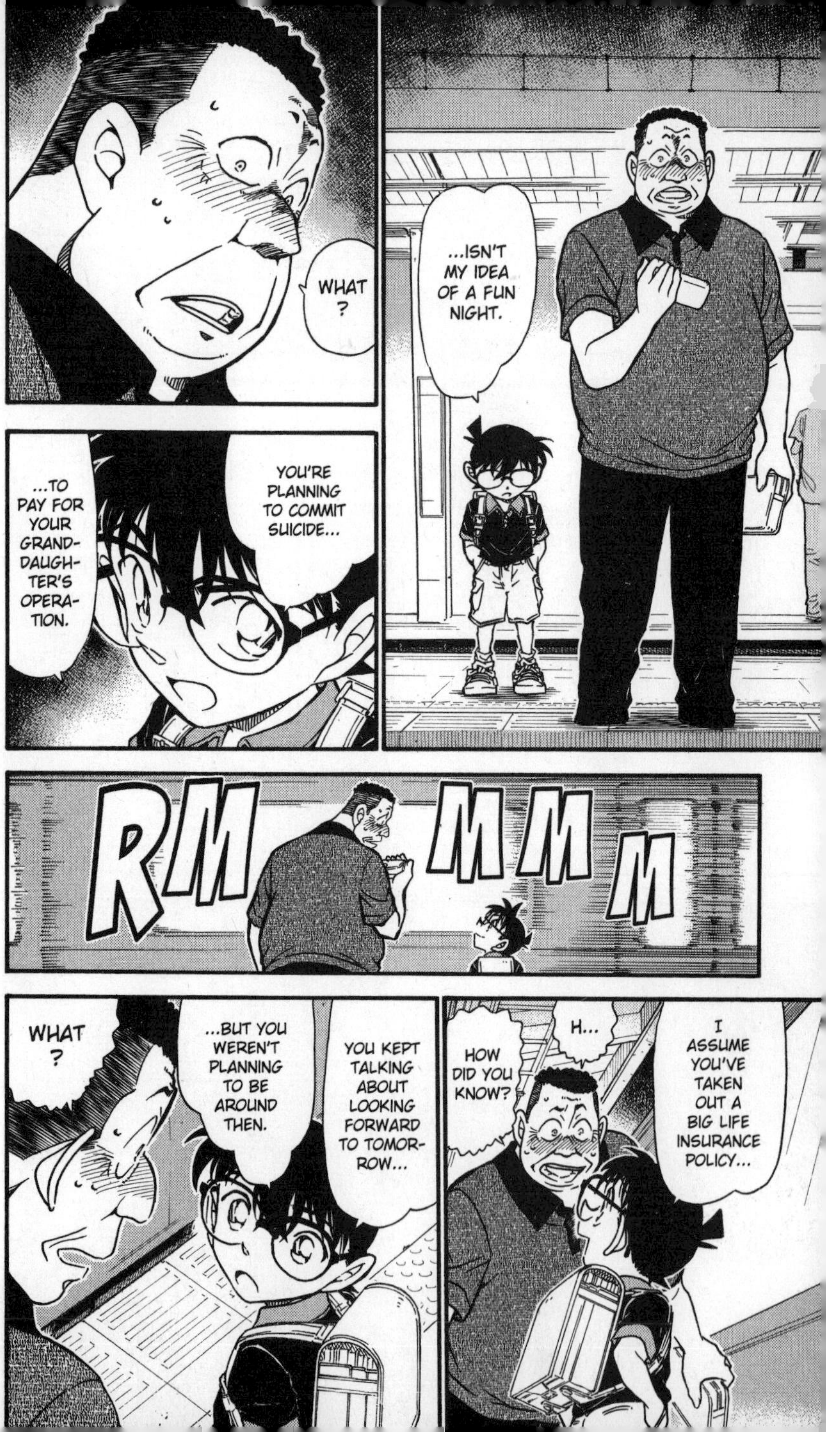
...ISN'T MY IDEA OF A FUN NIGHT.
WHAT?
YOU'RE PLANNING TO COMMIT SUICIDE...
...TO PAY FOR YOUR GRAND-DAUGHTER'S OPERA-TION.
RMMMMM
I ASSUME YOU'VE TAKEN OUT A BIG LIFE INSURANCE POLICY...
H...
HOW DID YOU KNOW?
YOU KEPT TALKING ABOUT LOOKING FORWARD TO TOMOR-ROW...
...BUT YOU WEREN'T PLANNING TO BE AROUND THEN.
WHAT?

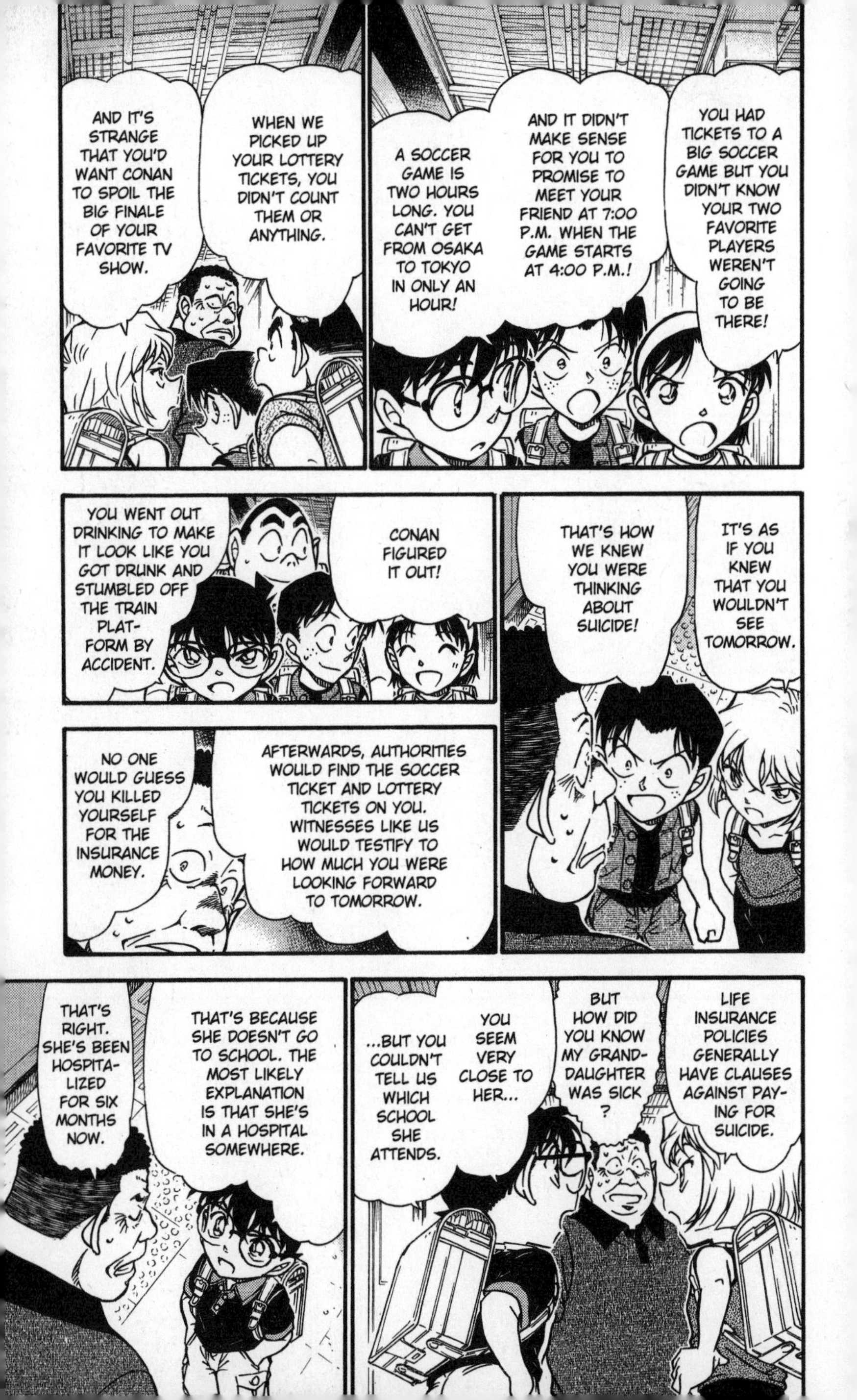
YOU HAD TICKETS TO A BIG SOCCER GAME BUT YOU DIDN'T KNOW YOUR TWO FAVORITE PLAYERS WEREN'T GOING TO BE THERE!
AND IT DIDN'T MAKE SENSE FOR YOU TO PROMISE TO MEET YOUR FRIEND AT 7:00 P.M. WHEN THE GAME STARTS AT 4:00 P.M.!
A SOCCER GAME IS TWO HOURS LONG. YOU CAN'T GET FROM OSAKA TO TOKYO IN ONLY AN HOUR!
WHEN WE PICKED UP YOUR LOTTERY TICKETS, YOU DIDN'T COUNT THEM OR ANYTHING.
AND IT'S STRANGE THAT YOU'D WANT CONAN TO SPOIL THE BIG FINALE OF YOUR FAVORITE TV SHOW.
IT'S AS IF YOU KNEW THAT YOU WOULDN'T SEE TOMORROW.
THAT'S HOW WE KNEW YOU WERE THINKING ABOUT SUICIDE!
CONAN FIGURED IT OUT!
YOU WENT OUT DRINKING TO MAKE IT LOOK LIKE YOU GOT DRUNK AND STUMBLED OFF THE TRAIN PLAT-FORM BY ACCIDENT.
AFTERWARDS, AUTHORITIES WOULD FIND THE SOCCER TICKET AND LOTTERY TICKETS ON YOU. WITNESSES LIKE US WOULD TESTIFY TO HOW MUCH YOU WERE LOOKING FORWARD TO TOMORROW.
NO ONE WOULD GUESS YOU KILLED YOURSELF FOR THE INSURANCE MONEY.
LIFE INSURANCE POLICIES GENERALLY HAVE CLAUSES AGAINST PAY-ING FOR SUICIDE.
BUT HOW DID YOU KNOW MY GRAND-DAUGHTER WAS SICK?
YOU SEEM VERY CLOSE TO HER...
...BUT YOU COULDN'T TELL US WHICH SCHOOL SHE ATTENDS.
THAT'S BECAUSE SHE DOESN'T GO TO SCHOOL. THE MOST LIKELY EXPLANATION IS THAT SHE'S IN A HOSPITAL SOMEWHERE.
THAT'S RIGHT. SHE'S BEEN HOSPITA-LIZED FOR SIX MONTHS NOW.

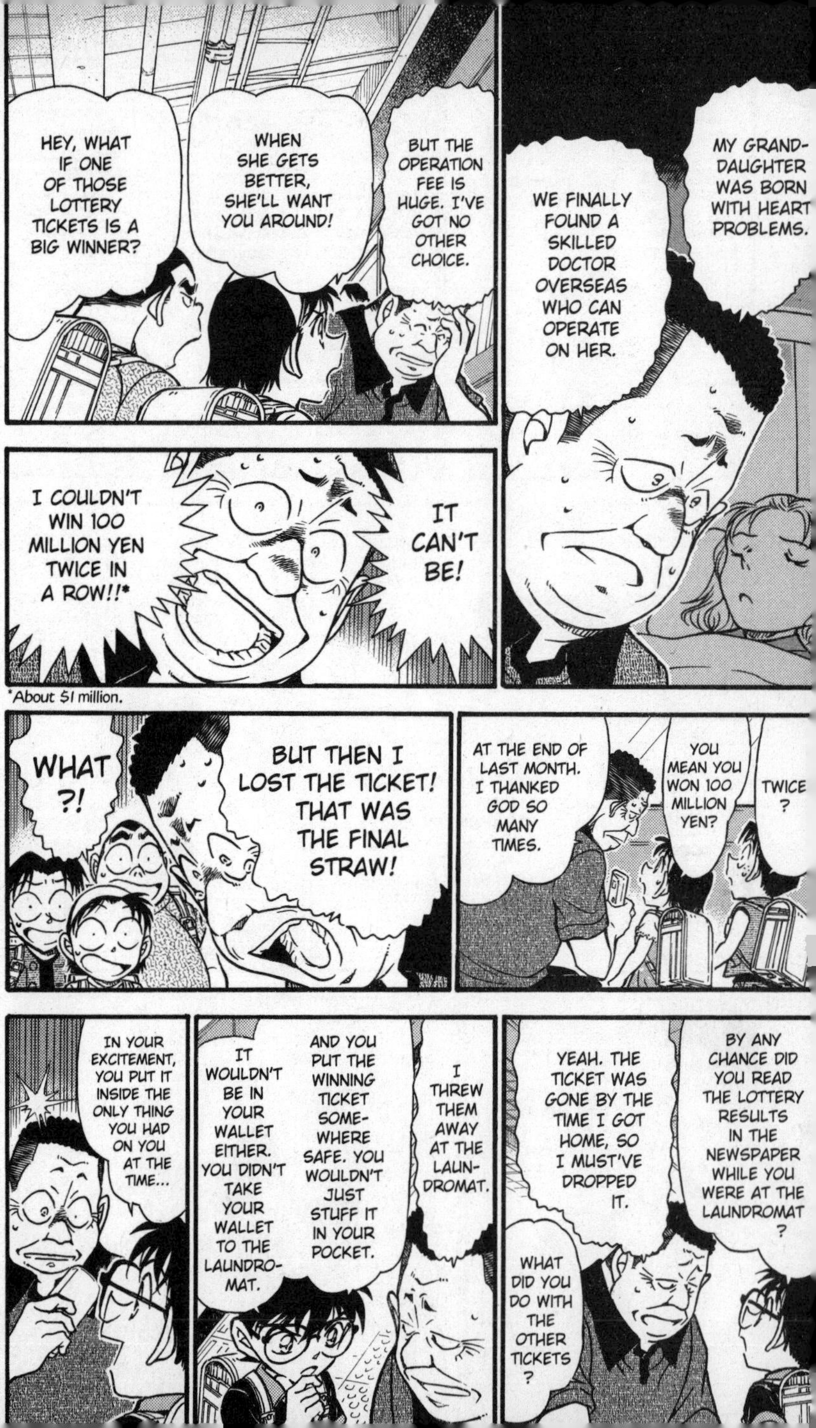
MY GRAND-DAUGHTER WAS BORN WITH HEART PROBLEMS.
WE FINALLY FOUND A SKILLED DOCTOR OVERSEAS WHO CAN OPERATE ON HER.
BUT THE OPERATION FEE IS HUGE. I'VE GOT NO OTHER CHOICE.
WHEN SHE GETS BETTER, SHE'LL WANT YOU AROUND!
HEY, WHAT IF ONE OF THOSE LOTTERY TICKETS IS A BIG WINNER?
IT CAN'T BE!
I COULDN'T WIN 100 MILLION YEN TWICE IN A ROW!!*
TWICE?
YOU MEAN YOU WON 100 MILLION YEN?
AT THE END OF LAST MONTH. I THANKED GOD SO MANY TIMES.
BUT THEN I LOST THE TICKET! THAT WAS THE FINAL STRAW!
WHAT?!
BY ANY CHANCE DID YOU READ THE LOTTERY RESULTS IN THE NEWSPAPER WHILE YOU WERE AT THE LAUNDROMAT?
YEAH. THE TICKET WAS GONE BY THE TIME I GOT HOME, SO I MUST'VE DROPPED IT.
WHAT DID YOU DO WITH THE OTHER TICKETS?
I THREW THEM AWAY AT THE LAUNDROMAT.
AND YOU PUT THE WINNING TICKET SOMEWHERE SAFE. YOU WOULDN'T JUST STUFF IT IN YOUR POCKET.
IT WOULDN'T BE IN YOUR WALLET EITHER. YOU DIDN'T TAKE YOUR WALLET TO THE LAUNDROMAT.
IN YOUR EXCITEMENT, YOU PUT IT INSIDE THE ONLY THING YOU HAD ON YOU AT THE TIME...

*About $1 million.

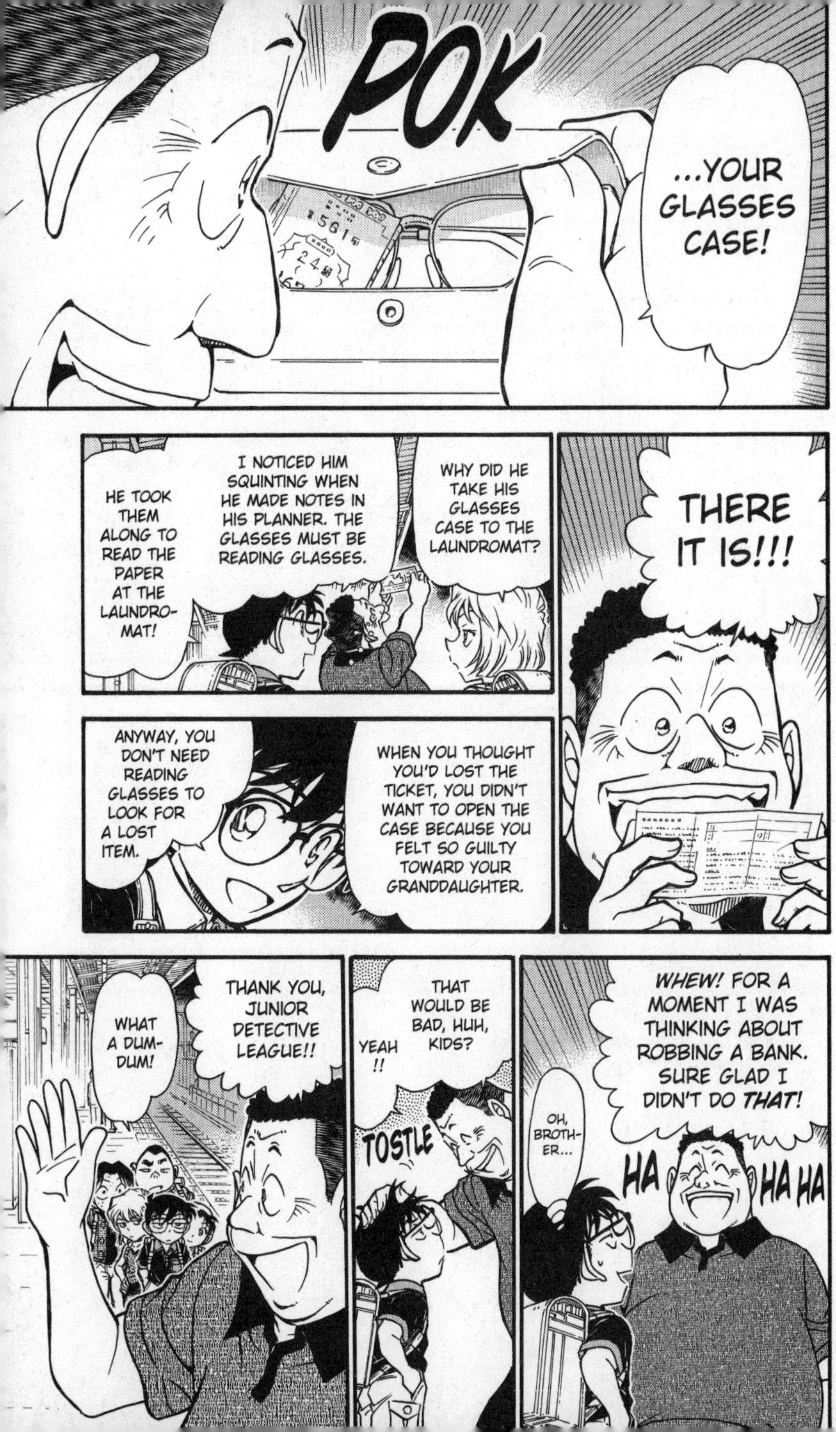
...YOUR GLASSES CASE!
POK
THERE IT IS!!!
WHY DID HE TAKE HIS GLASSES CASE TO THE LAUNDROMAT?
I NOTICED HIM SQUINTING WHEN HE MADE NOTES IN HIS PLANNER. THE GLASSES MUST BE READING GLASSES.
HE TOOK THEM ALONG TO READ THE PAPER AT THE LAUNDRO-MAT!
WHEN YOU THOUGHT YOU'D LOST THE TICKET, YOU DIDN'T WANT TO OPEN THE CASE BECAUSE YOU FELT SO GUILTY TOWARD YOUR GRANDDAUGHTER.
ANYWAY, YOU DON'T NEED READING GLASSES TO LOOK FOR A LOST ITEM.
WHEW! FOR A MOMENT I WAS THINKING ABOUT ROBBING A BANK. SURE GLAD I DIDN'T DO THAT!
HA HA HA
OH, BROTHER-ER...
THAT WOULD BE BAD, HUH, KIDS?
YEAH !!
TOSTLE
THANK YOU, JUNIOR DETECTIVE LEAGUE!!
WHAT A DUM-DUM!

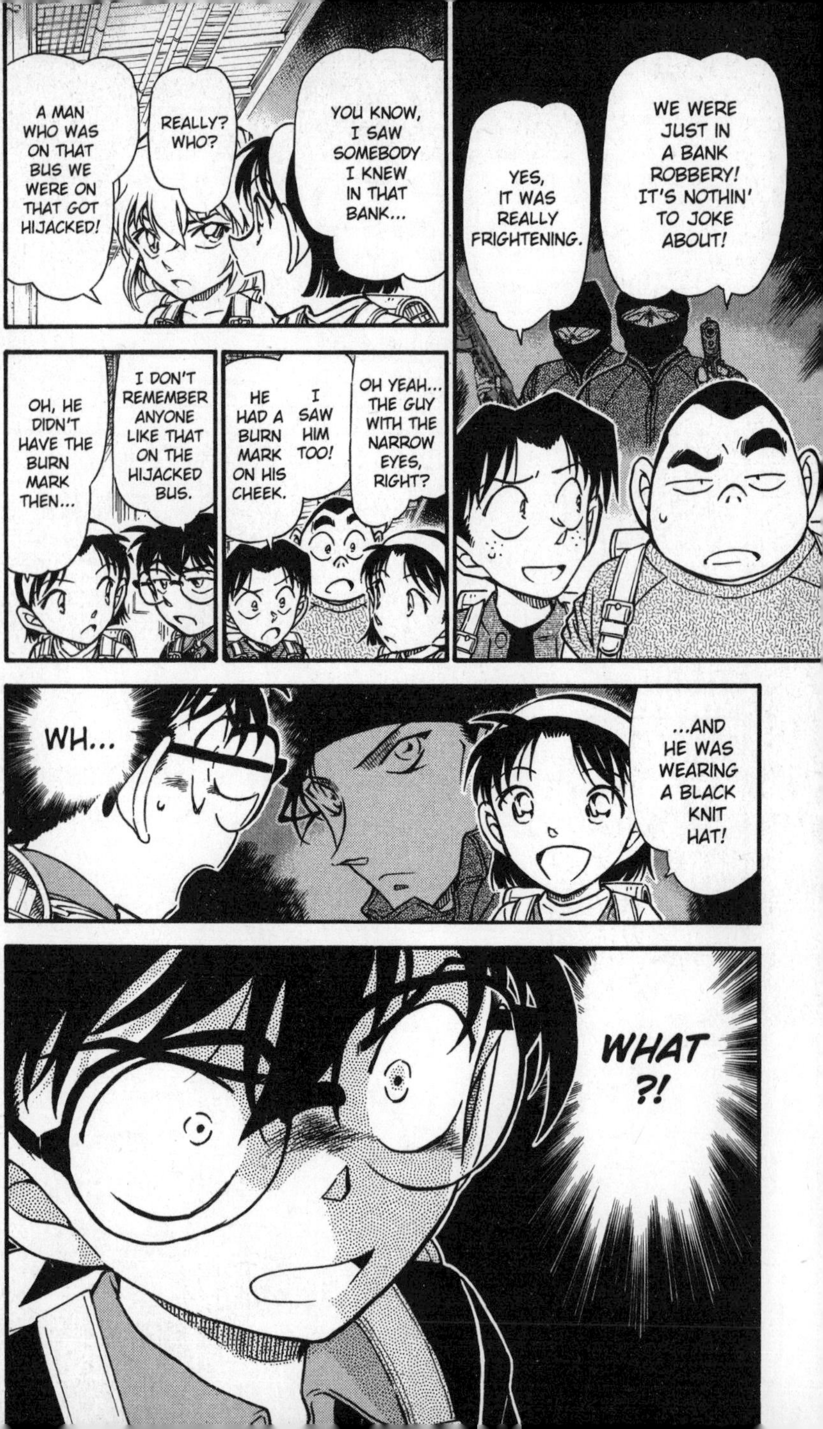
WE WERE JUST IN A BANK ROBBERY! IT'S NOTHIN' TO JOKE ABOUT!
YES, IT WAS REALLY FRIGHTENING.
YOU KNOW, I SAW SOMEBODY I KNEW IN THAT BANK...
REALLY? WHO?
A MAN WHO WAS ON THAT BUS WE WERE ON THAT GOT HIJACKED!
OH YEAH... THE GUY WITH THE NARROW EYES, RIGHT?
I SAW HIM TOO!
HE HAD A BURN MARK ON HIS CHEEK.
I DON'T REMEMBER ANYONE LIKE THAT ON THE HIJACKED BUS.
OH, HE DIDN'T HAVE THE BURN MARK THEN...
...AND HE WAS WEARING A BLACK KNIT HAT!
WH...
WHAT ?!

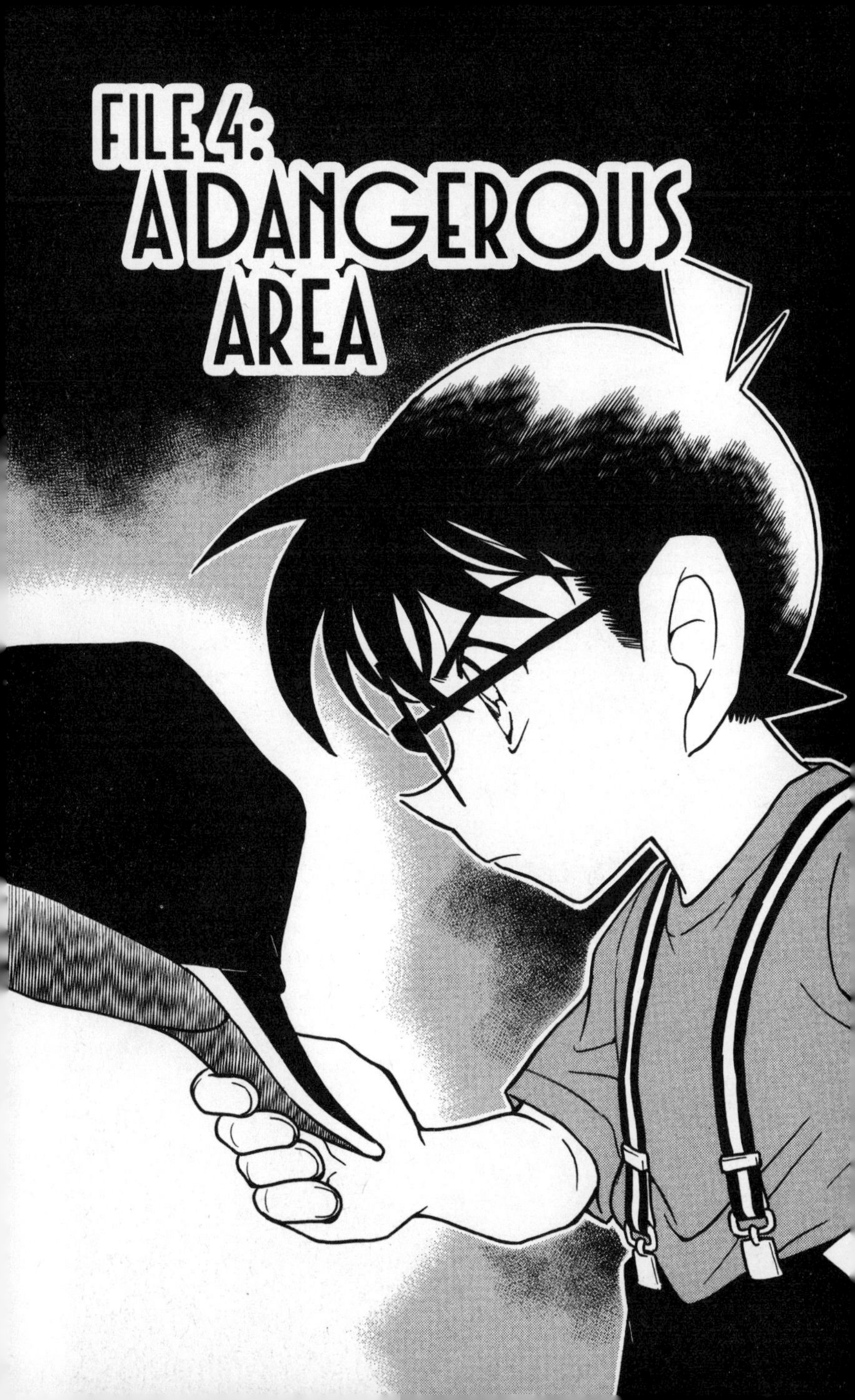
FILE 4:
A DANGEROUS AREA

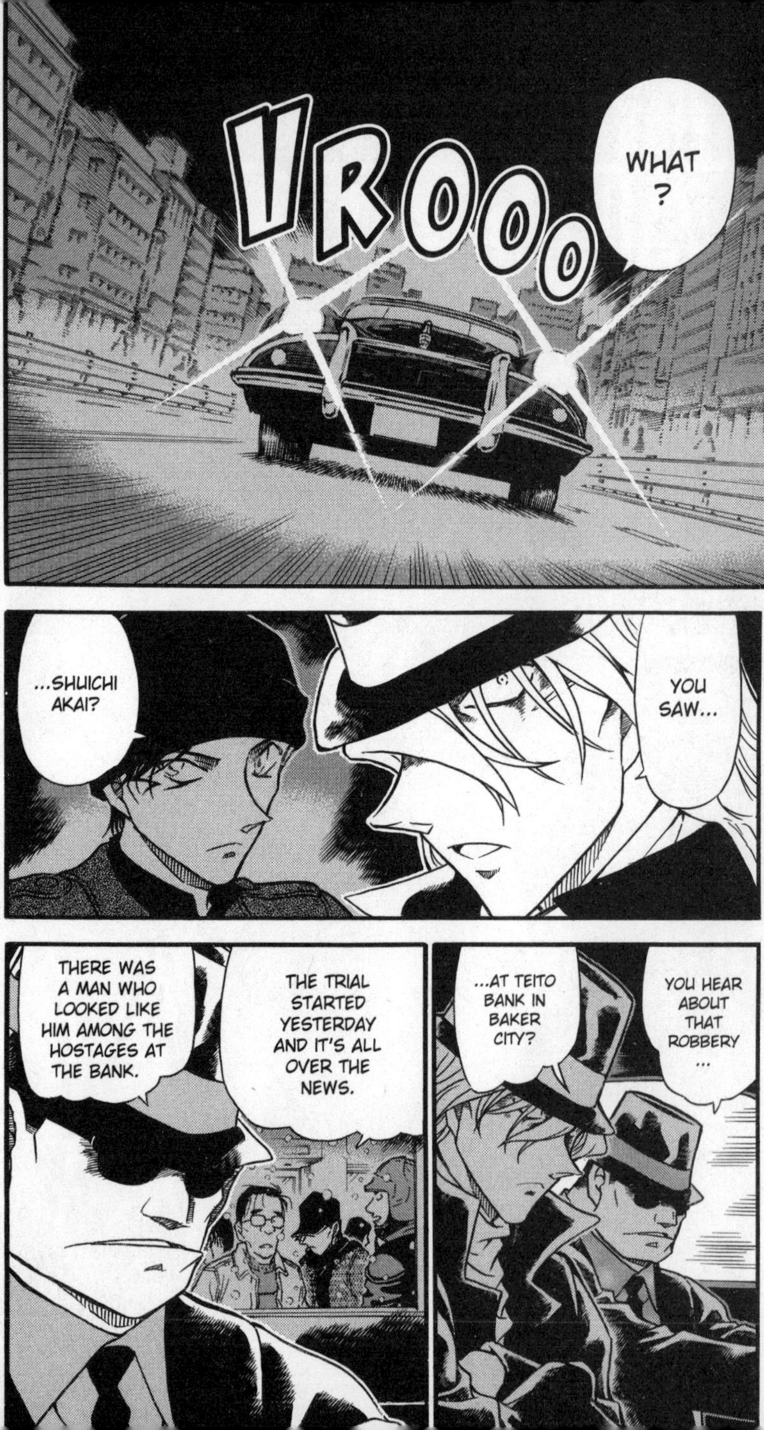
VROOOO
WHAT?
YOU SAW...
...SHUICHI AKAI?
YOU HEAR ABOUT THAT ROBBERY...
...AT TEITO BANK IN BAKER CITY?
THE TRIAL STARTED YESTERDAY AND IT'S ALL OVER THE NEWS.
THERE WAS A MAN WHO LOOKED LIKE HIM AMONG THE HOSTAGES AT THE BANK.

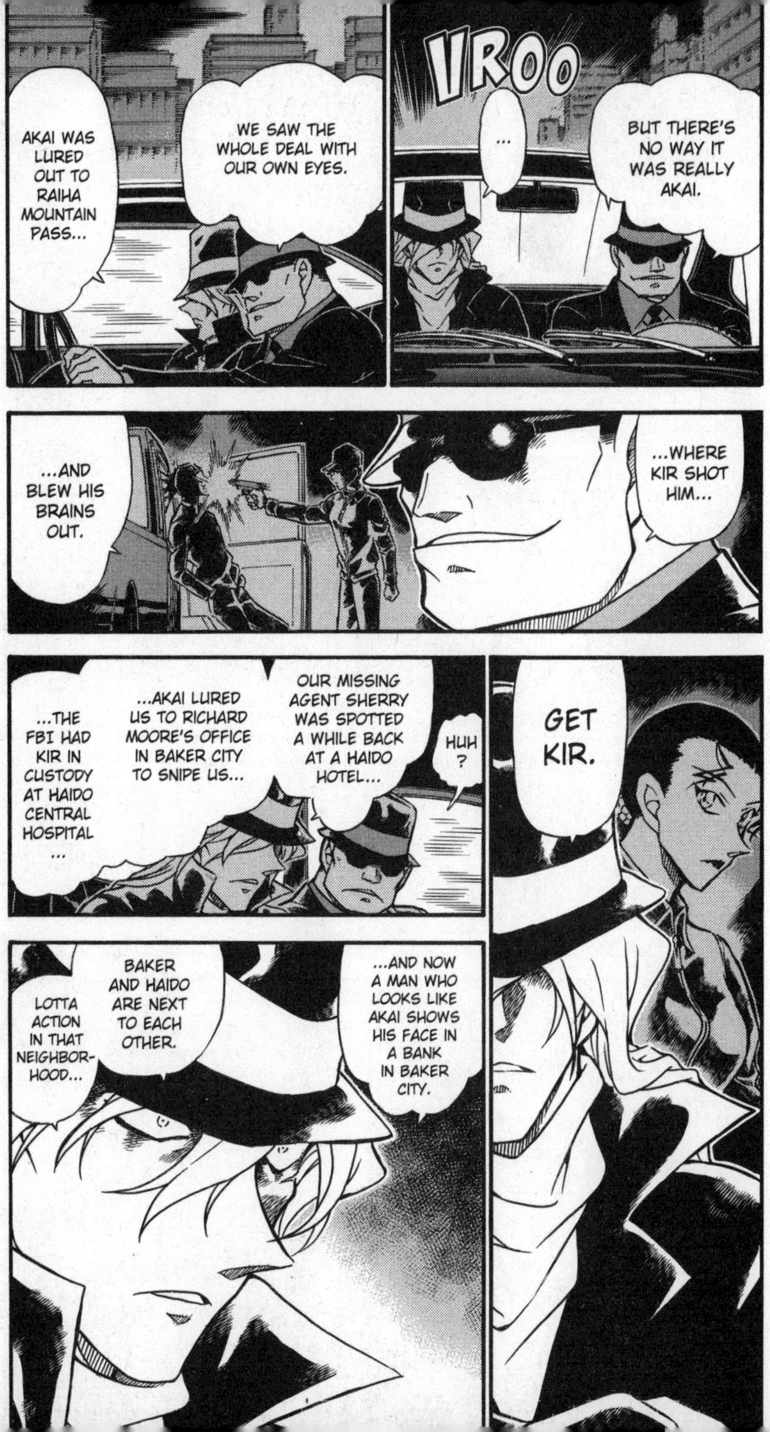
VROO
...
BUT THERE'S NO WAY IT WAS REALLY AKAI.
WE SAW THE WHOLE DEAL WITH OUR OWN EYES.
AKAI WAS LURED OUT TO RAIHA MOUNTAIN PASS...
...WHERE KIR SHOT HIM...
...AND BLEW HIS BRAINS OUT.
HUH?
OUR MISSING AGENT SHERRY WAS SPOTTED A WHILE BACK AT A HAIDO HOTEL...
...AKAI LURED US TO RICHARD MOORE'S OFFICE IN BAKER CITY TO SNIPE US...
...THE FBI HAD KIR IN CUSTODY AT HAIDO CENTRAL HOSPITAL...
...AND NOW A MAN WHO LOOKS LIKE AKAI SHOWS HIS FACE IN A BANK IN BAKER CITY.
BAKER AND HAIDO ARE NEXT TO EACH OTHER.
LOTTA ACTION IN THAT NEIGHBOR-HOOD...
GET KIR.

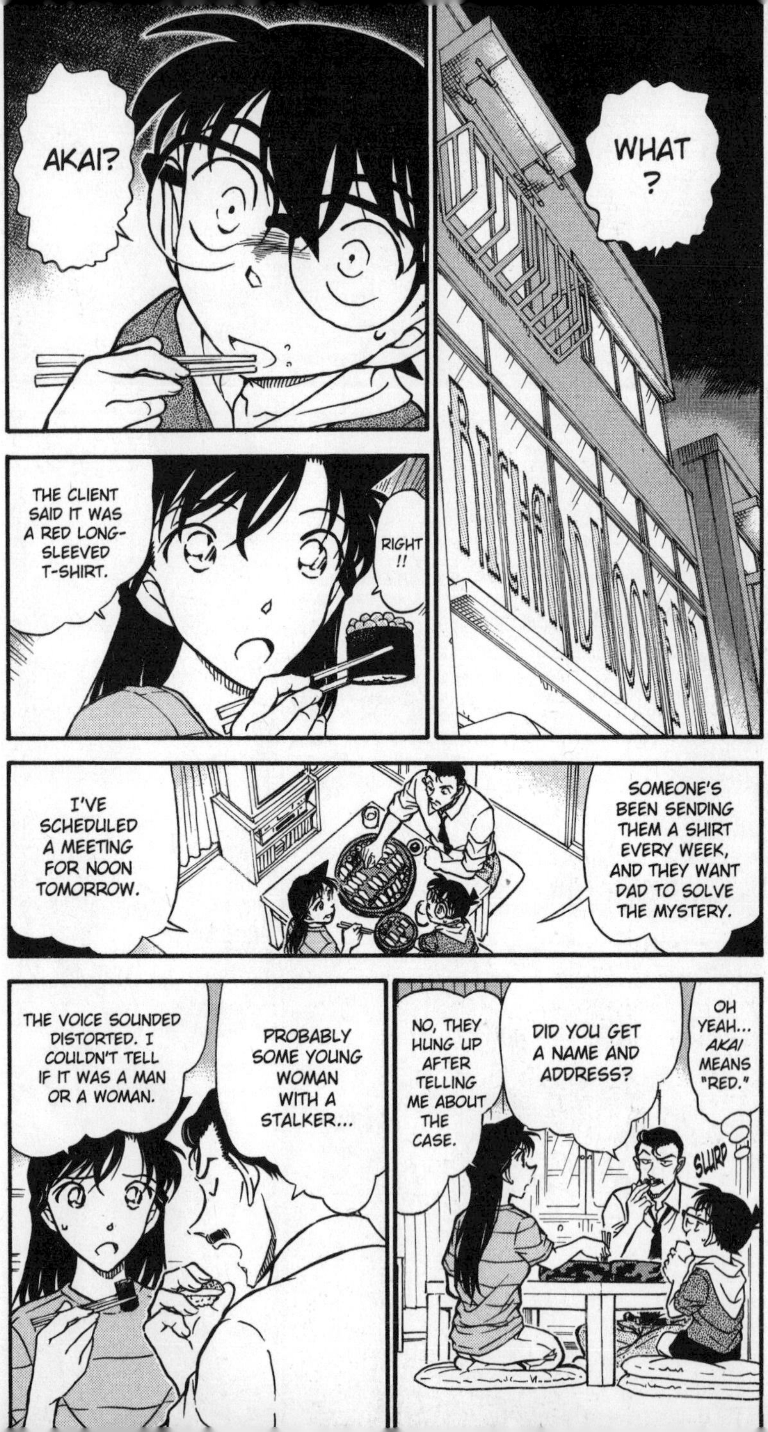
WHAT ?
AKAI?
RIGHT !!
THE CLIENT SAID IT WAS A RED LONG-SLEEVED T-SHIRT.
SOMEONE'S BEEN SENDING THEM A SHIRT EVERY WEEK, AND THEY WANT DAD TO SOLVE THE MYSTERY.
I'VE SCHEDULED A MEETING FOR NOON TOMORROW.
OH YEAH... AKAI MEANS "RED."
DID YOU GET A NAME AND ADDRESS?
NO, THEY HUNG UP AFTER TELLING ME ABOUT THE CASE.
SLURP
PROBABLY SOME YOUNG WOMAN WITH A STALKER...
THE VOICE SOUNDED DISTORTED. I COULDN'T TELL IF IT WAS A MAN OR A WOMAN.

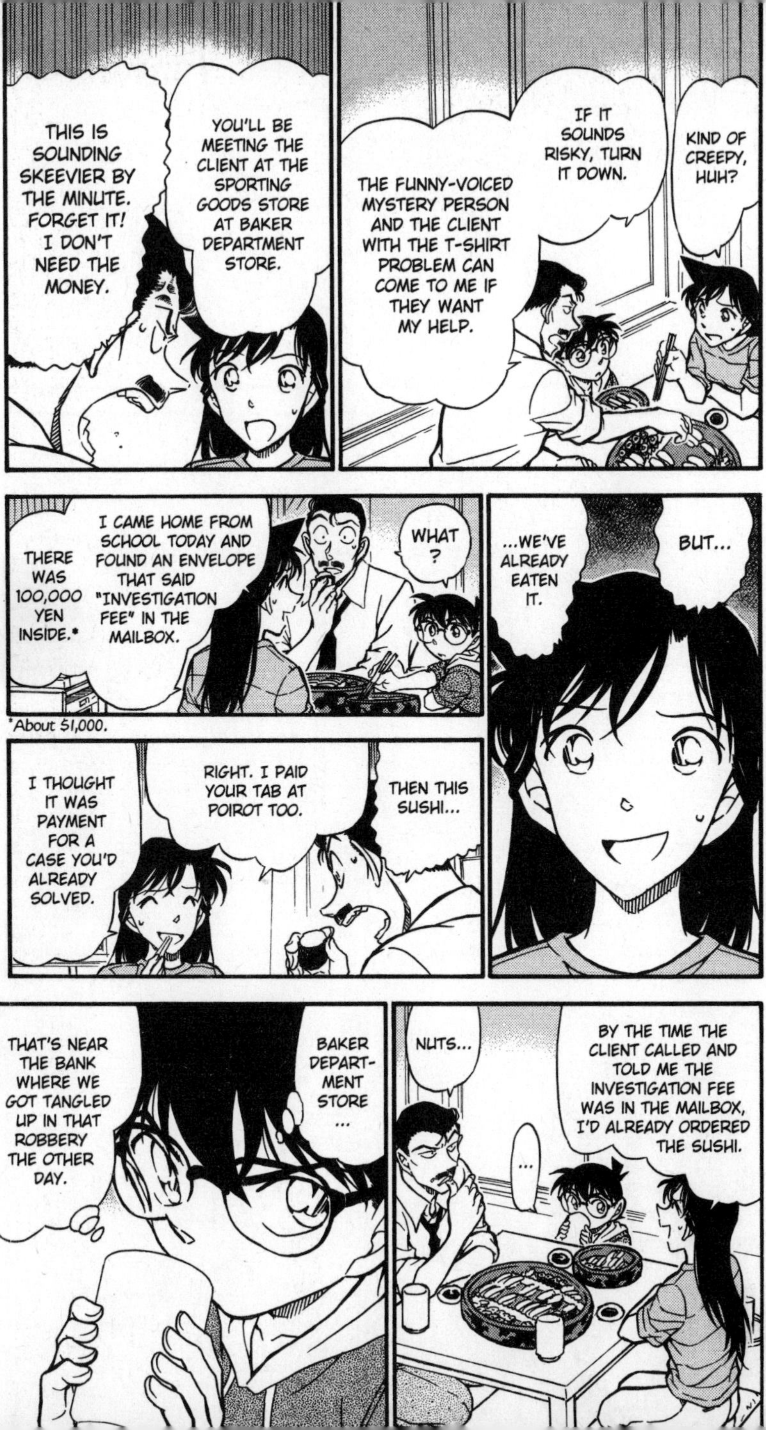
KIND OF CREEPY, HUH?
IF IT SOUNDS RISKY, TURN IT DOWN.
THE FUNNY-VOICED MYSTERY PERSON AND THE CLIENT WITH THE T-SHIRT PROBLEM CAN COME TO ME IF THEY WANT MY HELP.
YOU'LL BE MEETING THE CLIENT AT THE SPORTING GOODS STORE AT BAKER DEPARTMENT STORE.
THIS IS SOUNDING SKEEVIER BY THE MINUTE. FORGET IT! I DON'T NEED THE MONEY.
BUT...
...WE'VE ALREADY EATEN IT.
WHAT?
I CAME HOME FROM SCHOOL TODAY AND FOUND AN ENVELOPE THAT SAID "INVESTIGATION FEE" IN THE MAILBOX.
THERE WAS 100,000 YEN INSIDE.*
*About $1,000.
THEN THIS SUSHI...
RIGHT. I PAID YOUR TAB AT POIROT TOO.
I THOUGHT IT WAS PAYMENT FOR A CASE YOU'D ALREADY SOLVED.
BY THE TIME THE CLIENT CALLED AND TOLD ME THE INVESTIGATION FEE WAS IN THE MAILBOX, I'D ALREADY ORDERED THE SUSHI.
NUTS...
...
BAKER DEPARTMENT STORE...
THAT'S NEAR THE BANK WHERE WE GOT TANGLED UP IN THAT ROBBERY THE OTHER DAY.

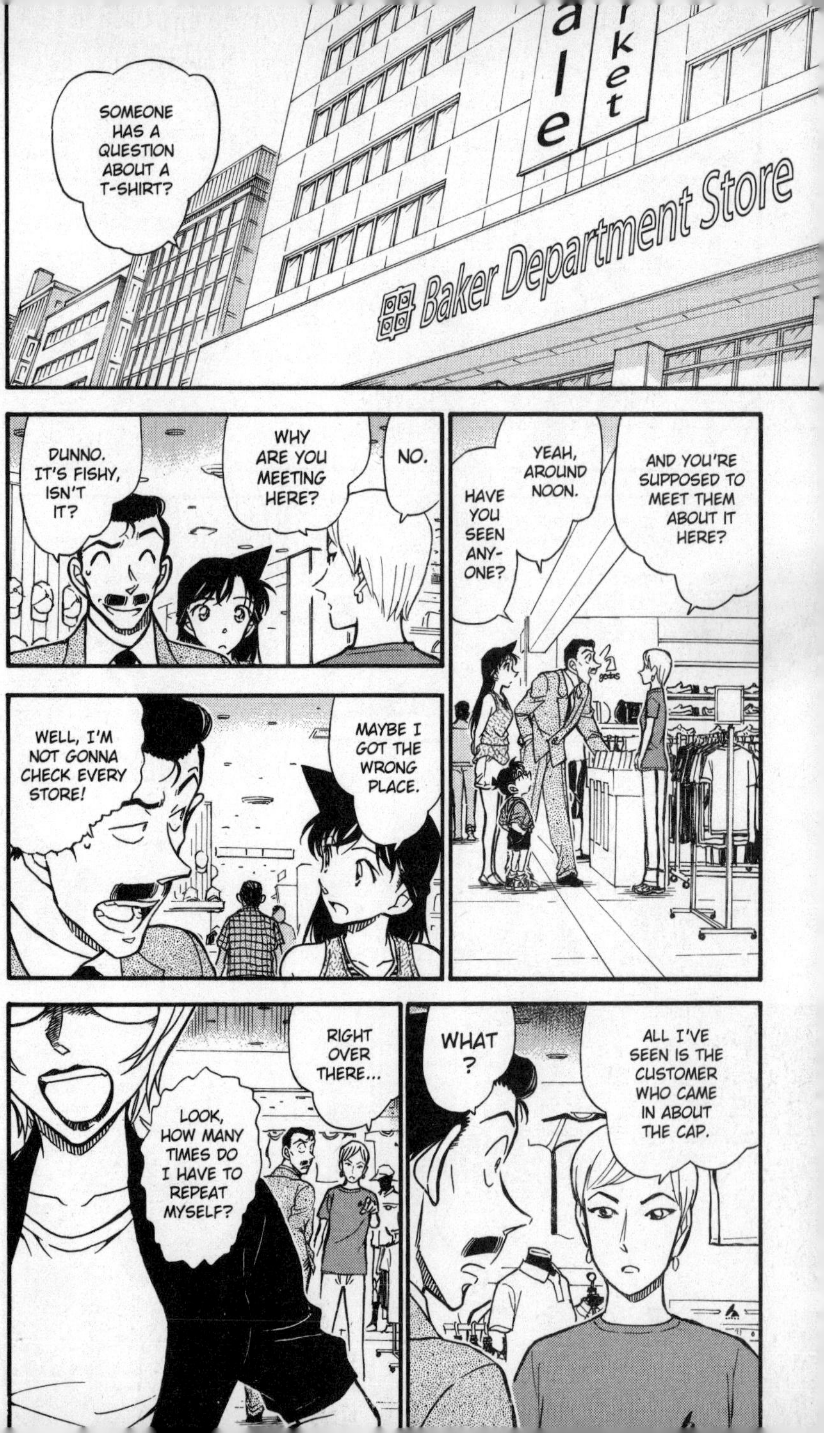
SOMEONE HAS A QUESTION ABOUT A T-SHIRT?
Baker Department Store
AND YOU'RE SUPPOSED TO MEET THEM ABOUT IT HERE?
YEAH, AROUND NOON.
HAVE YOU SEEN ANYONE?
NO.
WHY ARE YOU MEETING HERE?
DUNNO. IT'S FISHY, ISN'T IT?
MAYBE I GOT THE WRONG PLACE.
WELL, I'M NOT GONNA CHECK EVERY STORE!
ALL I'VE SEEN IS THE CUSTOMER WHO CAME IN ABOUT THE CAP.
WHAT?
RIGHT OVER THERE...
LOOK, HOW MANY TIMES DO I HAVE TO REPEAT MYSELF?

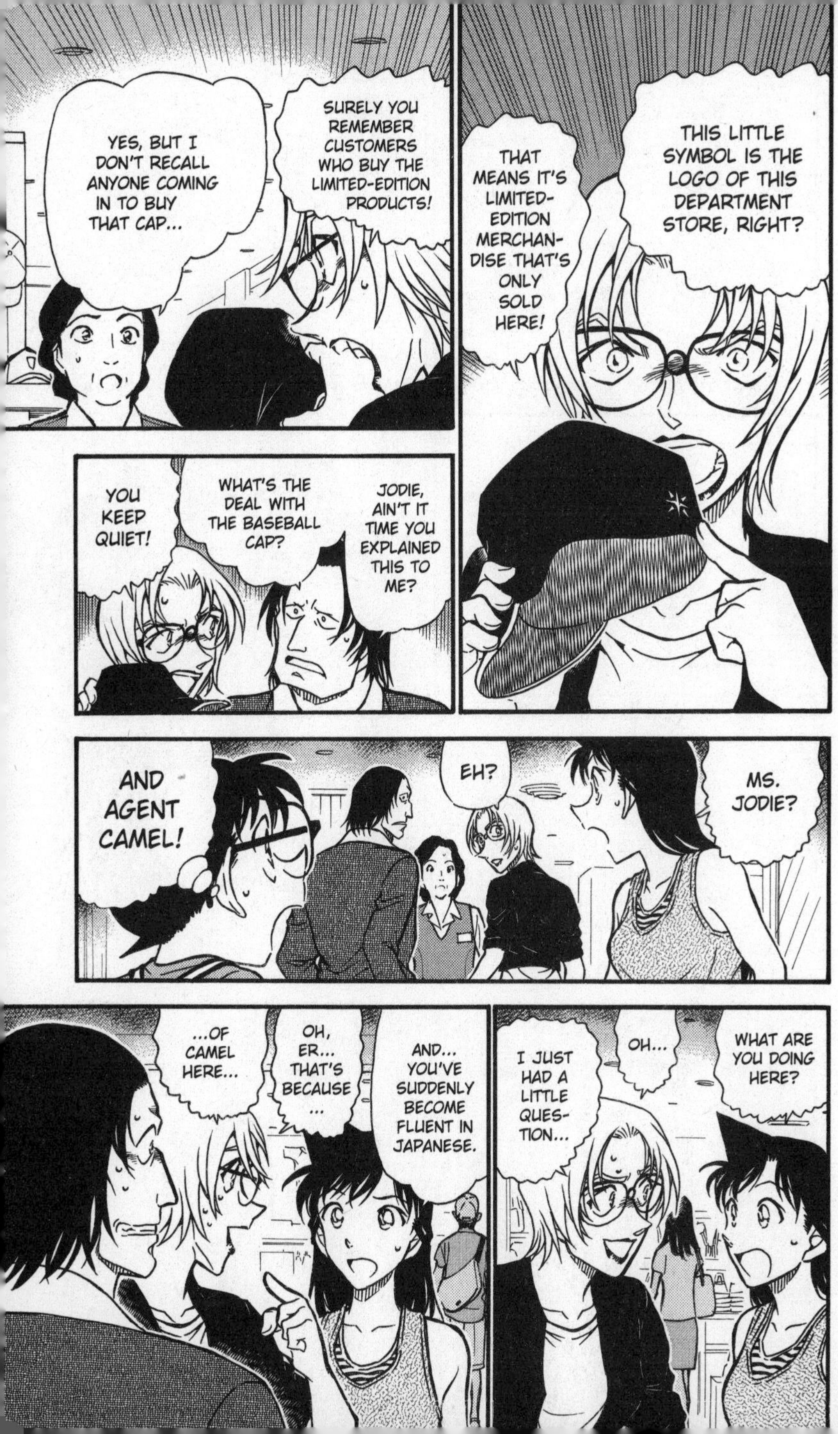
THIS LITTLE SYMBOL IS THE LOGO OF THIS DEPARTMENT STORE, RIGHT?
THAT MEANS IT'S LIMITED-EDITION MERCHANDISE THAT'S ONLY SOLD HERE!
SURELY YOU REMEMBER CUSTOMERS WHO BUY THE LIMITED-EDITION PRODUCTS!
YES, BUT I DON'T RECALL ANYONE COMING IN TO BUY THAT CAP...
JODIE, AIN'T IT TIME YOU EXPLAINED THIS TO ME?
WHAT'S THE DEAL WITH THE BASEBALL CAP?
YOU KEEP QUIET!
MS. JODIE?
EH?
AND AGENT CAMEL!
WHAT ARE YOU DOING HERE?
OH...
I JUST HAD A LITTLE QUES-TION...
AND... YOU'VE SUDDENLY BECOME FLUENT IN JAPANESE.
OH, ER... THAT'S BECAUSE...
...OF CAMEL HERE...

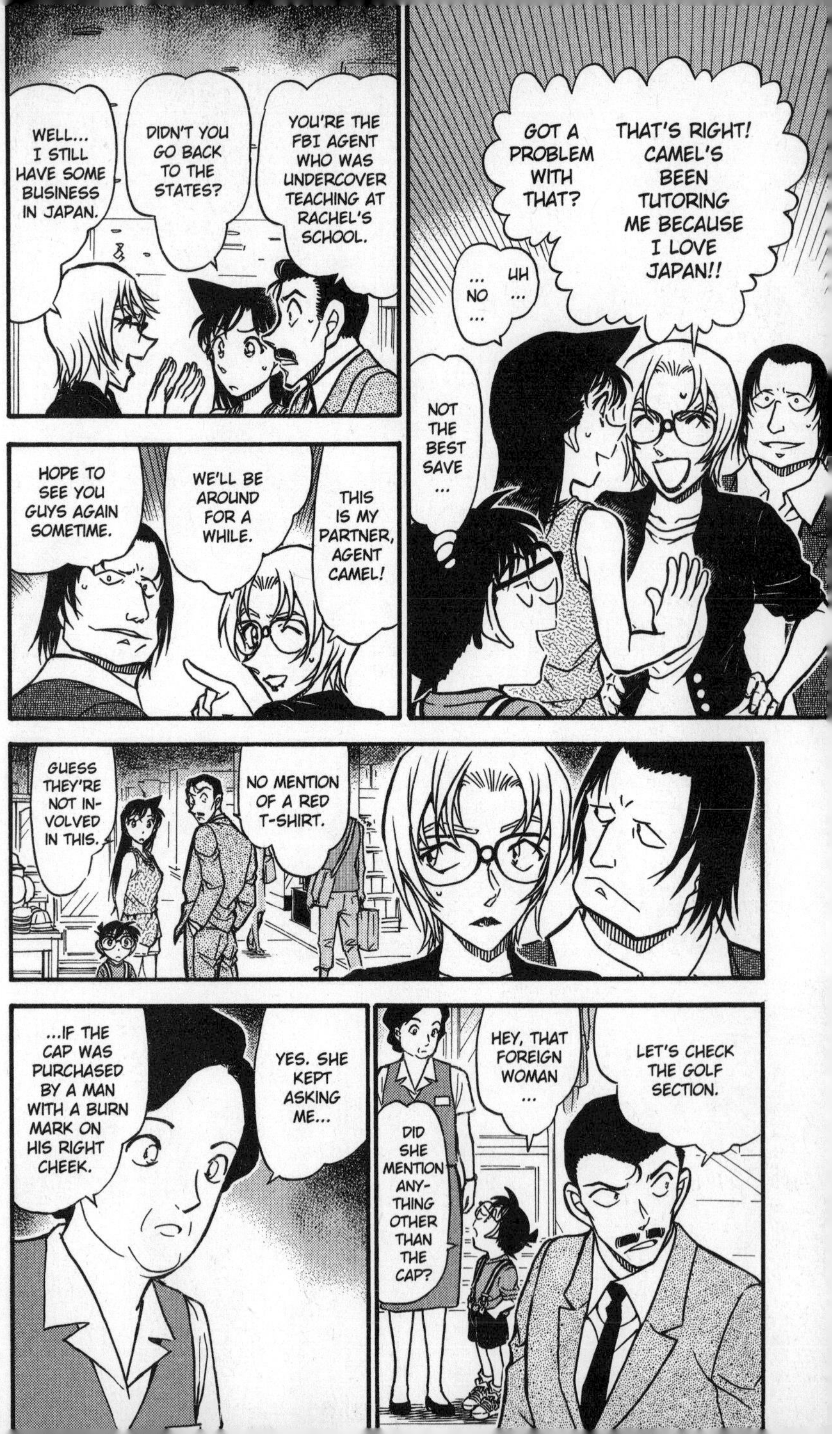
YOU'RE THE FBI AGENT WHO WAS UNDERCOVER TEACHING AT RACHEL'S SCHOOL.
DIDN'T YOU GO BACK TO THE STATES?
WELL... I STILL HAVE SOME BUSINESS IN JAPAN.
THIS IS MY PARTNER, AGENT CAMEL!
WE'LL BE AROUND FOR A WHILE.
HOPE TO SEE YOU GUYS AGAIN SOMETIME.
THAT'S RIGHT! CAMEL'S BEEN TUTORING ME BECAUSE I LOVE JAPAN!!
GOT A PROBLEM WITH THAT?
UH ... ... NO ...
NOT THE BEST SAVE ...
NO MENTION OF A RED T-SHIRT.
GUESS THEY'RE NOT IN-VOLVED IN THIS.
LET'S CHECK THE GOLF SECTION.
HEY, THAT FOREIGN WOMAN ...
DID SHE MENTION ANY-THING OTHER THAN THE CAP?
YES. SHE KEPT ASKING ME...
...IF THE CAP WAS PURCHASED BY A MAN WITH A BURN MARK ON HIS RIGHT CHEEK.

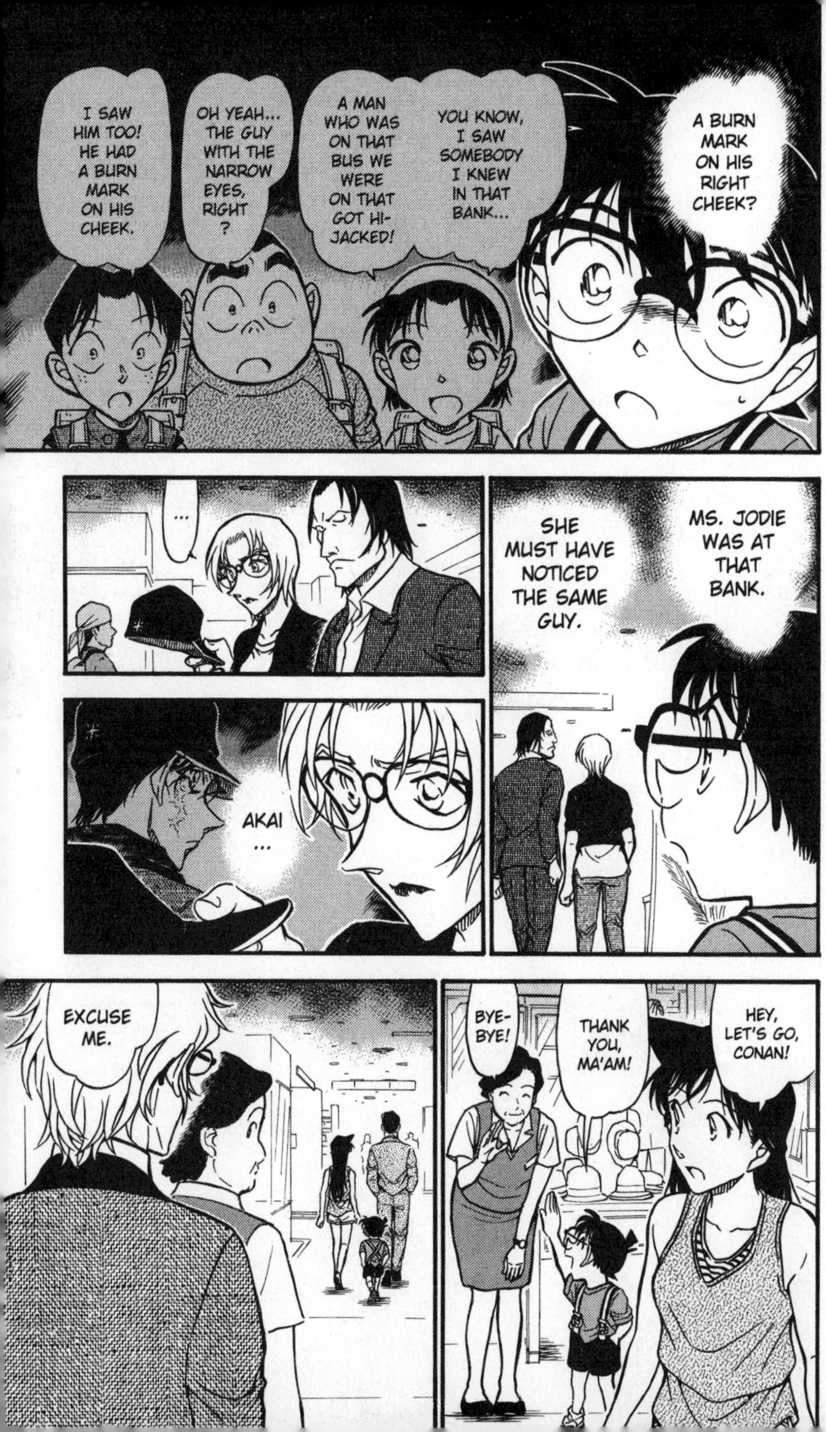
YOU KNOW, I SAW SOMEBODY I KNEW IN THAT BANK...
A MAN WHO WAS ON THAT BUS WE WERE ON THAT GOT HI-JACKED!
OH YEAH... THE GUY WITH THE NARROW EYES, RIGHT?
I SAW HIM TOO! HE HAD A BURN MARK ON HIS CHEEK.
A BURN MARK ON HIS RIGHT CHEEK?
MS. JODIE WAS AT THAT BANK.
SHE MUST HAVE NOTICED THE SAME GUY.
...
AKAI ...
HEY, LET'S GO, CONAN!
THANK YOU, MA'AM!
BYE-BYE!
EXCUSE ME.

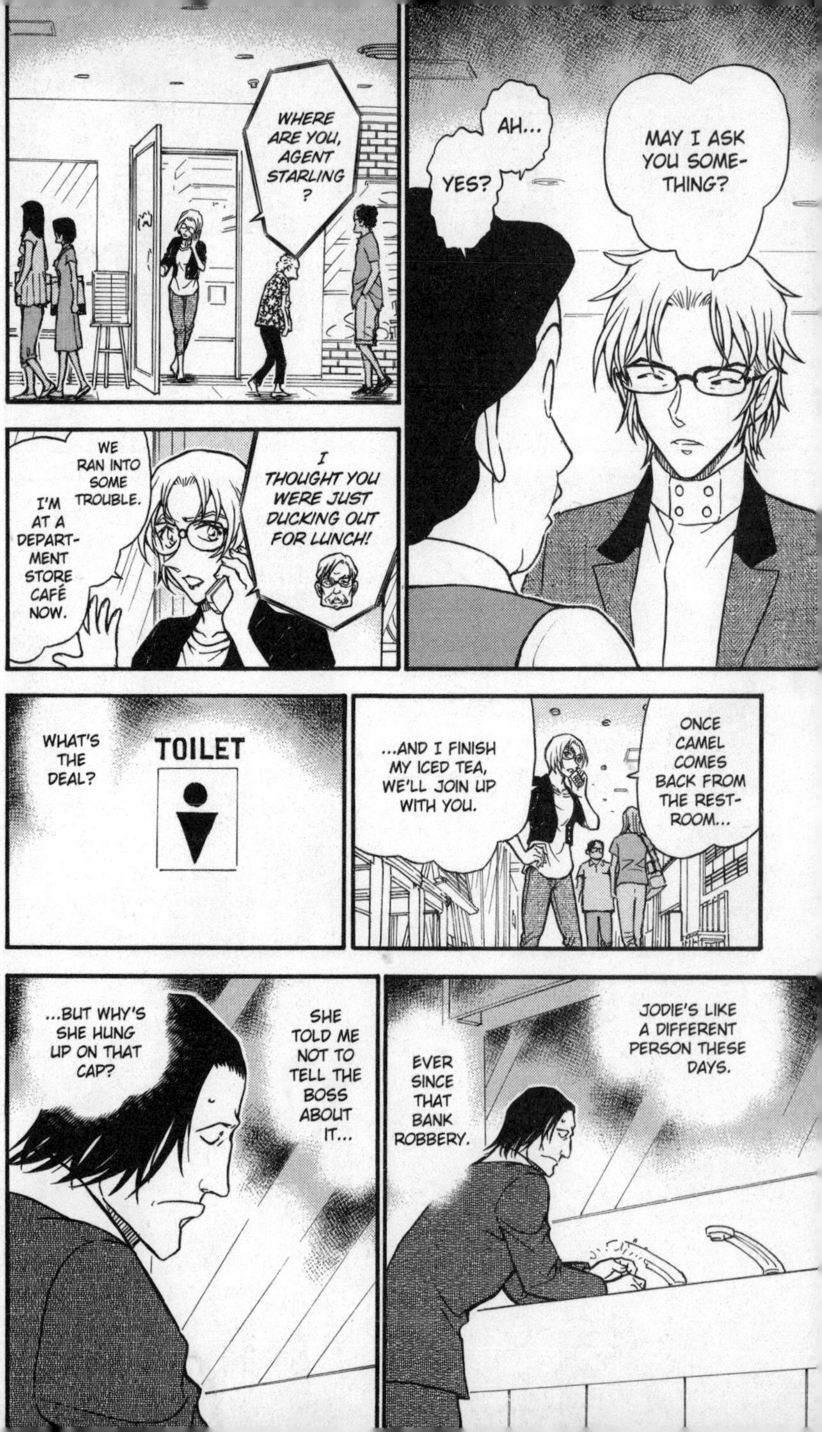
MAY I ASK YOU SOME-THING?
AH... YES?
WHERE ARE YOU, AGENT STARLING?
I THOUGHT YOU WERE JUST DUCKING OUT FOR LUNCH!
WE RAN INTO SOME TROUBLE.
I'M AT A DEPART-MENT STORE CAFÉ NOW.
ONCE CAMEL COMES BACK FROM THE REST-ROOM...
...AND I FINISH MY ICED TEA, WE'LL JOIN UP WITH YOU.
TOILET
WHAT'S THE DEAL?
JODIE'S LIKE A DIFFERENT PERSON THESE DAYS.
EVER SINCE THAT BANK ROBBERY.
SHE TOLD ME NOT TO TELL THE BOSS ABOUT IT...
...BUT WHY'S SHE HUNG UP ON THAT CAP?

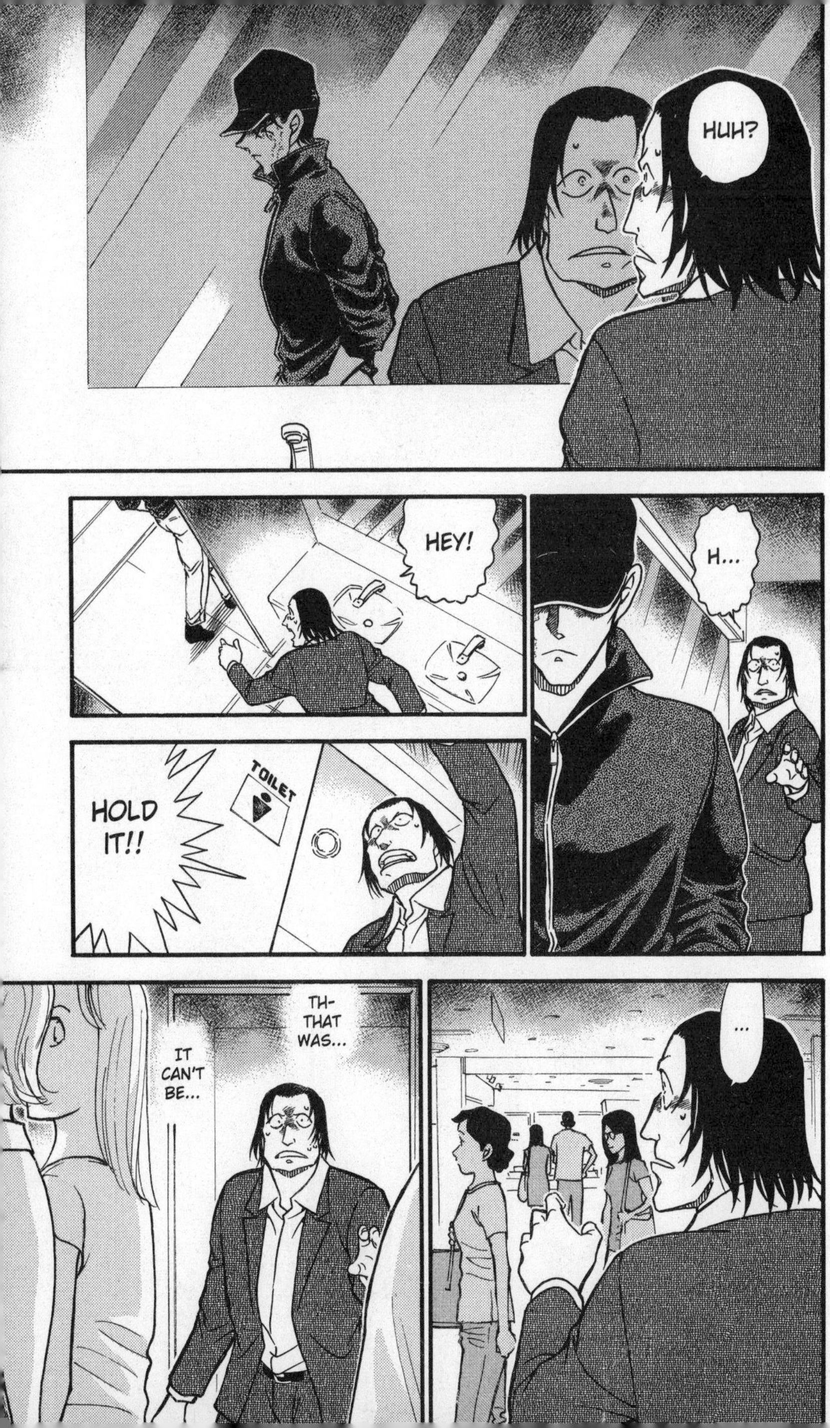
HUH?
H...
HEY!
HOLD IT!!
...
TH- THAT WAS...
IT CAN'T BE...

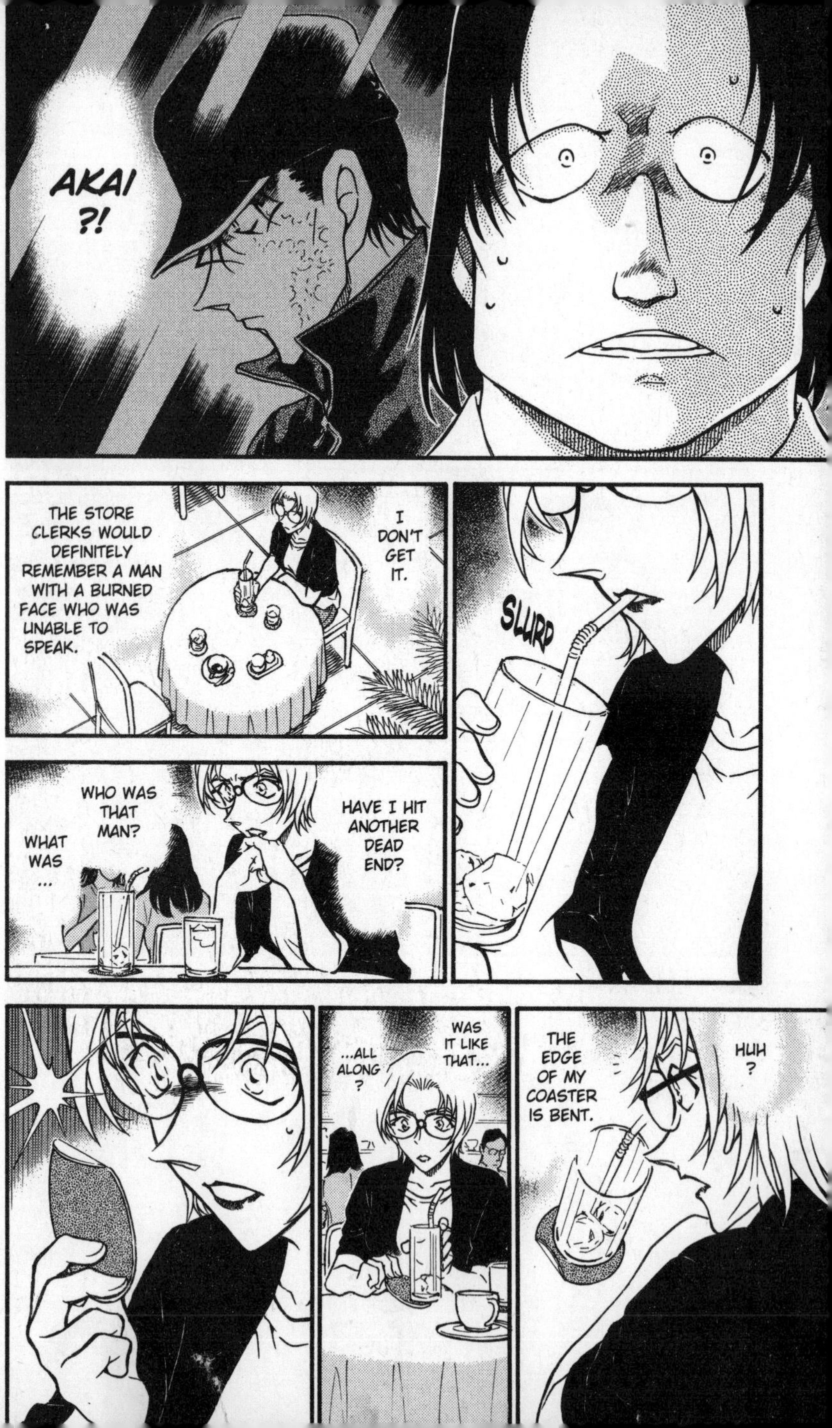
AKAI ?!
SLURP
I DON'T GET IT.
THE STORE CLERKS WOULD DEFINITELY REMEMBER A MAN WITH A BURNED FACE WHO WAS UNABLE TO SPEAK.
HAVE I HIT ANOTHER DEAD END?
WHO WAS THAT MAN?
WHAT WAS ...
HUH ?
THE EDGE OF MY COASTER IS BENT.
WAS IT LIKE THAT...
...ALL ALONG ?

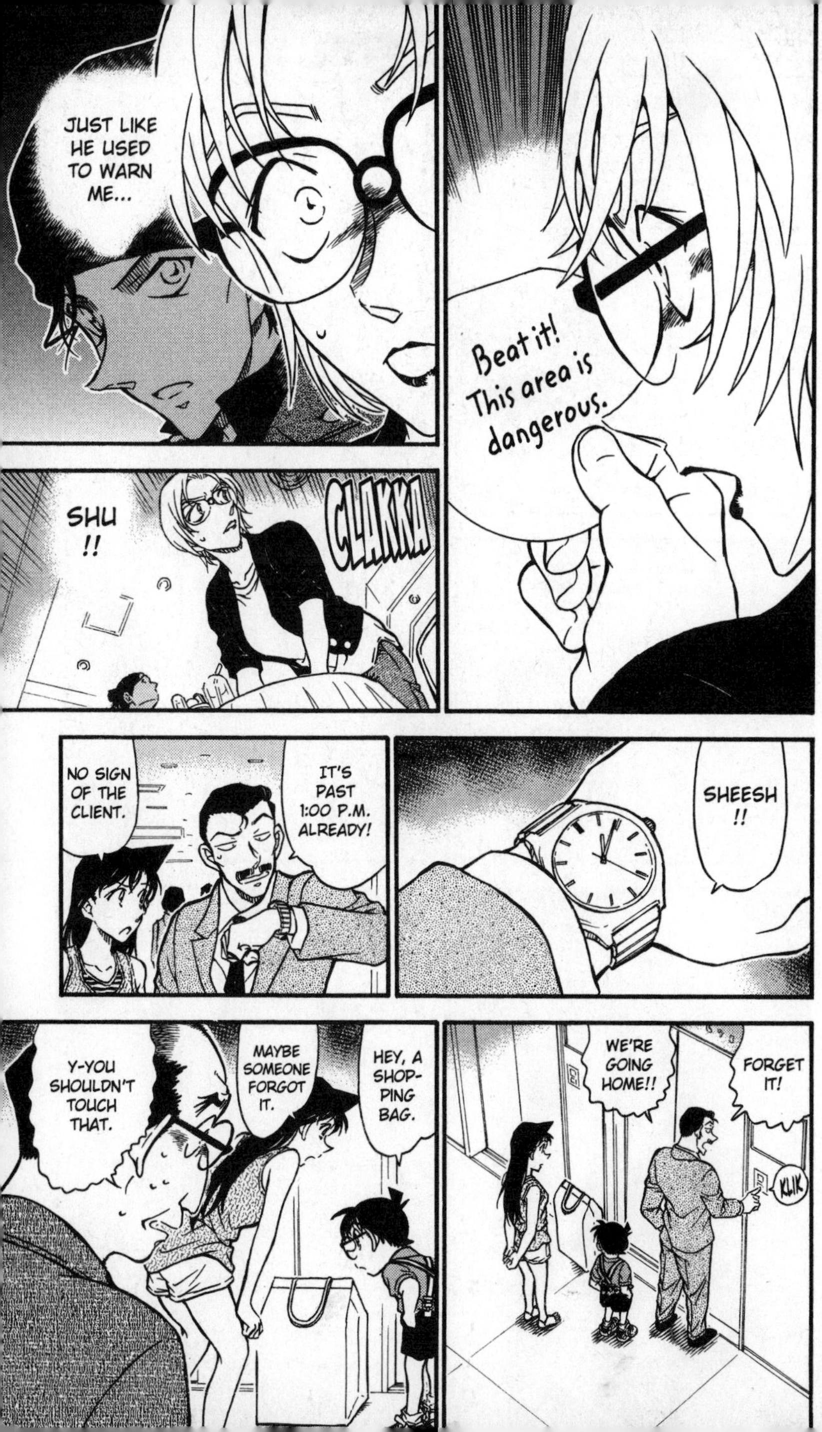
Beat it! This area is dangerous.
JUST LIKE HE USED TO WARN ME...
CLAKKA
SHU !!
SHEESH !!
IT'S PAST 1:00 P.M. ALREADY!
NO SIGN OF THE CLIENT.
FORGET IT!
KLIK
WE'RE GOING HOME!!
HEY, A SHOP-PING BAG.
MAYBE SOMEONE FORGOT IT.
Y-YOU SHOULDN'T TOUCH THAT.

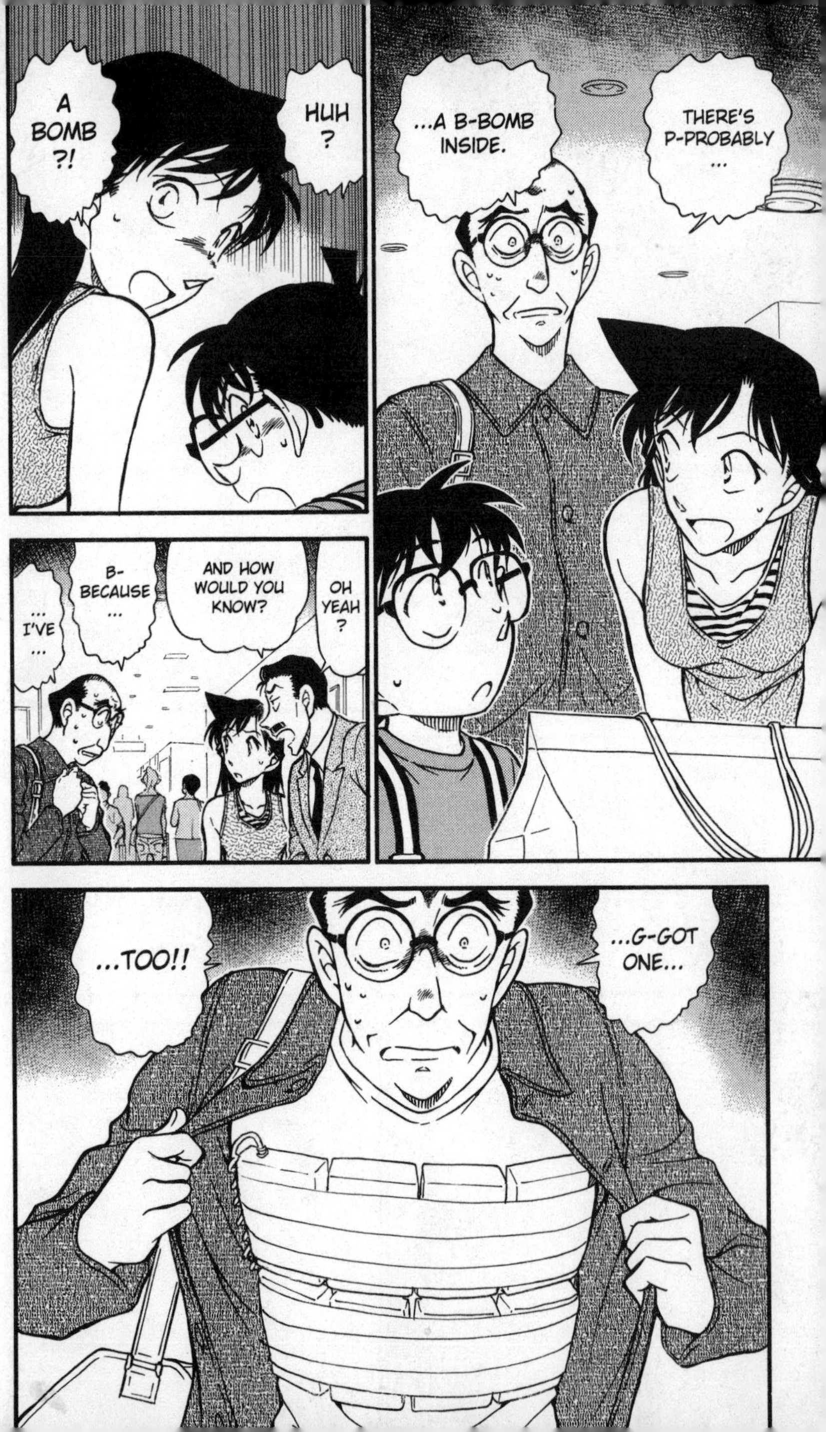
THERE'S P-PROBABLY ...
...A B-BOMB INSIDE.
HUH ?
A BOMB ?!
OH YEAH ?
AND HOW WOULD YOU KNOW?
B-BECAUSE ...
... I'VE ...
...G-GOT ONE...
...TOO!!

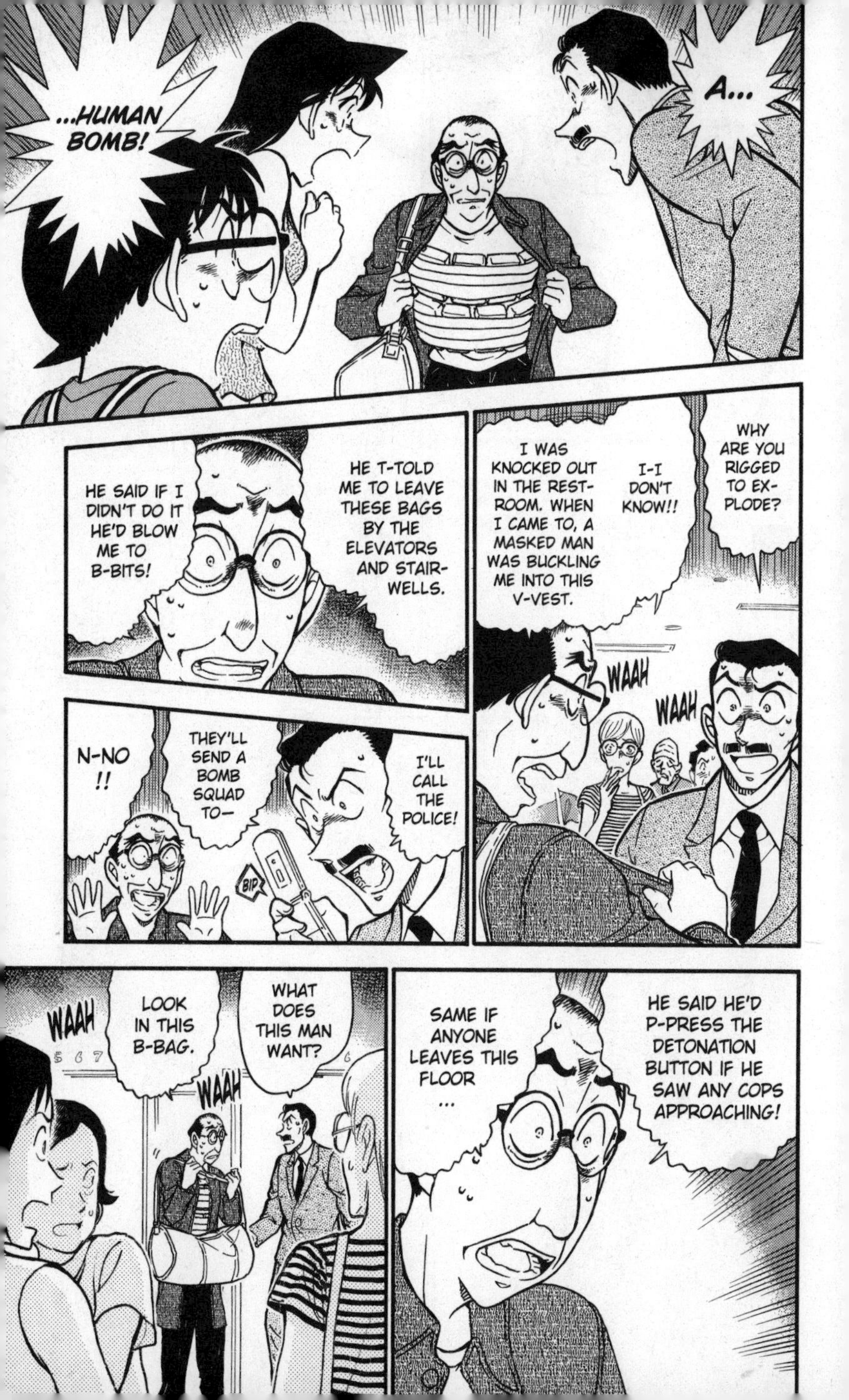
A...
...HUMAN BOMB!
WHY ARE YOU RIGGED TO EX-PLODE?
I-I DON'T KNOW!!
I WAS KNOCKED OUT IN THE REST-ROOM. WHEN I CAME TO, A MASKED MAN WAS BUCKLING ME INTO THIS V-VEST.
WAAH
WAAH
HE T-TOLD ME TO LEAVE THESE BAGS BY THE ELEVATORS AND STAIR-WELLS.
HE SAID IF I DIDN'T DO IT HE'D BLOW ME TO B-BITS!
I'LL CALL THE POLICE!
BIP
THEY'LL SEND A BOMB SQUAD TO—
N-NO!!
HE SAID HE'D P-PRESS THE DETONATION BUTTON IF HE SAW ANY COPS APPROACHING!
SAME IF ANYONE LEAVES THIS FLOOR ...
WHAT DOES THIS MAN WANT?
LOOK IN THIS B-BAG.
WAAH
WAAH

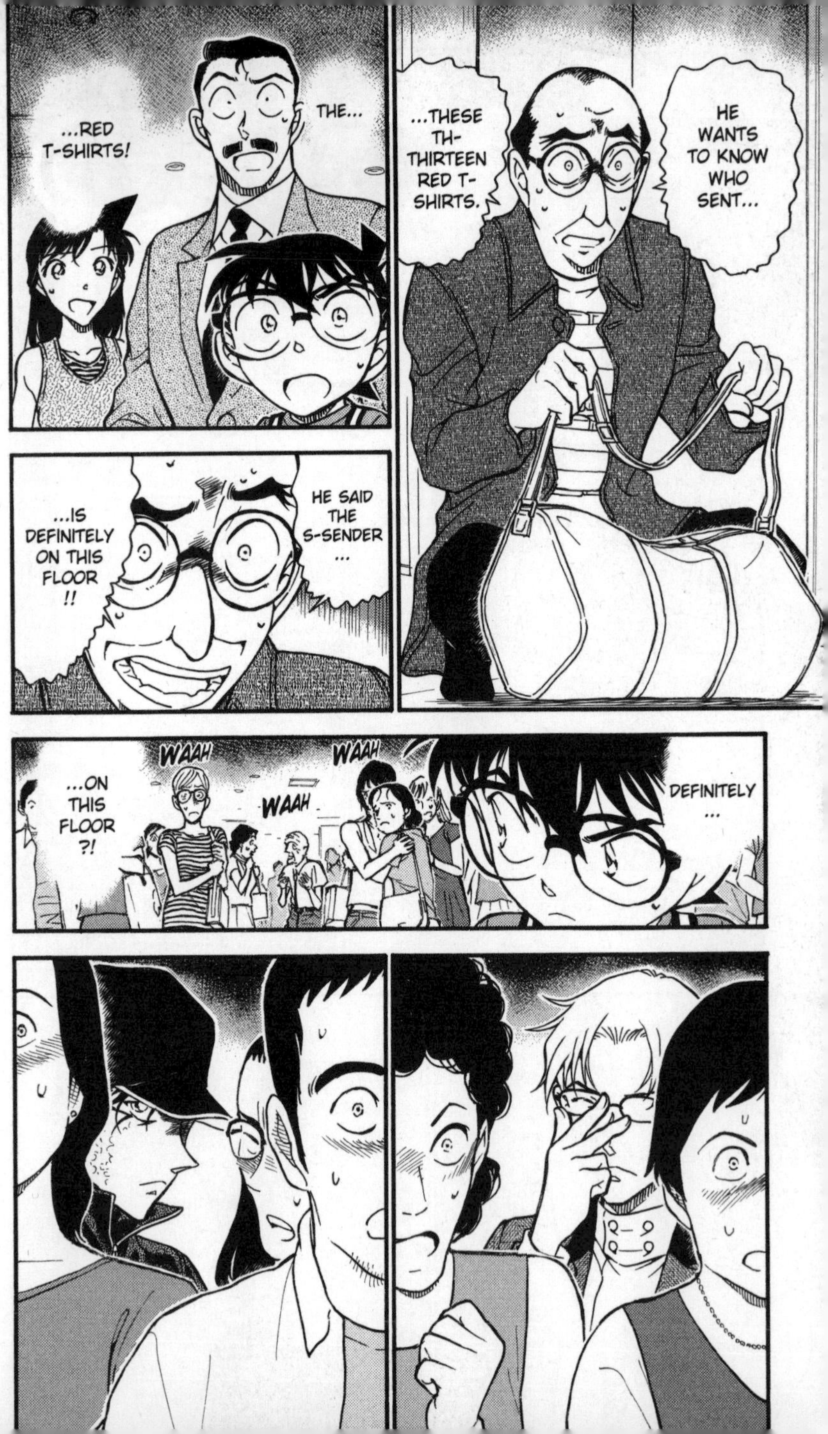
HE WANTS TO KNOW WHO SENT...
...THESE TH-THIRTEEN RED T-SHIRTS.
THE...
...RED T-SHIRTS!
HE SAID THE S-SENDER ...
...IS DEFINITELY ON THIS FLOOR !!
DEFINITELY ...
WAAH
WAAH
WAAH
...ON THIS FLOOR ?!

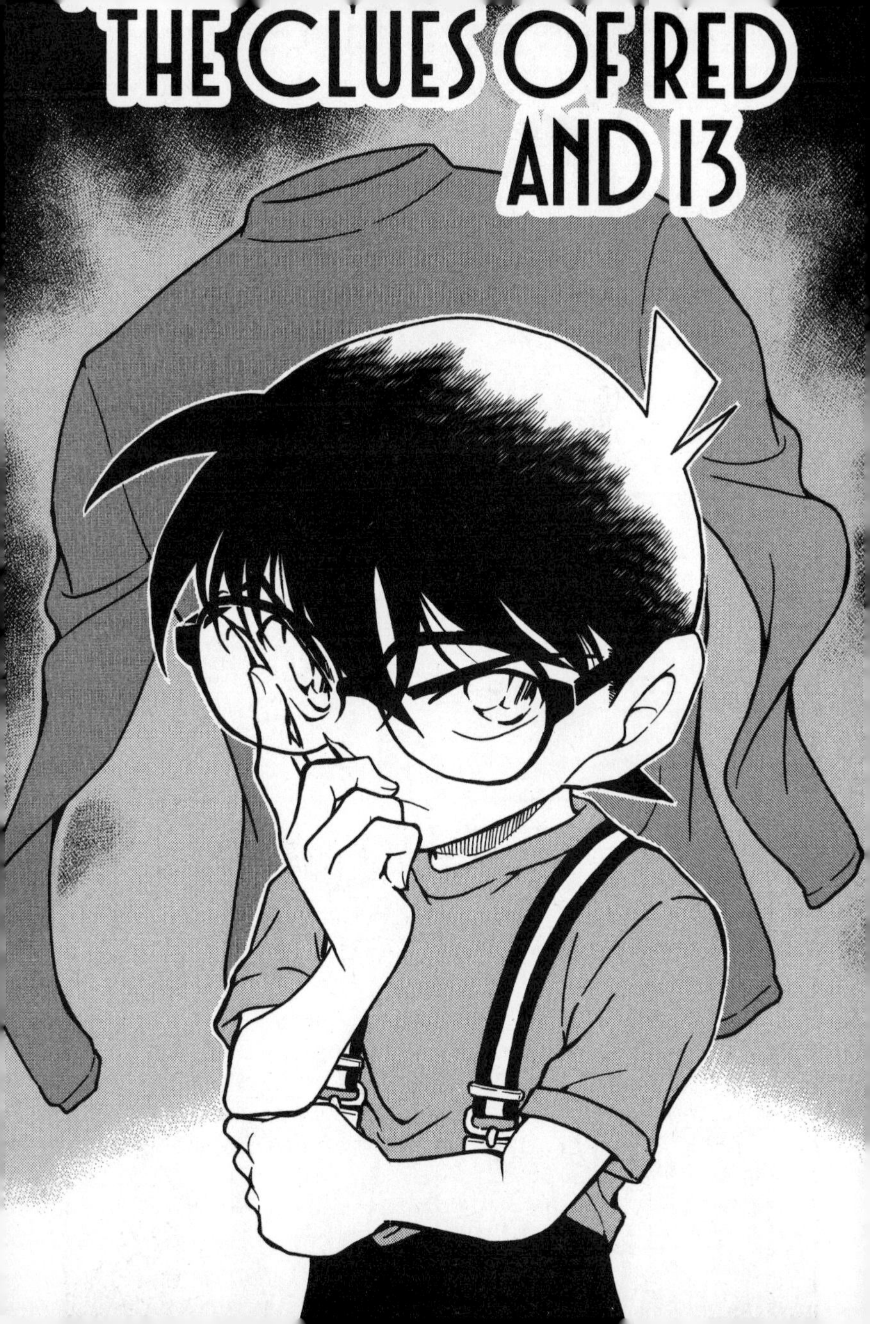
THE CLUES OF RED AND 13

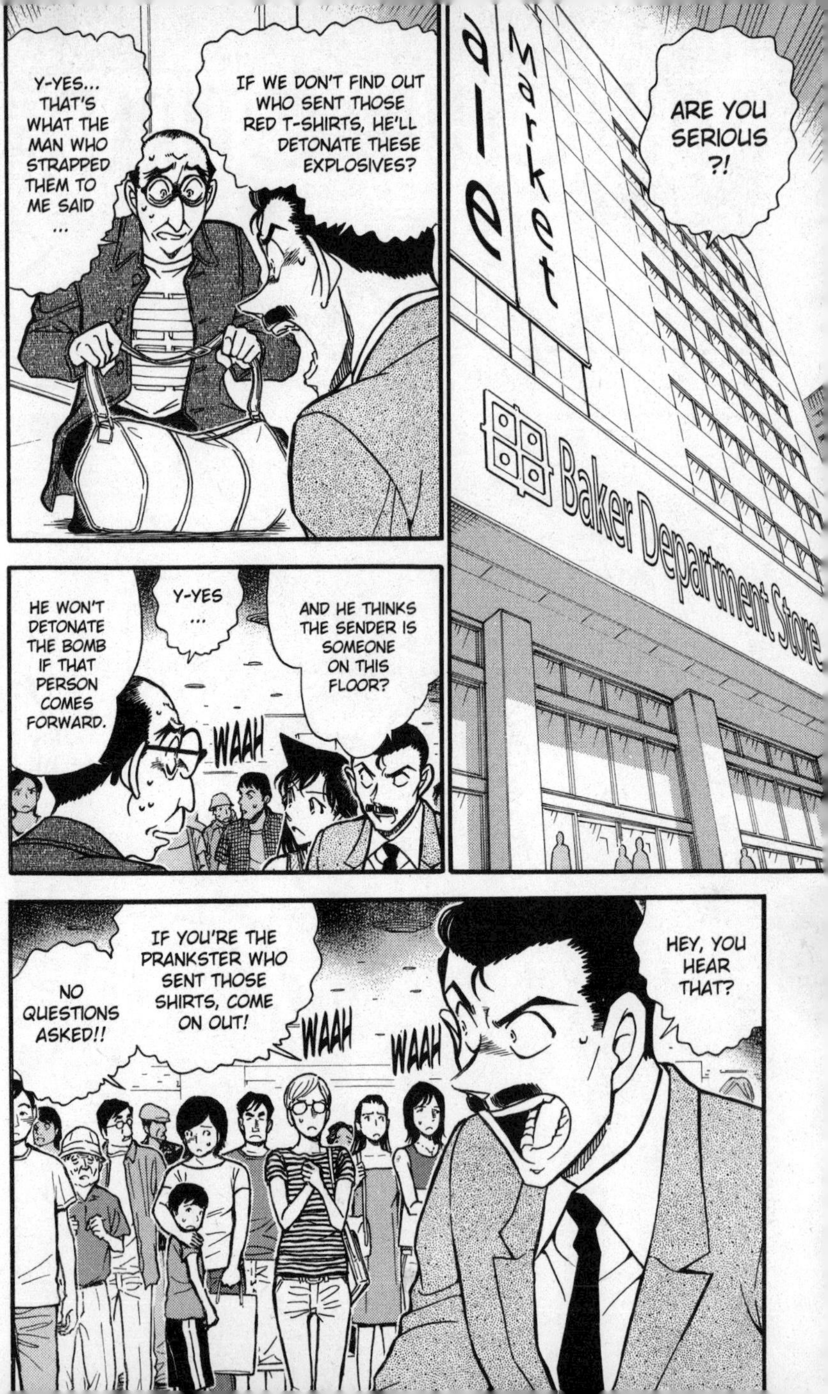
Market
Baker Department Store
ARE YOU SERIOUS ?!
IF WE DON'T FIND OUT WHO SENT THOSE RED T-SHIRTS, HE'LL DETONATE THESE EXPLOSIVES?
Y-YES... THAT'S WHAT THE MAN WHO STRAPPED THEM TO ME SAID ...
AND HE THINKS THE SENDER IS SOMEONE ON THIS FLOOR?
Y-YES ...
HE WON'T DETONATE THE BOMB IF THAT PERSON COMES FORWARD.
WAAH
HEY, YOU HEAR THAT?
WAAH
WAAH
IF YOU'RE THE PRANKSTER WHO SENT THOSE SHIRTS, COME ON OUT!
NO QUESTIONS ASKED!!

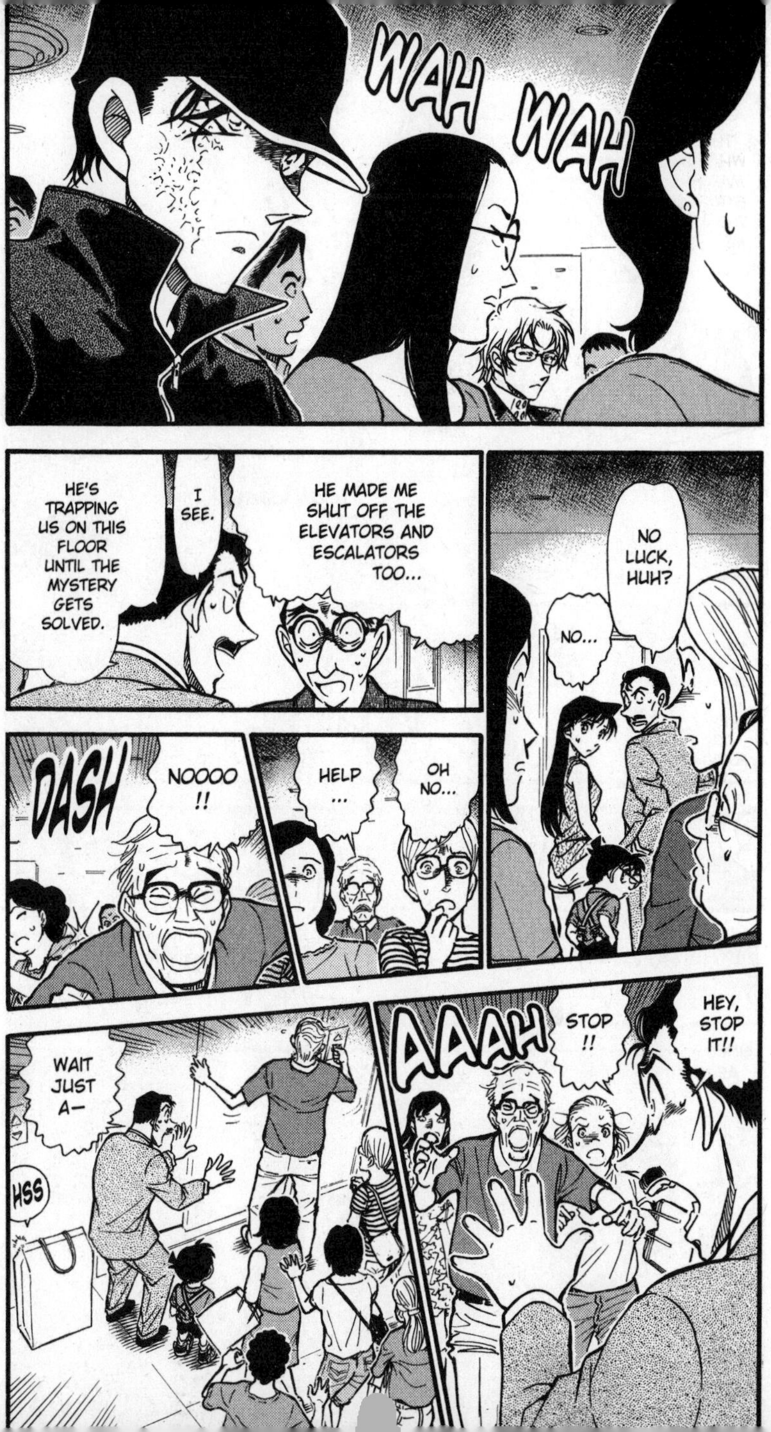
WAH WAH
NO LUCK, HUH?
NO...
HE MADE ME SHUT OFF THE ELEVATORS AND ESCALATORS TOO...
I SEE.
HE'S TRAPPING US ON THIS FLOOR UNTIL THE MYSTERY GETS SOLVED.
OH NO...
HELP...
NOOOO!!
DASH
HEY, STOP IT!!
STOP!!
AAAH
WAIT JUST A—
HSS

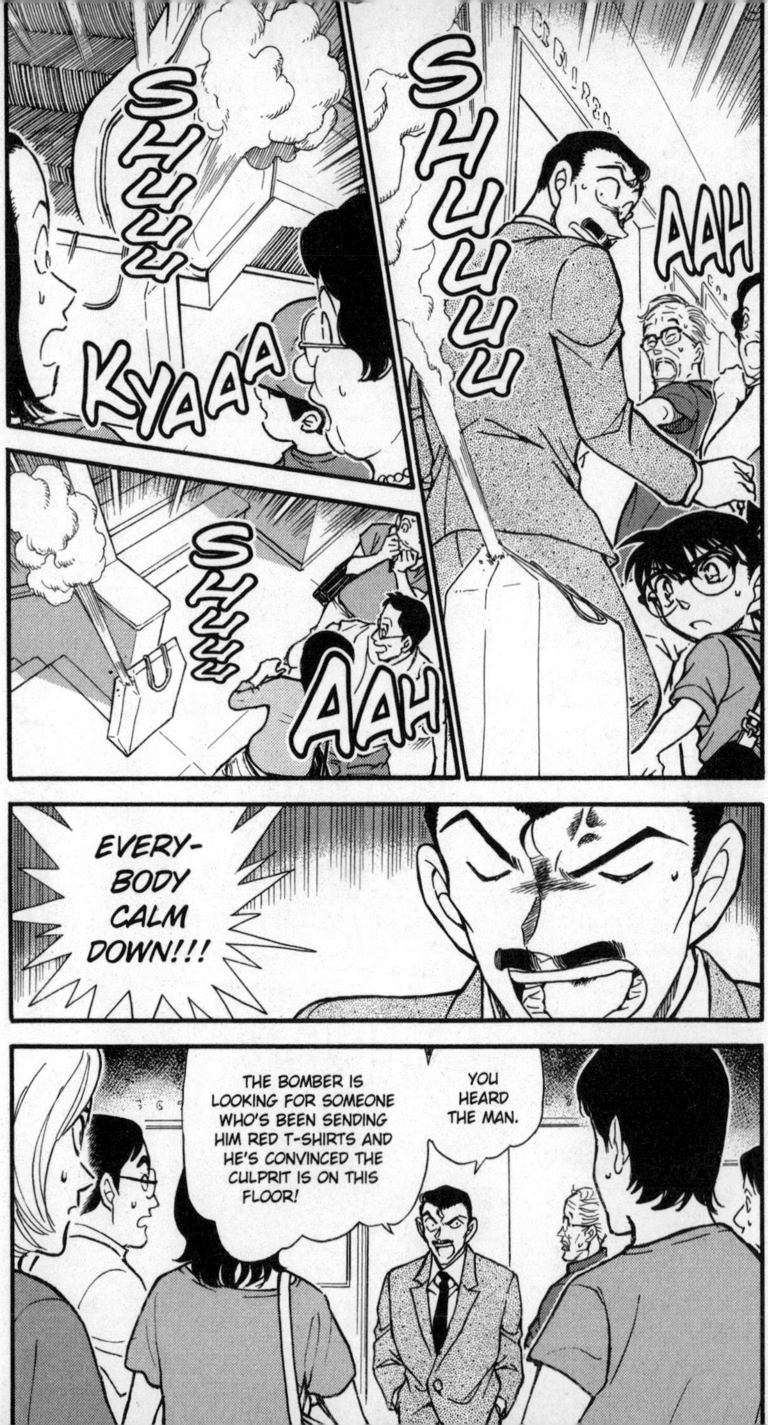
SHUUUUU
AAH
SHUUUU
KYAAA
SHUUU
AAH
EVERY-BODY CALM DOWN!!!
YOU HEARD THE MAN.
THE BOMBER IS LOOKING FOR SOMEONE WHO'S BEEN SENDING HIM RED T-SHIRTS AND HE'S CONVINCED THE CULPRIT IS ON THIS FLOOR!

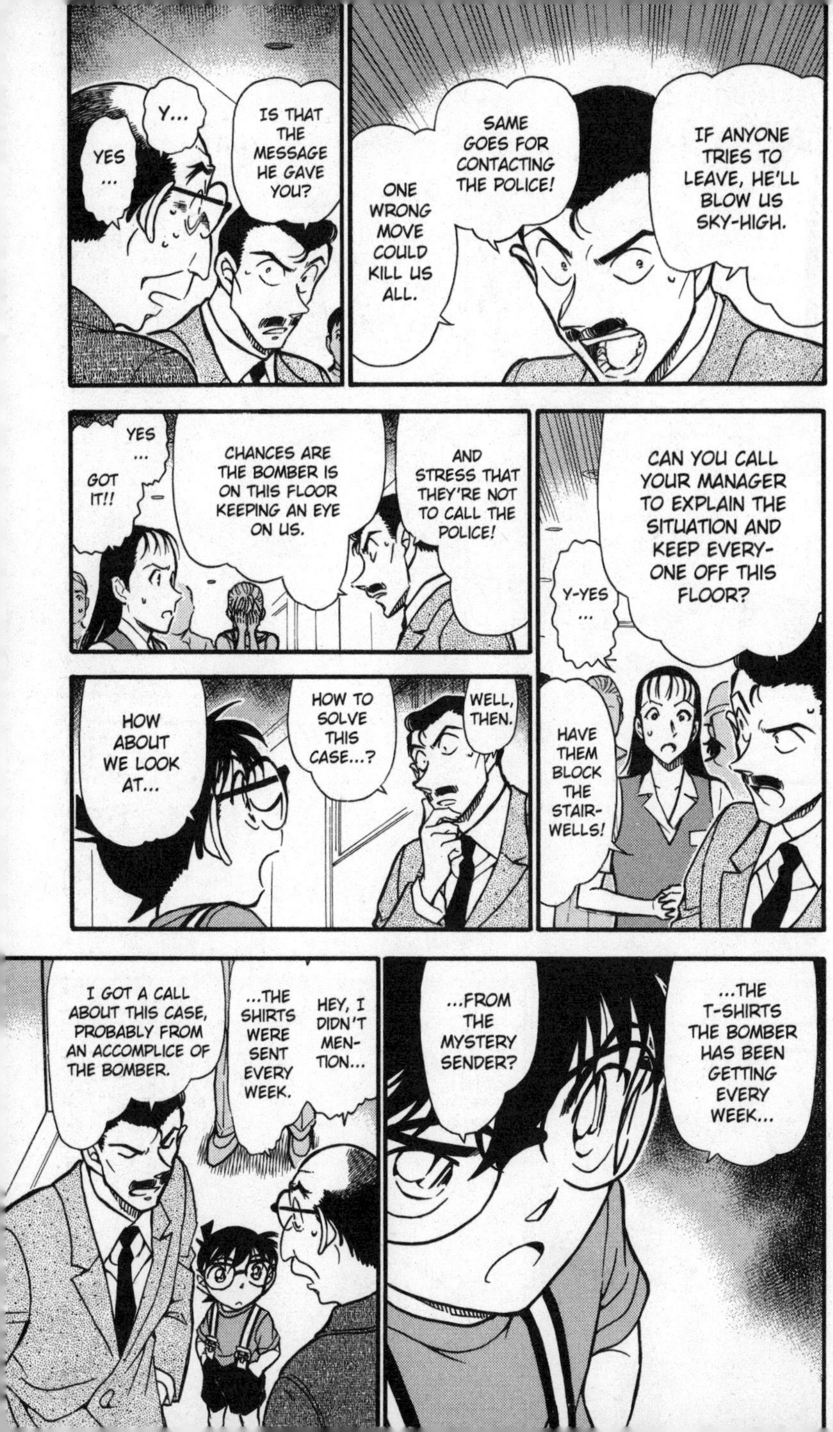
IF ANYONE TRIES TO LEAVE, HE'LL BLOW US SKY-HIGH.
SAME GOES FOR CONTACTING THE POLICE!
ONE WRONG MOVE COULD KILL US ALL.
IS THAT THE MESSAGE HE GAVE YOU?
Y...
YES ...
CAN YOU CALL YOUR MANAGER TO EXPLAIN THE SITUATION AND KEEP EVERY-ONE OFF THIS FLOOR?
Y-YES ...
HAVE THEM BLOCK THE STAIR-WELLS!
AND STRESS THAT THEY'RE NOT TO CALL THE POLICE!
CHANCES ARE THE BOMBER IS ON THIS FLOOR KEEPING AN EYE ON US.
YES ...
GOT IT!!
WELL, THEN.
HOW TO SOLVE THIS CASE...?
HOW ABOUT WE LOOK AT...
...THE T-SHIRTS THE BOMBER HAS BEEN GETTING EVERY WEEK...
...FROM THE MYSTERY SENDER?
HEY, I DIDN'T MEN-TION...
...THE SHIRTS WERE SENT EVERY WEEK.
I GOT A CALL ABOUT THIS CASE, PROBABLY FROM AN ACCOMPLICE OF THE BOMBER.

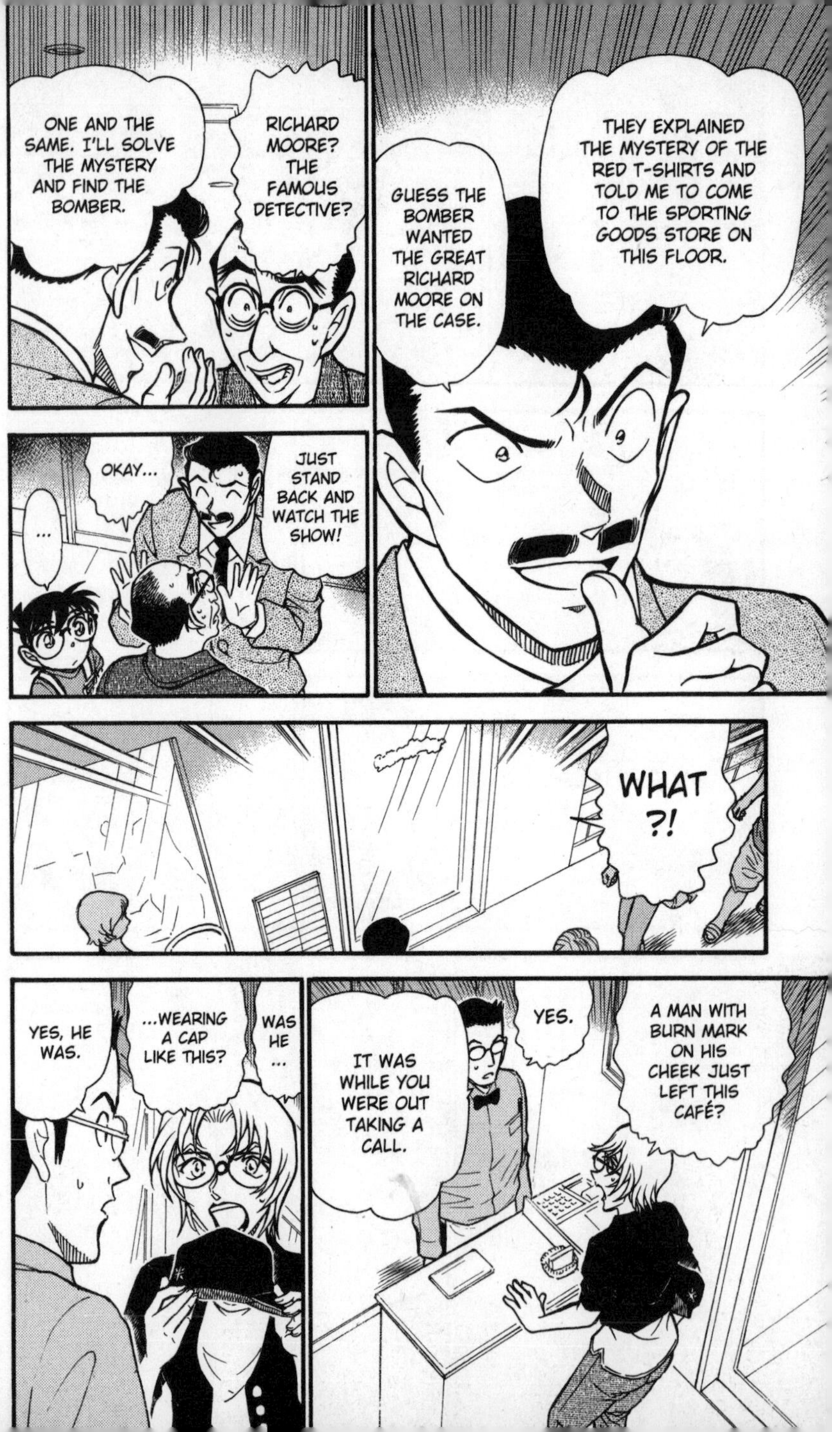
THEY EXPLAINED THE MYSTERY OF THE RED T-SHIRTS AND TOLD ME TO COME TO THE SPORTING GOODS STORE ON THIS FLOOR.
GUESS THE BOMBER WANTED THE GREAT RICHARD MOORE ON THE CASE.
RICHARD MOORE? THE FAMOUS DETECTIVE?
ONE AND THE SAME. I'LL SOLVE THE MYSTERY AND FIND THE BOMBER.
JUST STAND BACK AND WATCH THE SHOW!
OKAY...
...
WHAT ?!
A MAN WITH BURN MARK ON HIS CHEEK JUST LEFT THIS CAFÉ?
YES.
IT WAS WHILE YOU WERE OUT TAKING A CALL.
WAS HE ...
...WEARING A CAP LIKE THIS?
YES, HE WAS.

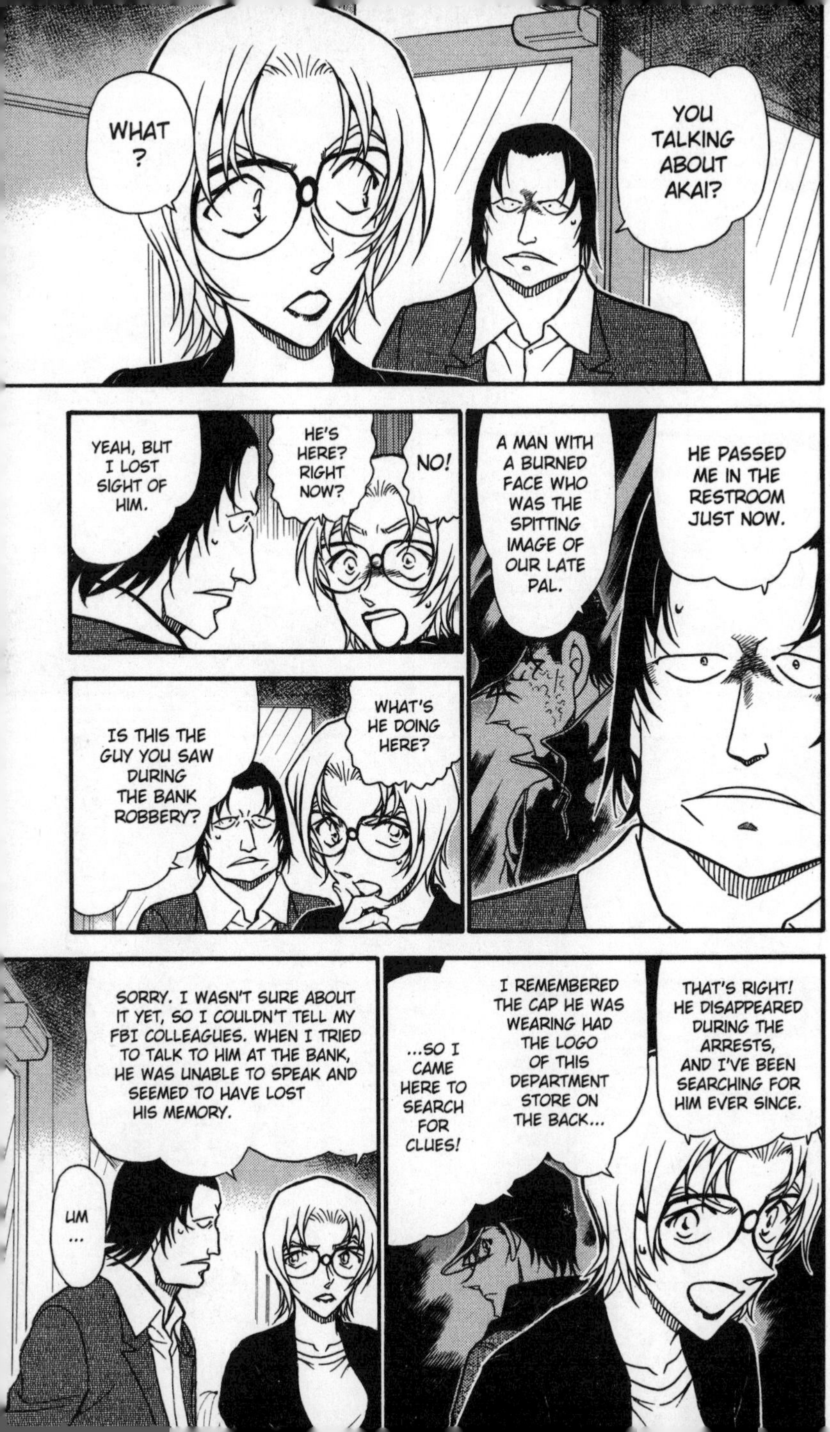
YOU TALKING ABOUT AKAI?
WHAT ?
HE PASSED ME IN THE RESTROOM JUST NOW.
A MAN WITH A BURNED FACE WHO WAS THE SPITTING IMAGE OF OUR LATE PAL.
NO!
HE'S HERE? RIGHT NOW?
YEAH, BUT I LOST SIGHT OF HIM.
WHAT'S HE DOING HERE?
IS THIS THE GUY YOU SAW DURING THE BANK ROBBERY?
THAT'S RIGHT! HE DISAPPEARED DURING THE ARRESTS, AND I'VE BEEN SEARCHING FOR HIM EVER SINCE.
I REMEMBERED THE CAP HE WAS WEARING HAD THE LOGO OF THIS DEPARTMENT STORE ON THE BACK...
...SO I CAME HERE TO SEARCH FOR CLUES!
SORRY. I WASN'T SURE ABOUT IT YET, SO I COULDN'T TELL MY FBI COLLEAGUES. WHEN I TRIED TO TALK TO HIM AT THE BANK, HE WAS UNABLE TO SPEAK AND SEEMED TO HAVE LOST HIS MEMORY.
UM ...

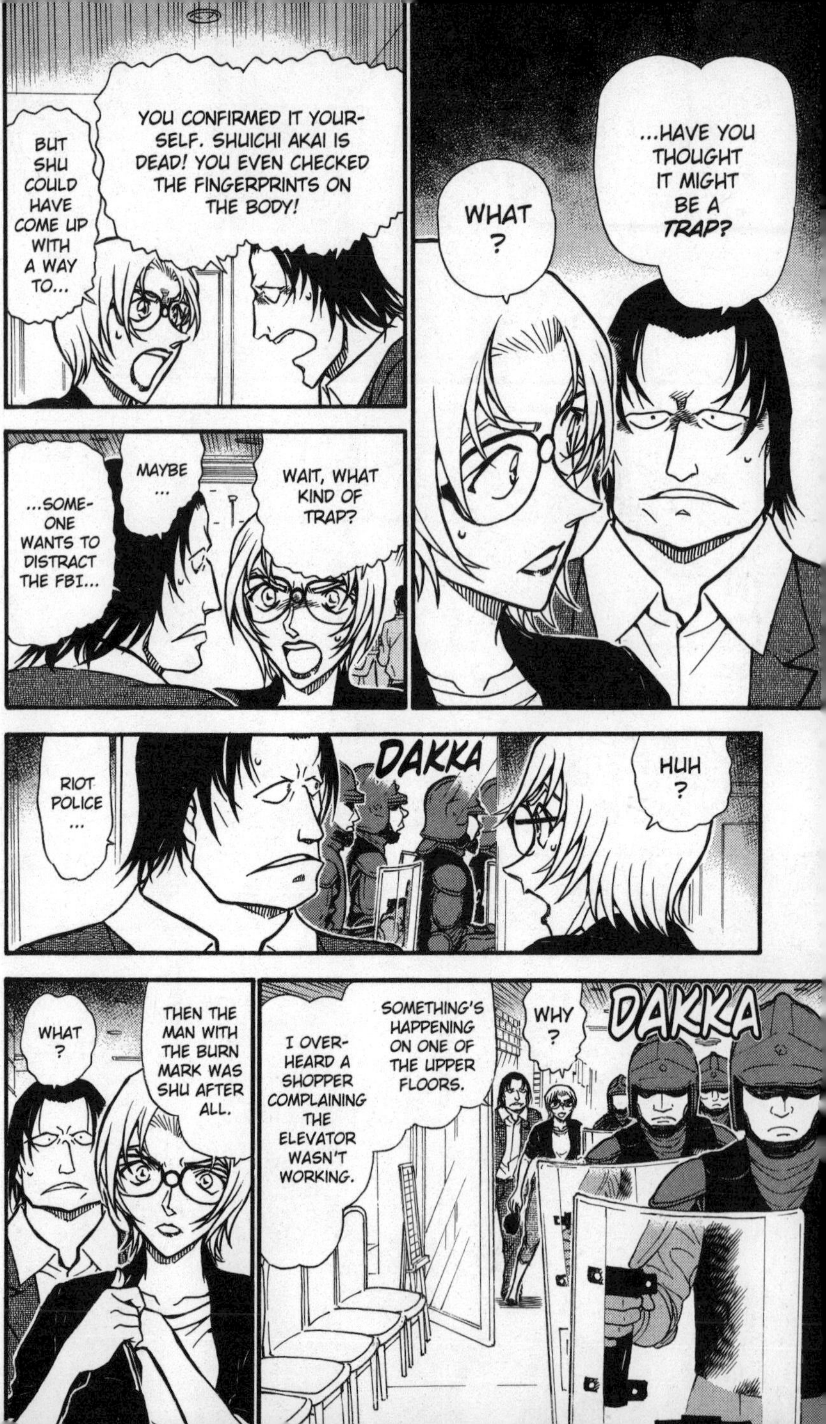
...HAVE YOU THOUGHT IT MIGHT BE A *TRAP?*
WHAT ?
YOU CONFIRMED IT YOURSELF. SHUICHI AKAI IS DEAD! YOU EVEN CHECKED THE FINGERPRINTS ON THE BODY!
BUT SHU COULD HAVE COME UP WITH A WAY TO...
WAIT, WHAT KIND OF TRAP?
MAYBE ...
...SOMEONE WANTS TO DISTRACT THE FBI...
HUH ?
DAKKA
RIOT POLICE ...
DAKKA
WHY ?
SOMETHING'S HAPPENING ON ONE OF THE UPPER FLOORS.
I OVERHEARD A SHOPPER COMPLAINING THE ELEVATOR WASN'T WORKING.
THEN THE MAN WITH THE BURN MARK WAS SHU AFTER ALL.
WHAT ?

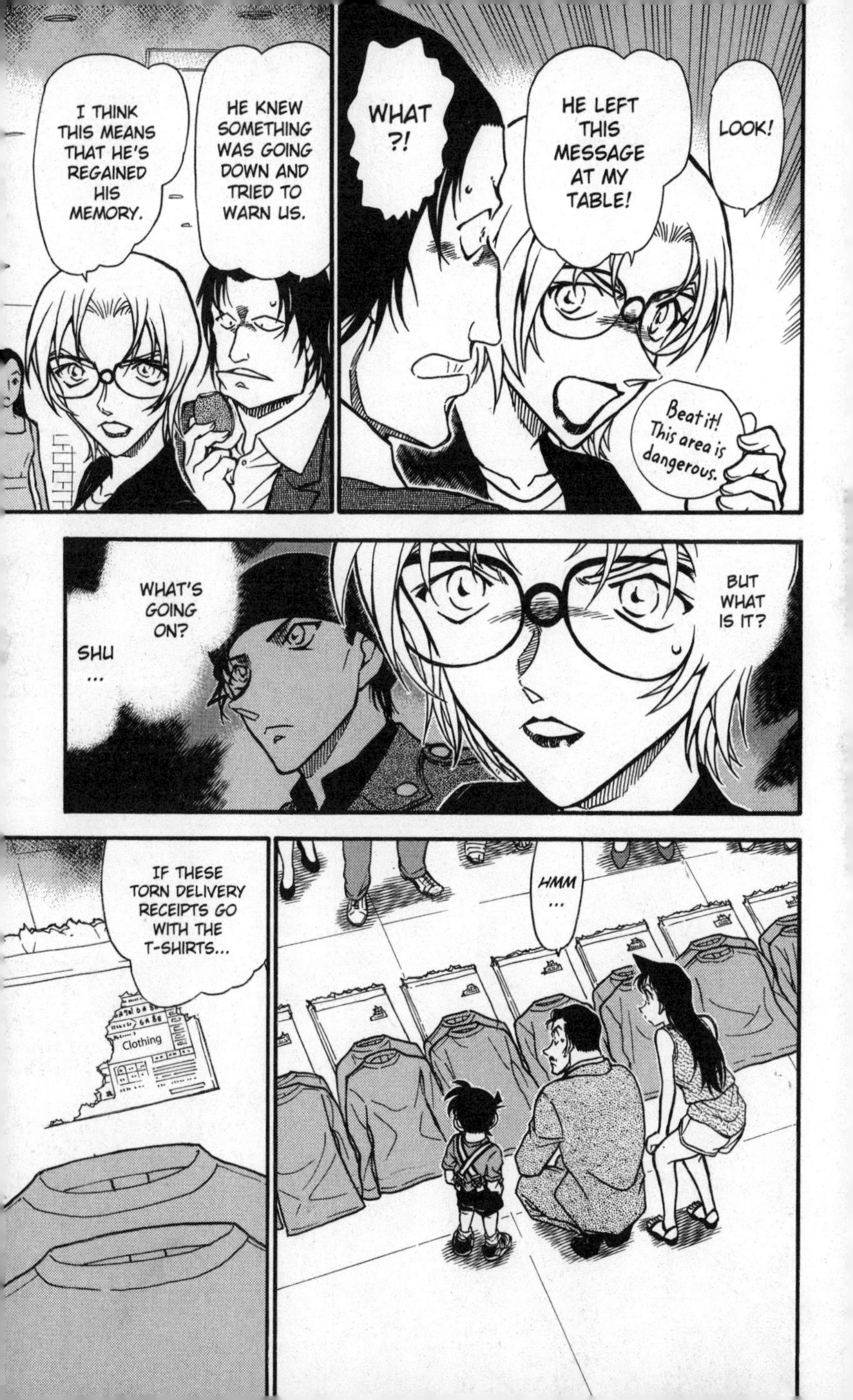
LOOK!
HE LEFT THIS MESSAGE AT MY TABLE!
Beat it! This area is dangerous.
WHAT ?!
HE KNEW SOMETHING WAS GOING DOWN AND TRIED TO WARN US.
I THINK THIS MEANS THAT HE'S REGAINED HIS MEMORY.
BUT WHAT IS IT?
WHAT'S GOING ON?
SHU ...
HMM ...
IF THESE TORN DELIVERY RECEIPTS GO WITH THE T-SHIRTS...
Clothing

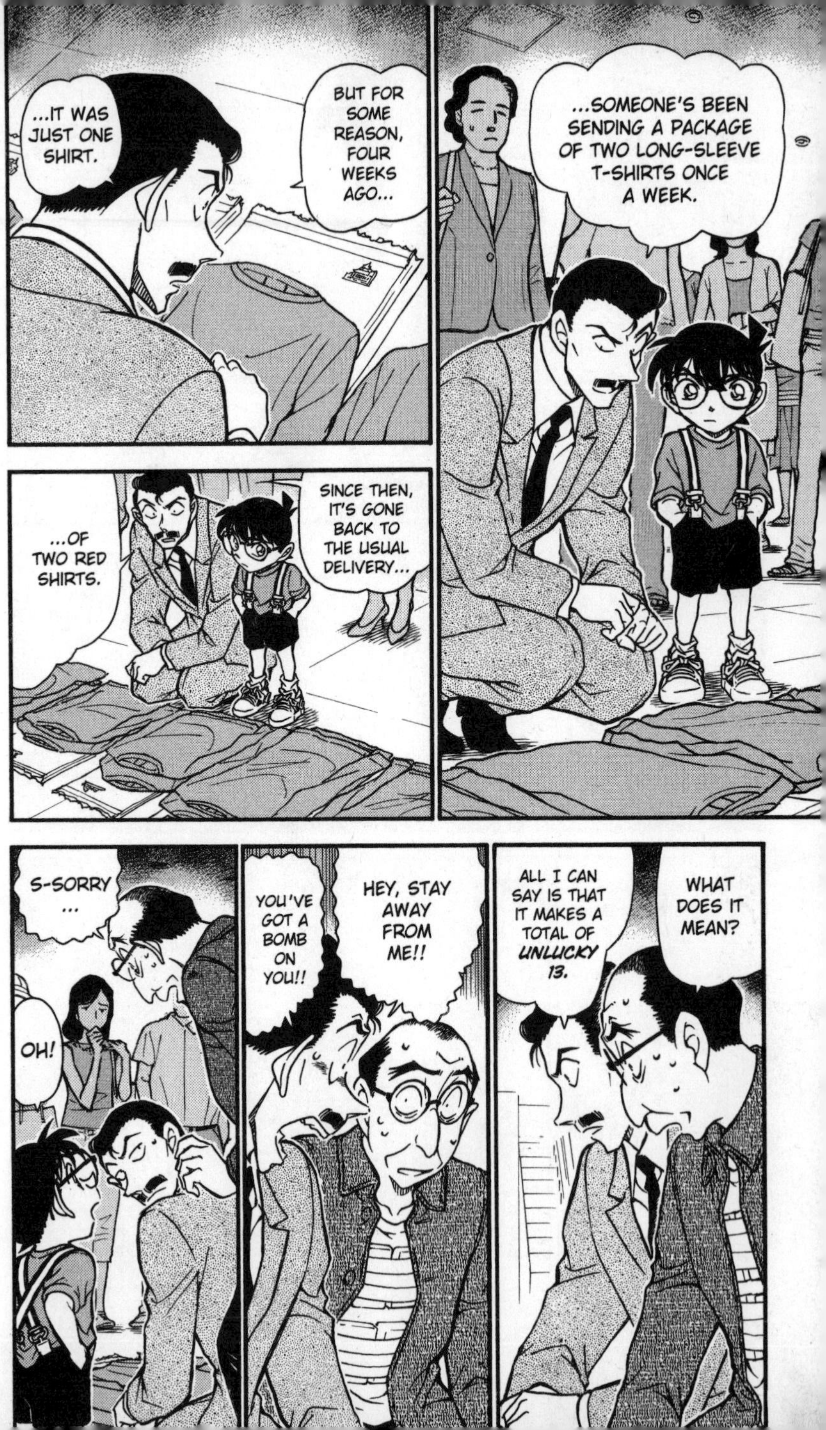
...SOMEONE'S BEEN SENDING A PACKAGE OF TWO LONG-SLEEVE T-SHIRTS ONCE A WEEK.
BUT FOR SOME REASON, FOUR WEEKS AGO...
...IT WAS JUST ONE SHIRT.
SINCE THEN, IT'S GONE BACK TO THE USUAL DELIVERY...
...OF TWO RED SHIRTS.
WHAT DOES IT MEAN?
ALL I CAN SAY IS THAT IT MAKES A TOTAL OF *UNLUCKY* 13.
HEY, STAY AWAY FROM ME!!
YOU'VE GOT A BOMB ON YOU!!
S-SORRY ...
OH!

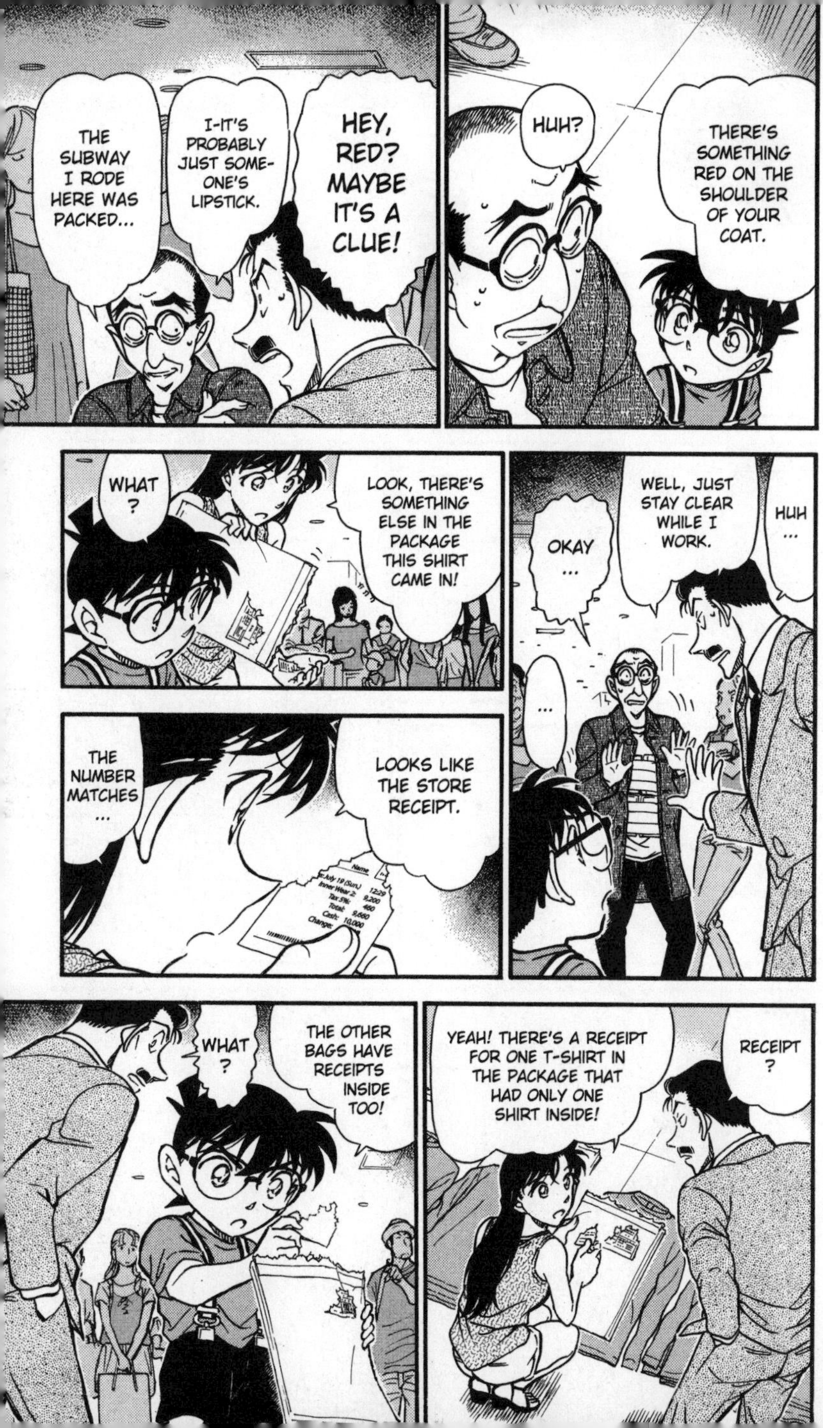
THERE'S SOMETHING RED ON THE SHOULDER OF YOUR COAT.
HUH?
HEY, RED? MAYBE IT'S A CLUE!
I-IT'S PROBABLY JUST SOME-ONE'S LIPSTICK.
THE SUBWAY I RODE HERE WAS PACKED...
HUH ...
WELL, JUST STAY CLEAR WHILE I WORK.
OKAY ...
...
LOOK, THERE'S SOMETHING ELSE IN THE PACKAGE THIS SHIRT CAME IN!
WHAT ?
LOOKS LIKE THE STORE RECEIPT.
THE NUMBER MATCHES ...
Name
July 19 (Sun.) 12:29
Inner Wear 2: 9,200
Tax 5%: 460
Total: 9,660
Cash: 10,000
Change:
RECEIPT ?
YEAH! THERE'S A RECEIPT FOR ONE T-SHIRT IN THE PACKAGE THAT HAD ONLY ONE SHIRT INSIDE!
THE OTHER BAGS HAVE RECEIPTS INSIDE TOO!
WHAT ?

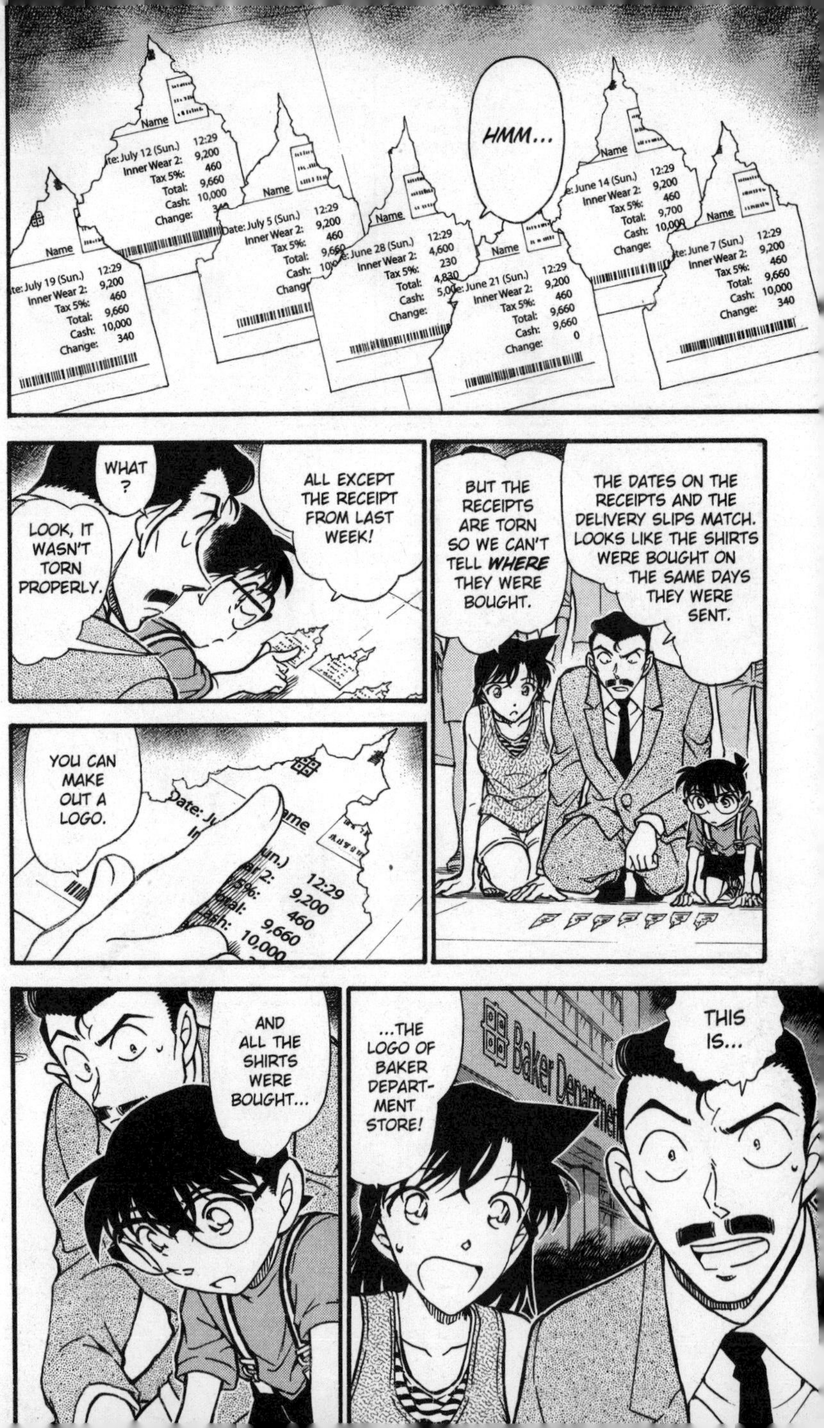
HMM...
Name
te: June 7 (Sun.) 12:29
Inner Wear 2: 9,200
Tax 5%: 460
Total: 9,660
Cash: 10,000
Change: 340
Name
e: June 14 (Sun.) 12:29
Inner Wear 2: 9,200
Tax 5%: 460
Total: 9,700
Cash: 10,000
Change:
Name
e: June 21 (Sun.) 12:29
Inner Wear 2: 9,200
Tax 5%: 460
Total: 9,660
Cash: 9,660
Change: 0
Name
e: June 28 (Sun.) 12:29
Inner Wear 2: 4,600
Tax 5%: 230
Total: 4,830
Cash: 5,00
Change:
Name
Date: July 5 (Sun.) 12:29
Inner Wear 2: 9,200
Tax 5%: 460
Total: 9,66
Cash: 10
Change
Name
te: July 12 (Sun.) 12:29
Inner Wear 2: 9,200
Tax 5%: 460
Total: 9,660
Cash: 10,000
Change: 340
Name
te: July 19 (Sun.) 12:29
Inner Wear 2: 9,200
Tax 5%: 460
Total: 9,660
Cash: 10,000
Change: 340
THE DATES ON THE RECEIPTS AND THE DELIVERY SLIPS MATCH. LOOKS LIKE THE SHIRTS WERE BOUGHT ON THE SAME DAYS THEY WERE SENT.
BUT THE RECEIPTS ARE TORN SO WE CAN'T TELL *WHERE* THEY WERE BOUGHT.
ALL EXCEPT THE RECEIPT FROM LAST WEEK!
WHAT ?
LOOK, IT WASN'T TORN PROPERLY.
YOU CAN MAKE OUT A LOGO.
Date: Ju
ame
12:29
9,200
460
9,660
10,000
THIS IS...
Baker Department
...THE LOGO OF BAKER DEPARTMENT STORE!
AND ALL THE SHIRTS WERE BOUGHT...

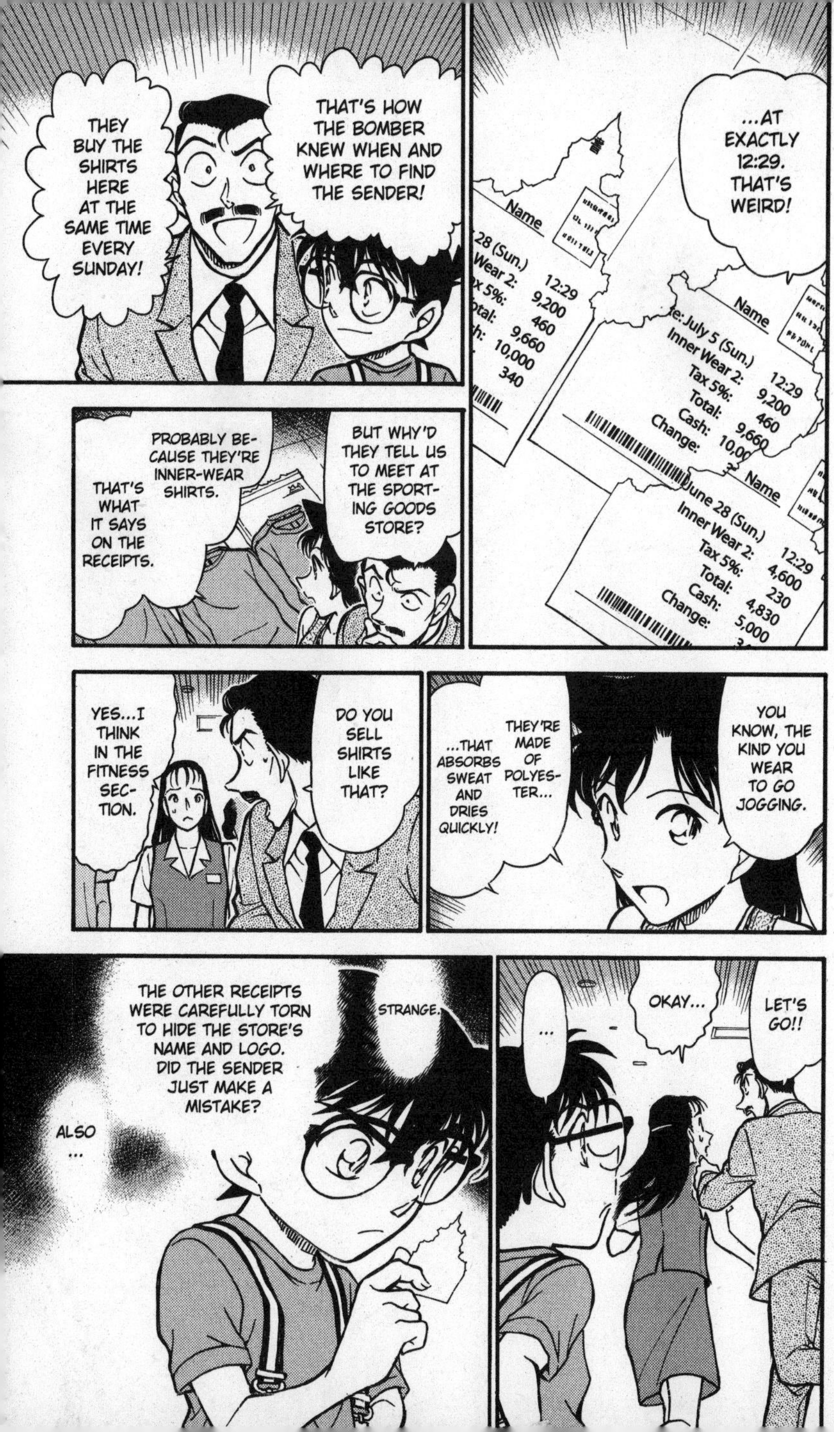
...AT EXACTLY 12:29. THAT'S WEIRD!
Name
28 (Sun.)
Wear 2: 12:29
ax 5%: 9,200
otal: 460
h: 9,660
10,000
340
Name
e: July 5 (Sun.)
Inner Wear 2: 12:29
Tax 5%: 9,200
Total: 460
Cash: 9,660
Change: 10,00
Name
June 28 (Sun.)
Inner Wear 2: 12:29
Tax 5%: 4,600
Total: 230
Cash: 4,830
Change: 5,000
THEY BUY THE SHIRTS HERE AT THE SAME TIME EVERY SUNDAY!
THAT'S HOW THE BOMBER KNEW WHEN AND WHERE TO FIND THE SENDER!
BUT WHY'D THEY TELL US TO MEET AT THE SPORTING GOODS STORE?
PROBABLY BECAUSE THEY'RE INNER-WEAR SHIRTS.
THAT'S WHAT IT SAYS ON THE RECEIPTS.
YOU KNOW, THE KIND YOU WEAR TO GO JOGGING.
THEY'RE MADE OF POLYESTER...
...THAT ABSORBS SWEAT AND DRIES QUICKLY!
DO YOU SELL SHIRTS LIKE THAT?
YES...I THINK IN THE FITNESS SECTION.
LET'S GO!!
OKAY...
...
STRANGE.
THE OTHER RECEIPTS WERE CAREFULLY TORN TO HIDE THE STORE'S NAME AND LOGO. DID THE SENDER JUST MAKE A MISTAKE?
ALSO ...

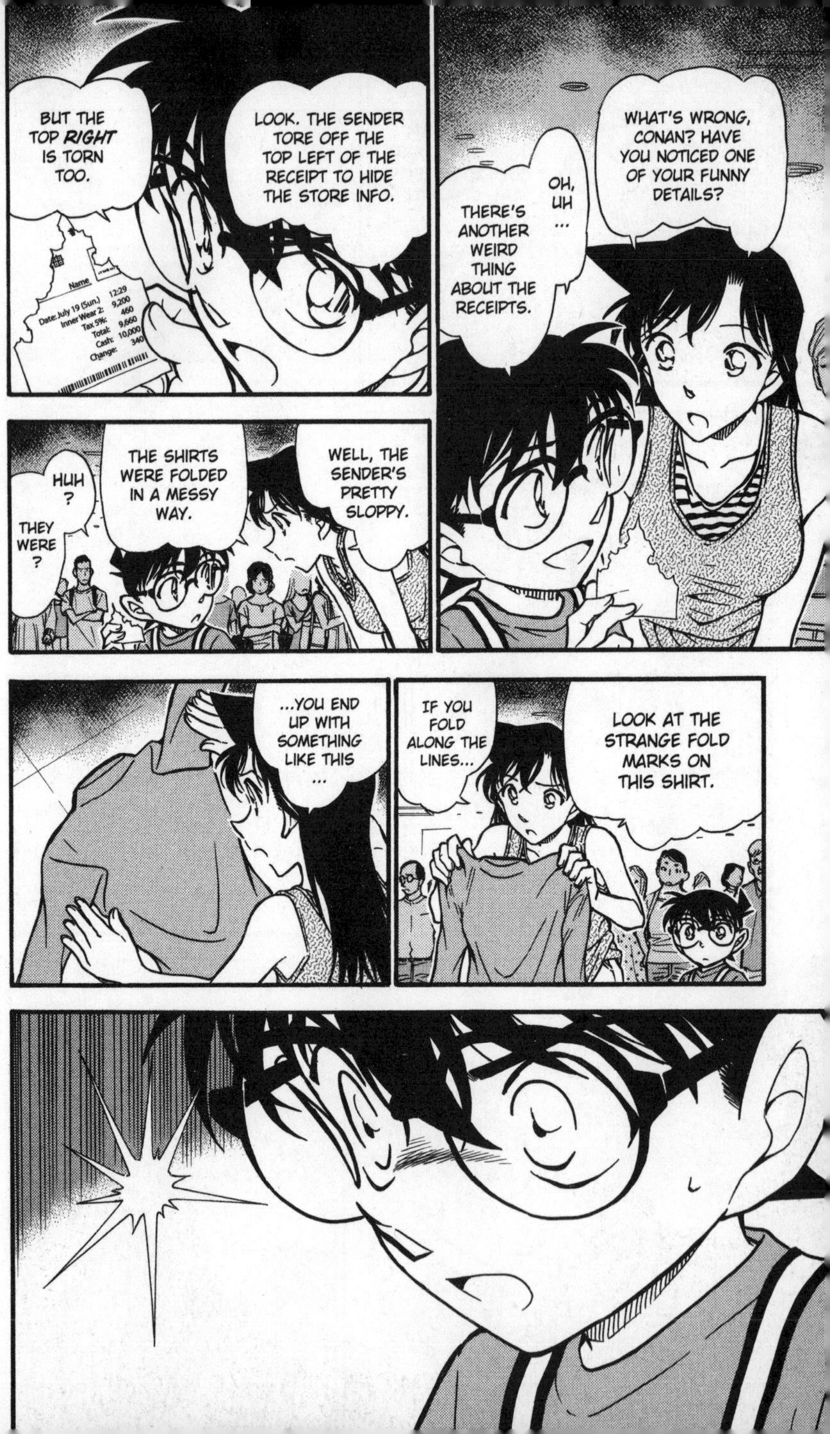
WHAT'S WRONG, CONAN? HAVE YOU NOTICED ONE OF YOUR FUNNY DETAILS?
OH, UH ...
THERE'S ANOTHER WEIRD THING ABOUT THE RECEIPTS.
LOOK. THE SENDER TORE OFF THE TOP LEFT OF THE RECEIPT TO HIDE THE STORE INFO.
BUT THE TOP *RIGHT* IS TORN TOO.
Name
Date: July 19 (Sun.) 12:29
Inner Wear 2: 9,200
Tax 5%: 460
Total: 9,660
Cash: 10,000
Change: 340
WELL, THE SENDER'S PRETTY SLOPPY.
THE SHIRTS WERE FOLDED IN A MESSY WAY.
HUH?
THEY WERE?
LOOK AT THE STRANGE FOLD MARKS ON THIS SHIRT.
IF YOU FOLD ALONG THE LINES...
...YOU END UP WITH SOMETHING LIKE THIS ...

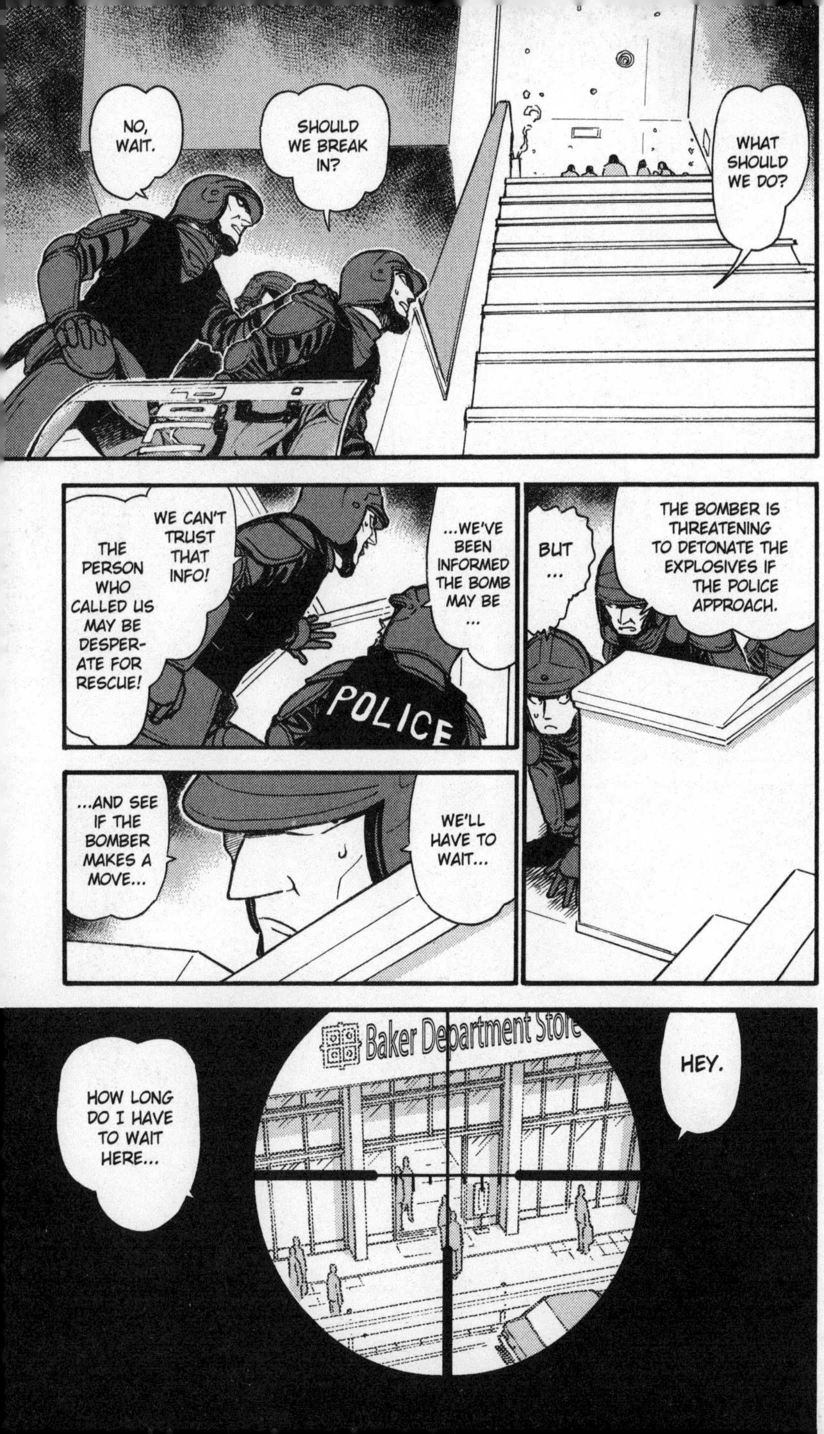
WHAT SHOULD WE DO?
SHOULD WE BREAK IN?
NO, WAIT.
THE BOMBER IS THREATENING TO DETONATE THE EXPLOSIVES IF THE POLICE APPROACH.
BUT ...
...WE'VE BEEN INFORMED THE BOMB MAY BE ...
WE CAN'T TRUST THAT INFO!
THE PERSON WHO CALLED US MAY BE DESPERATE FOR RESCUE!
WE'LL HAVE TO WAIT...
...AND SEE IF THE BOMBER MAKES A MOVE...
HEY.
Baker Department Store
HOW LONG DO I HAVE TO WAIT HERE...

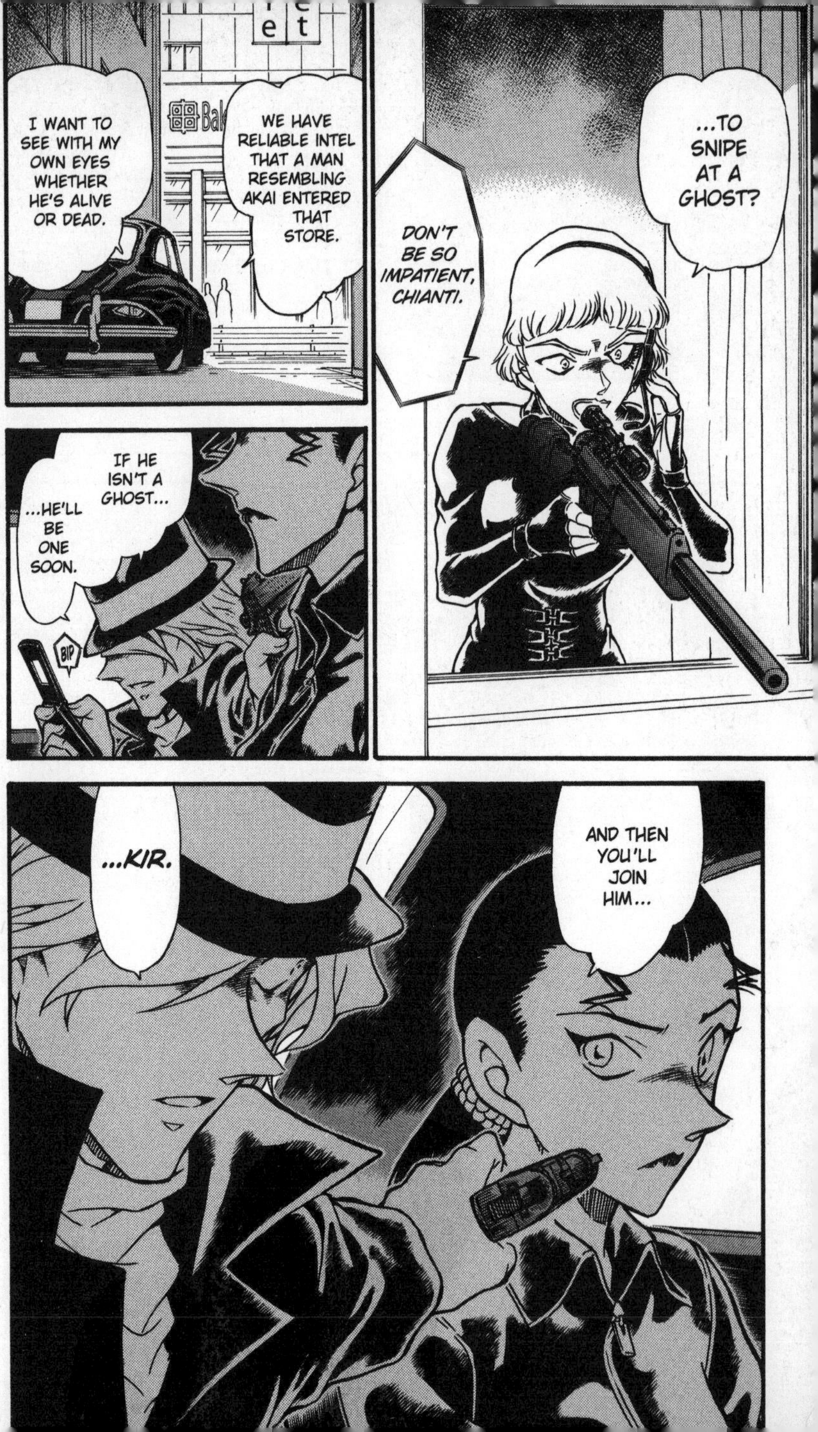
...TO SNIPE AT A GHOST?
DON'T BE SO IMPATIENT, CHIANTI.
WE HAVE RELIABLE INTEL THAT A MAN RESEMBLING AKAI ENTERED THAT STORE.
I WANT TO SEE WITH MY OWN EYES WHETHER HE'S ALIVE OR DEAD.
IF HE ISN'T A GHOST...
...HE'LL BE ONE SOON.
BIP
AND THEN YOU'LL JOIN HIM...
...KIR.

FILE 6: THE BOMBER'S AIM

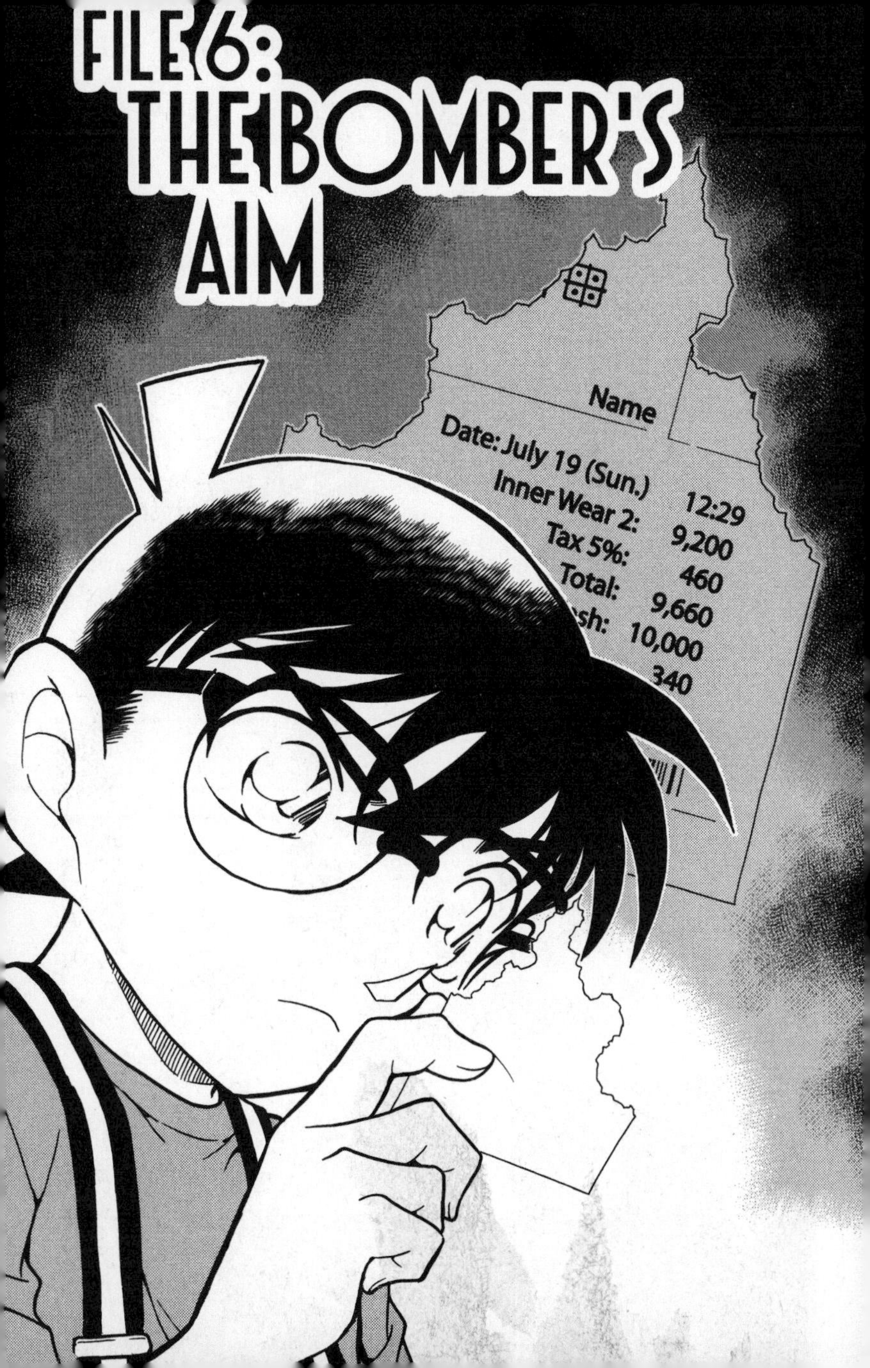
Name
Date: July 19 (Sun.) 12:29
Inner Wear 2: 9,200
Tax 5%: 460
Total: 9,660
10,000
340

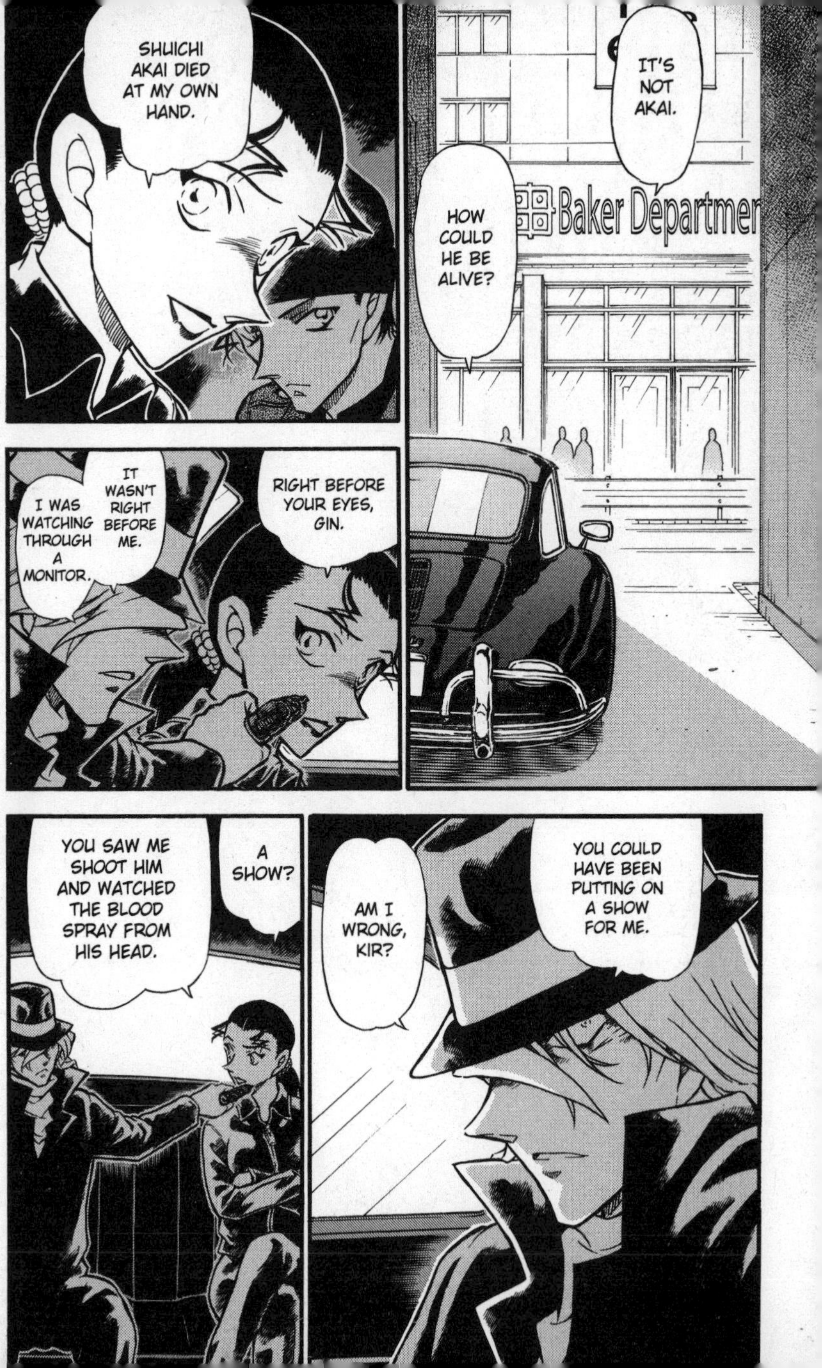
IT'S NOT AKAI.
Baker Departmer
HOW COULD HE BE ALIVE?
SHUICHI AKAI DIED AT MY OWN HAND.
RIGHT BEFORE YOUR EYES, GIN.
IT WASN'T RIGHT BEFORE ME.
I WAS WATCHING THROUGH A MONITOR.
YOU COULD HAVE BEEN PUTTING ON A SHOW FOR ME.
AM I WRONG, KIR?
A SHOW?
YOU SAW ME SHOOT HIM AND WATCHED THE BLOOD SPRAY FROM HIS HEAD.

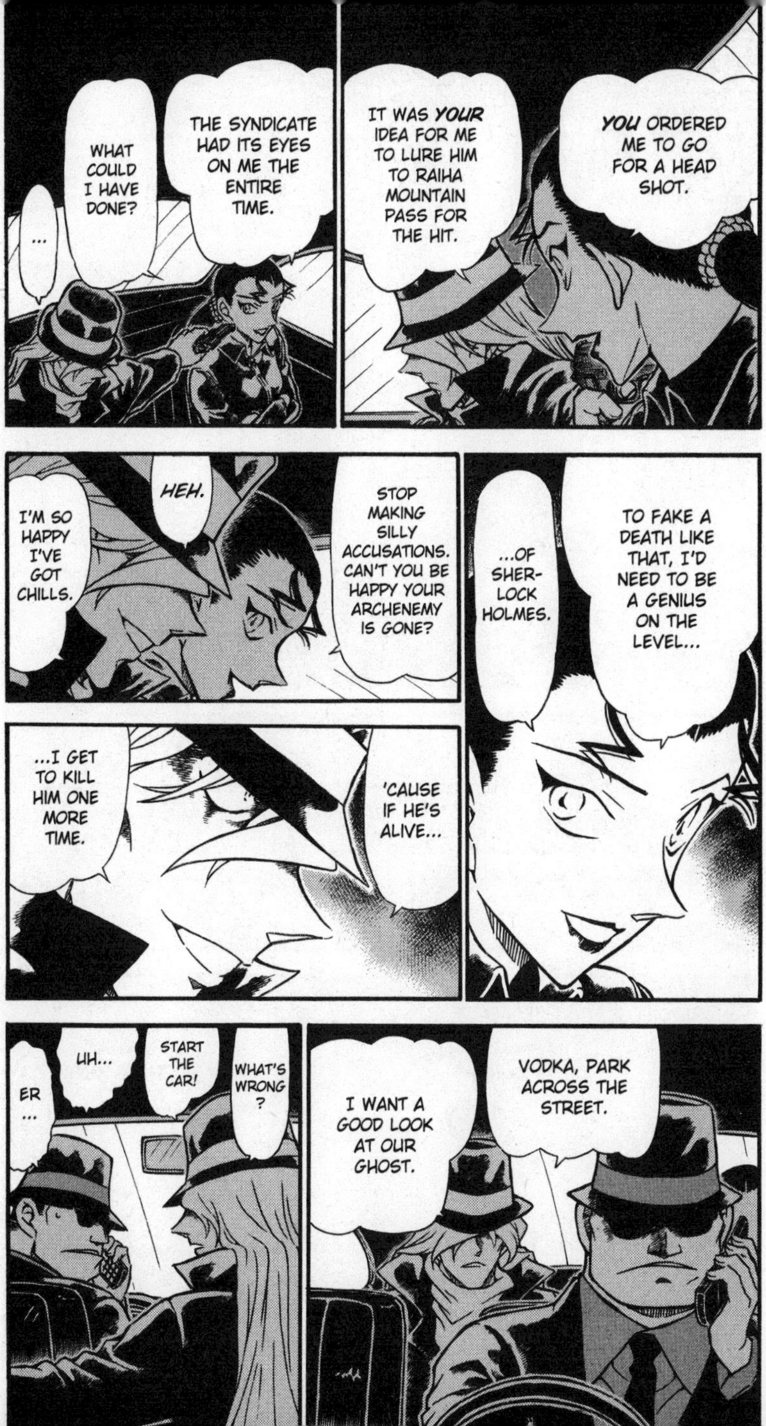
YOU ORDERED ME TO GO FOR A HEAD SHOT.
IT WAS YOUR IDEA FOR ME TO LURE HIM TO RAIHA MOUNTAIN PASS FOR THE HIT.
THE SYNDICATE HAD ITS EYES ON ME THE ENTIRE TIME.
WHAT COULD I HAVE DONE?
...
TO FAKE A DEATH LIKE THAT, I'D NEED TO BE A GENIUS ON THE LEVEL...
...OF SHER-LOCK HOLMES.
STOP MAKING SILLY ACCUSATIONS. CAN'T YOU BE HAPPY YOUR ARCHENEMY IS GONE?
HEH.
I'M SO HAPPY I'VE GOT CHILLS.
'CAUSE IF HE'S ALIVE...
...I GET TO KILL HIM ONE MORE TIME.
VODKA, PARK ACROSS THE STREET.
I WANT A GOOD LOOK AT OUR GHOST.
WHAT'S WRONG?
START THE CAR!
UH...
ER...

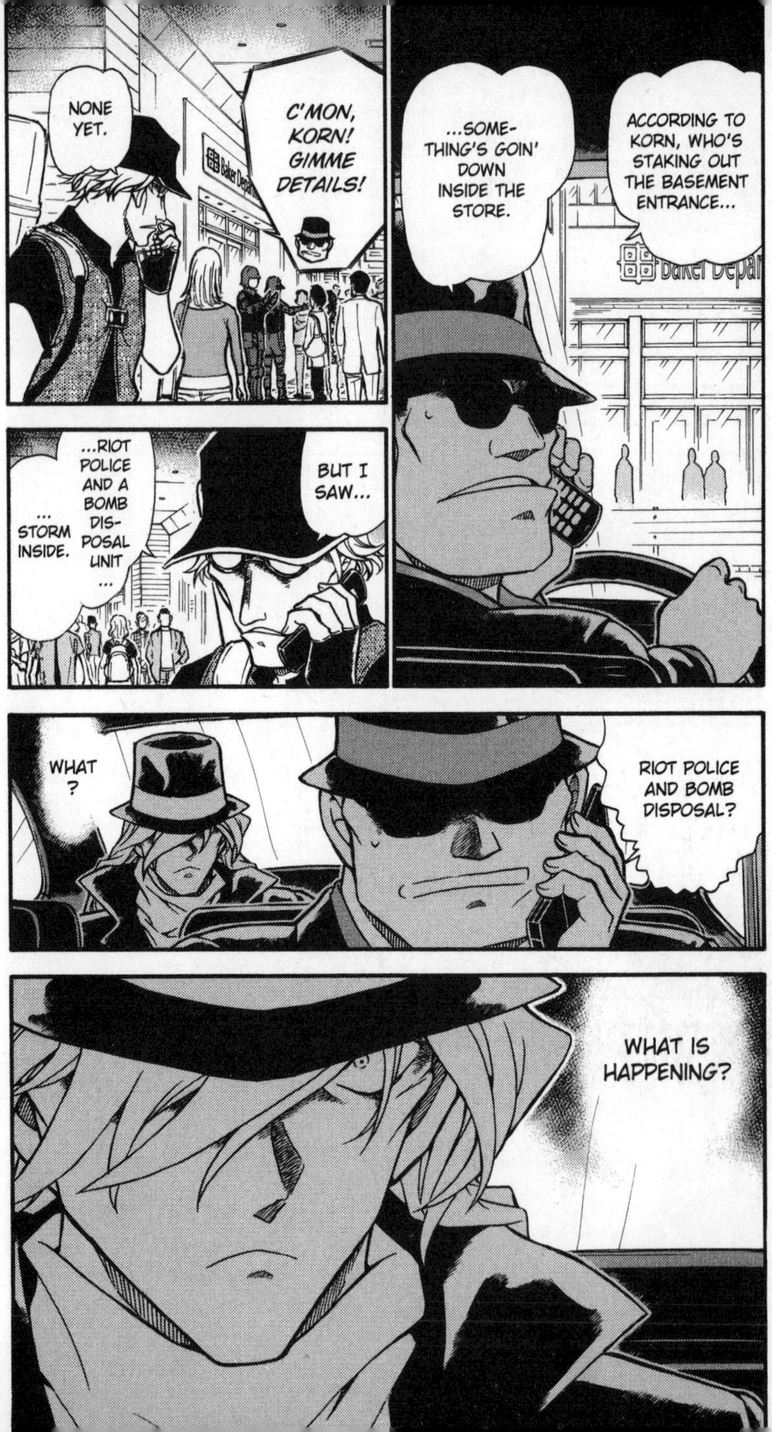
ACCORDING TO KORN, WHO'S STAKING OUT THE BASEMENT ENTRANCE...
...SOME-THING'S GOIN' DOWN INSIDE THE STORE.
C'MON, KORN! GIMME DETAILS!
NONE YET.
BUT I SAW...
...RIOT POLICE AND A BOMB DIS-POSAL UNIT...
...STORM INSIDE.
RIOT POLICE AND BOMB DISPOSAL?
WHAT?
WHAT IS HAPPENING?

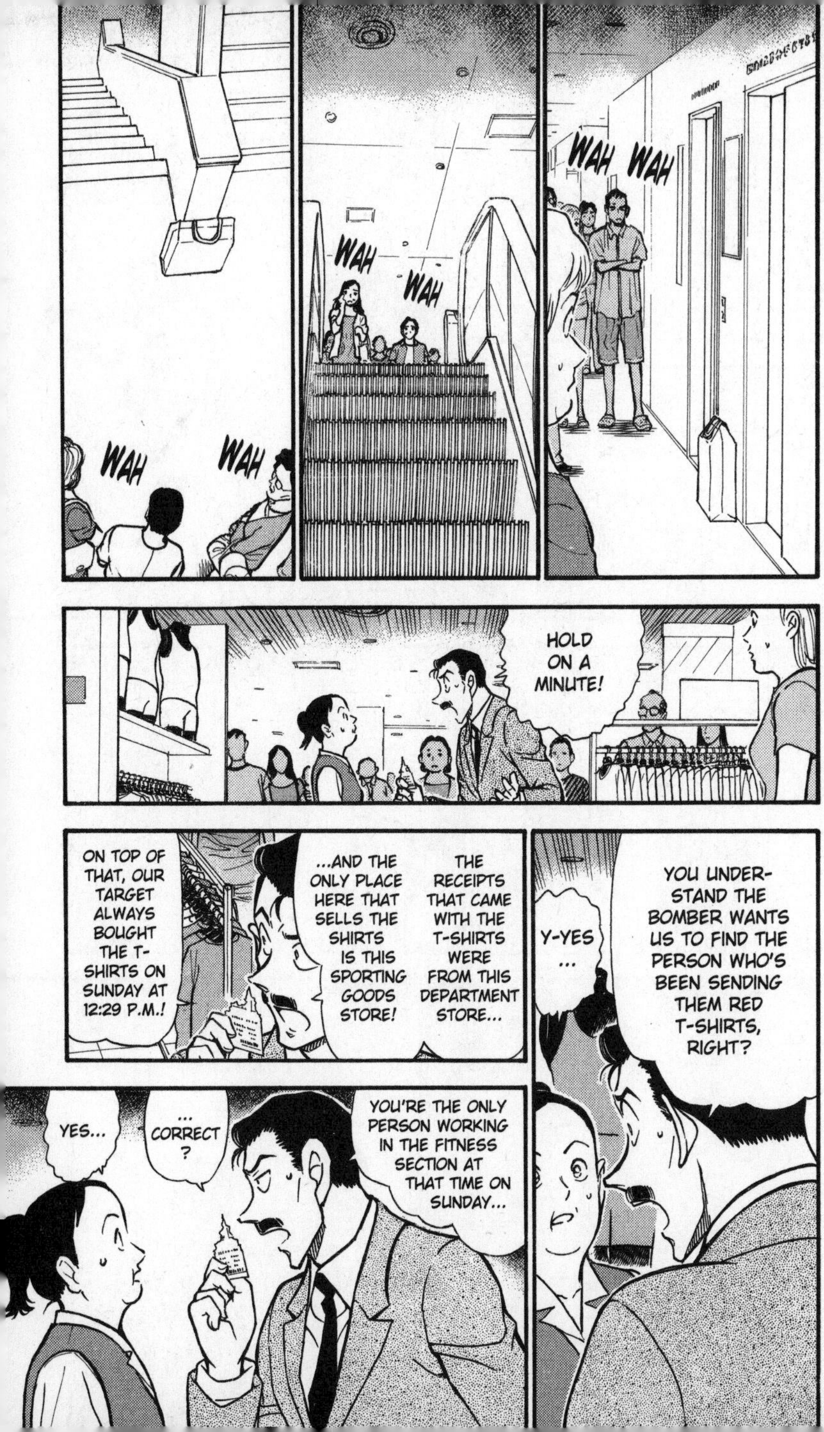
WAH WAH
WAH
WAH
WAH
WAH
HOLD ON A MINUTE!
YOU UNDER-STAND THE BOMBER WANTS US TO FIND THE PERSON WHO'S BEEN SENDING THEM RED T-SHIRTS, RIGHT?
Y-YES...
THE RECEIPTS THAT CAME WITH THE T-SHIRTS WERE FROM THIS DEPARTMENT STORE...
...AND THE ONLY PLACE HERE THAT SELLS THE SHIRTS IS THIS SPORTING GOODS STORE!
ON TOP OF THAT, OUR TARGET ALWAYS BOUGHT THE T-SHIRTS ON SUNDAY AT 12:29 P.M.!
YOU'RE THE ONLY PERSON WORKING IN THE FITNESS SECTION AT THAT TIME ON SUNDAY...
...CORRECT?
YES...

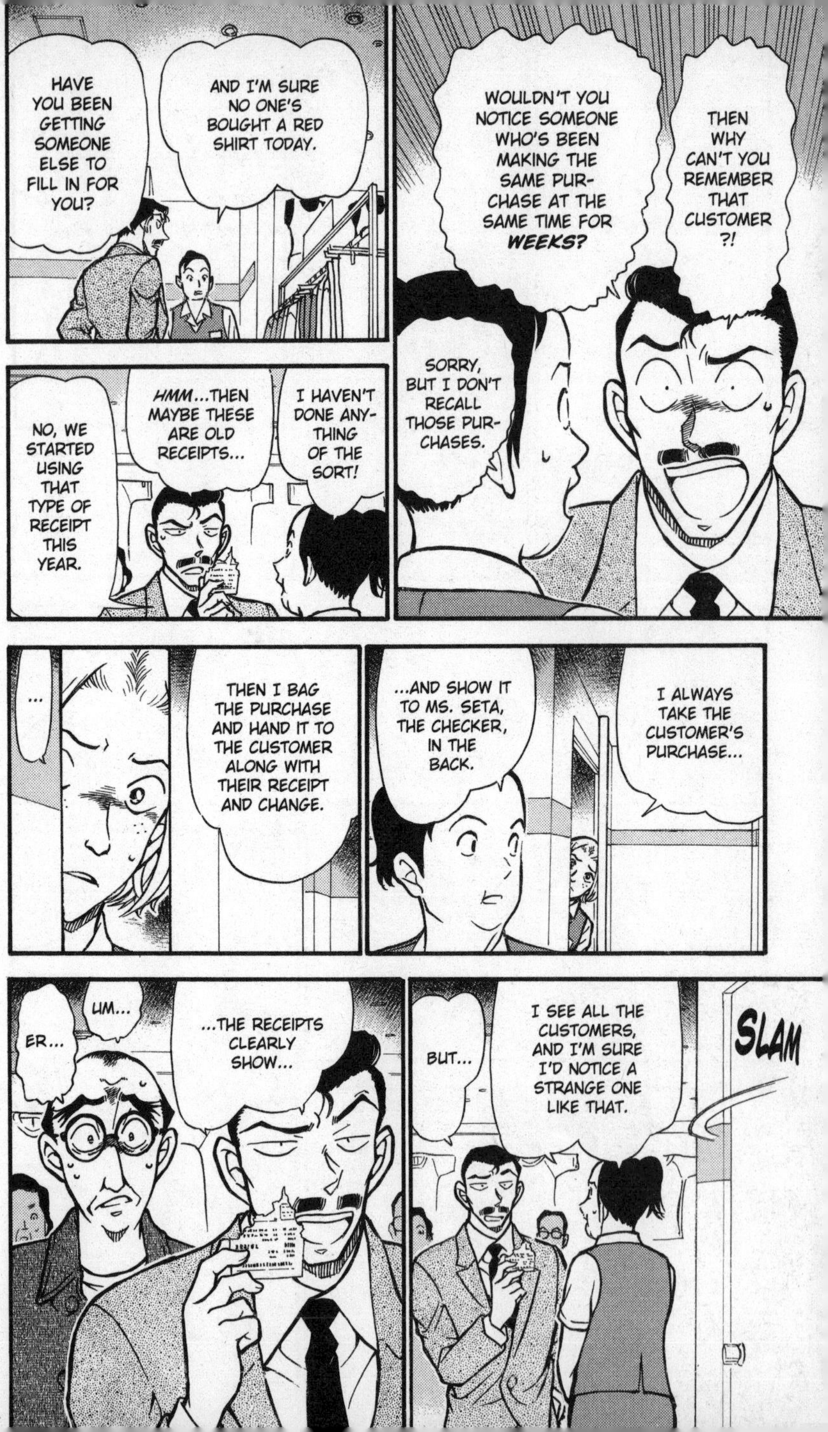
THEN WHY CAN'T YOU REMEMBER THAT CUSTOMER ?!
WOULDN'T YOU NOTICE SOMEONE WHO'S BEEN MAKING THE SAME PUR-CHASE AT THE SAME TIME FOR WEEKS?
SORRY, BUT I DON'T RECALL THOSE PUR-CHASES.
AND I'M SURE NO ONE'S BOUGHT A RED SHIRT TODAY.
HAVE YOU BEEN GETTING SOMEONE ELSE TO FILL IN FOR YOU?
I HAVEN'T DONE ANY-THING OF THE SORT!
HMM...THEN MAYBE THESE ARE OLD RECEIPTS...
NO, WE STARTED USING THAT TYPE OF RECEIPT THIS YEAR.
I ALWAYS TAKE THE CUSTOMER'S PURCHASE...
...AND SHOW IT TO MS. SETA, THE CHECKER, IN THE BACK.
THEN I BAG THE PURCHASE AND HAND IT TO THE CUSTOMER ALONG WITH THEIR RECEIPT AND CHANGE.
...
SLAM
I SEE ALL THE CUSTOMERS, AND I'M SURE I'D NOTICE A STRANGE ONE LIKE THAT.
BUT...
...THE RECEIPTS CLEARLY SHOW...
UM...
ER...

I'M JUST AN ORDINARY CITIZEN WHO'S BEEN STRAPPED TO A BOMB!

I-I'M NOT THE BOMBER.

P-PLEASE DON'T CALL ME THAT!

BOMB MAN!!

WHOA!

...WITH THE RED T-SHIRTS.

...HAS BEEN FOOLING AROUND...

I'M SORRY!

BUT YOUR LITTLE BOY...

YEAH, THAT'S WHY I ASKED YOU TO STAND WAY BACK!

HIM AGAIN?

WAH

WAH

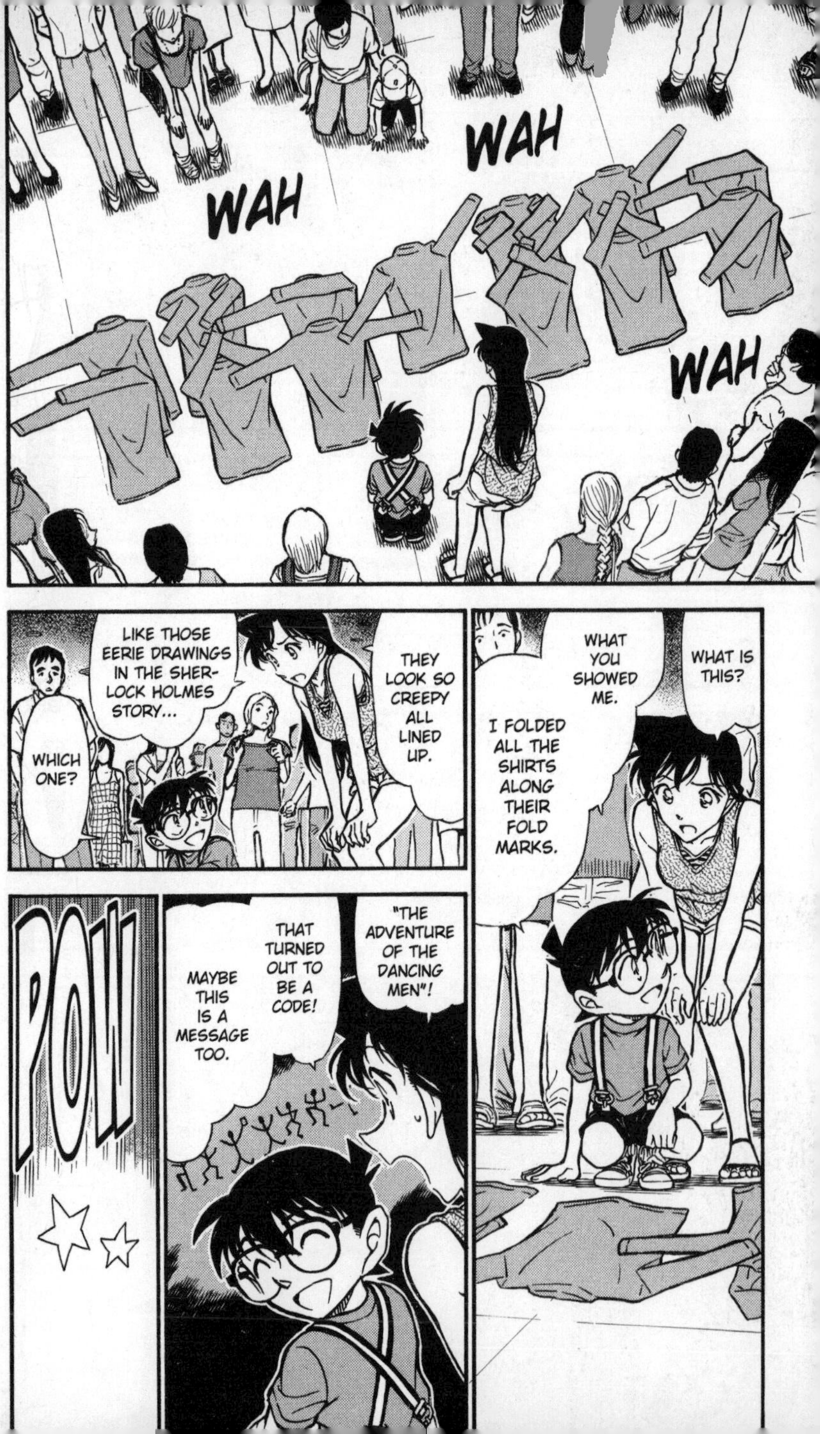
WAH
WAH
WAH
WHAT IS THIS?
WHAT YOU SHOWED ME.
I FOLDED ALL THE SHIRTS ALONG THEIR FOLD MARKS.
THEY LOOK SO CREEPY ALL LINED UP.
LIKE THOSE EERIE DRAWINGS IN THE SHER-LOCK HOLMES STORY...
WHICH ONE?
"THE ADVENTURE OF THE DANCING MEN"!
THAT TURNED OUT TO BE A CODE!
MAYBE THIS IS A MESSAGE TOO.
POW

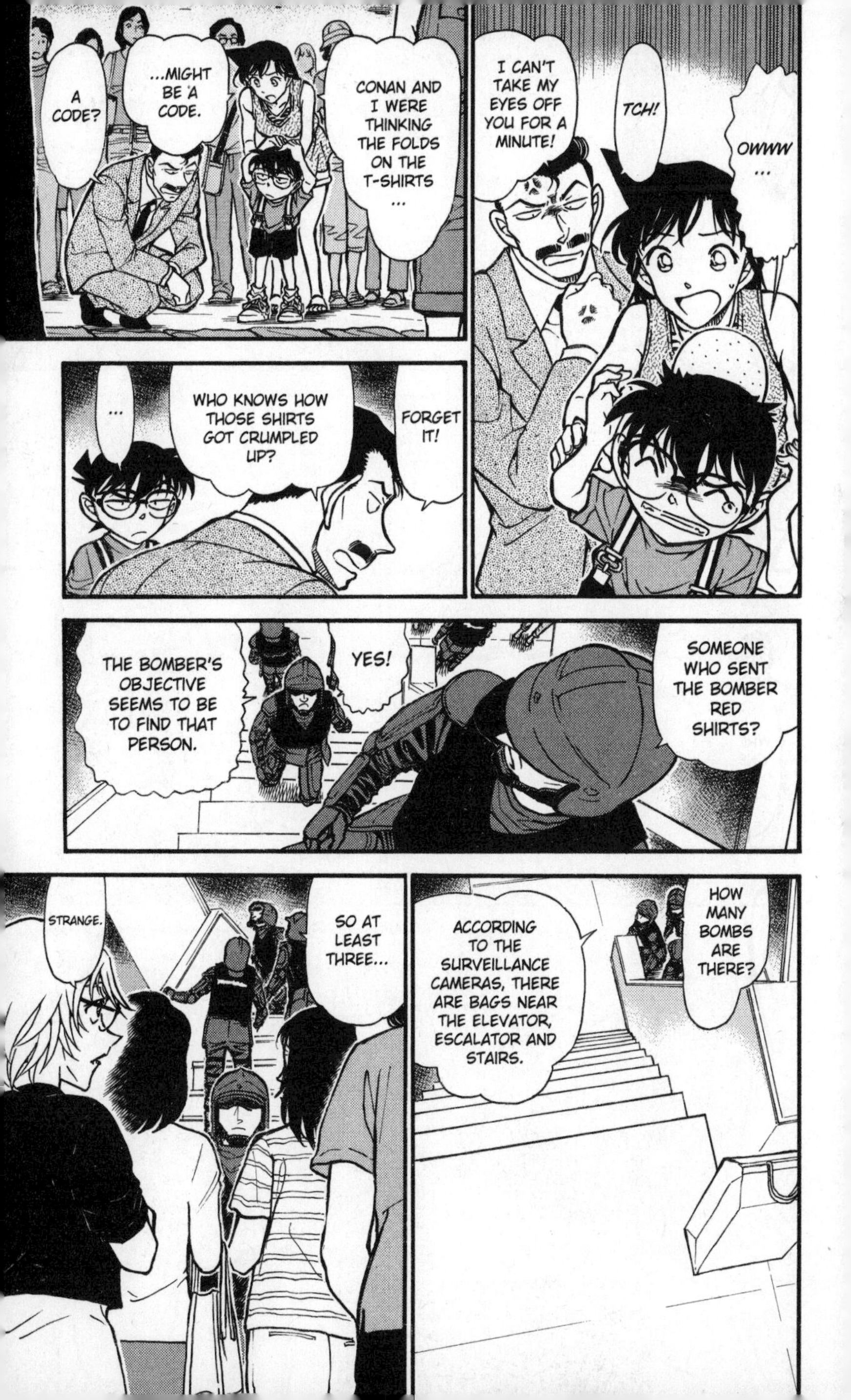
CONAN AND I WERE THINKING THE FOLDS ON THE T-SHIRTS ...
...MIGHT BE A CODE.
A CODE?
OWWW ...
TCH!
I CAN'T TAKE MY EYES OFF YOU FOR A MINUTE!
FORGET IT!
WHO KNOWS HOW THOSE SHIRTS GOT CRUMPLED UP?
...
SOMEONE WHO SENT THE BOMBER RED SHIRTS?
YES!
THE BOMBER'S OBJECTIVE SEEMS TO BE TO FIND THAT PERSON.
HOW MANY BOMBS ARE THERE?
ACCORDING TO THE SURVEILLANCE CAMERAS, THERE ARE BAGS NEAR THE ELEVATOR, ESCALATOR AND STAIRS.
SO AT LEAST THREE...
STRANGE.

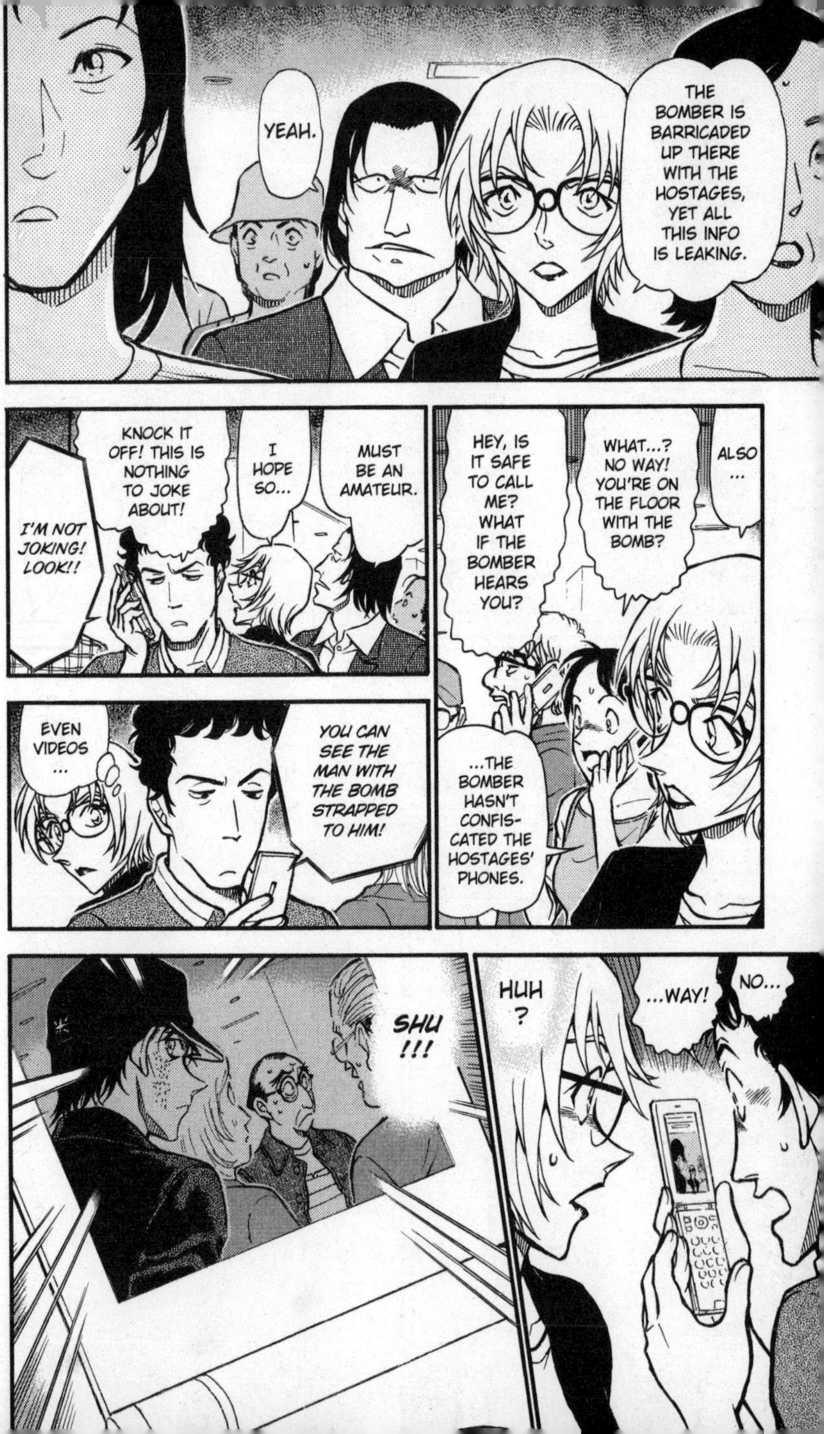
THE BOMBER IS BARRICADED UP THERE WITH THE HOSTAGES, YET ALL THIS INFO IS LEAKING.
YEAH.
ALSO ...
WHAT...? NO WAY! YOU'RE ON THE FLOOR WITH THE BOMB?
HEY, IS IT SAFE TO CALL ME? WHAT IF THE BOMBER HEARS YOU?
...THE BOMBER HASN'T CONFISCATED THE HOSTAGES' PHONES.
MUST BE AN AMATEUR.
I HOPE SO...
KNOCK IT OFF! THIS IS NOTHING TO JOKE ABOUT!
I'M NOT JOKING! LOOK!!
YOU CAN SEE THE MAN WITH THE BOMB STRAPPED TO HIM!
EVEN VIDEOS ...
NO...
...WAY!
HUH ?
SHU !!!

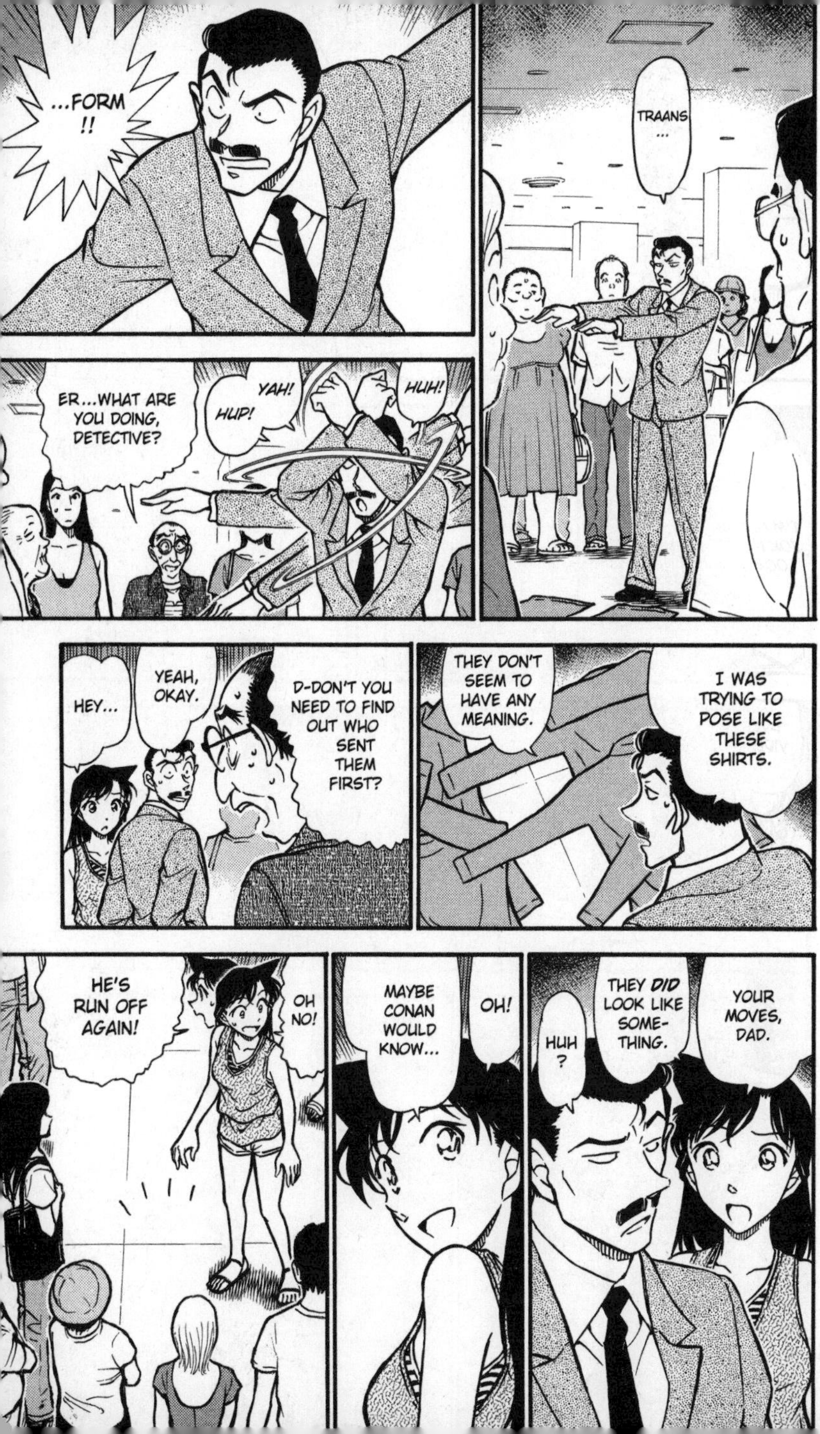
TRAANS...
...FORM!!
HUH!
YAH!
HUP!
ER...WHAT ARE YOU DOING, DETECTIVE?
I WAS TRYING TO POSE LIKE THESE SHIRTS.
THEY DON'T SEEM TO HAVE ANY MEANING.
D-DON'T YOU NEED TO FIND OUT WHO SENT THEM FIRST?
YEAH, OKAY.
HEY...
YOUR MOVES, DAD.
THEY *DID* LOOK LIKE SOME-THING.
HUH?
OH!
MAYBE CONAN WOULD KNOW...
OH NO!
HE'S RUN OFF AGAIN!

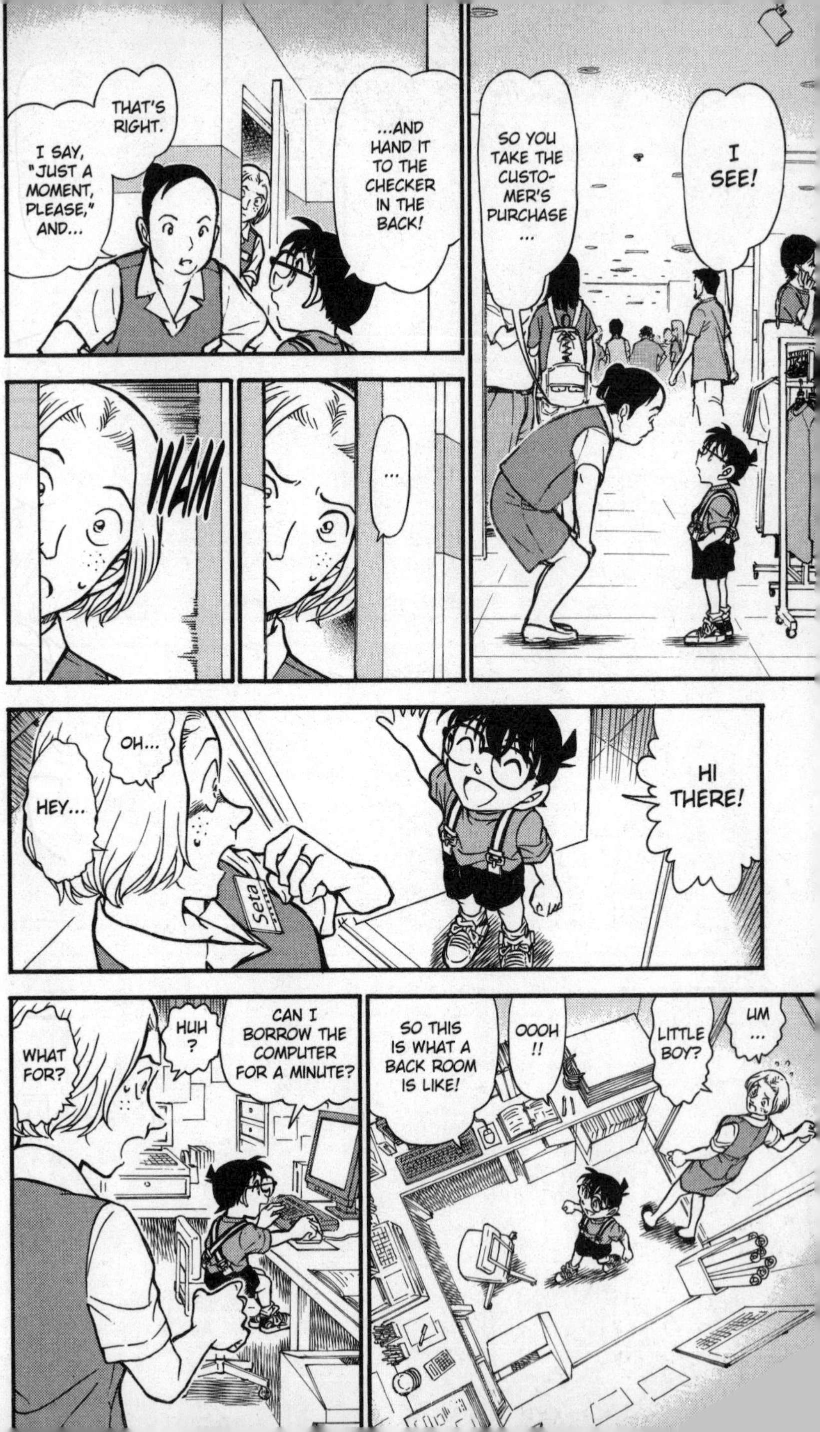
I SEE!
SO YOU TAKE THE CUSTOMER'S PURCHASE ...
...AND HAND IT TO THE CHECKER IN THE BACK!
THAT'S RIGHT.
I SAY, "JUST A MOMENT, PLEASE," AND...
...
WAM
HI THERE!
OH...
HEY...
Seta
UM ...
LITTLE BOY?
OOOH !!
SO THIS IS WHAT A BACK ROOM IS LIKE!
CAN I BORROW THE COMPUTER FOR A MINUTE?
HUH ?
WHAT FOR?

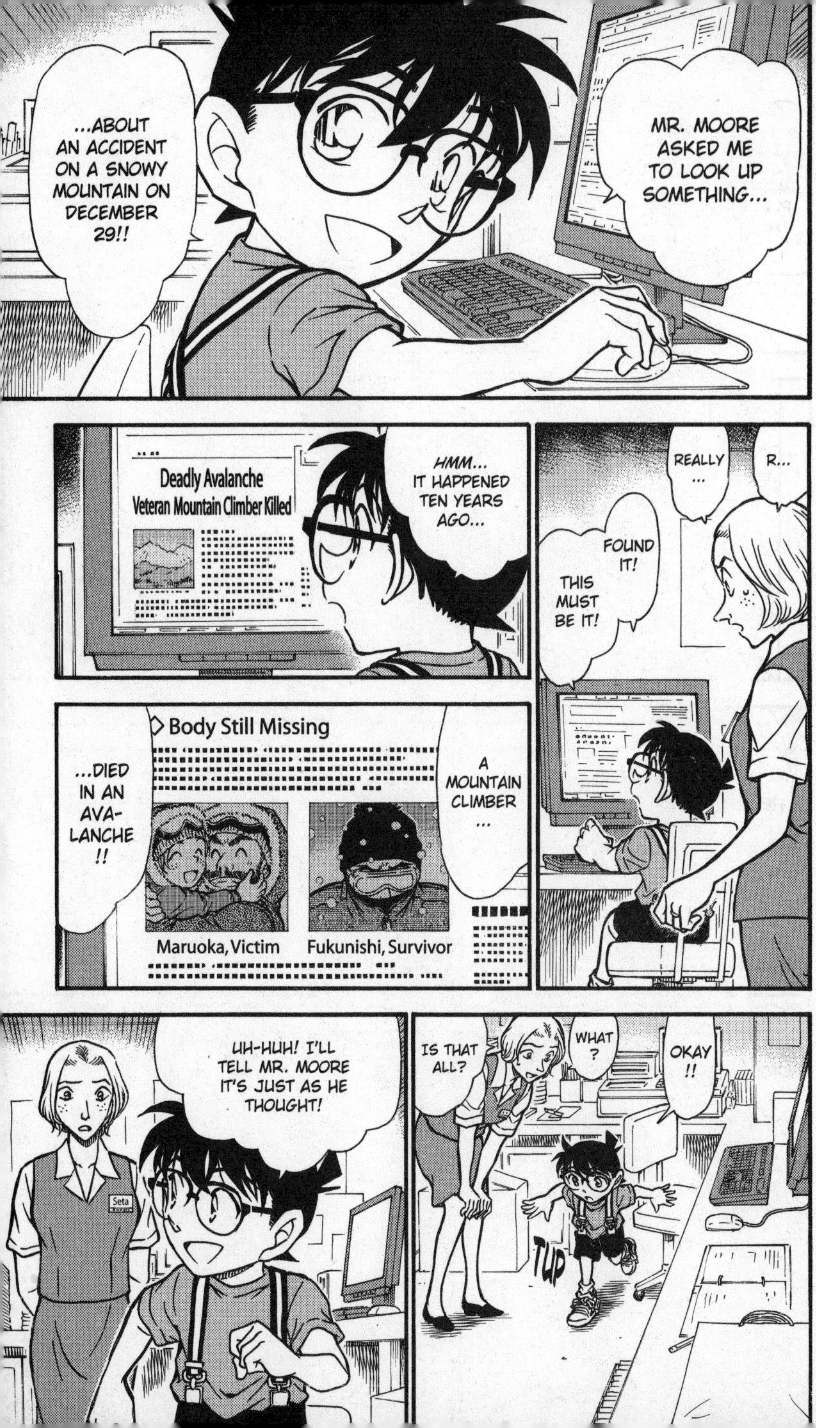
MR. MOORE ASKED ME TO LOOK UP SOMETHING...
...ABOUT AN ACCIDENT ON A SNOWY MOUNTAIN ON DECEMBER 29!!
R...
REALLY ...
FOUND IT!
THIS MUST BE IT!
HMM... IT HAPPENED TEN YEARS AGO...
Deadly Avalanche
Veteran Mountain Climber Killed
A MOUNTAIN CLIMBER ...
Body Still Missing
Maruoka, Victim
Fukunishi, Survivor
...DIED IN AN AVA-LANCHE !!
OKAY !!
WHAT ?
IS THAT ALL?
TUP
UH-HUH! I'LL TELL MR. MOORE IT'S JUST AS HE THOUGHT!
Seta

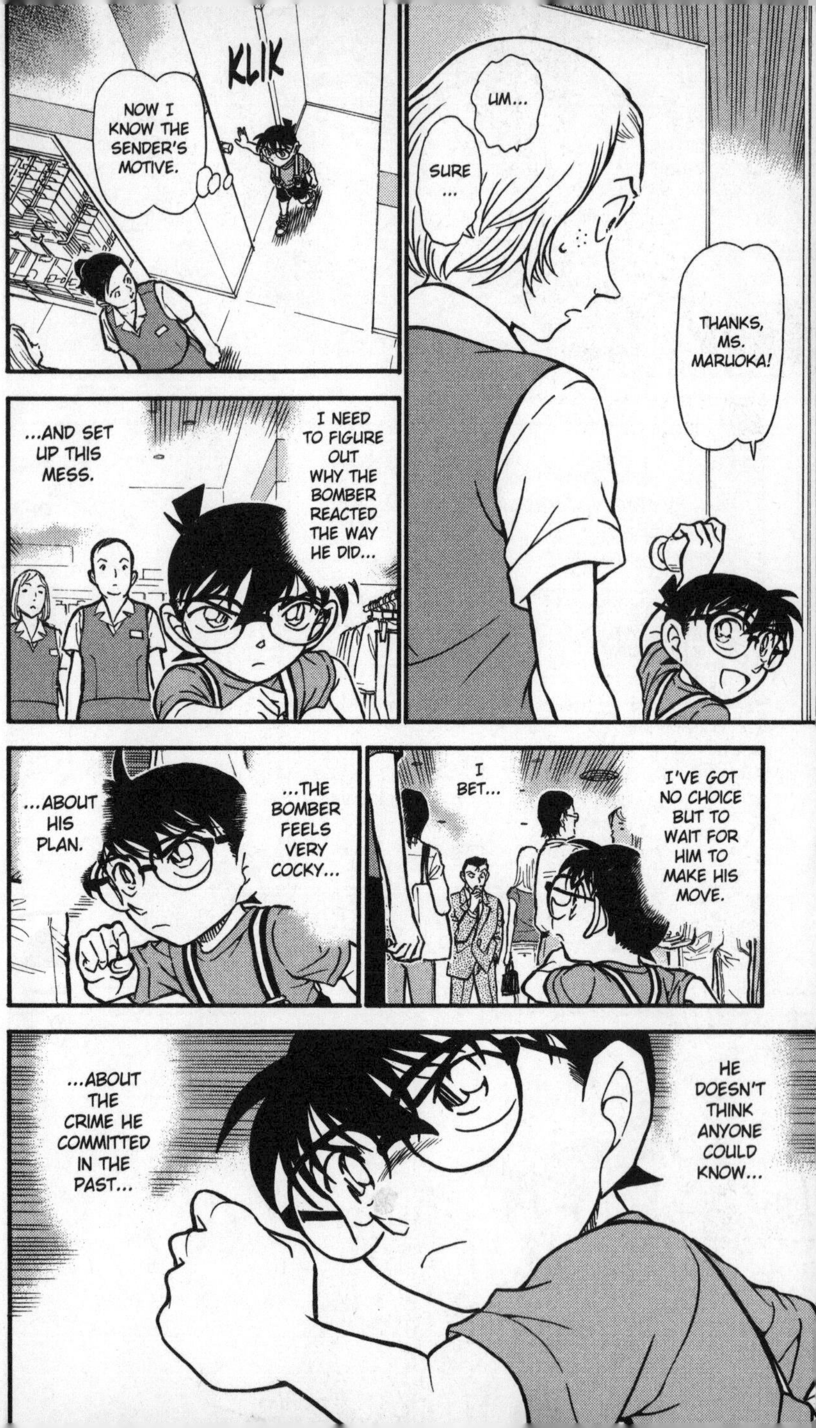
UM...
SURE...
THANKS, MS. MARUOKA!
KLIK
NOW I KNOW THE SENDER'S MOTIVE.
I NEED TO FIGURE OUT WHY THE BOMBER REACTED THE WAY HE DID...
...AND SET UP THIS MESS.
I'VE GOT NO CHOICE BUT TO WAIT FOR HIM TO MAKE HIS MOVE.
I BET...
...THE BOMBER FEELS VERY COCKY...
...ABOUT HIS PLAN.
HE DOESN'T THINK ANYONE COULD KNOW...
...ABOUT THE CRIME HE COMMITTED IN THE PAST...

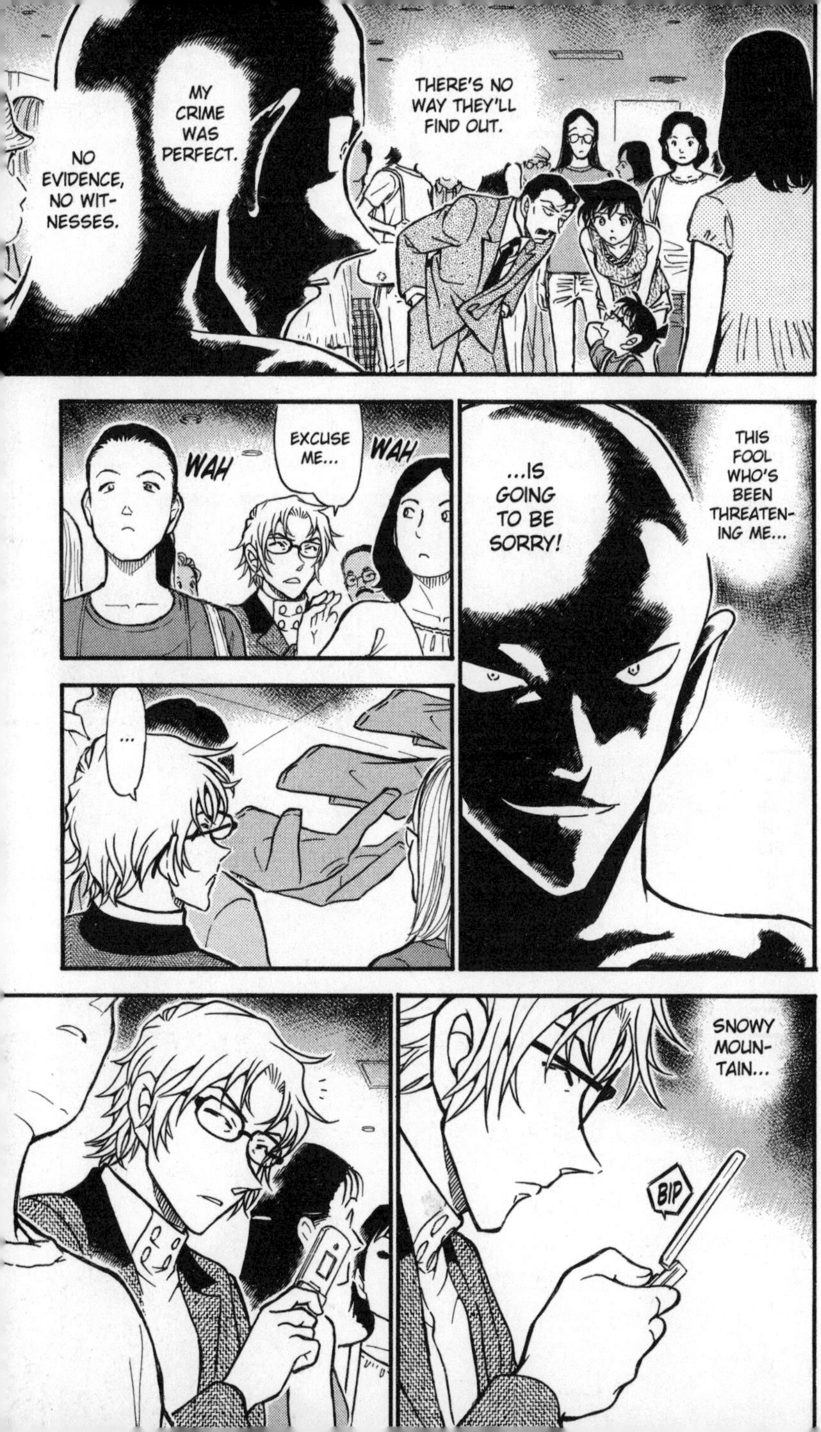
THERE'S NO WAY THEY'LL FIND OUT.
MY CRIME WAS PERFECT.
NO EVIDENCE, NO WIT-NESSES.
THIS FOOL WHO'S BEEN THREATEN-ING ME...
...IS GOING TO BE SORRY!
WAH
EXCUSE ME...
WAH
...
SNOWY MOUN-TAIN...
BIP

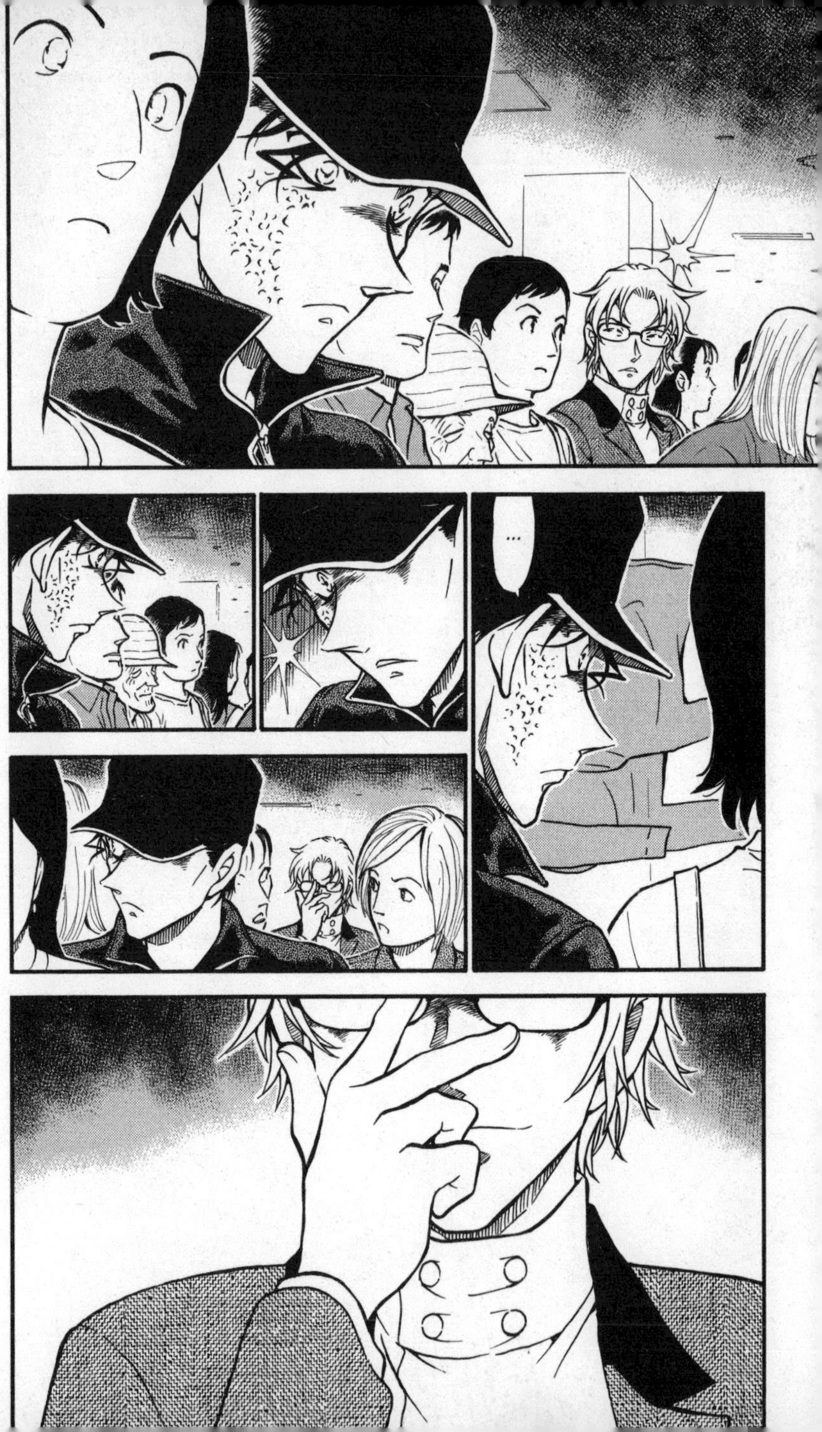
...

FILE 7: THE TRUTH IN THE BLIZZARD

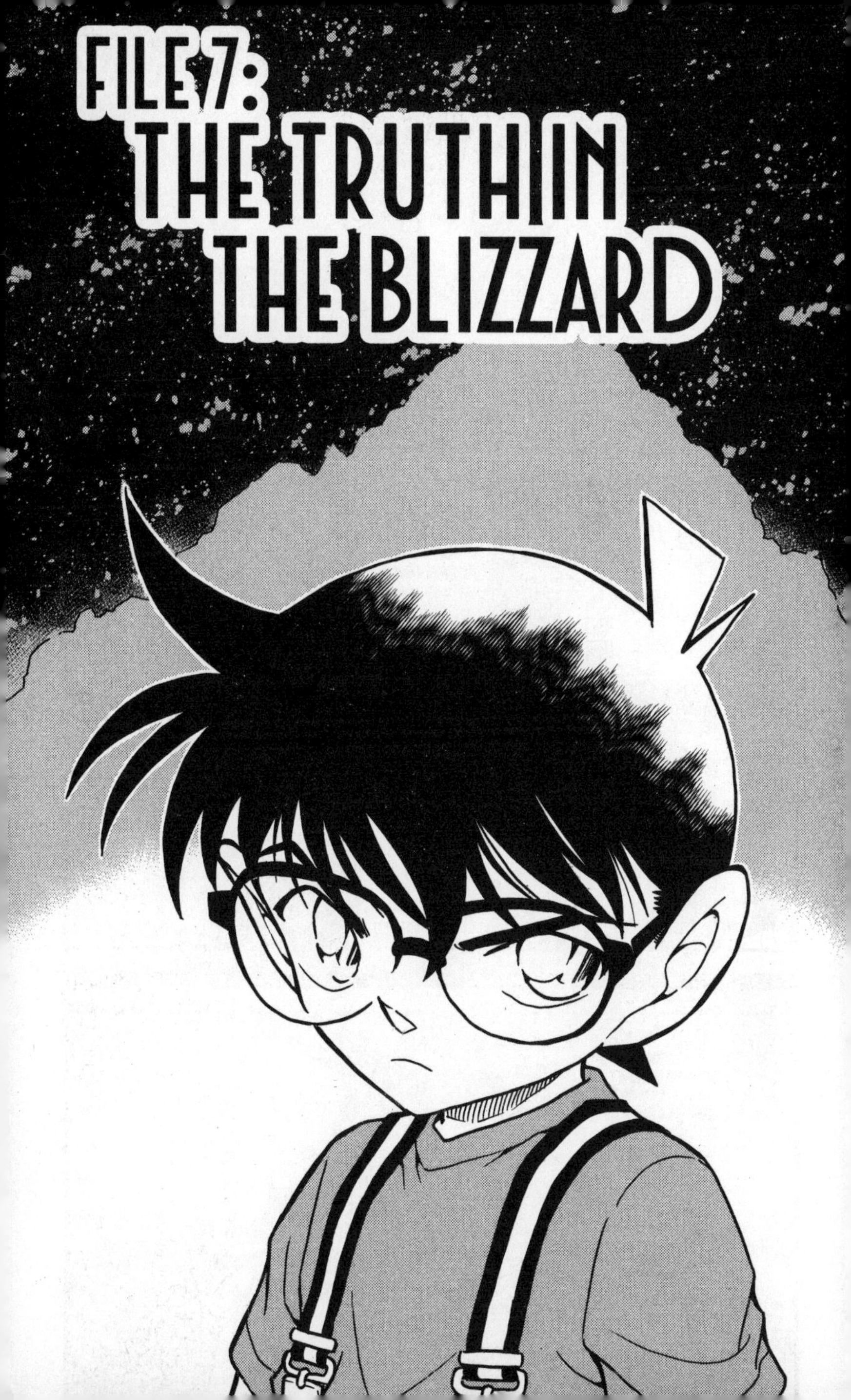

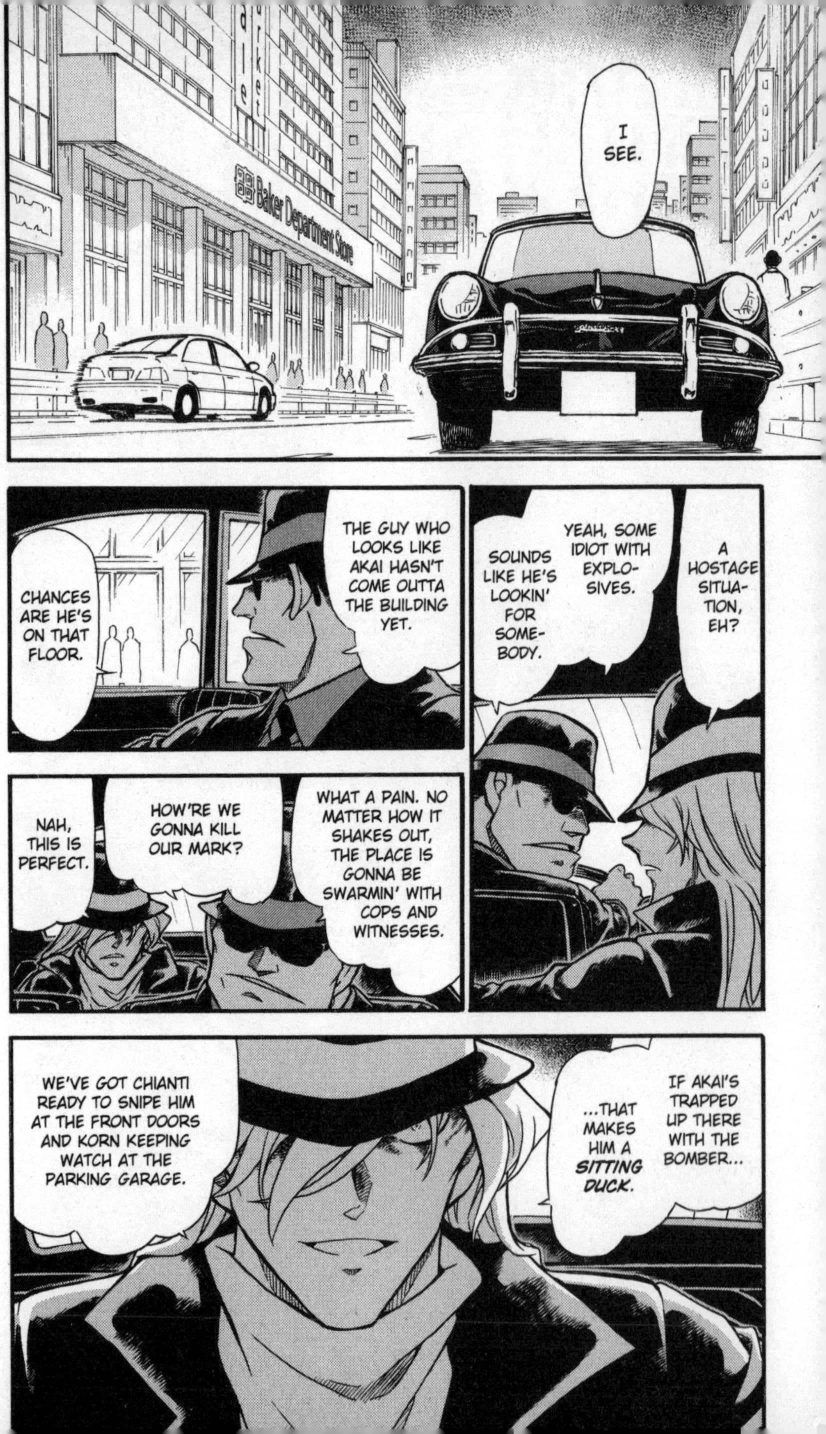
Baker Department Store
I SEE.
A HOSTAGE SITUATION, EH?
YEAH, SOME IDIOT WITH EXPLOSIVES.
SOUNDS LIKE HE'S LOOKIN' FOR SOMEBODY.
THE GUY WHO LOOKS LIKE AKAI HASN'T COME OUTTA THE BUILDING YET.
CHANCES ARE HE'S ON THAT FLOOR.
WHAT A PAIN. NO MATTER HOW IT SHAKES OUT, THE PLACE IS GONNA BE SWARMIN' WITH COPS AND WITNESSES.
HOW'RE WE GONNA KILL OUR MARK?
NAH, THIS IS PERFECT.
IF AKAI'S TRAPPED UP THERE WITH THE BOMBER...
...THAT MAKES HIM A *SITTING DUCK.*
WE'VE GOT CHIANTI READY TO SNIPE HIM AT THE FRONT DOORS AND KORN KEEPING WATCH AT THE PARKING GARAGE.

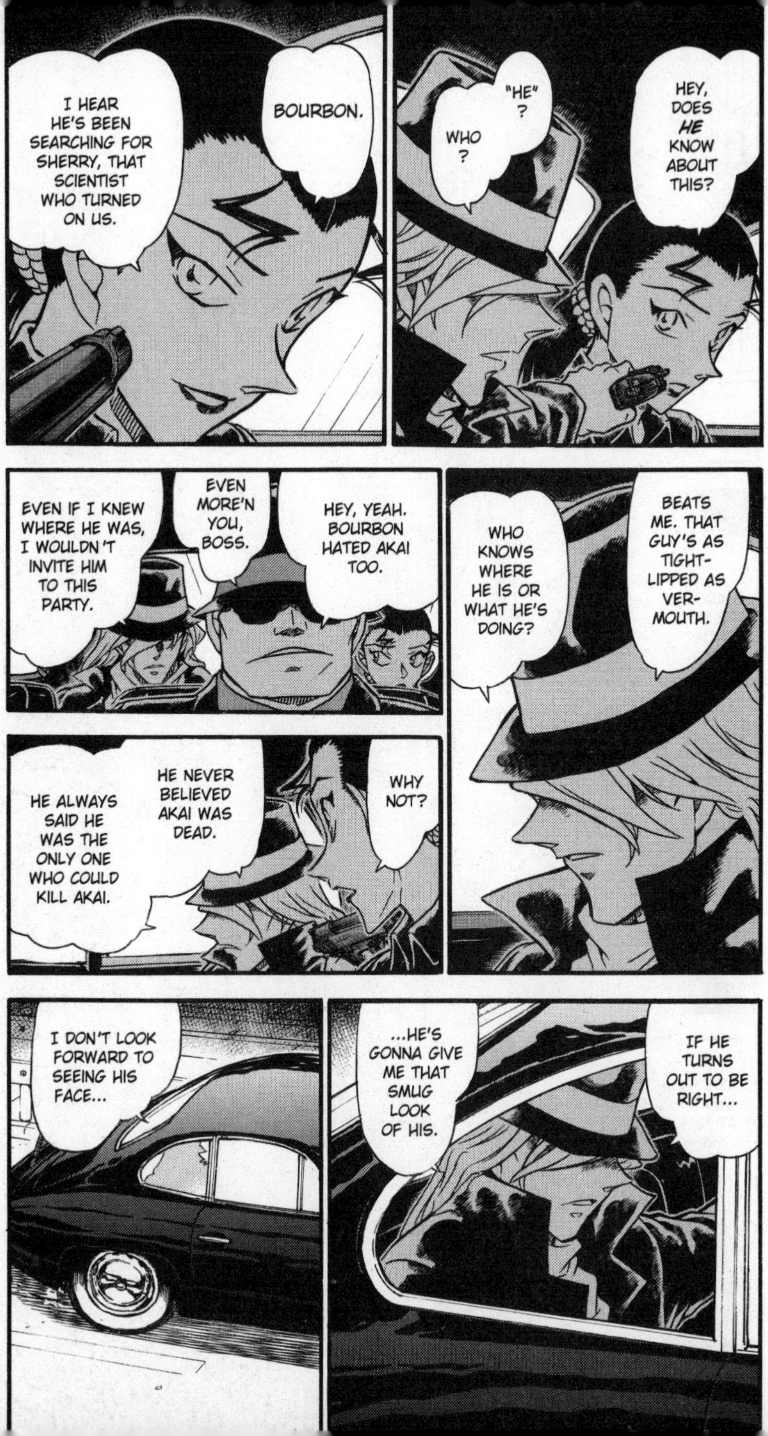
HEY, DOES *HE* KNOW ABOUT THIS?
"HE"?
WHO?
BOURBON.
I HEAR HE'S BEEN SEARCHING FOR SHERRY, THAT SCIENTIST WHO TURNED ON US.
BEATS ME. THAT GUY'S AS TIGHT-LIPPED AS VERMOUTH.
WHO KNOWS WHERE HE IS OR WHAT HE'S DOING?
HEY, YEAH. BOURBON HATED AKAI TOO.
EVEN MORE'N YOU, BOSS.
EVEN IF I KNEW WHERE HE WAS, I WOULDN'T INVITE HIM TO THIS PARTY.
WHY NOT?
HE NEVER BELIEVED AKAI WAS DEAD.
HE ALWAYS SAID HE WAS THE ONLY ONE WHO COULD KILL AKAI.
IF HE TURNS OUT TO BE RIGHT...
...HE'S GONNA GIVE ME THAT SMUG LOOK OF HIS.
I DON'T LOOK FORWARD TO SEEING HIS FACE...

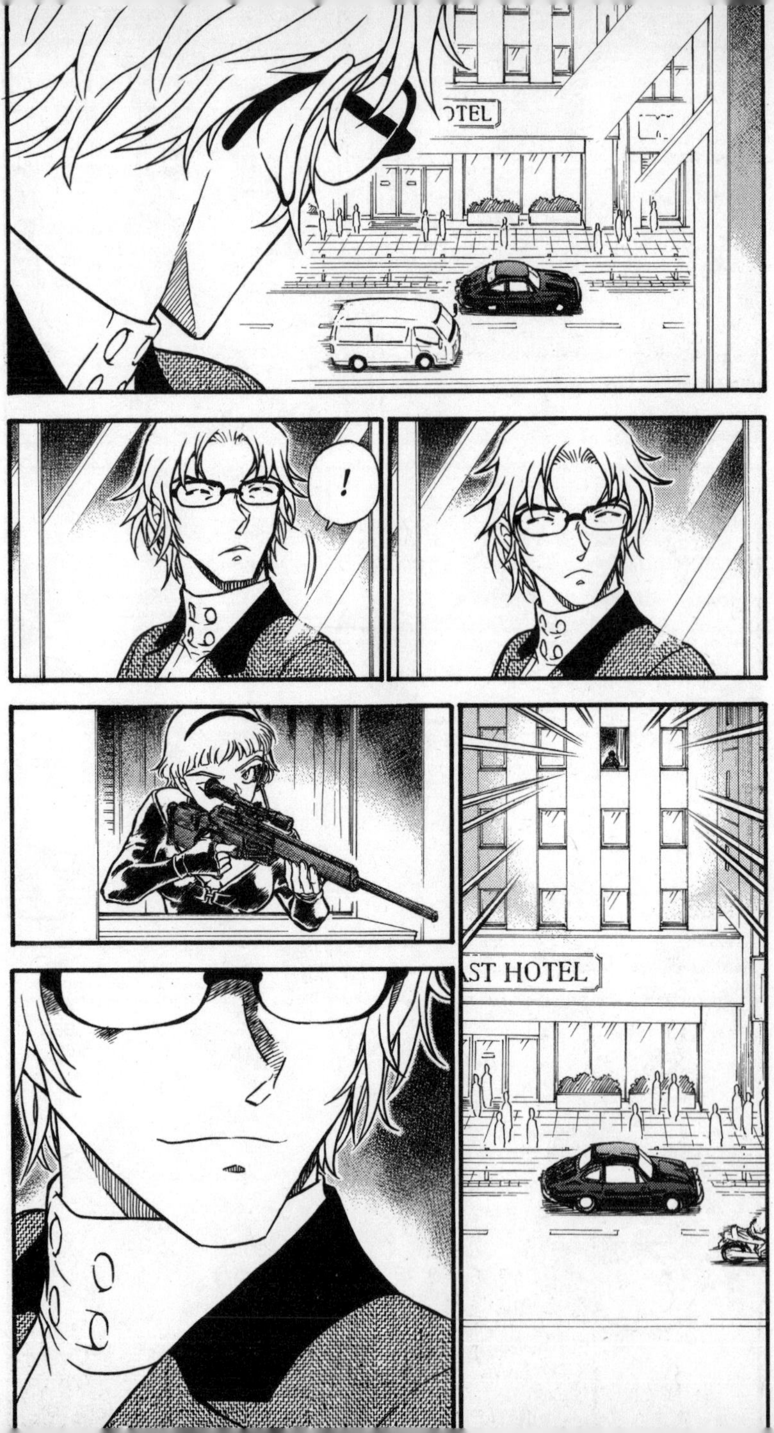
OTEL
!
AST HOTEL

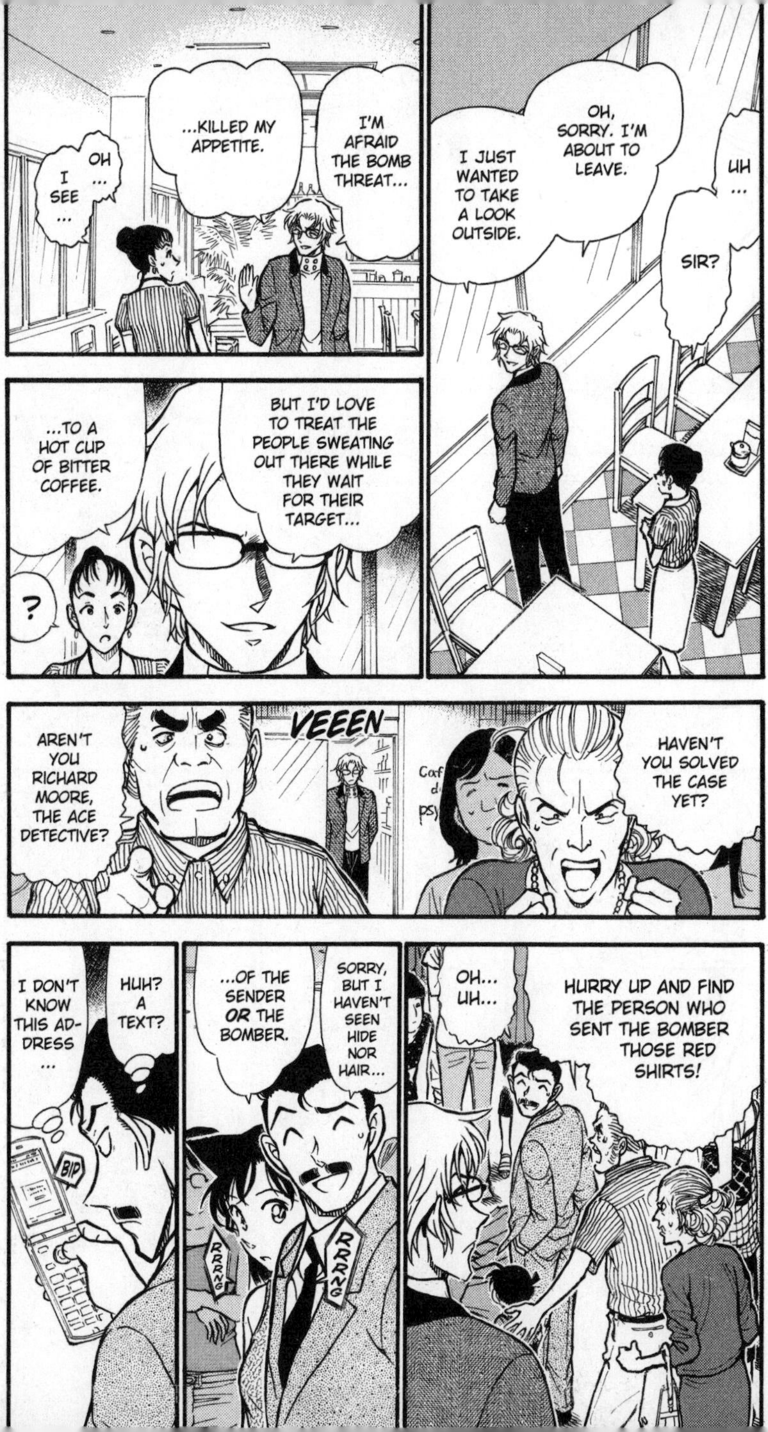
UH ... SIR?
OH, SORRY. I'M ABOUT TO LEAVE.
I JUST WANTED TO TAKE A LOOK OUTSIDE.
I'M AFRAID THE BOMB THREAT...
...KILLED MY APPETITE.
OH ... I SEE ...
BUT I'D LOVE TO TREAT THE PEOPLE SWEATING OUT THERE WHILE THEY WAIT FOR THEIR TARGET...
...TO A HOT CUP OF BITTER COFFEE.
?
HAVEN'T YOU SOLVED THE CASE YET?
VEEEN
AREN'T YOU RICHARD MOORE, THE ACE DETECTIVE?
HURRY UP AND FIND THE PERSON WHO SENT THE BOMBER THOSE RED SHIRTS!
OH... UH...
SORRY, BUT I HAVEN'T SEEN HIDE NOR HAIR...
...OF THE SENDER OR THE BOMBER.
RRRNG
RRRNG
HUH? A TEXT?
I DON'T KNOW THIS ADDRESS ...
BIP

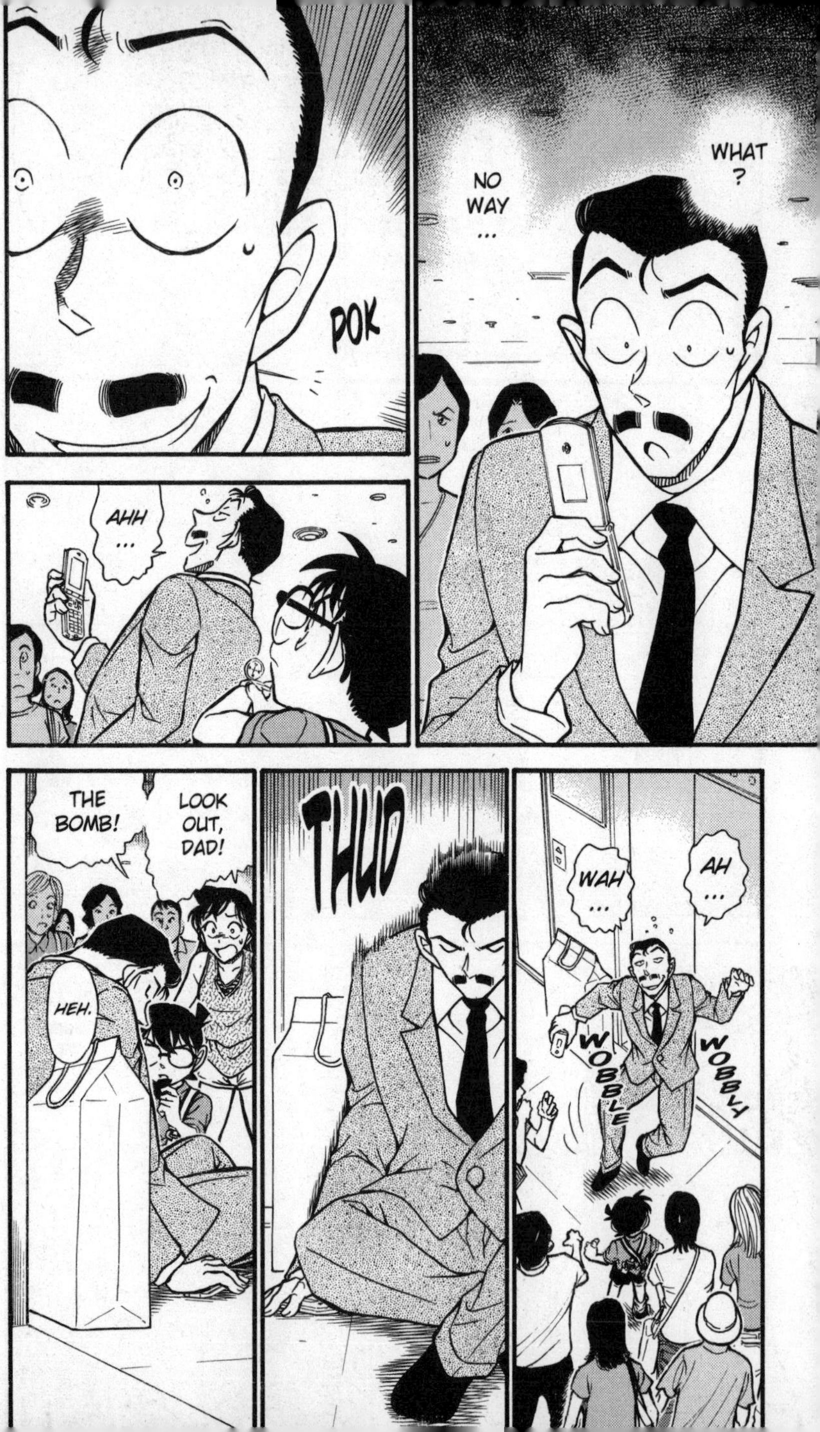
WHAT ?
NO WAY ...
POK
AHH ...
AH ...
WAH ...
WOBBLY
WOBBLE
THUD
LOOK OUT, DAD!
THE BOMB!
HEH.

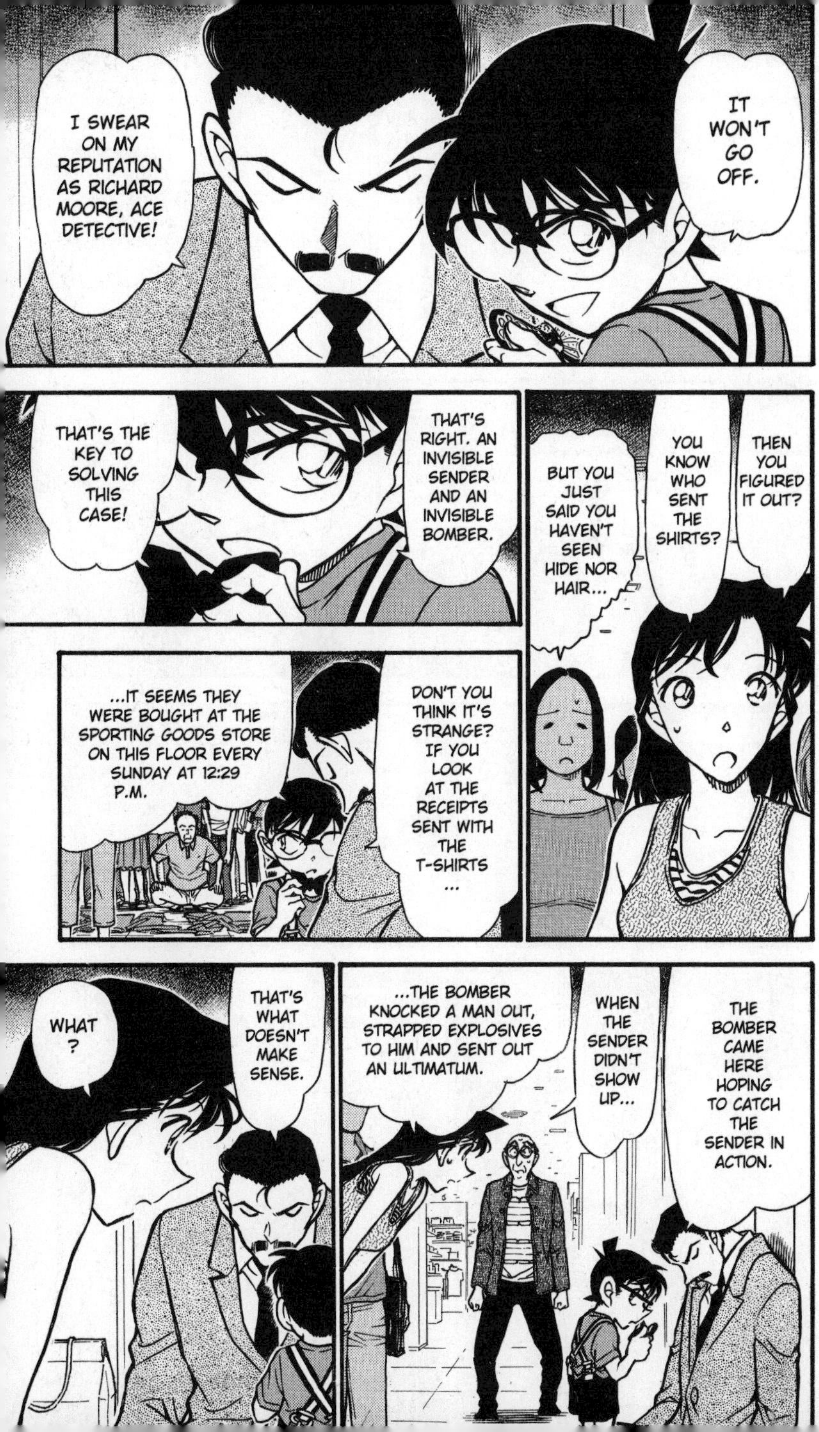
IT WON'T GO OFF.
I SWEAR ON MY REPUTATION AS RICHARD MOORE, ACE DETECTIVE!
THEN YOU FIGURED IT OUT?
YOU KNOW WHO SENT THE SHIRTS?
BUT YOU JUST SAID YOU HAVEN'T SEEN HIDE NOR HAIR...
THAT'S RIGHT. AN INVISIBLE SENDER AND AN INVISIBLE BOMBER.
THAT'S THE KEY TO SOLVING THIS CASE!
DON'T YOU THINK IT'S STRANGE? IF YOU LOOK AT THE RECEIPTS SENT WITH THE T-SHIRTS ...
...IT SEEMS THEY WERE BOUGHT AT THE SPORTING GOODS STORE ON THIS FLOOR EVERY SUNDAY AT 12:29 P.M.
THE BOMBER CAME HERE HOPING TO CATCH THE SENDER IN ACTION.
WHEN THE SENDER DIDN'T SHOW UP...
...THE BOMBER KNOCKED A MAN OUT, STRAPPED EXPLOSIVES TO HIM AND SENT OUT AN ULTIMATUM.
THAT'S WHAT DOESN'T MAKE SENSE.
WHAT?

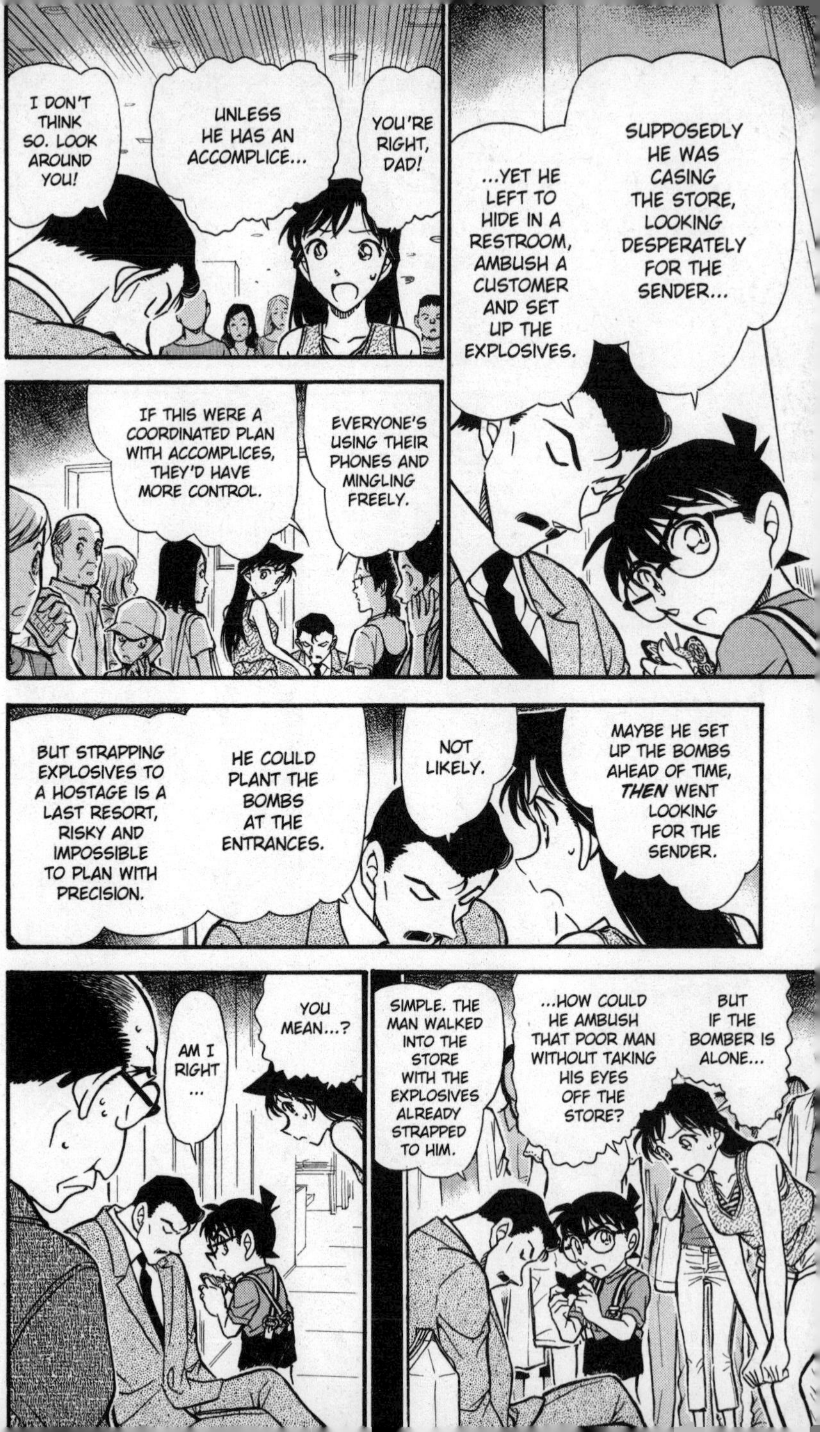
SUPPOSEDLY HE WAS CASING THE STORE, LOOKING DESPERATELY FOR THE SENDER...
...YET HE LEFT TO HIDE IN A RESTROOM, AMBUSH A CUSTOMER AND SET UP THE EXPLOSIVES.
YOU'RE RIGHT, DAD!
UNLESS HE HAS AN ACCOMPLICE...
I DON'T THINK SO. LOOK AROUND YOU!
EVERYONE'S USING THEIR PHONES AND MINGLING FREELY.
IF THIS WERE A COORDINATED PLAN WITH ACCOMPLICES, THEY'D HAVE MORE CONTROL.
MAYBE HE SET UP THE BOMBS AHEAD OF TIME, *THEN* WENT LOOKING FOR THE SENDER.
NOT LIKELY.
HE COULD PLANT THE BOMBS AT THE ENTRANCES.
BUT STRAPPING EXPLOSIVES TO A HOSTAGE IS A LAST RESORT, RISKY AND IMPOSSIBLE TO PLAN WITH PRECISION.
BUT IF THE BOMBER IS ALONE...
...HOW COULD HE AMBUSH THAT POOR MAN WITHOUT TAKING HIS EYES OFF THE STORE?
SIMPLE. THE MAN WALKED INTO THE STORE WITH THE EXPLOSIVES ALREADY STRAPPED TO HIM.
YOU MEAN...?
AM I RIGHT ...

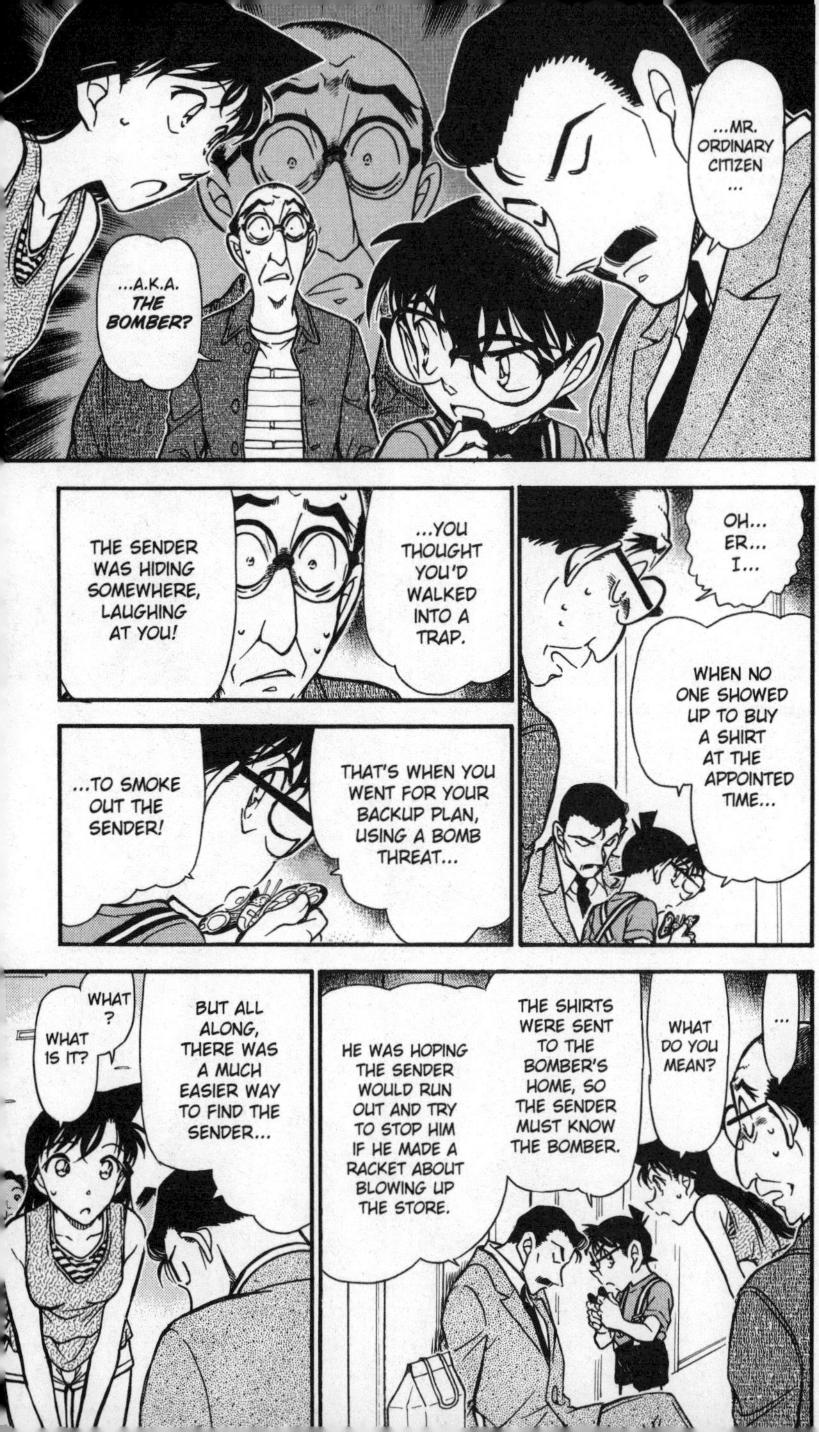
...MR. ORDINARY CITIZEN ...
...A.K.A. THE BOMBER?
OH... ER... I...
WHEN NO ONE SHOWED UP TO BUY A SHIRT AT THE APPOINTED TIME...
...YOU THOUGHT YOU'D WALKED INTO A TRAP.
THE SENDER WAS HIDING SOMEWHERE, LAUGHING AT YOU!
THAT'S WHEN YOU WENT FOR YOUR BACKUP PLAN, USING A BOMB THREAT...
...TO SMOKE OUT THE SENDER!
...
WHAT DO YOU MEAN?
THE SHIRTS WERE SENT TO THE BOMBER'S HOME, SO THE SENDER MUST KNOW THE BOMBER.
HE WAS HOPING THE SENDER WOULD RUN OUT AND TRY TO STOP HIM IF HE MADE A RACKET ABOUT BLOWING UP THE STORE.
BUT ALL ALONG, THERE WAS A MUCH EASIER WAY TO FIND THE SENDER...
WHAT? WHAT IS IT?

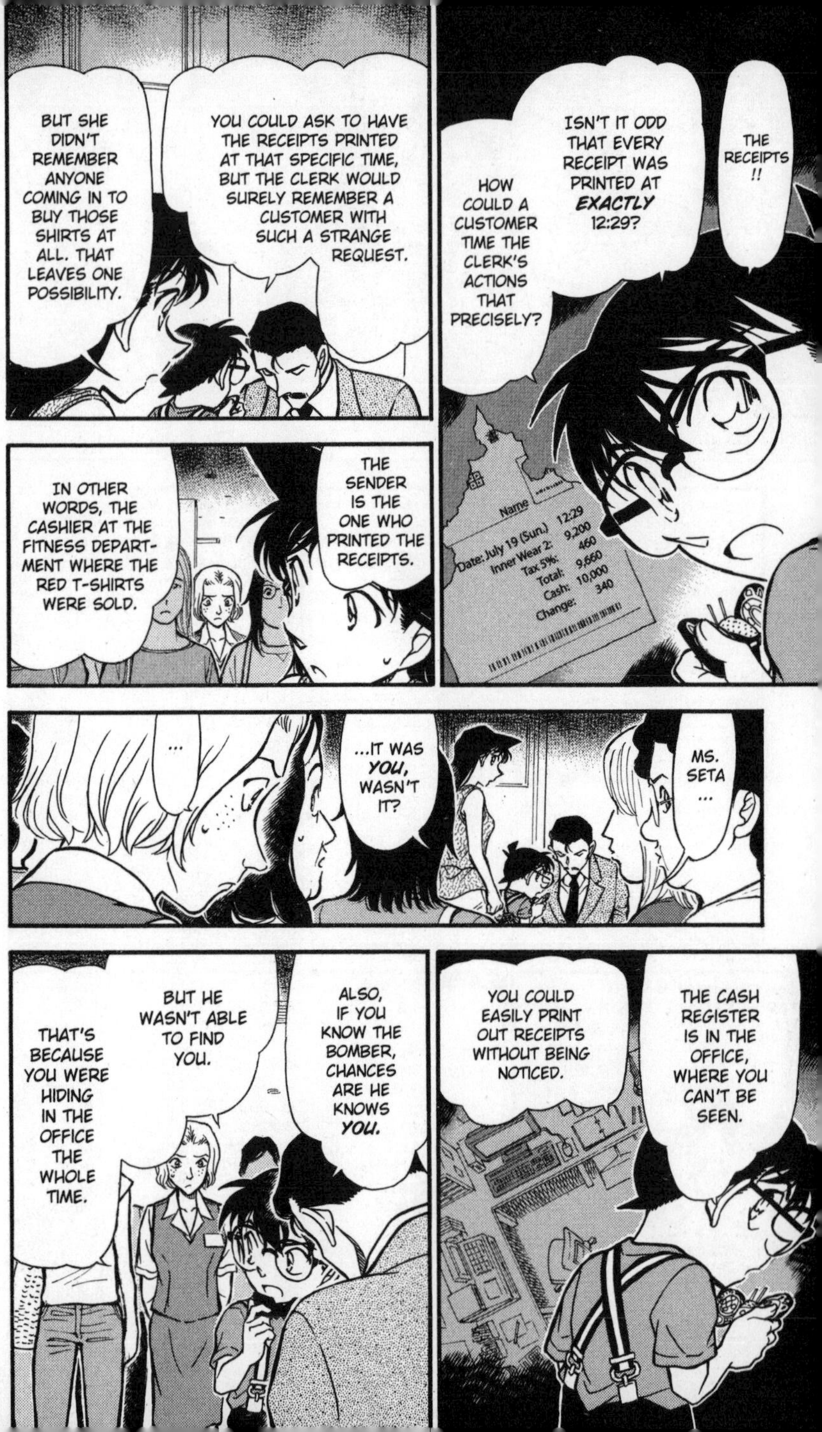
THE RECEIPTS !!
ISN'T IT ODD THAT EVERY RECEIPT WAS PRINTED AT *EXACTLY* 12:29?
HOW COULD A CUSTOMER TIME THE CLERK'S ACTIONS THAT PRECISELY?
Name
Date: July 19 (Sun.) 12:29
Inner Wear 2: 9,200
Tax 5%: 460
Total: 9,660
Cash: 10,000
Change: 340
YOU COULD ASK TO HAVE THE RECEIPTS PRINTED AT THAT SPECIFIC TIME, BUT THE CLERK WOULD SURELY REMEMBER A CUSTOMER WITH SUCH A STRANGE REQUEST.
BUT SHE DIDN'T REMEMBER ANYONE COMING IN TO BUY THOSE SHIRTS AT ALL. THAT LEAVES ONE POSSIBILITY.
THE SENDER IS THE ONE WHO PRINTED THE RECEIPTS.
IN OTHER WORDS, THE CASHIER AT THE FITNESS DEPARTMENT WHERE THE RED T-SHIRTS WERE SOLD.
MS. SETA ...
...IT WAS *YOU,* WASN'T IT?
...
THE CASH REGISTER IS IN THE OFFICE, WHERE YOU CAN'T BE SEEN.
YOU COULD EASILY PRINT OUT RECEIPTS WITHOUT BEING NOTICED.
ALSO, IF YOU KNOW THE BOMBER, CHANCES ARE HE KNOWS *YOU.*
BUT HE WASN'T ABLE TO FIND YOU.
THAT'S BECAUSE YOU WERE HIDING IN THE OFFICE THE WHOLE TIME.

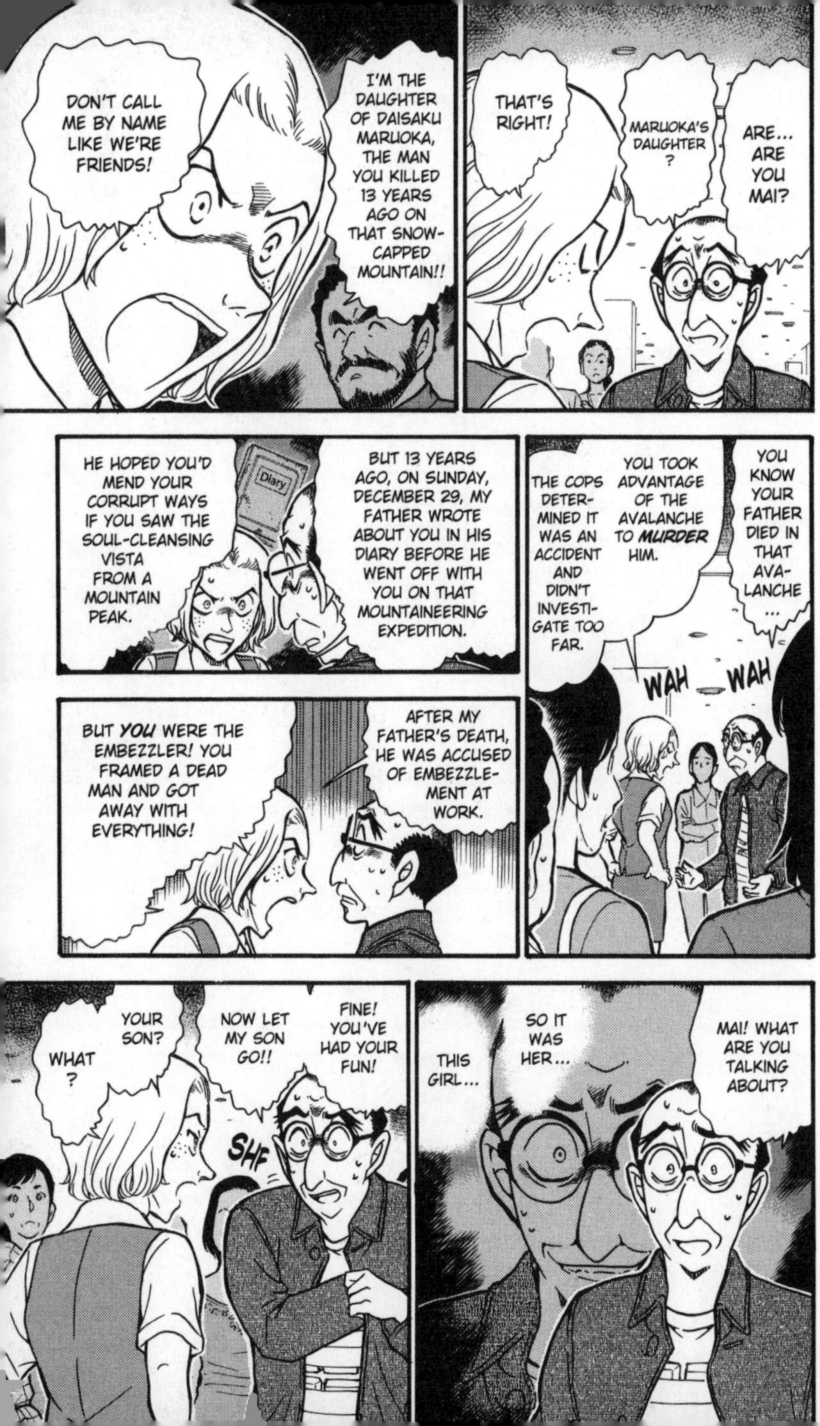
ARE... ARE YOU MAI?
MARUOKA'S DAUGHTER?
THAT'S RIGHT!
I'M THE DAUGHTER OF DAISAKU MARUOKA, THE MAN YOU KILLED 13 YEARS AGO ON THAT SNOW-CAPPED MOUNTAIN!!
DON'T CALL ME BY NAME LIKE WE'RE FRIENDS!
YOU KNOW YOUR FATHER DIED IN THAT AVALANCHE...
YOU TOOK ADVANTAGE OF THE AVALANCHE TO ***MURDER*** HIM.
THE COPS DETERMINED IT WAS AN ACCIDENT AND DIDN'T INVESTIGATE TOO FAR.
WAH WAH
BUT 13 YEARS AGO, ON SUNDAY, DECEMBER 29, MY FATHER WROTE ABOUT YOU IN HIS DIARY BEFORE HE WENT OFF WITH YOU ON THAT MOUNTAINEERING EXPEDITION.
Diary
HE HOPED YOU'D MEND YOUR CORRUPT WAYS IF YOU SAW THE SOUL-CLEANSING VISTA FROM A MOUNTAIN PEAK.
AFTER MY FATHER'S DEATH, HE WAS ACCUSED OF EMBEZZLEMENT AT WORK.
BUT ***YOU*** WERE THE EMBEZZLER! YOU FRAMED A DEAD MAN AND GOT AWAY WITH EVERYTHING!
MAI! WHAT ARE YOU TALKING ABOUT?
SO IT WAS HER...
THIS GIRL...
FINE! YOU'VE HAD YOUR FUN!
NOW LET MY SON GO!!
SHF
YOUR SON?
WHAT?

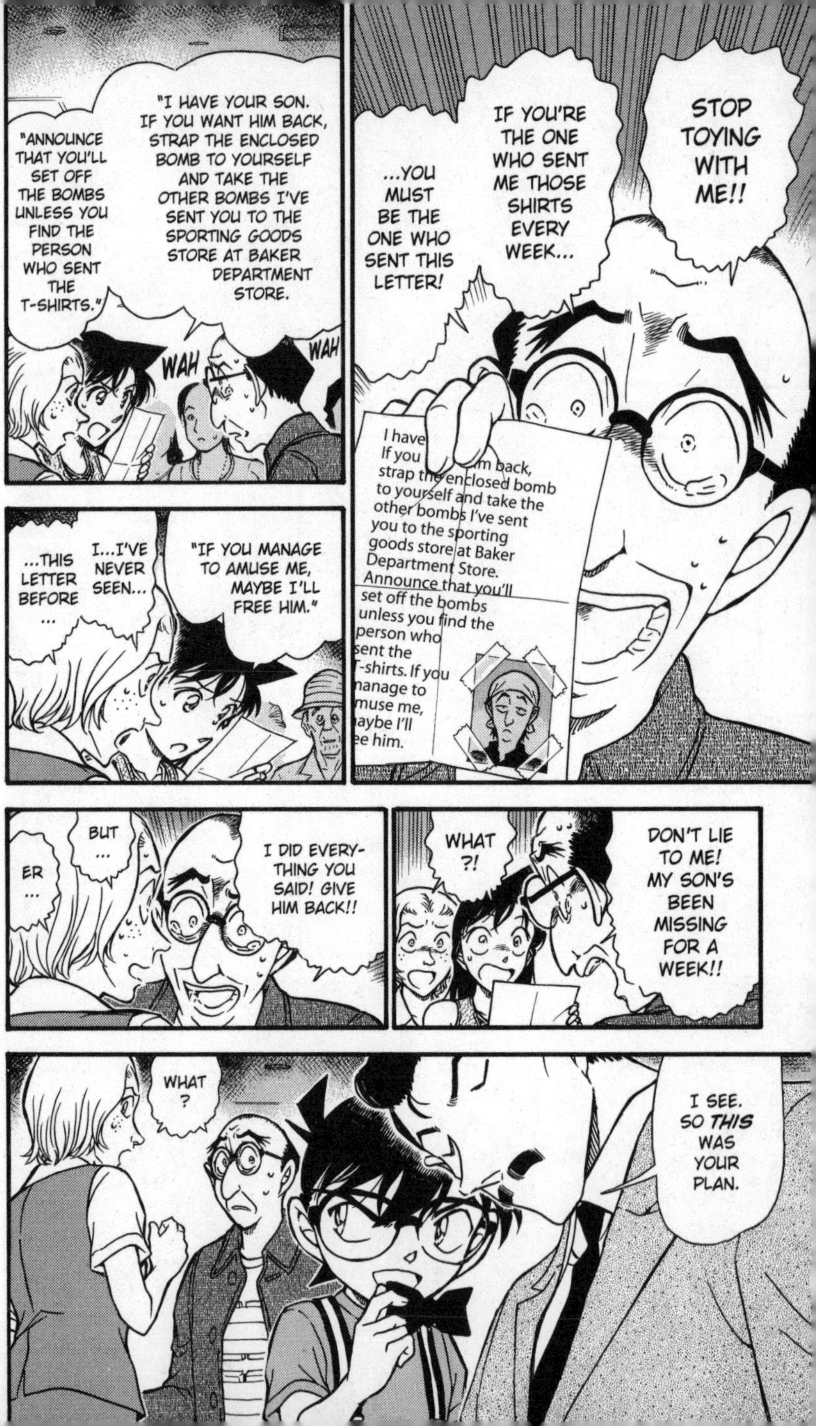
STOP TOYING WITH ME!!
IF YOU'RE THE ONE WHO SENT ME THOSE SHIRTS EVERY WEEK...
...YOU MUST BE THE ONE WHO SENT THIS LETTER!
I have
If you m back,
strap the enclosed bomb
to yourself and take the
other bombs I've sent
you to the sporting
goods store at Baker
Department Store.
Announce that you'll
set off the bombs
unless you find the
person who
sent the
T-shirts. If you
anage to
muse me,
aybe I'll
ee him.
"I HAVE YOUR SON. IF YOU WANT HIM BACK, STRAP THE ENCLOSED BOMB TO YOURSELF AND TAKE THE OTHER BOMBS I'VE SENT YOU TO THE SPORTING GOODS STORE AT BAKER DEPARTMENT STORE.
"ANNOUNCE THAT YOU'LL SET OFF THE BOMBS UNLESS YOU FIND THE PERSON WHO SENT THE T-SHIRTS."
WAH
WAH
"IF YOU MANAGE TO AMUSE ME, MAYBE I'LL FREE HIM."
I...I'VE NEVER SEEN...
...THIS LETTER BEFORE...
DON'T LIE TO ME! MY SON'S BEEN MISSING FOR A WEEK!!
WHAT ?!
I DID EVERY-THING YOU SAID! GIVE HIM BACK!!
BUT ...
ER ...
I SEE. SO *THIS* WAS YOUR PLAN.
WHAT ?

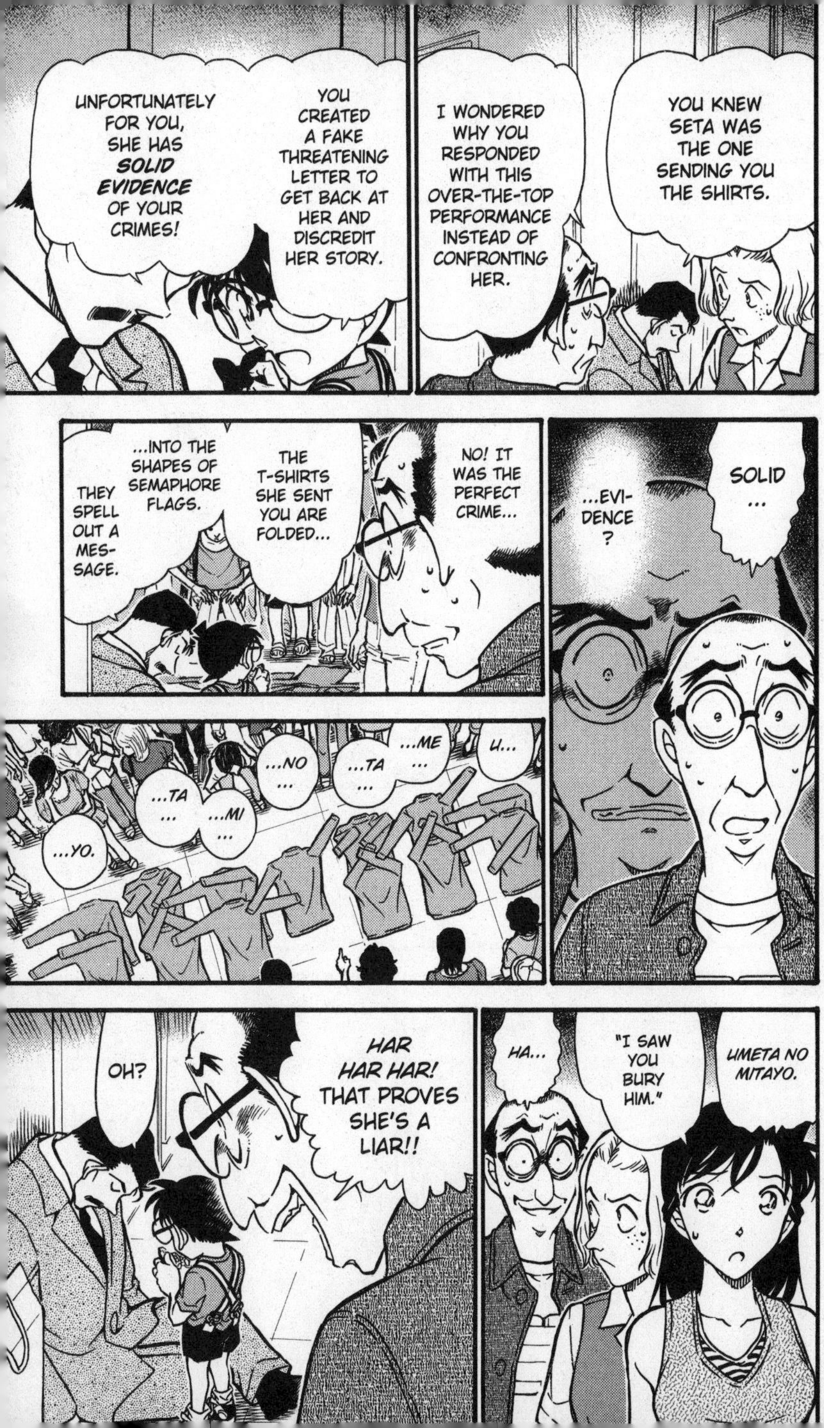
YOU KNEW SETA WAS THE ONE SENDING YOU THE SHIRTS.
I WONDERED WHY YOU RESPONDED WITH THIS OVER-THE-TOP PERFORMANCE INSTEAD OF CONFRONTING HER.
YOU CREATED A FAKE THREATENING LETTER TO GET BACK AT HER AND DISCREDIT HER STORY.
UNFORTUNATELY FOR YOU, SHE HAS **SOLID EVIDENCE** OF YOUR CRIMES!
SOLID ...
...EVI-DENCE ?
NO! IT WAS THE PERFECT CRIME...
THE T-SHIRTS SHE SENT YOU ARE FOLDED...
...INTO THE SHAPES OF SEMAPHORE FLAGS.
THEY SPELL OUT A MES-SAGE.
U...
...ME ...
...TA ...
...NO ...
...TA ...
...MI ...
...YO.
UMETA NO MITAYO.
"I SAW YOU BURY HIM."
HA...
HAR HAR HAR! THAT PROVES SHE'S A LIAR!!
OH?

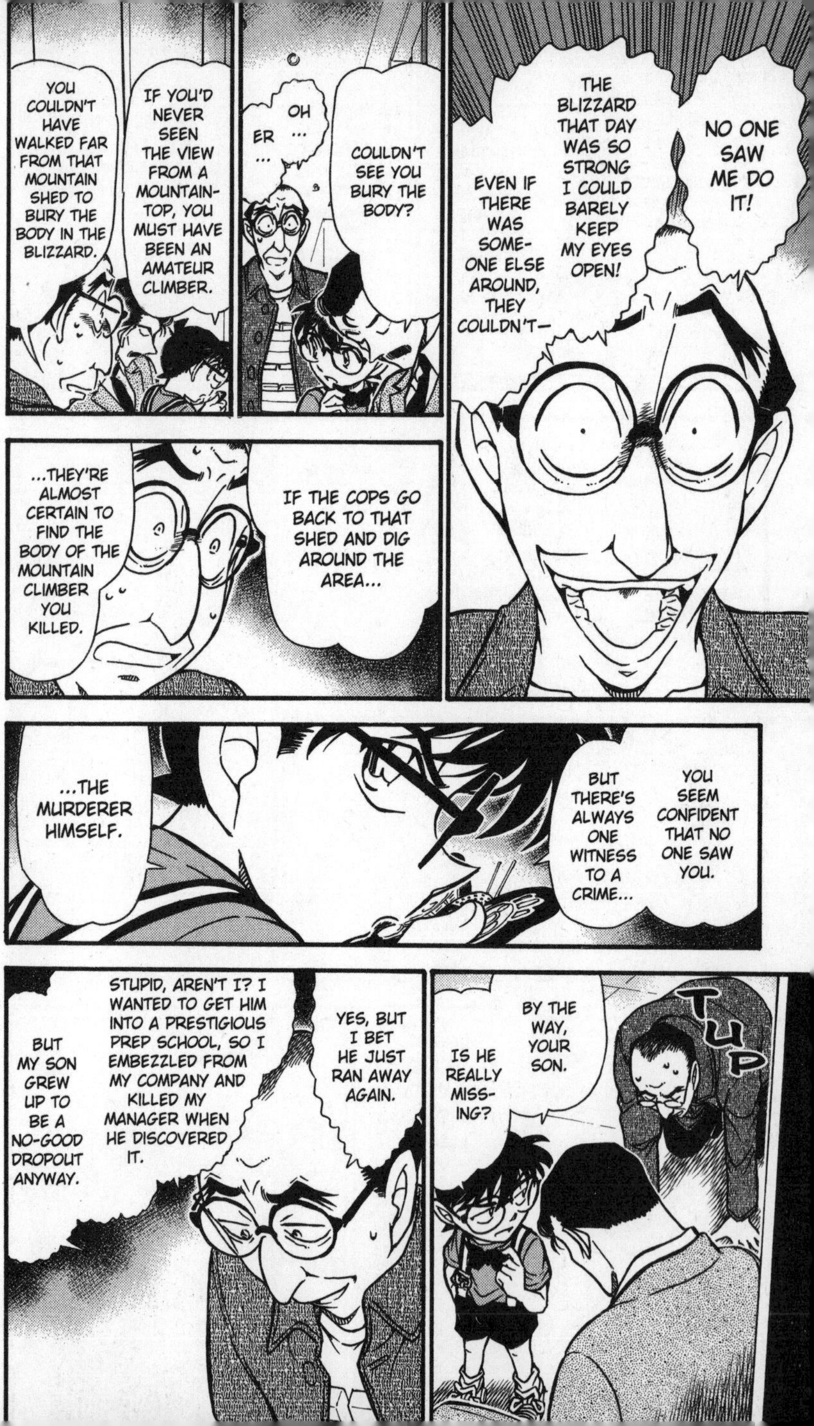
NO ONE SAW ME DO IT!
THE BLIZZARD THAT DAY WAS SO STRONG I COULD BARELY KEEP MY EYES OPEN!
EVEN IF THERE WAS SOME-ONE ELSE AROUND, THEY COULDN'T—
COULDN'T SEE YOU BURY THE BODY?
OH ...
ER ...
IF YOU'D NEVER SEEN THE VIEW FROM A MOUNTAIN-TOP, YOU MUST HAVE BEEN AN AMATEUR CLIMBER.
YOU COULDN'T HAVE WALKED FAR FROM THAT MOUNTAIN SHED TO BURY THE BODY IN THE BLIZZARD.
IF THE COPS GO BACK TO THAT SHED AND DIG AROUND THE AREA...
...THEY'RE ALMOST CERTAIN TO FIND THE BODY OF THE MOUNTAIN CLIMBER YOU KILLED.
YOU SEEM CONFIDENT THAT NO ONE SAW YOU.
BUT THERE'S ALWAYS ONE WITNESS TO A CRIME...
...THE MURDERER HIMSELF.
TUP
BY THE WAY, YOUR SON.
IS HE REALLY MISS-ING?
YES, BUT I BET HE JUST RAN AWAY AGAIN.
STUPID, AREN'T I? I WANTED TO GET HIM INTO A PRESTIGIOUS PREP SCHOOL, SO I EMBEZZLED FROM MY COMPANY AND KILLED MY MANAGER WHEN HE DISCOVERED IT.
BUT MY SON GREW UP TO BE A NO-GOOD DROPOUT ANYWAY.

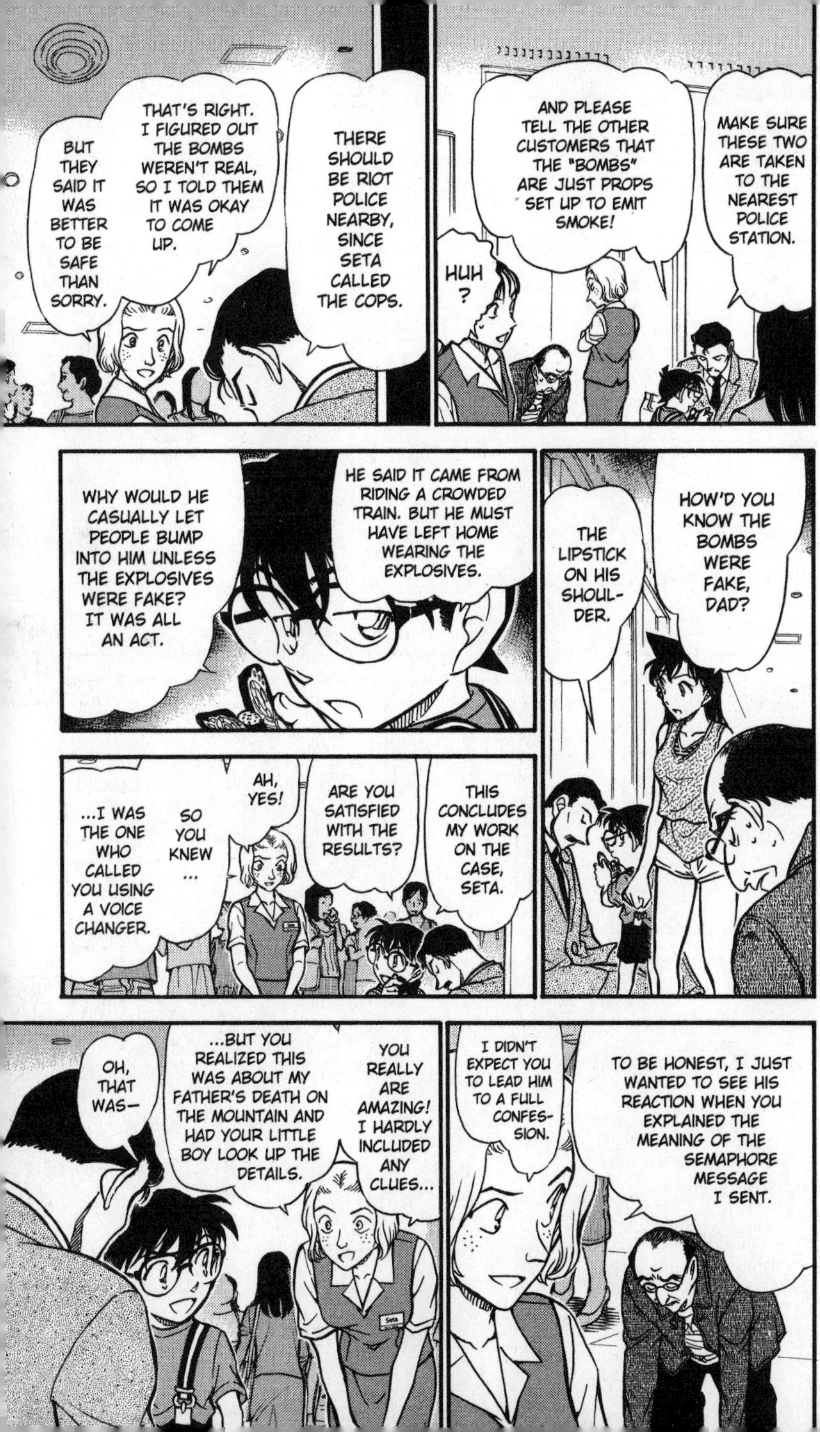
MAKE SURE THESE TWO ARE TAKEN TO THE NEAREST POLICE STATION.
AND PLEASE TELL THE OTHER CUSTOMERS THAT THE "BOMBS" ARE JUST PROPS SET UP TO EMIT SMOKE!
HUH?
THERE SHOULD BE RIOT POLICE NEARBY, SINCE SETA CALLED THE COPS.
THAT'S RIGHT. I FIGURED OUT THE BOMBS WEREN'T REAL, SO I TOLD THEM IT WAS OKAY TO COME UP.
BUT THEY SAID IT WAS BETTER TO BE SAFE THAN SORRY.
HOW'D YOU KNOW THE BOMBS WERE FAKE, DAD?
THE LIPSTICK ON HIS SHOULDER.
HE SAID IT CAME FROM RIDING A CROWDED TRAIN. BUT HE MUST HAVE LEFT HOME WEARING THE EXPLOSIVES.
WHY WOULD HE CASUALLY LET PEOPLE BUMP INTO HIM UNLESS THE EXPLOSIVES WERE FAKE? IT WAS ALL AN ACT.
THIS CONCLUDES MY WORK ON THE CASE, SETA.
ARE YOU SATISFIED WITH THE RESULTS?
AH, YES!
SO YOU KNEW ...
...I WAS THE ONE WHO CALLED YOU USING A VOICE CHANGER.
TO BE HONEST, I JUST WANTED TO SEE HIS REACTION WHEN YOU EXPLAINED THE MEANING OF THE SEMAPHORE MESSAGE I SENT.
I DIDN'T EXPECT YOU TO LEAD HIM TO A FULL CONFESSION.
YOU REALLY ARE AMAZING! I HARDLY INCLUDED ANY CLUES...
...BUT YOU REALIZED THIS WAS ABOUT MY FATHER'S DEATH ON THE MOUNTAIN AND HAD YOUR LITTLE BOY LOOK UP THE DETAILS.
OH, THAT WAS—

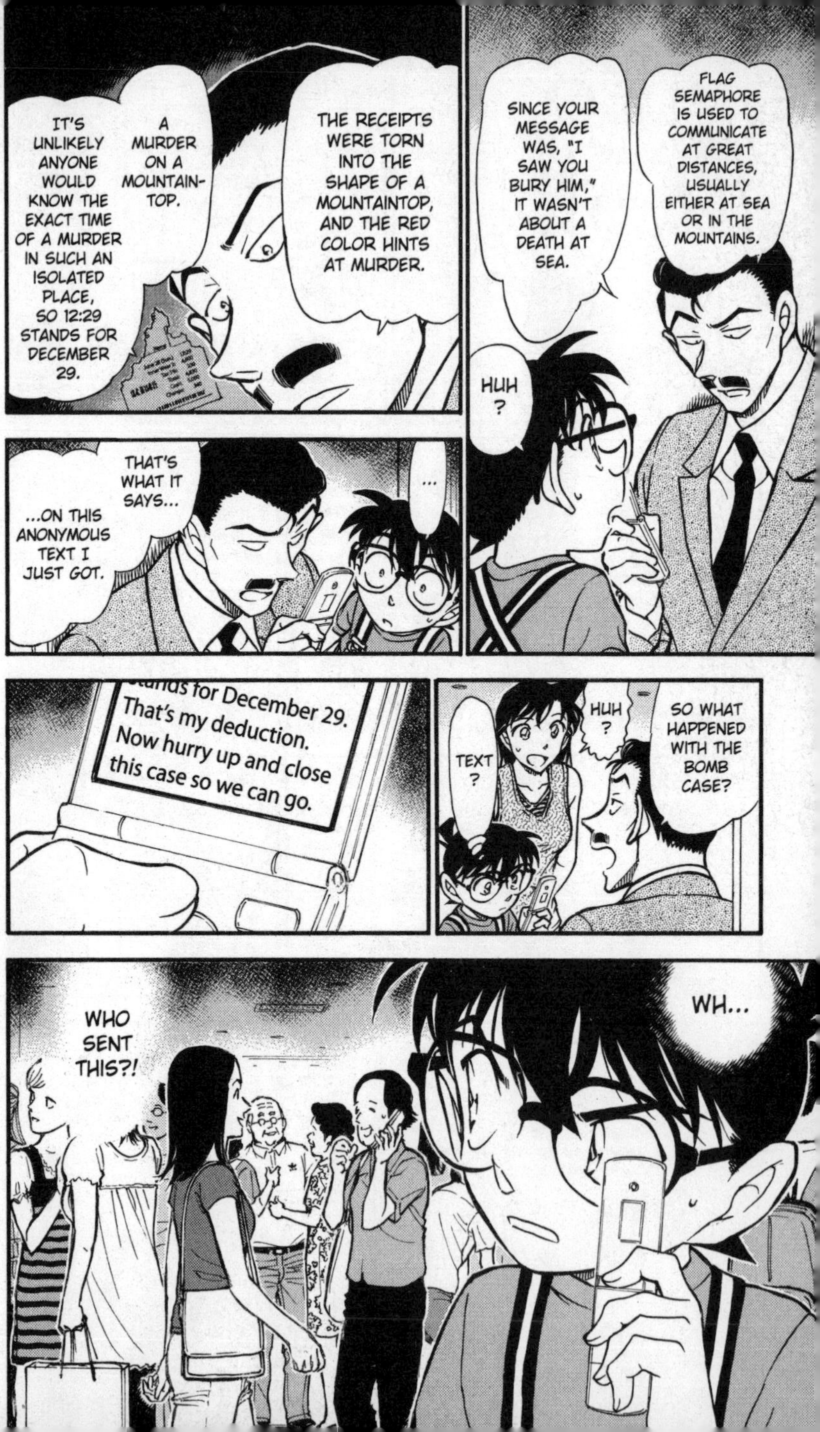
FLAG SEMAPHORE IS USED TO COMMUNICATE AT GREAT DISTANCES, USUALLY EITHER AT SEA OR IN THE MOUNTAINS.
SINCE YOUR MESSAGE WAS, "I SAW YOU BURY HIM," IT WASN'T ABOUT A DEATH AT SEA.
HUH?
THE RECEIPTS WERE TORN INTO THE SHAPE OF A MOUNTAINTOP, AND THE RED COLOR HINTS AT MURDER.
A MURDER ON A MOUNTAINTOP.
IT'S UNLIKELY ANYONE WOULD KNOW THE EXACT TIME OF A MURDER IN SUCH AN ISOLATED PLACE, SO 12:29 STANDS FOR DECEMBER 29.
...
THAT'S WHAT IT SAYS...
...ON THIS ANONYMOUS TEXT I JUST GOT.
SO WHAT HAPPENED WITH THE BOMB CASE?
HUH?
TEXT?
stands for December 29. That's my deduction. Now hurry up and close this case so we can go.
WH...
WHO SENT THIS?!

FILE 8: A SILENT BATTLE

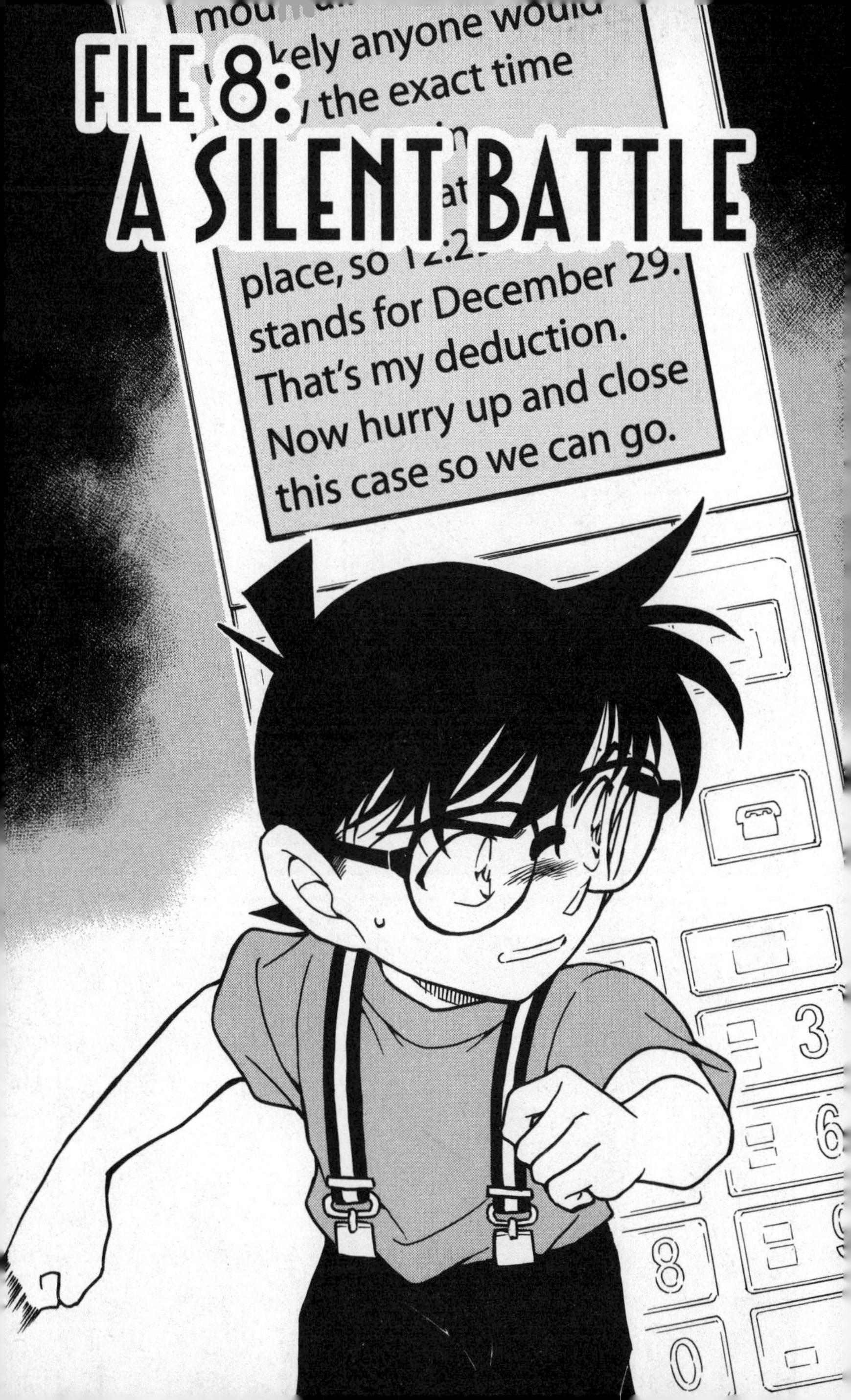
the exact time
stands for December 29.
That's my deduction.
Now hurry up and close
this case so we can go.

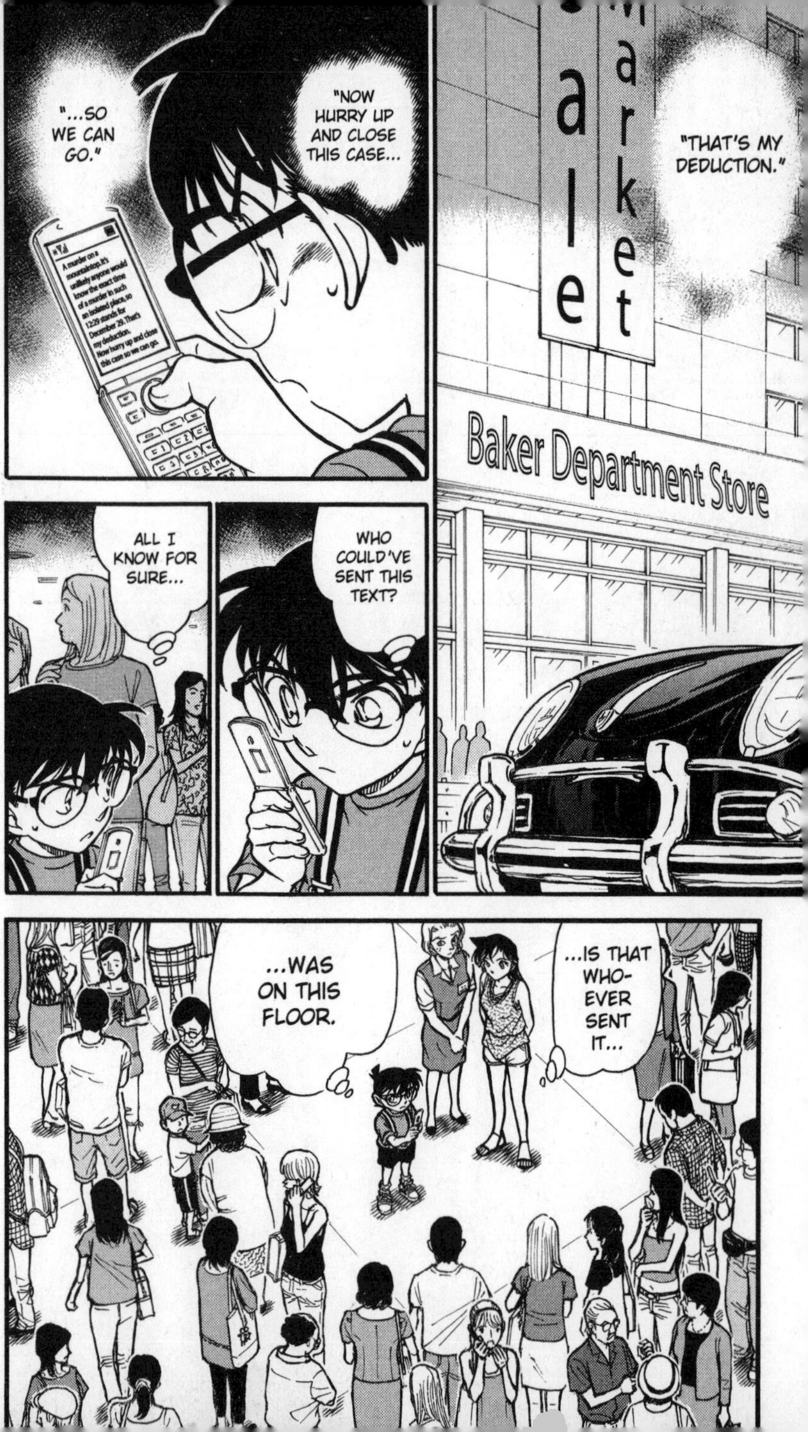
"THAT'S MY DEDUCTION."
Baker Department Store
"NOW HURRY UP AND CLOSE THIS CASE...
"...SO WE CAN GO."
A murder on a mountaintop. It's unlikely anyone would know the exact time of a murder in such an isolated place, so 1229 stands for December 29. That's my deduction. Now hurry up and close this case so we can go.
WHO COULD'VE SENT THIS TEXT?
ALL I KNOW FOR SURE...
...IS THAT WHO-EVER SENT IT...
...WAS ON THIS FLOOR.

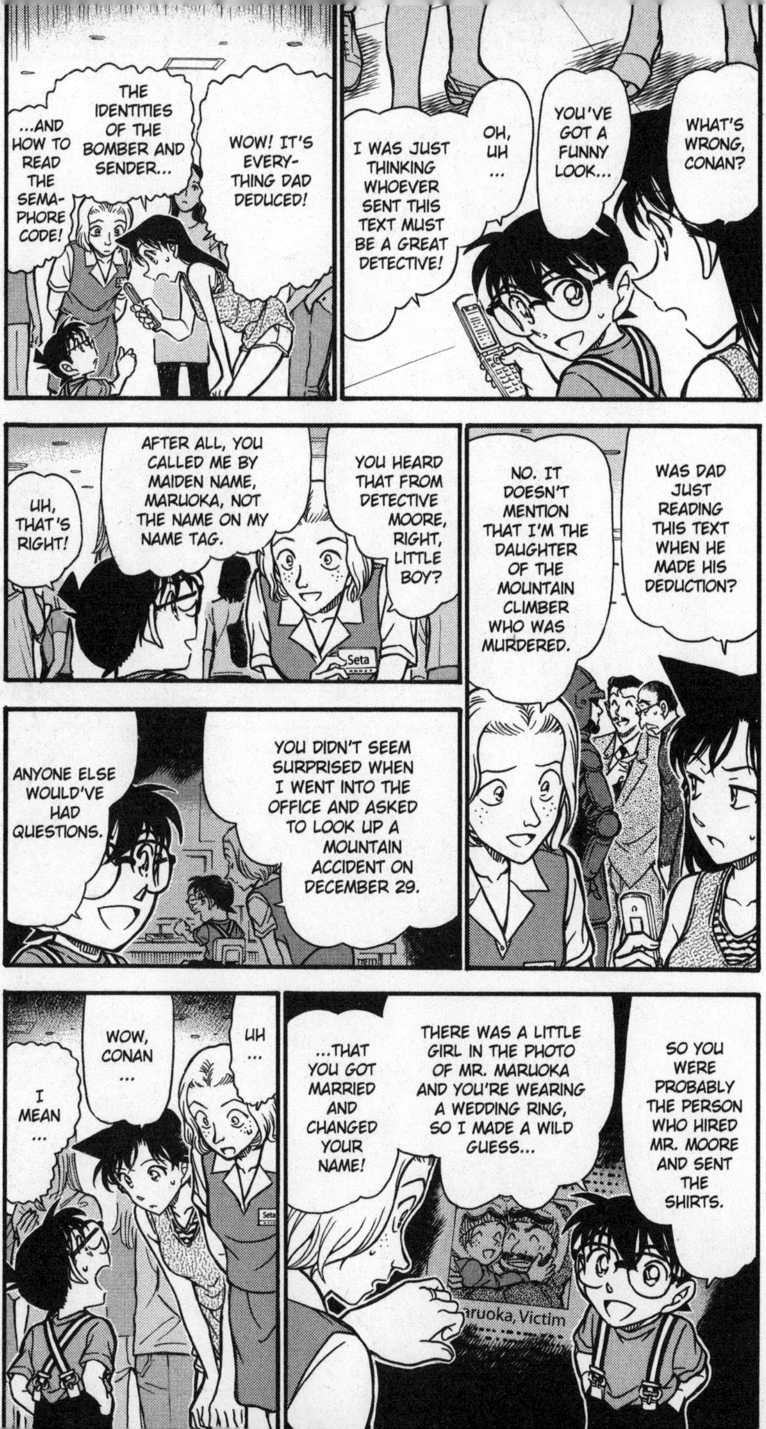
WHAT'S WRONG, CONAN?
YOU'VE GOT A FUNNY LOOK...
OH, UH ...
I WAS JUST THINKING WHOEVER SENT THIS TEXT MUST BE A GREAT DETECTIVE!
WOW! IT'S EVERY-THING DAD DEDUCED!
THE IDENTITIES OF THE BOMBER AND SENDER...
...AND HOW TO READ THE SEMA-PHORE CODE!
WAS DAD JUST READING THIS TEXT WHEN HE MADE HIS DEDUCTION?
NO. IT DOESN'T MENTION THAT I'M THE DAUGHTER OF THE MOUNTAIN CLIMBER WHO WAS MURDERED.
YOU HEARD THAT FROM DETECTIVE MOORE, RIGHT, LITTLE BOY?
AFTER ALL, YOU CALLED ME BY MAIDEN NAME, MARUOKA, NOT THE NAME ON MY NAME TAG.
UH, THAT'S RIGHT!
Seta
YOU DIDN'T SEEM SURPRISED WHEN I WENT INTO THE OFFICE AND ASKED TO LOOK UP A MOUNTAIN ACCIDENT ON DECEMBER 29.
ANYONE ELSE WOULD'VE HAD QUESTIONS.
SO YOU WERE PROBABLY THE PERSON WHO HIRED MR. MOORE AND SENT THE SHIRTS.
THERE WAS A LITTLE GIRL IN THE PHOTO OF MR. MARUOKA AND YOU'RE WEARING A WEDDING RING, SO I MADE A WILD GUESS...
...THAT YOU GOT MARRIED AND CHANGED YOUR NAME!
aruoka, Victim
UH ...
WOW, CONAN ...
I MEAN ...

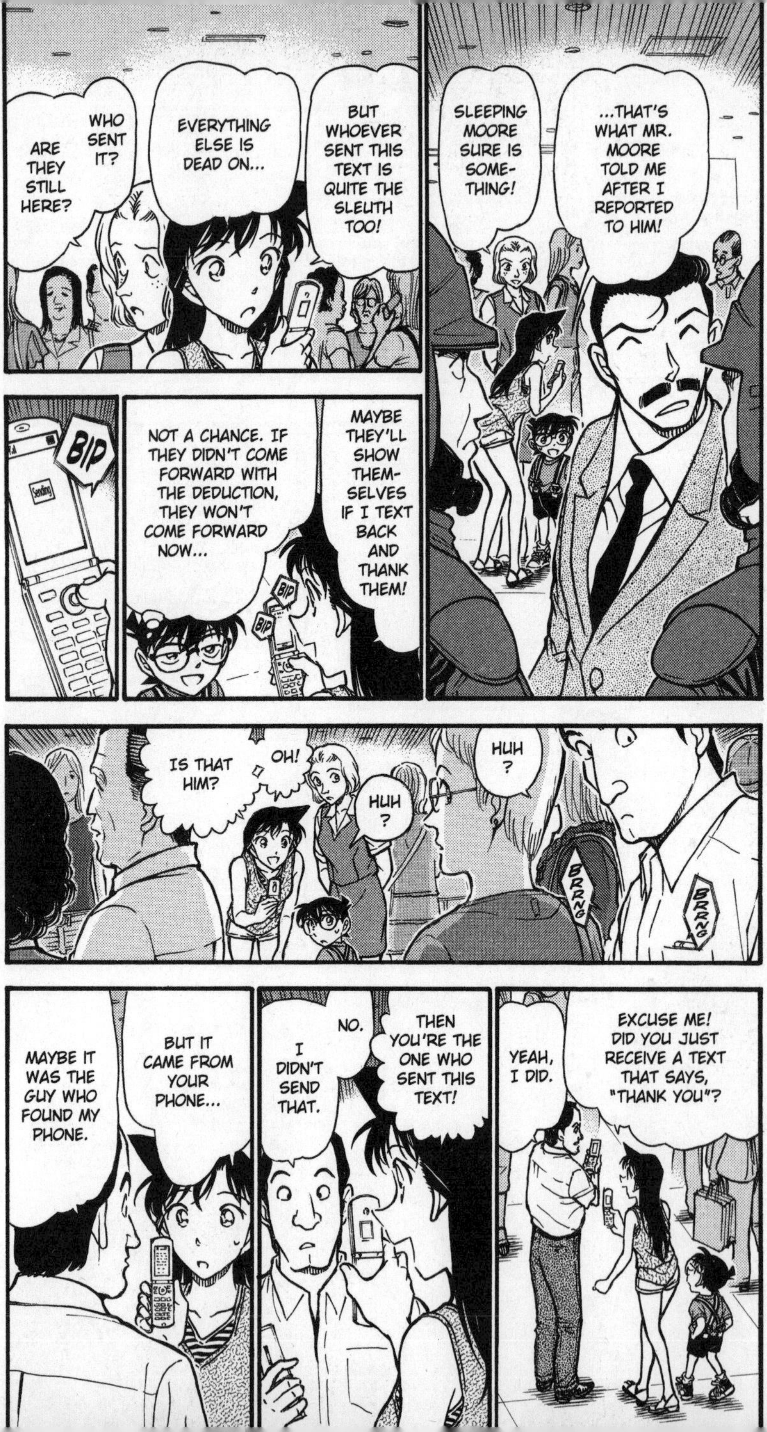
...THAT'S WHAT MR. MOORE TOLD ME AFTER I REPORTED TO HIM!
SLEEPING MOORE SURE IS SOMETHING!
BUT WHOEVER SENT THIS TEXT IS QUITE THE SLEUTH TOO!
EVERYTHING ELSE IS DEAD ON...
WHO SENT IT?
ARE THEY STILL HERE?
MAYBE THEY'LL SHOW THEMSELVES IF I TEXT BACK AND THANK THEM!
NOT A CHANCE. IF THEY DIDN'T COME FORWARD WITH THE DEDUCTION, THEY WON'T COME FORWARD NOW...
BIP
BIP
BIP
Sending
HUH?
BRRNG
BRRNG
HUH?
OH!
IS THAT HIM?
EXCUSE ME! DID YOU JUST RECEIVE A TEXT THAT SAYS, "THANK YOU"?
YEAH, I DID.
THEN YOU'RE THE ONE WHO SENT THIS TEXT!
NO.
I DIDN'T SEND THAT.
BUT IT CAME FROM YOUR PHONE...
MAYBE IT WAS THE GUY WHO FOUND MY PHONE.

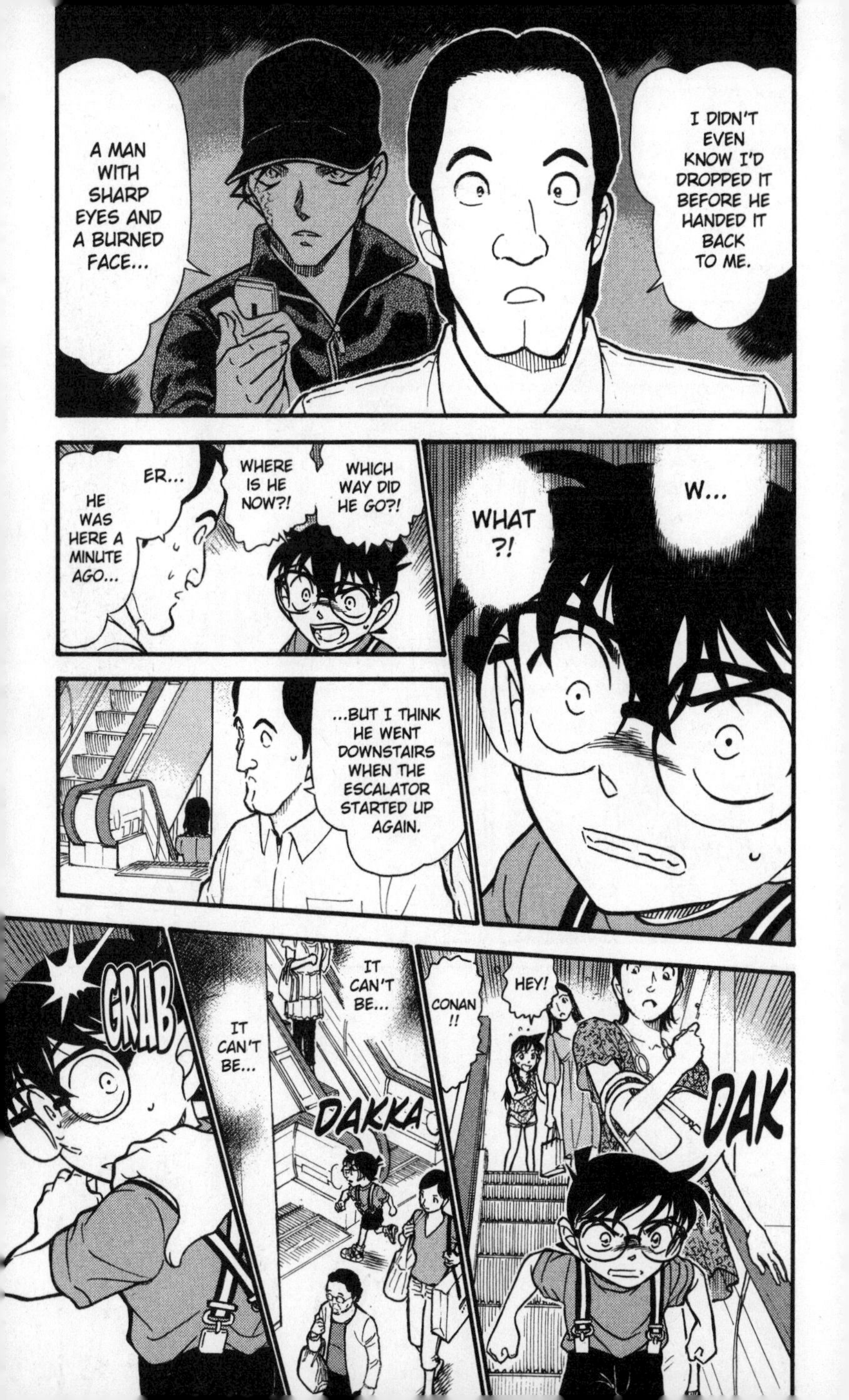
I DIDN'T EVEN KNOW I'D DROPPED IT BEFORE HE HANDED IT BACK TO ME.
A MAN WITH SHARP EYES AND A BURNED FACE...
W...
WHAT ?!
WHICH WAY DID HE GO?!
WHERE IS HE NOW?!
ER...
HE WAS HERE A MINUTE AGO...
...BUT I THINK HE WENT DOWNSTAIRS WHEN THE ESCALATOR STARTED UP AGAIN.
HEY!
CONAN !!
DAK
IT CAN'T BE...
DAKKA
IT CAN'T BE...
GRAB

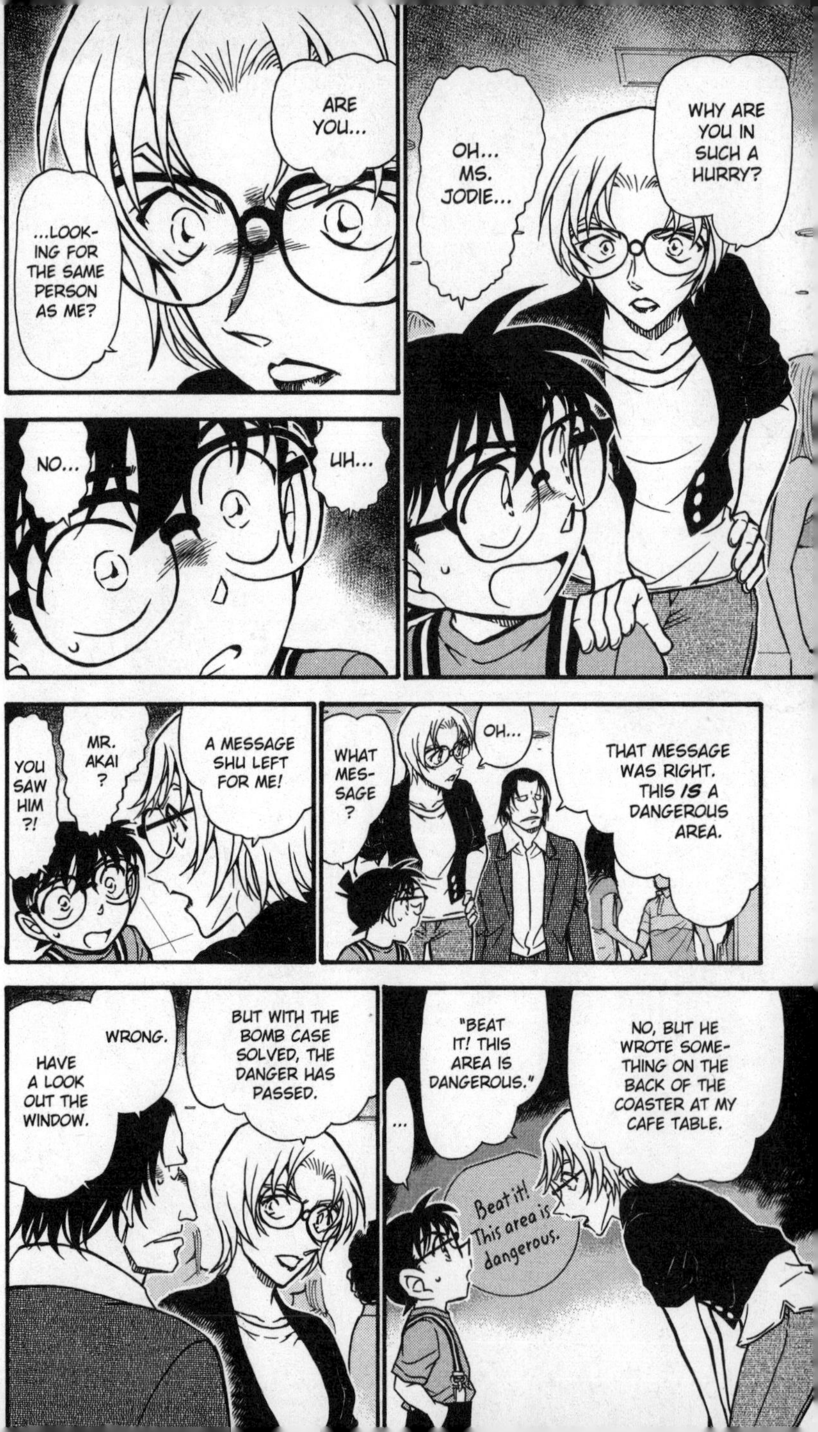
WHY ARE YOU IN SUCH A HURRY?
OH... MS. JODIE...
ARE YOU...
...LOOKING FOR THE SAME PERSON AS ME?
UH...
NO...
THAT MESSAGE WAS RIGHT. THIS *IS* A DANGEROUS AREA.
OH...
WHAT MESSAGE?
A MESSAGE SHU LEFT FOR ME!
MR. AKAI?
YOU SAW HIM?!
NO, BUT HE WROTE SOMETHING ON THE BACK OF THE COASTER AT MY CAFE TABLE.
"BEAT IT! THIS AREA IS DANGEROUS."
...
Beat it! This area is dangerous.
BUT WITH THE BOMB CASE SOLVED, THE DANGER HAS PASSED.
WRONG.
HAVE A LOOK OUT THE WINDOW.

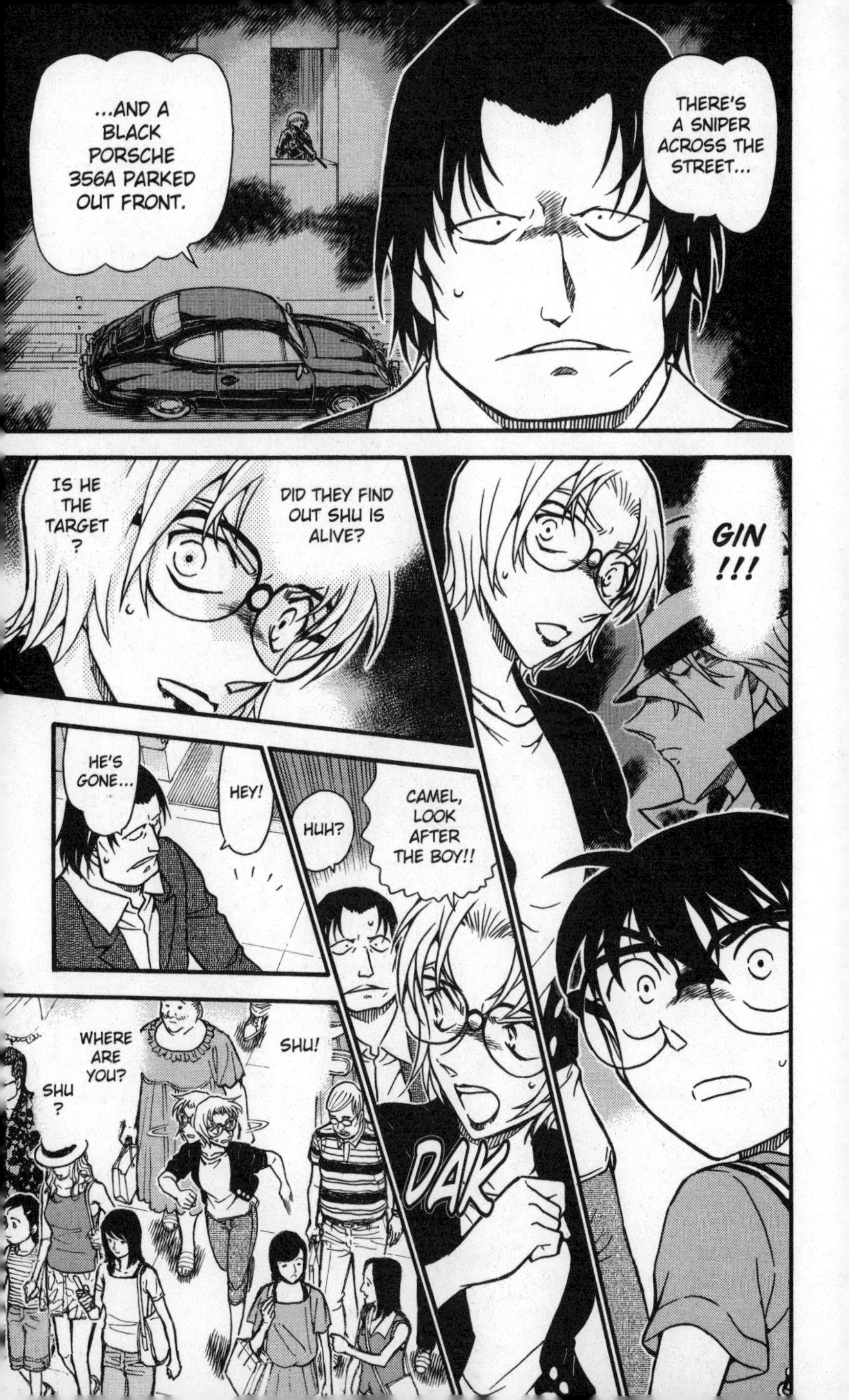
THERE'S A SNIPER ACROSS THE STREET...
...AND A BLACK PORSCHE 356A PARKED OUT FRONT.
GIN !!!
DID THEY FIND OUT SHU IS ALIVE?
IS HE THE TARGET?
CAMEL, LOOK AFTER THE BOY!!
HUH?
HEY!
HE'S GONE...
DAK
SHU!
WHERE ARE YOU?
SHU?

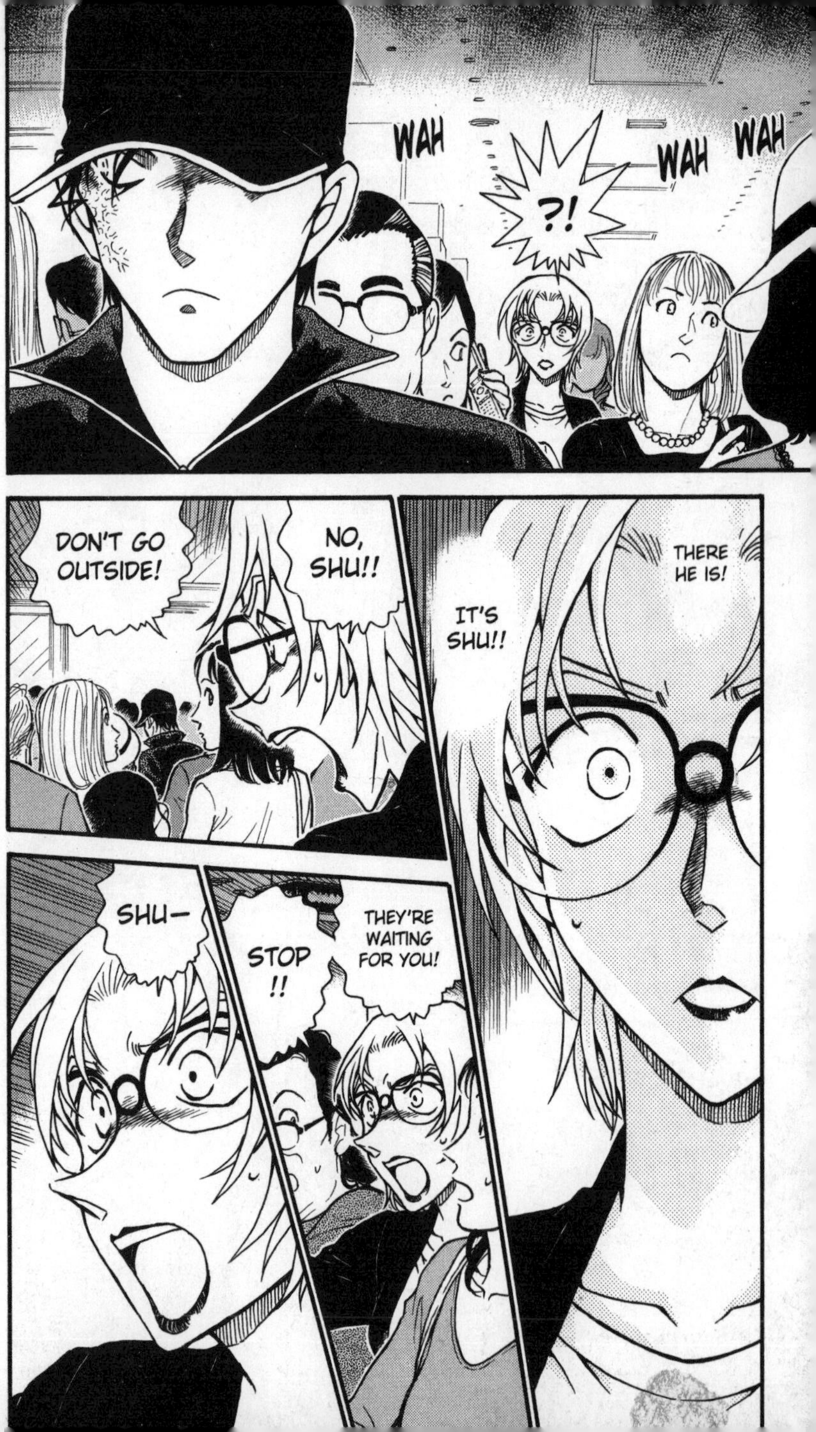
WAH
WAH
?!
WAH
THERE HE IS!
IT'S SHU!!
NO, SHU!!
DON'T GO OUTSIDE!
THEY'RE WAITING FOR YOU!
STOP !!
SHU—

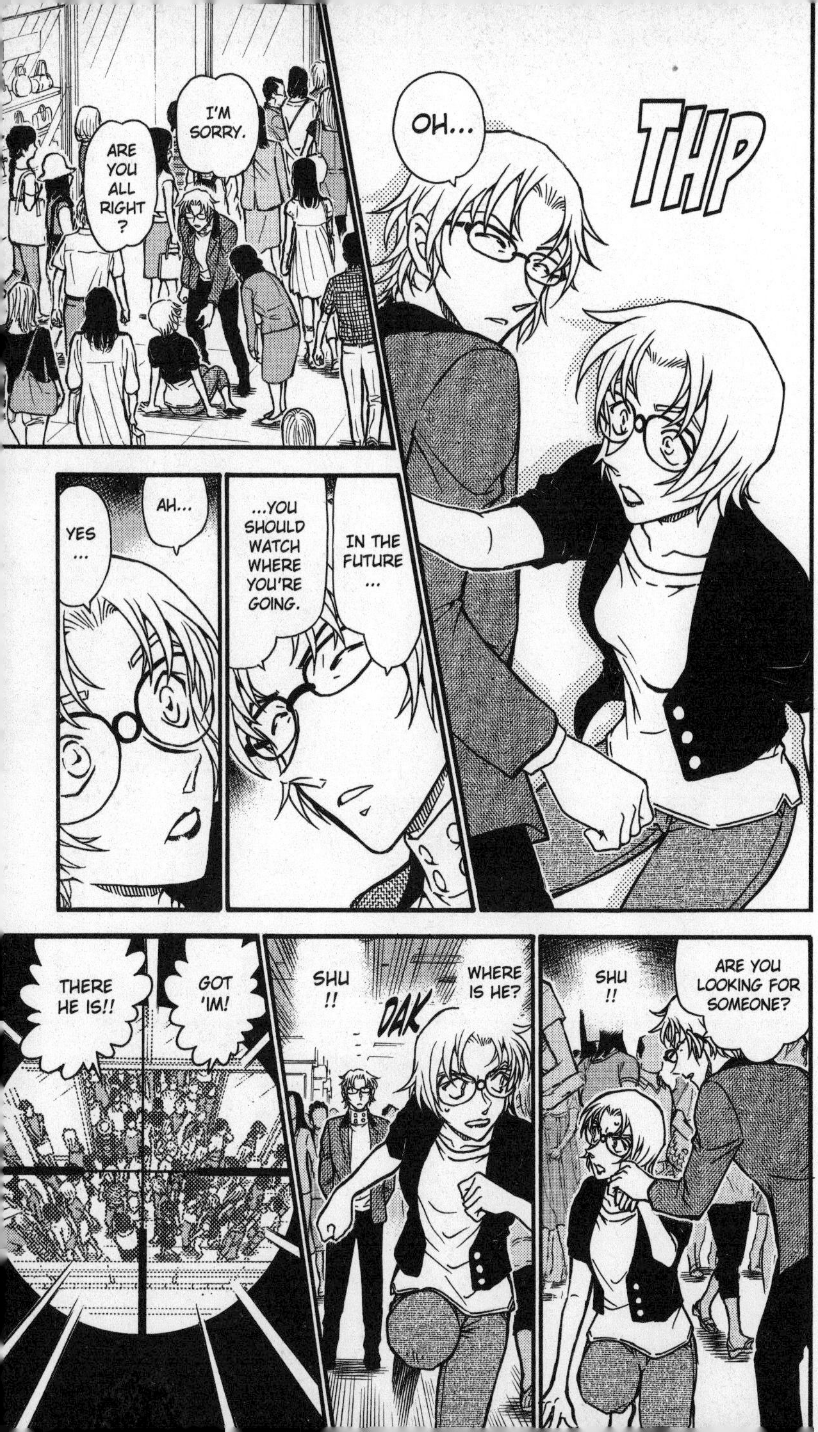
THP
OH...
I'M SORRY.
ARE YOU ALL RIGHT?
IN THE FUTURE...
...YOU SHOULD WATCH WHERE YOU'RE GOING.
AH...
YES...
ARE YOU LOOKING FOR SOMEONE?
SHU!!
WHERE IS HE?
SHU!!
DAK
GOT 'IM!
THERE HE IS!!

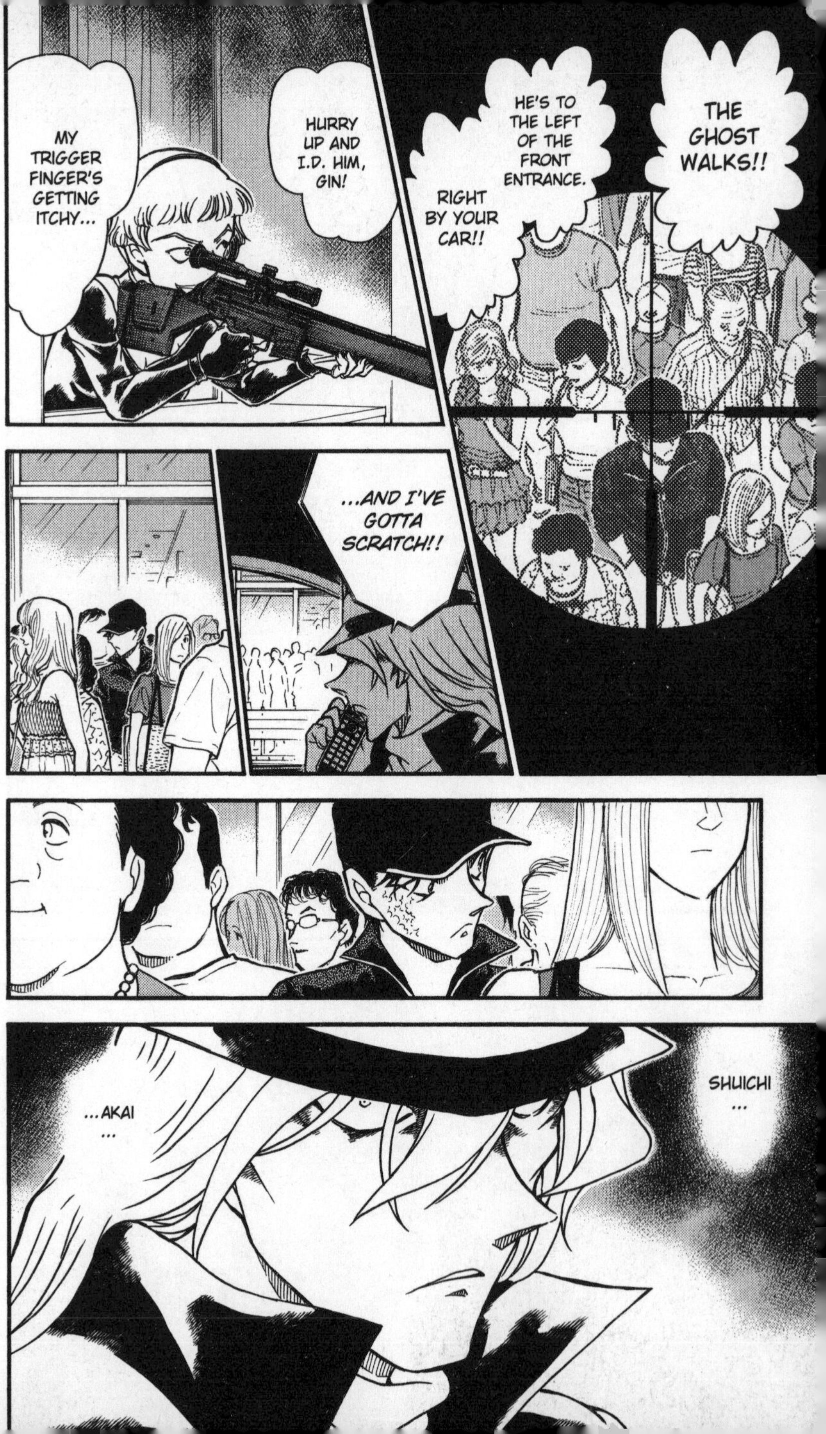
THE GHOST WALKS!!
HE'S TO THE LEFT OF THE FRONT ENTRANCE.
RIGHT BY YOUR CAR!!
HURRY UP AND I.D. HIM, GIN!
MY TRIGGER FINGER'S GETTING ITCHY...
...AND I'VE GOTTA SCRATCH!!
SHUICHI ...
...AKAI ...

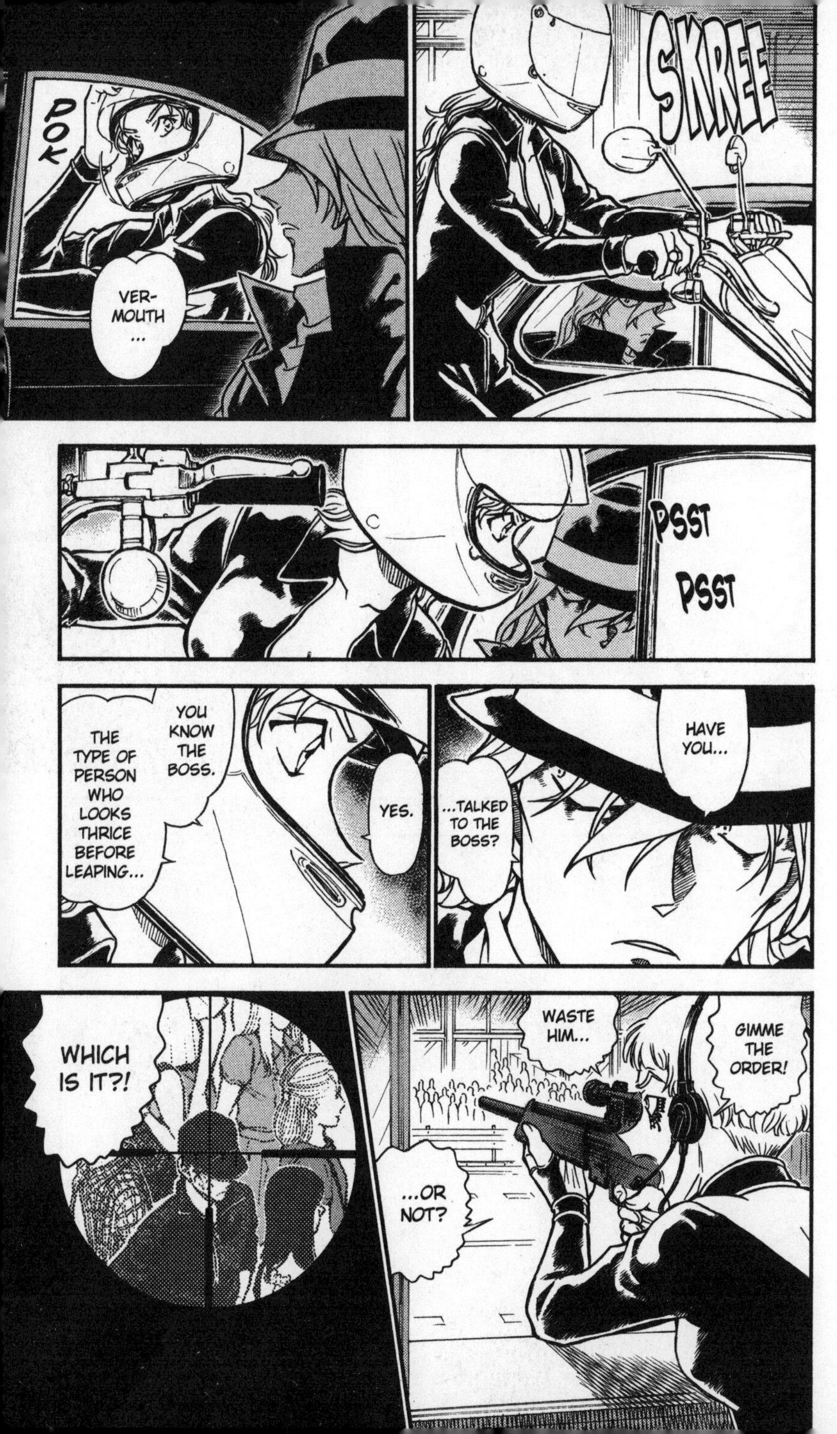
SKREE
POK
VER-MOUTH...
PSST
PSST
HAVE YOU...
...TALKED TO THE BOSS?
YES.
YOU KNOW THE BOSS.
THE TYPE OF PERSON WHO LOOKS THRICE BEFORE LEAPING...
GIMME THE ORDER!
WASTE HIM...
...OR NOT?
WHICH IS IT?!

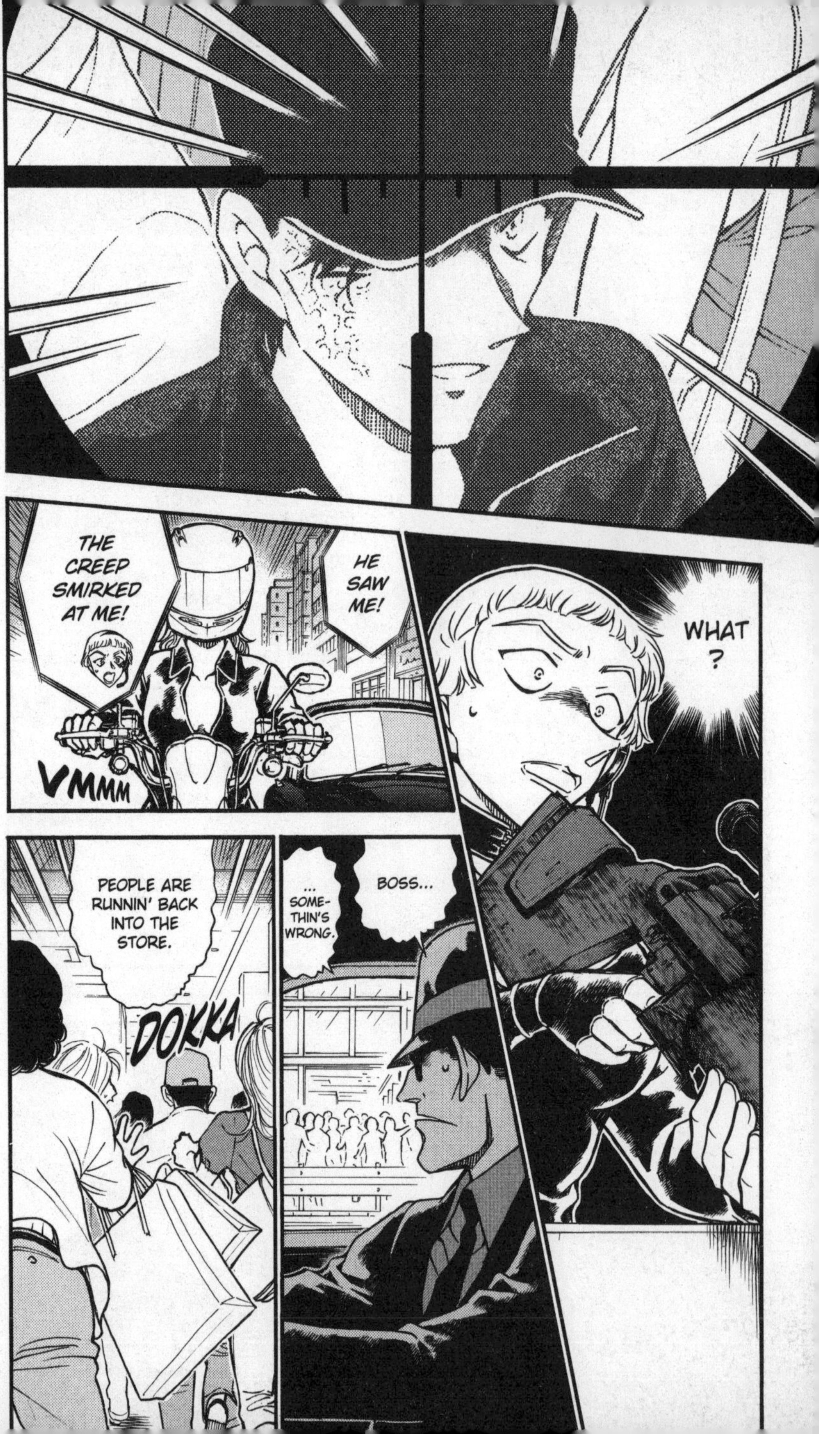
WHAT ?
HE SAW ME!
THE CREEP SMIRKED AT ME!
VMMM
BOSS...
... SOMETHIN'S WRONG.
PEOPLE ARE RUNNIN' BACK INTO THE STORE.
DOKKA

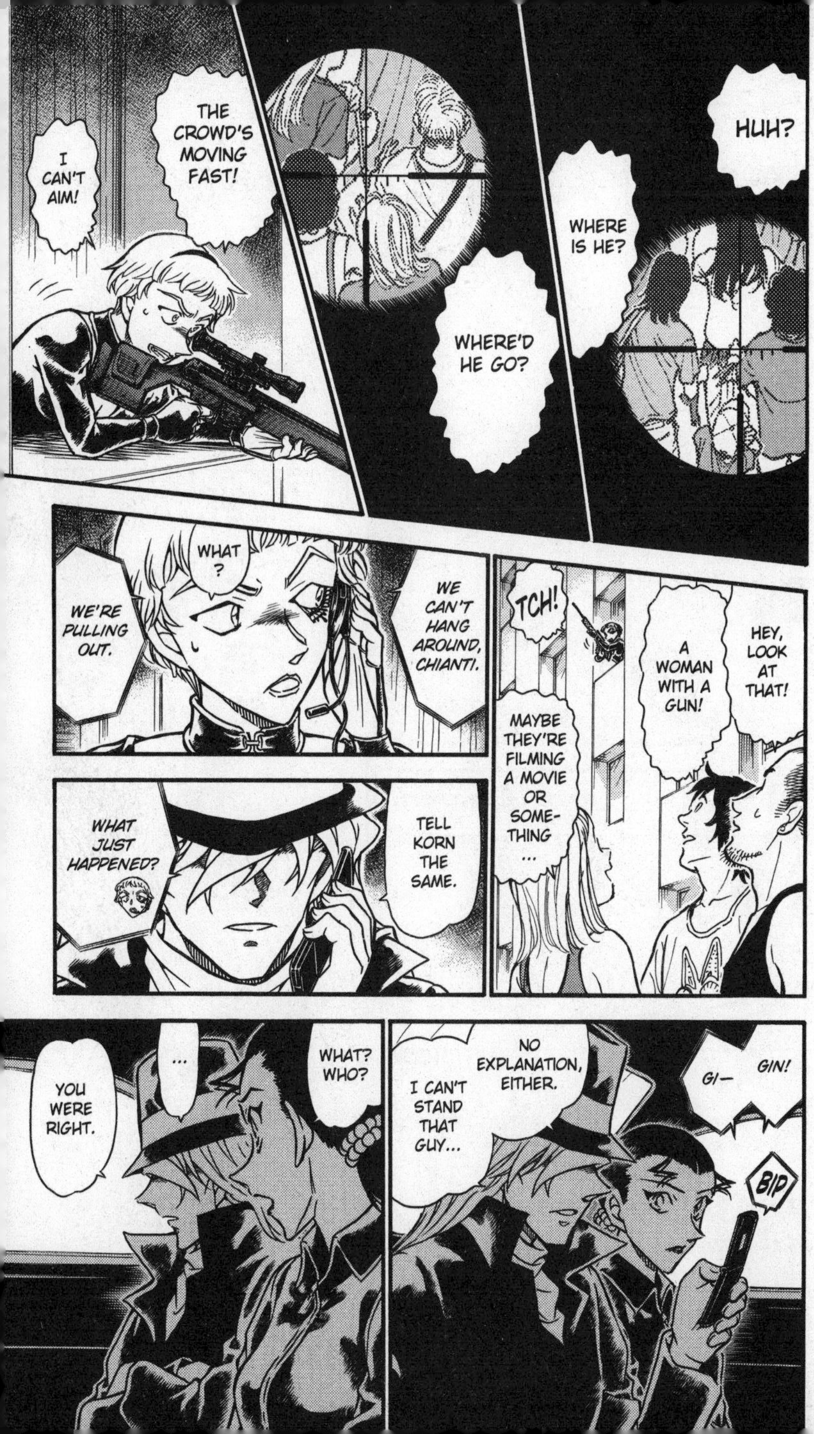
HUH?
WHERE IS HE?
WHERE'D HE GO?
THE CROWD'S MOVING FAST!
I CAN'T AIM!
HEY, LOOK AT THAT!
A WOMAN WITH A GUN!
TCH!
MAYBE THEY'RE FILMING A MOVIE OR SOMETHING...
WE CAN'T HANG AROUND, CHIANTI.
WHAT?
WE'RE PULLING OUT.
TELL KORN THE SAME.
WHAT JUST HAPPENED?
GIN!
GI—
BIP
NO EXPLANATION, EITHER.
I CAN'T STAND THAT GUY...
WHAT? WHO?
...
YOU WERE RIGHT.

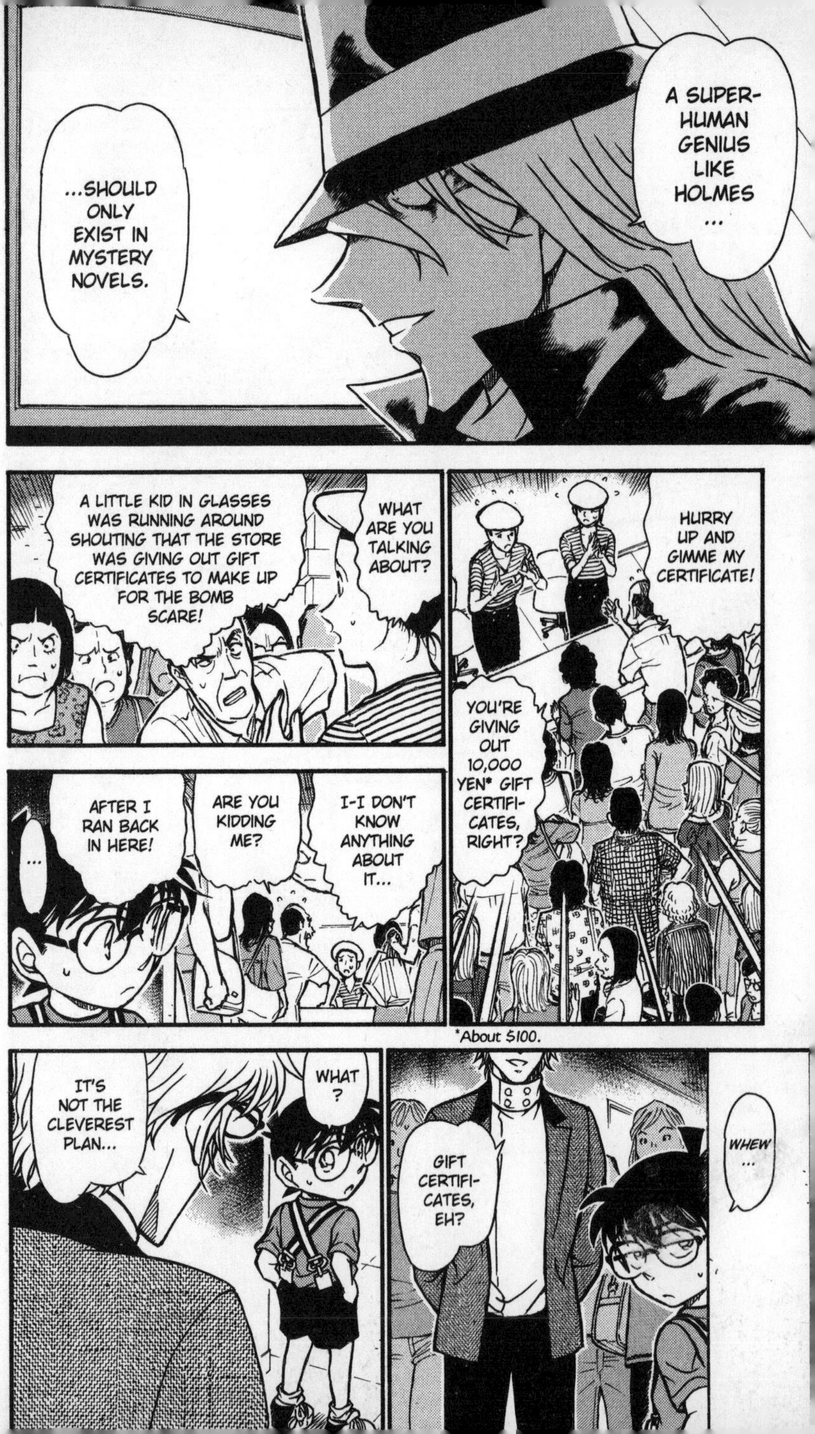
A SUPER-HUMAN GENIUS LIKE HOLMES...
...SHOULD ONLY EXIST IN MYSTERY NOVELS.
HURRY UP AND GIMME MY CERTIFICATE!
YOU'RE GIVING OUT 10,000 YEN* GIFT CERTIFI-CATES, RIGHT?
WHAT ARE YOU TALKING ABOUT?
A LITTLE KID IN GLASSES WAS RUNNING AROUND SHOUTING THAT THE STORE WAS GIVING OUT GIFT CERTIFICATES TO MAKE UP FOR THE BOMB SCARE!
I-I DON'T KNOW ANYTHING ABOUT IT...
ARE YOU KIDDING ME?
AFTER I RAN BACK IN HERE!
...
WHEW...
GIFT CERTIFI-CATES, EH?
WHAT?
IT'S NOT THE CLEVEREST PLAN...

*About $100.

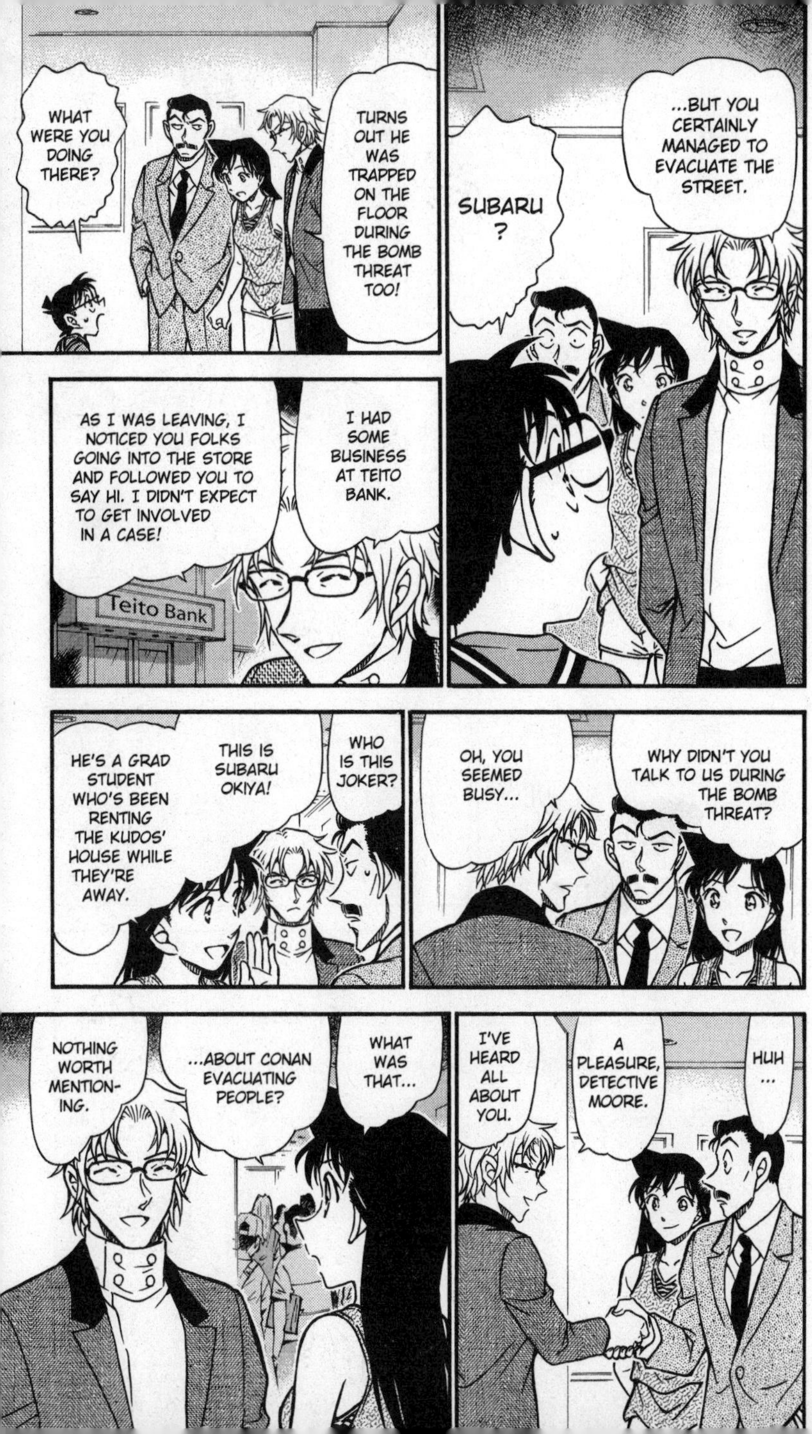
...BUT YOU CERTAINLY MANAGED TO EVACUATE THE STREET.
SUBARU?
TURNS OUT HE WAS TRAPPED ON THE FLOOR DURING THE BOMB THREAT TOO!
WHAT WERE YOU DOING THERE?
I HAD SOME BUSINESS AT TEITO BANK.
AS I WAS LEAVING, I NOTICED YOU FOLKS GOING INTO THE STORE AND FOLLOWED YOU TO SAY HI. I DIDN'T EXPECT TO GET INVOLVED IN A CASE!
Teito Bank
WHY DIDN'T YOU TALK TO US DURING THE BOMB THREAT?
OH, YOU SEEMED BUSY...
WHO IS THIS JOKER?
THIS IS SUBARU OKIYA!
HE'S A GRAD STUDENT WHO'S BEEN RENTING THE KUDOS' HOUSE WHILE THEY'RE AWAY.
HUH...
A PLEASURE, DETECTIVE MOORE.
I'VE HEARD ALL ABOUT YOU.
WHAT WAS THAT...
...ABOUT CONAN EVACUATING PEOPLE?
NOTHING WORTH MENTIONING.

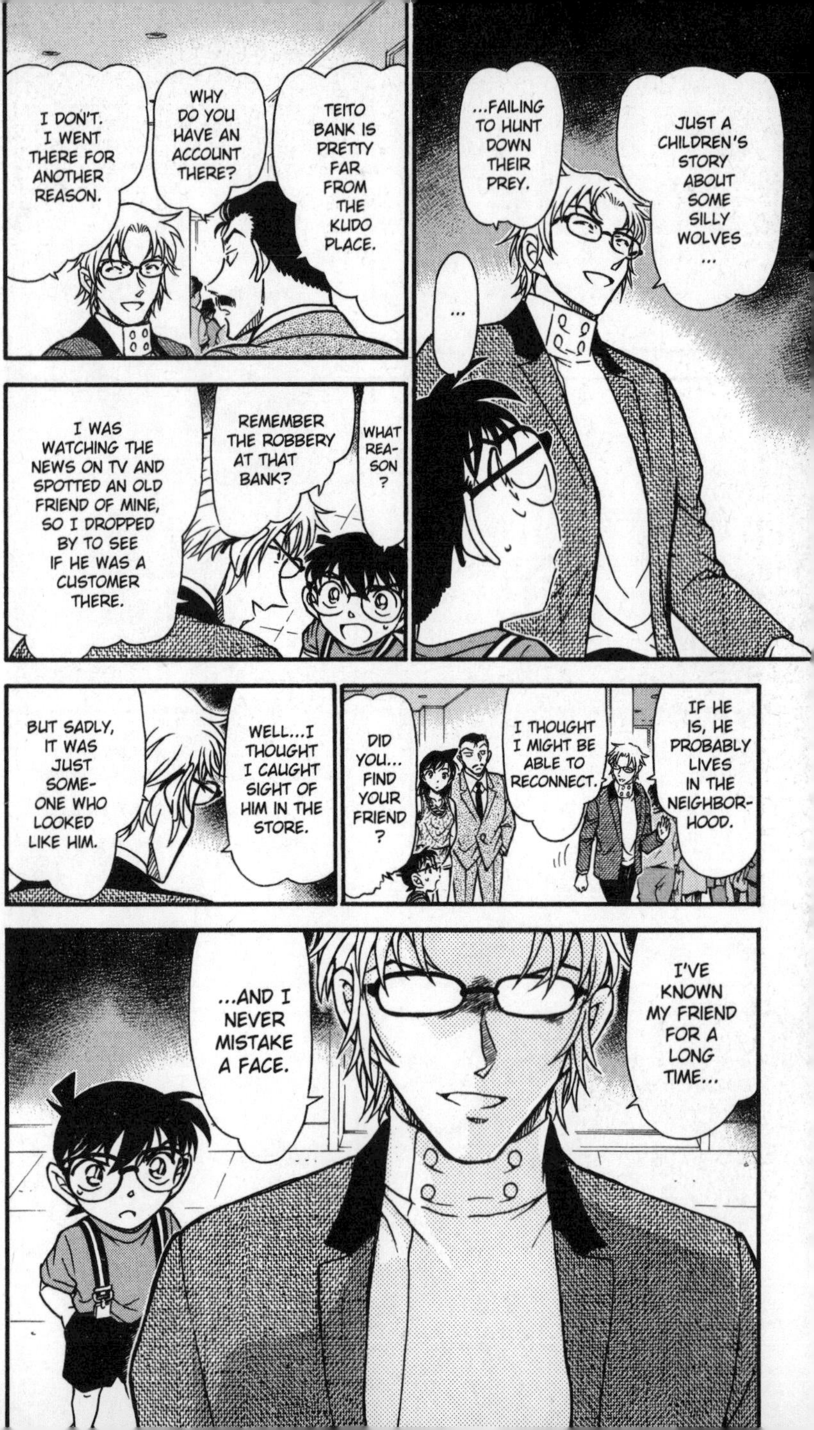
JUST A CHILDREN'S STORY ABOUT SOME SILLY WOLVES ...
...FAILING TO HUNT DOWN THEIR PREY.
...
TEITO BANK IS PRETTY FAR FROM THE KUDO PLACE.
WHY DO YOU HAVE AN ACCOUNT THERE?
I DON'T. I WENT THERE FOR ANOTHER REASON.
WHAT REA-SON?
REMEMBER THE ROBBERY AT THAT BANK?
I WAS WATCHING THE NEWS ON TV AND SPOTTED AN OLD FRIEND OF MINE, SO I DROPPED BY TO SEE IF HE WAS A CUSTOMER THERE.
IF HE IS, HE PROBABLY LIVES IN THE NEIGHBOR-HOOD.
I THOUGHT I MIGHT BE ABLE TO RECONNECT.
DID YOU... FIND YOUR FRIEND?
WELL...I THOUGHT I CAUGHT SIGHT OF HIM IN THE STORE.
BUT SADLY, IT WAS JUST SOME-ONE WHO LOOKED LIKE HIM.
I'VE KNOWN MY FRIEND FOR A LONG TIME...
...AND I NEVER MISTAKE A FACE.

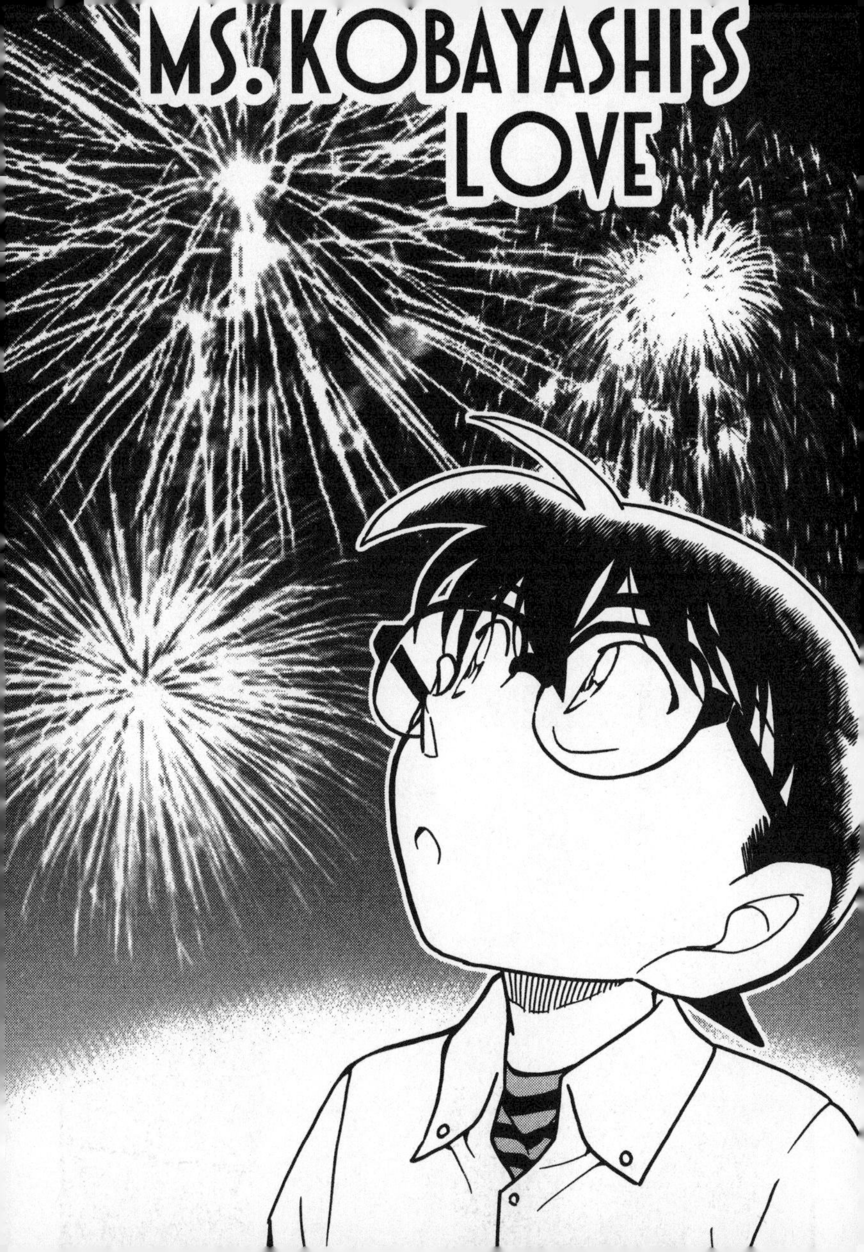
MS. KOBAYASHI'S LOVE

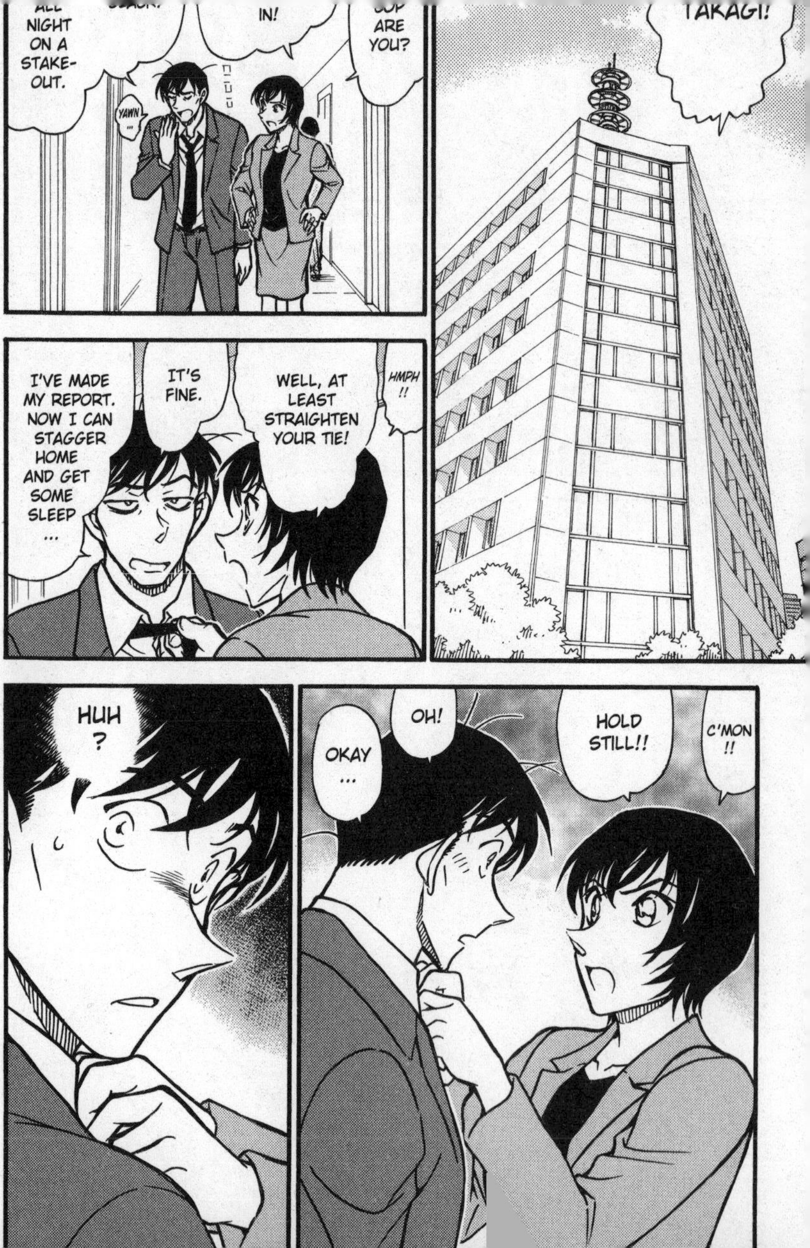
TAKAGI!
ARE YOU?
IN!
ALL NIGHT ON A STAKE-OUT.
YAWN ...
HMPH !!
WELL, AT LEAST STRAIGHTEN YOUR TIE!
IT'S FINE.
I'VE MADE MY REPORT. NOW I CAN STAGGER HOME AND GET SOME SLEEP ...
C'MON !!
HOLD STILL!!
OH!
OKAY ...
HUH ?

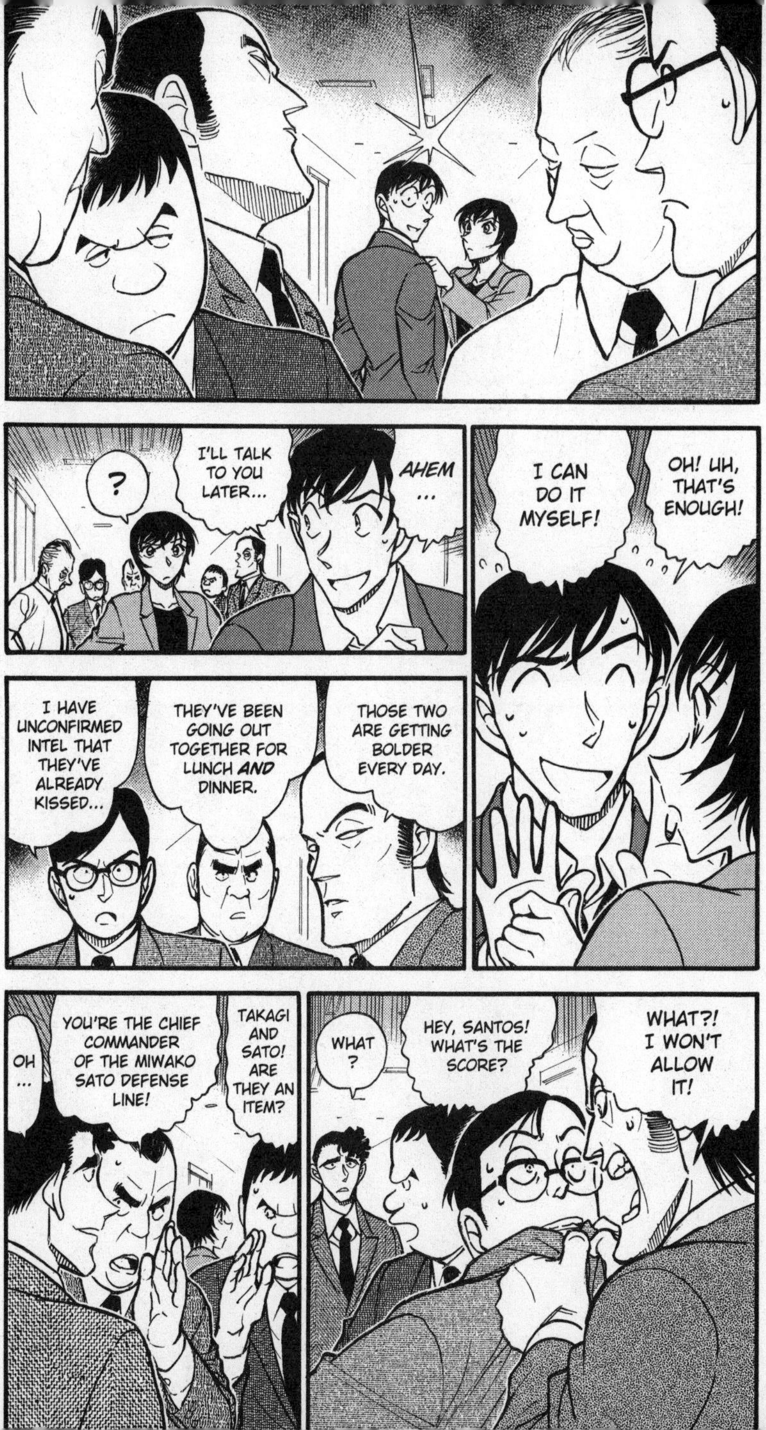
OH! UH, THAT'S ENOUGH!
I CAN DO IT MYSELF!
AHEM ...
I'LL TALK TO YOU LATER...
?
THOSE TWO ARE GETTING BOLDER EVERY DAY.
THEY'VE BEEN GOING OUT TOGETHER FOR LUNCH AND DINNER.
I HAVE UNCONFIRMED INTEL THAT THEY'VE ALREADY KISSED...
WHAT?! I WON'T ALLOW IT!
HEY, SANTOS! WHAT'S THE SCORE?
WHAT ?
TAKAGI AND SATO! ARE THEY AN ITEM?
YOU'RE THE CHIEF COMMANDER OF THE MIWAKO SATO DEFENSE LINE!
OH ...

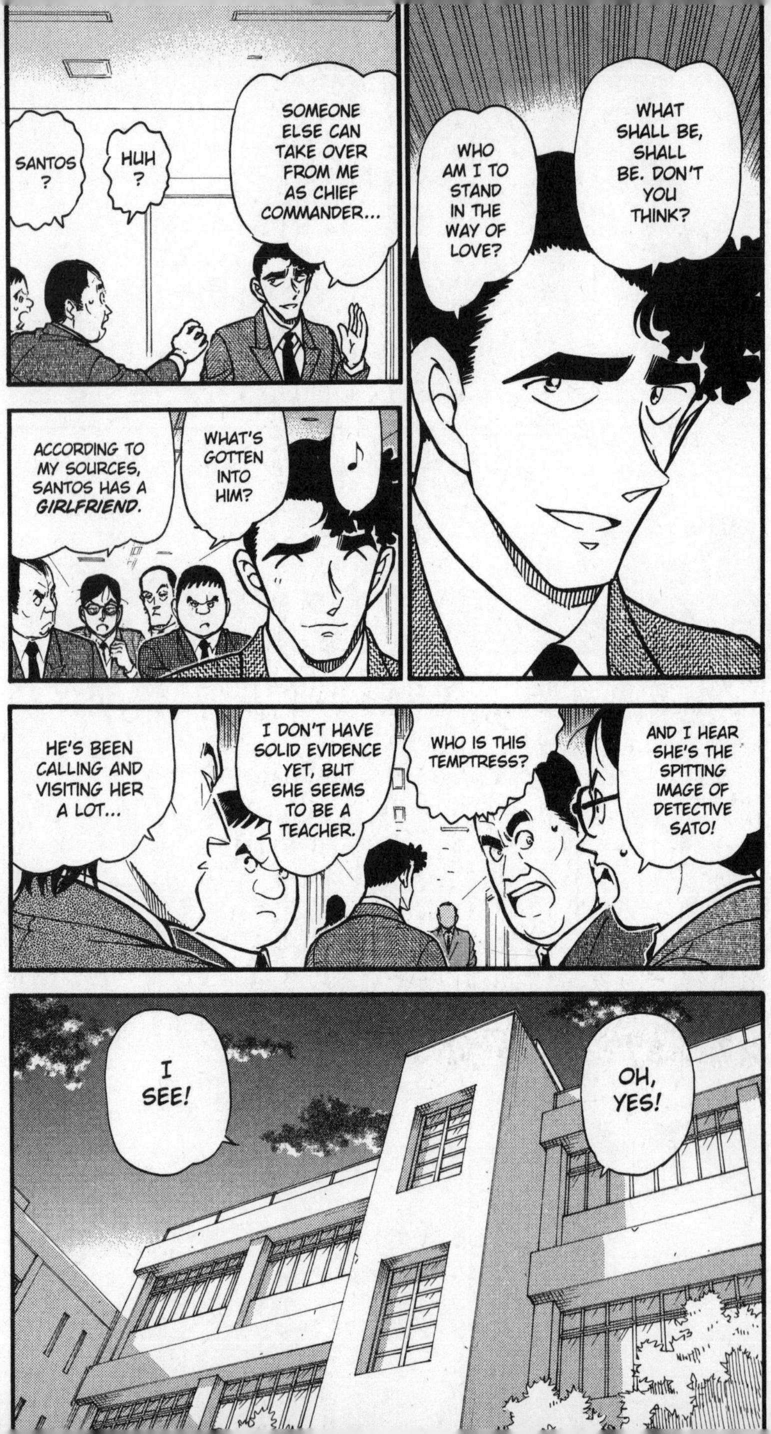
WHAT SHALL BE, SHALL BE. DON'T YOU THINK?
WHO AM I TO STAND IN THE WAY OF LOVE?
SOMEONE ELSE CAN TAKE OVER FROM ME AS CHIEF COMMANDER...
HUH ?
SANTOS ?
WHAT'S GOTTEN INTO HIM?
ACCORDING TO MY SOURCES, SANTOS HAS A *GIRLFRIEND*.
AND I HEAR SHE'S THE SPITTING IMAGE OF DETECTIVE SATO!
WHO IS THIS TEMPTRESS?
I DON'T HAVE SOLID EVIDENCE YET, BUT SHE SEEMS TO BE A TEACHER.
HE'S BEEN CALLING AND VISITING HER A LOT...
OH, YES!
I SEE!

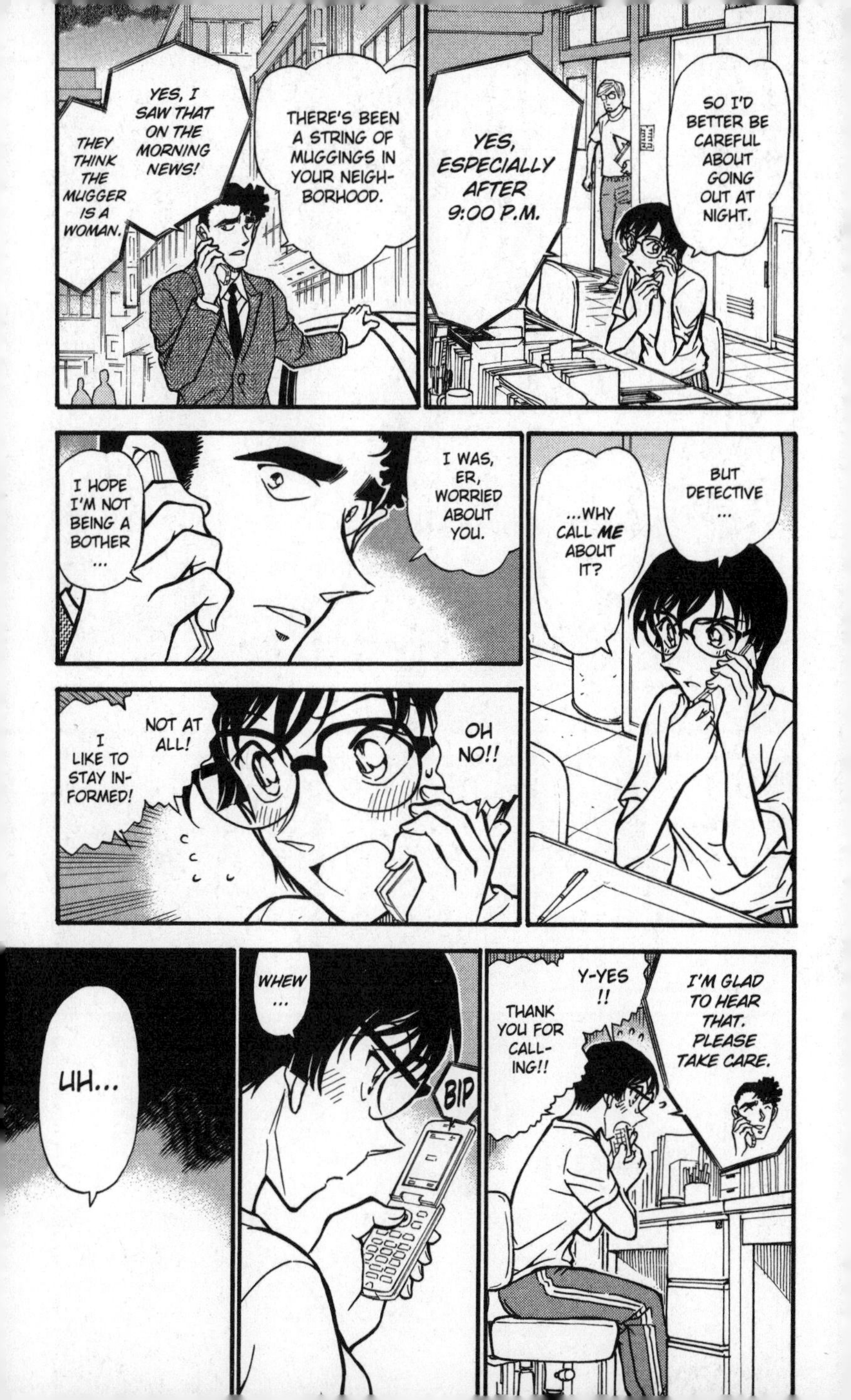
SO I'D BETTER BE CAREFUL ABOUT GOING OUT AT NIGHT.
YES, ESPECIALLY AFTER 9:00 P.M.
THERE'S BEEN A STRING OF MUGGINGS IN YOUR NEIGH-BORHOOD.
YES, I SAW THAT ON THE MORNING NEWS!
THEY THINK THE MUGGER IS A WOMAN.
BUT DETECTIVE ...
...WHY CALL ME ABOUT IT?
I WAS, ER, WORRIED ABOUT YOU.
I HOPE I'M NOT BEING A BOTHER ...
OH NO!!
NOT AT ALL!
I LIKE TO STAY IN-FORMED!
I'M GLAD TO HEAR THAT. PLEASE TAKE CARE.
Y-YES !!
THANK YOU FOR CALL-ING!!
WHEW ...
BIP
UH...

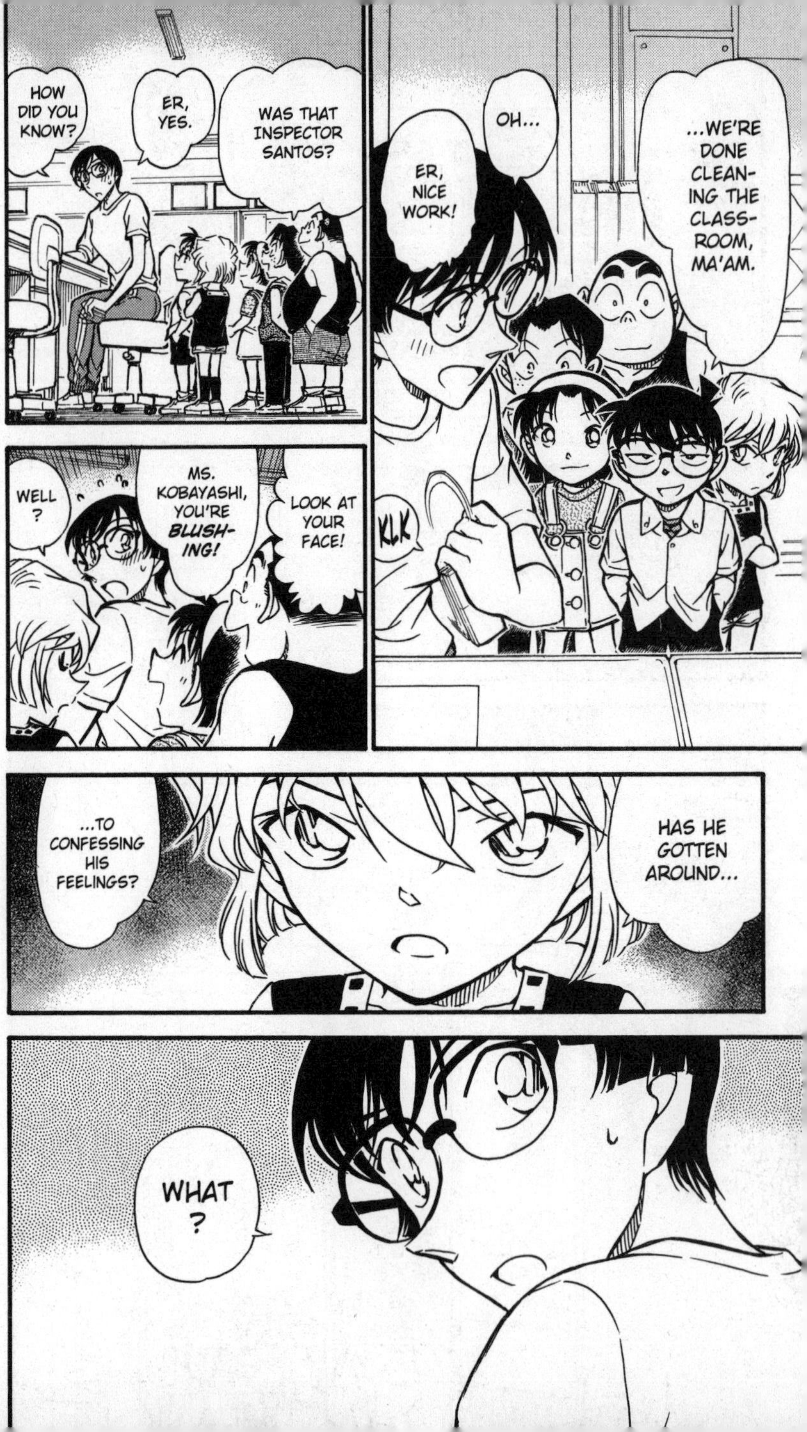
...WE'RE DONE CLEANING THE CLASSROOM, MA'AM.
OH...
ER, NICE WORK!
KLK
WAS THAT INSPECTOR SANTOS?
ER, YES.
HOW DID YOU KNOW?
LOOK AT YOUR FACE!
MS. KOBAYASHI, YOU'RE *BLUSHING!*
WELL?
HAS HE GOTTEN AROUND...
...TO CONFESSING HIS FEELINGS?
WHAT?

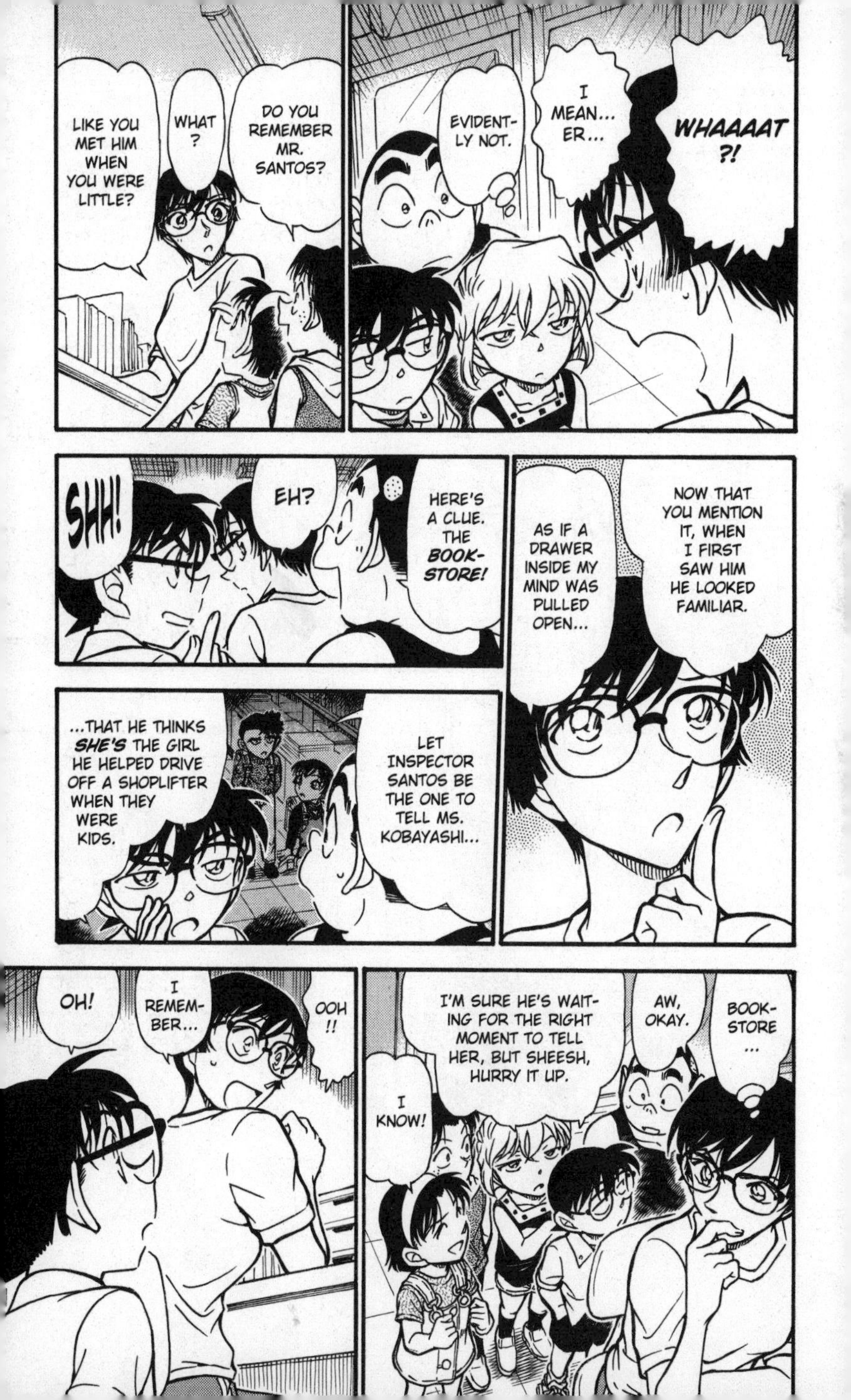
WHAAAAT ?!
I MEAN... ER...
EVIDENT-LY NOT.
DO YOU REMEMBER MR. SANTOS?
WHAT ?
LIKE YOU MET HIM WHEN YOU WERE LITTLE?
NOW THAT YOU MENTION IT, WHEN I FIRST SAW HIM HE LOOKED FAMILIAR.
AS IF A DRAWER INSIDE MY MIND WAS PULLED OPEN...
HERE'S A CLUE. THE *BOOK-STORE!*
EH?
SHH!
LET INSPECTOR SANTOS BE THE ONE TO TELL MS. KOBAYASHI...
...THAT HE THINKS *SHE'S* THE GIRL HE HELPED DRIVE OFF A SHOPLIFTER WHEN THEY WERE KIDS.
BOOK-STORE ...
AW, OKAY.
I'M SURE HE'S WAIT-ING FOR THE RIGHT MOMENT TO TELL HER, BUT SHEESH, HURRY IT UP.
I KNOW!
OOH !!
I REMEM-BER...
OH!

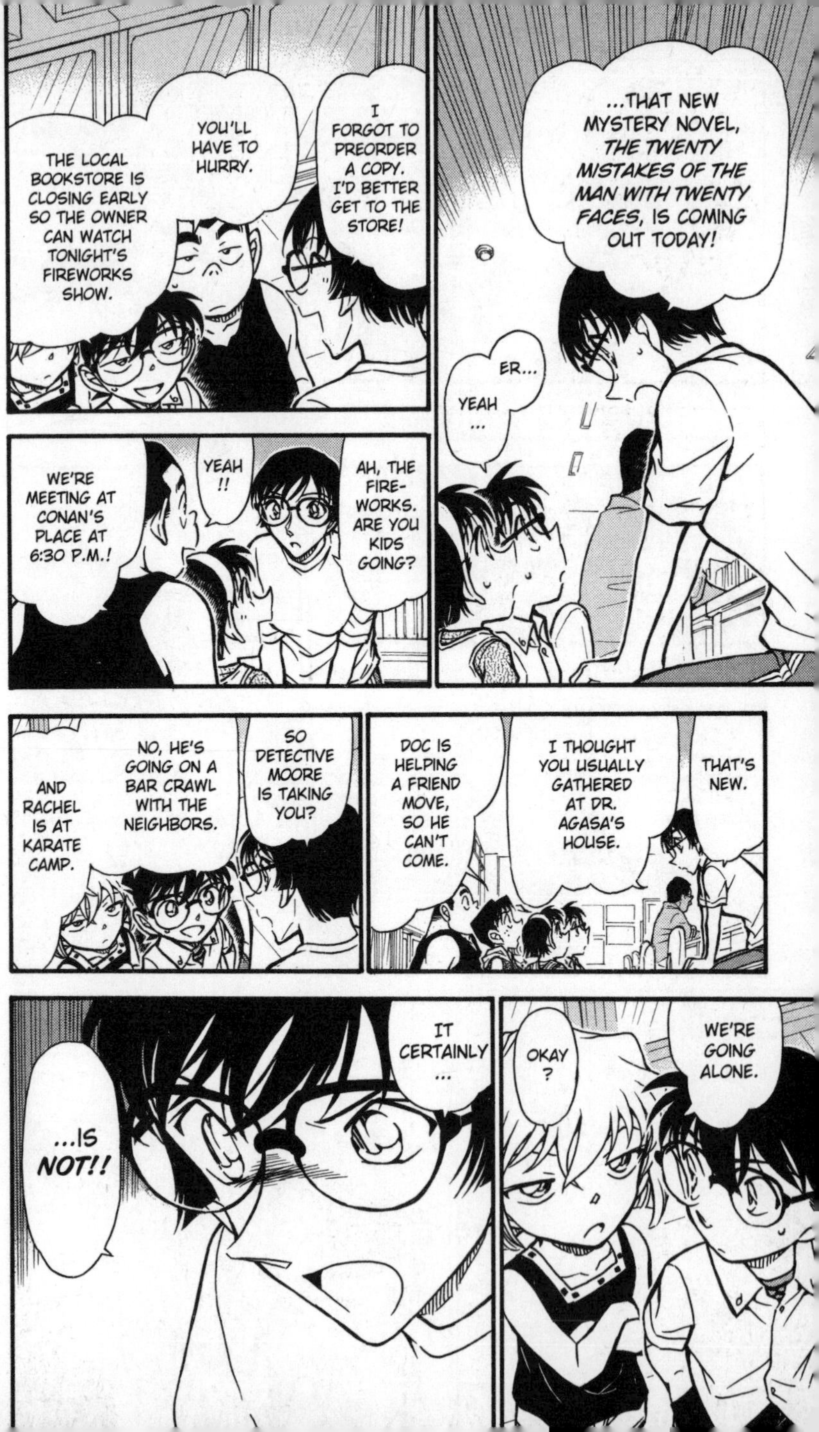
...THAT NEW MYSTERY NOVEL, *THE TWENTY MISTAKES OF THE MAN WITH TWENTY FACES*, IS COMING OUT TODAY!
ER... YEAH...
I FORGOT TO PREORDER A COPY. I'D BETTER GET TO THE STORE!
YOU'LL HAVE TO HURRY.
THE LOCAL BOOKSTORE IS CLOSING EARLY SO THE OWNER CAN WATCH TONIGHT'S FIREWORKS SHOW.
AH, THE FIRE-WORKS. ARE YOU KIDS GOING?
YEAH!!
WE'RE MEETING AT CONAN'S PLACE AT 6:30 P.M.!
THAT'S NEW.
I THOUGHT YOU USUALLY GATHERED AT DR. AGASA'S HOUSE.
DOC IS HELPING A FRIEND MOVE, SO HE CAN'T COME.
SO DETECTIVE MOORE IS TAKING YOU?
NO, HE'S GOING ON A BAR CRAWL WITH THE NEIGHBORS.
AND RACHEL IS AT KARATE CAMP.
WE'RE GOING ALONE.
OKAY?
IT CERTAINLY...
...IS **NOT!!**

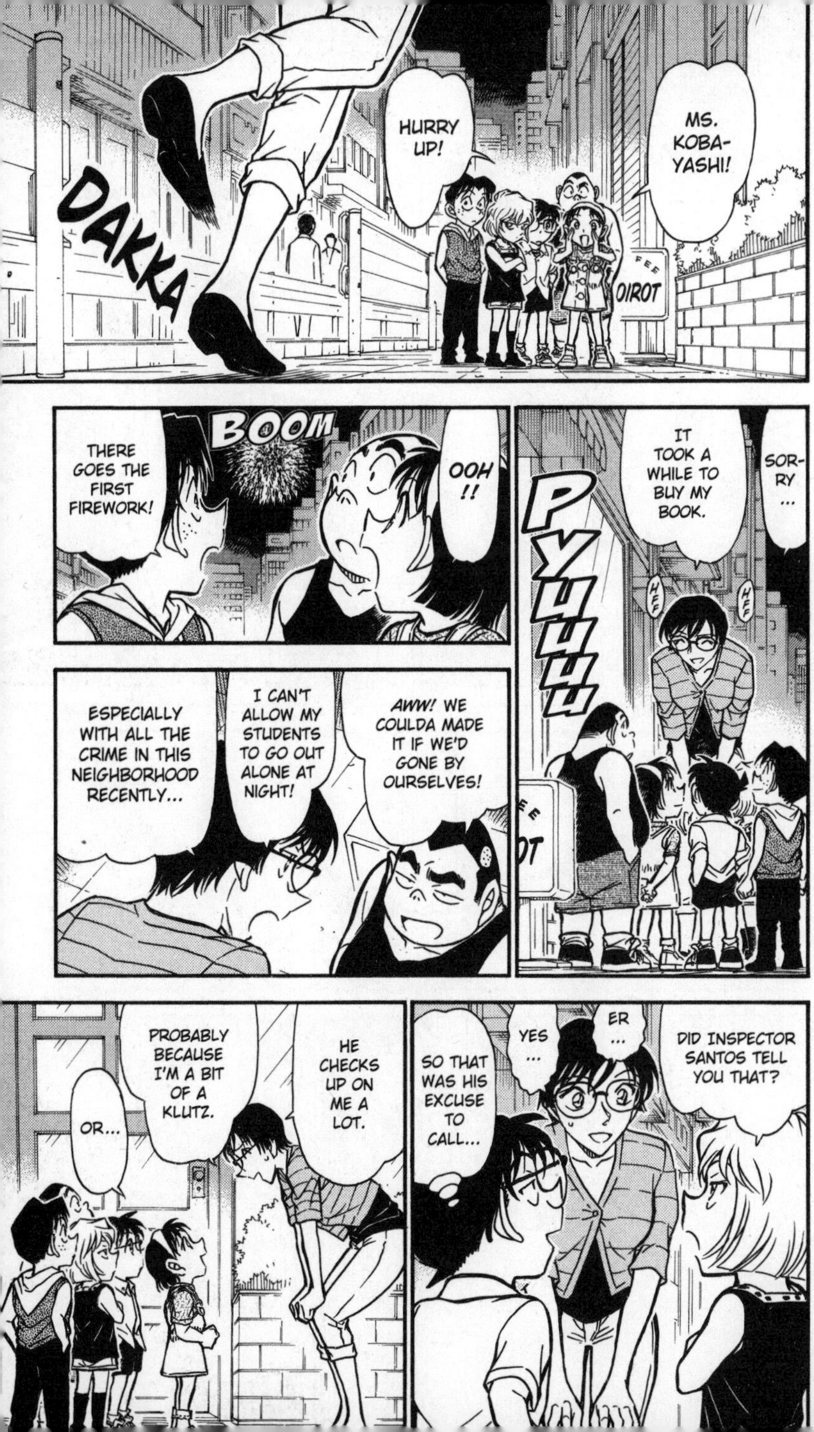
MS. KOBA-YASHI!
HURRY UP!
FEE
OIROT
DAKKA
SOR-RY...
IT TOOK A WHILE TO BUY MY BOOK.
HEF
HEF
PYUUUU
BOOM
OOH!!
THERE GOES THE FIRST FIREWORK!
AWW! WE COULDA MADE IT IF WE'D GONE BY OURSELVES!
I CAN'T ALLOW MY STUDENTS TO GO OUT ALONE AT NIGHT!
ESPECIALLY WITH ALL THE CRIME IN THIS NEIGHBORHOOD RECENTLY...
DID INSPECTOR SANTOS TELL YOU THAT?
ER...
YES...
SO THAT WAS HIS EXCUSE TO CALL...
HE CHECKS UP ON ME A LOT.
PROBABLY BECAUSE I'M A BIT OF A KLUTZ.
OR...

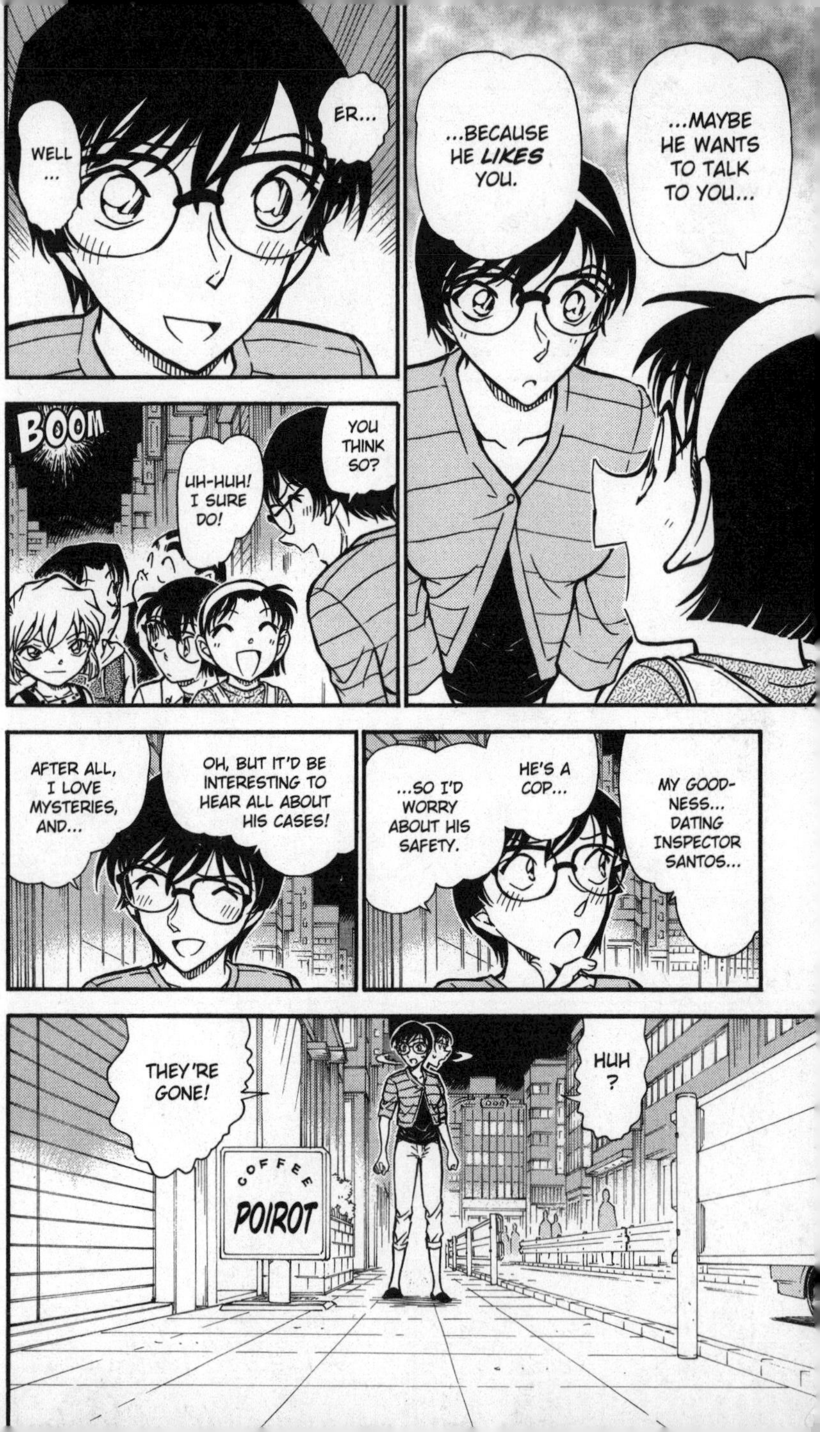
...MAYBE HE WANTS TO TALK TO YOU...
...BECAUSE HE LIKES YOU.
ER...
WELL ...
BOOM
YOU THINK SO?
UH-HUH! I SURE DO!
MY GOOD-NESS... DATING INSPECTOR SANTOS...
HE'S A COP...
...SO I'D WORRY ABOUT HIS SAFETY.
OH, BUT IT'D BE INTERESTING TO HEAR ALL ABOUT HIS CASES!
AFTER ALL, I LOVE MYSTERIES, AND...
HUH ?
THEY'RE GONE!
COFFEE POIROT

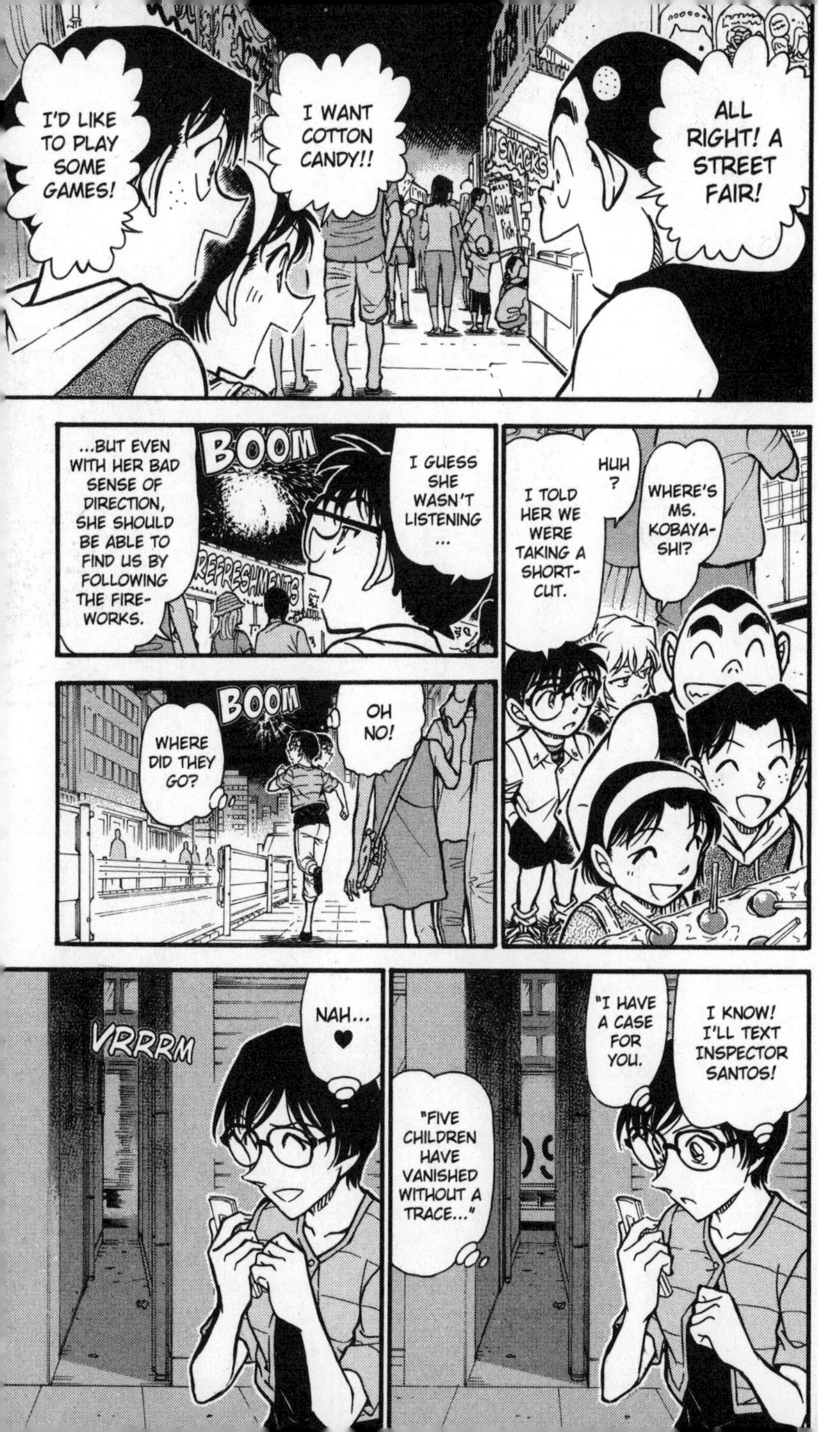
ALL RIGHT! A STREET FAIR!
SNACKS
Gold Fish
I WANT COTTON CANDY!!
I'D LIKE TO PLAY SOME GAMES!
WHERE'S MS. KOBAYASHI?
HUH?
I TOLD HER WE WERE TAKING A SHORT-CUT.
I GUESS SHE WASN'T LISTENING ...
BOOM
...BUT EVEN WITH HER BAD SENSE OF DIRECTION, SHE SHOULD BE ABLE TO FIND US BY FOLLOWING THE FIRE-WORKS.
REFRESHMENTS
OH NO!
BOOM
WHERE DID THEY GO?
I KNOW! I'LL TEXT INSPECTOR SANTOS!
"I HAVE A CASE FOR YOU.
"FIVE CHILDREN HAVE VANISHED WITHOUT A TRACE..."
NAH... ♥
VRRRM

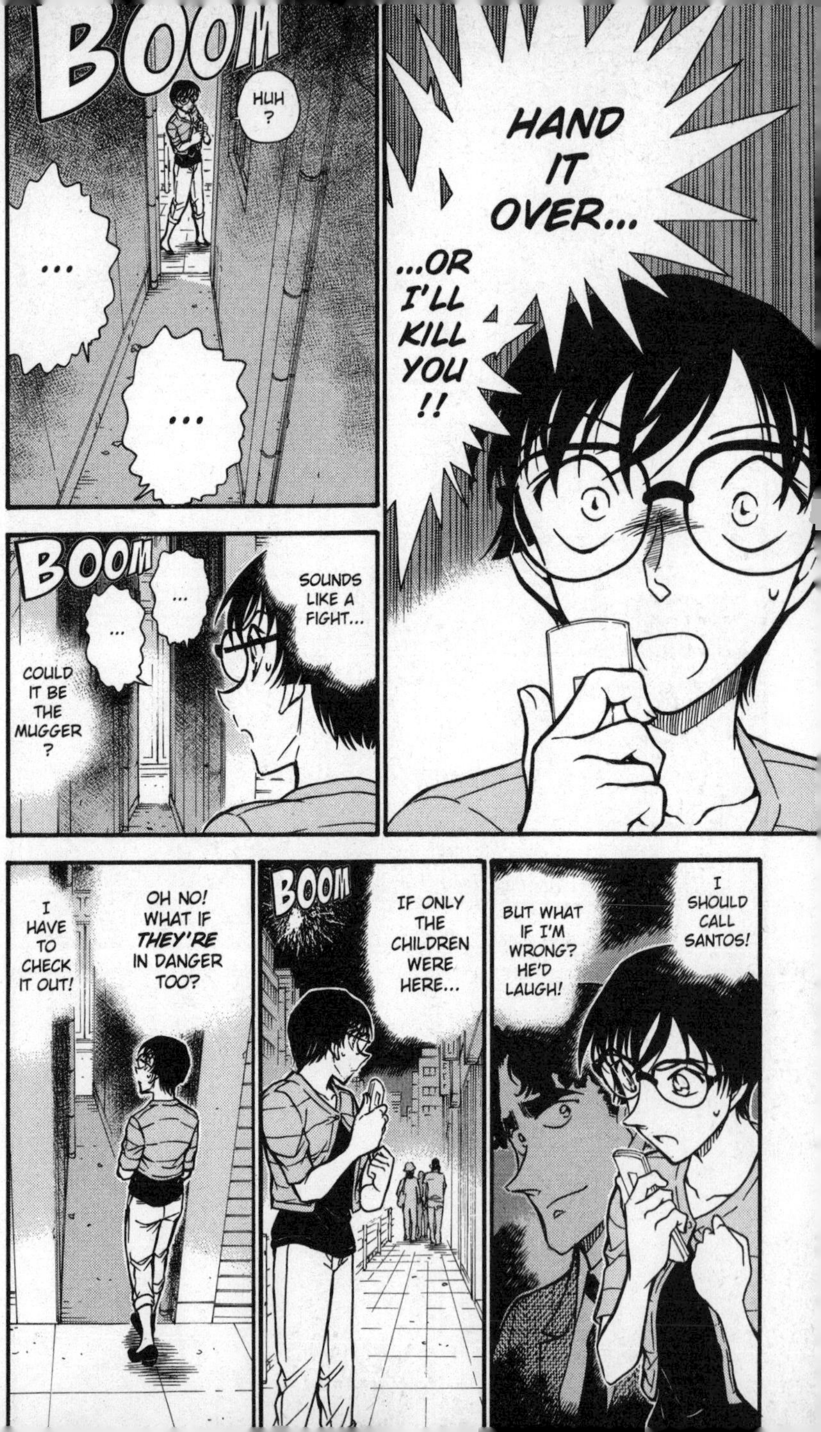
HAND IT OVER...
...OR I'LL KILL YOU!!
BOOM
HUH?
...
...
BOOM
SOUNDS LIKE A FIGHT...
...
...
COULD IT BE THE MUGGER?
I SHOULD CALL SANTOS!
BUT WHAT IF I'M WRONG? HE'D LAUGH!
BOOM
IF ONLY THE CHILDREN WERE HERE...
OH NO! WHAT IF *THEY'RE* IN DANGER TOO?
I HAVE TO CHECK IT OUT!

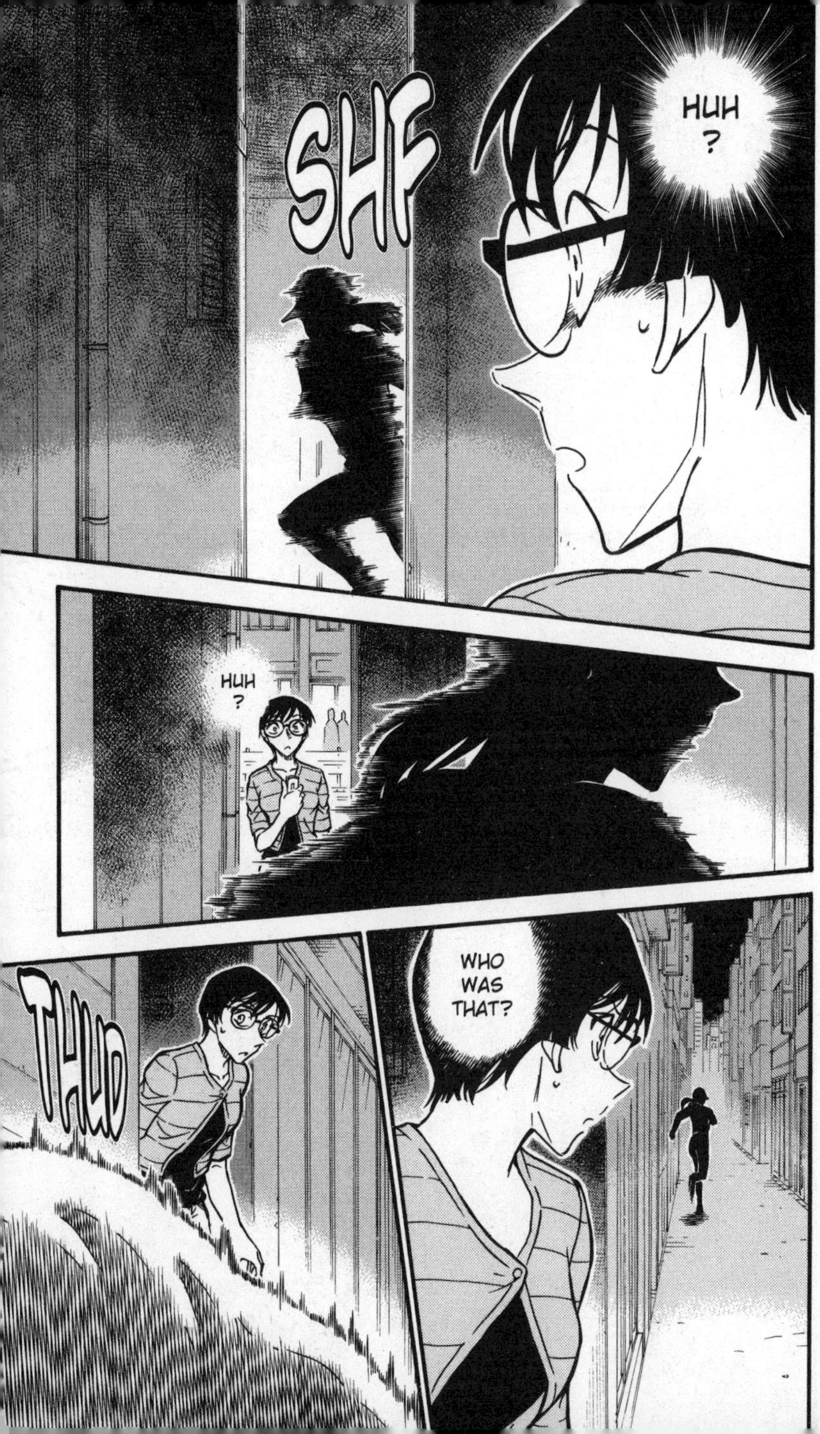
HUH?
SHF
HUH?
WHO WAS THAT?
THUD

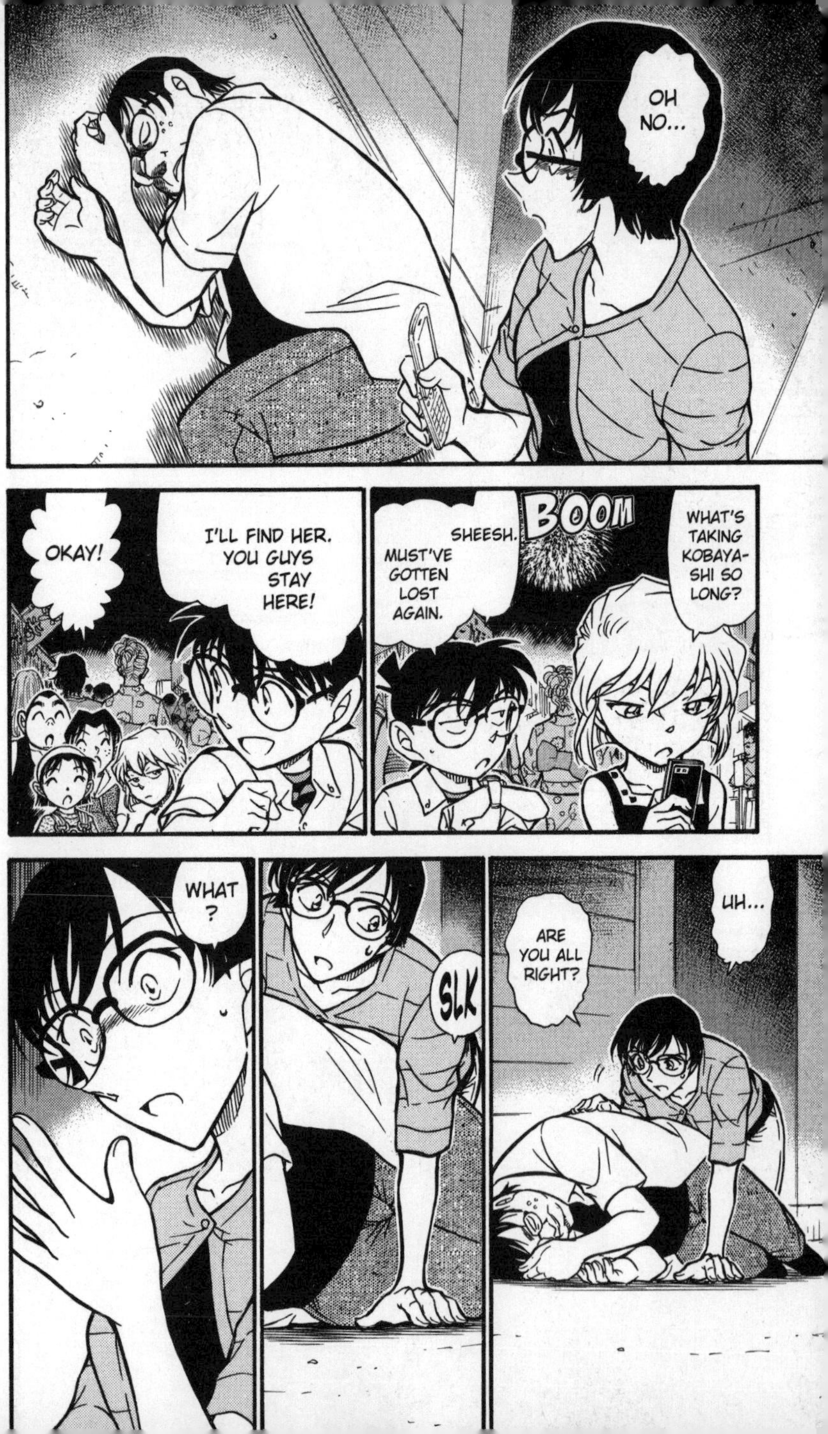
OH NO...
WHAT'S TAKING KOBAYASHI SO LONG?
BOOM
SHEESH. MUST'VE GOTTEN LOST AGAIN.
I'LL FIND HER. YOU GUYS STAY HERE!
OKAY!
UH...
ARE YOU ALL RIGHT?
SLK
WHAT?

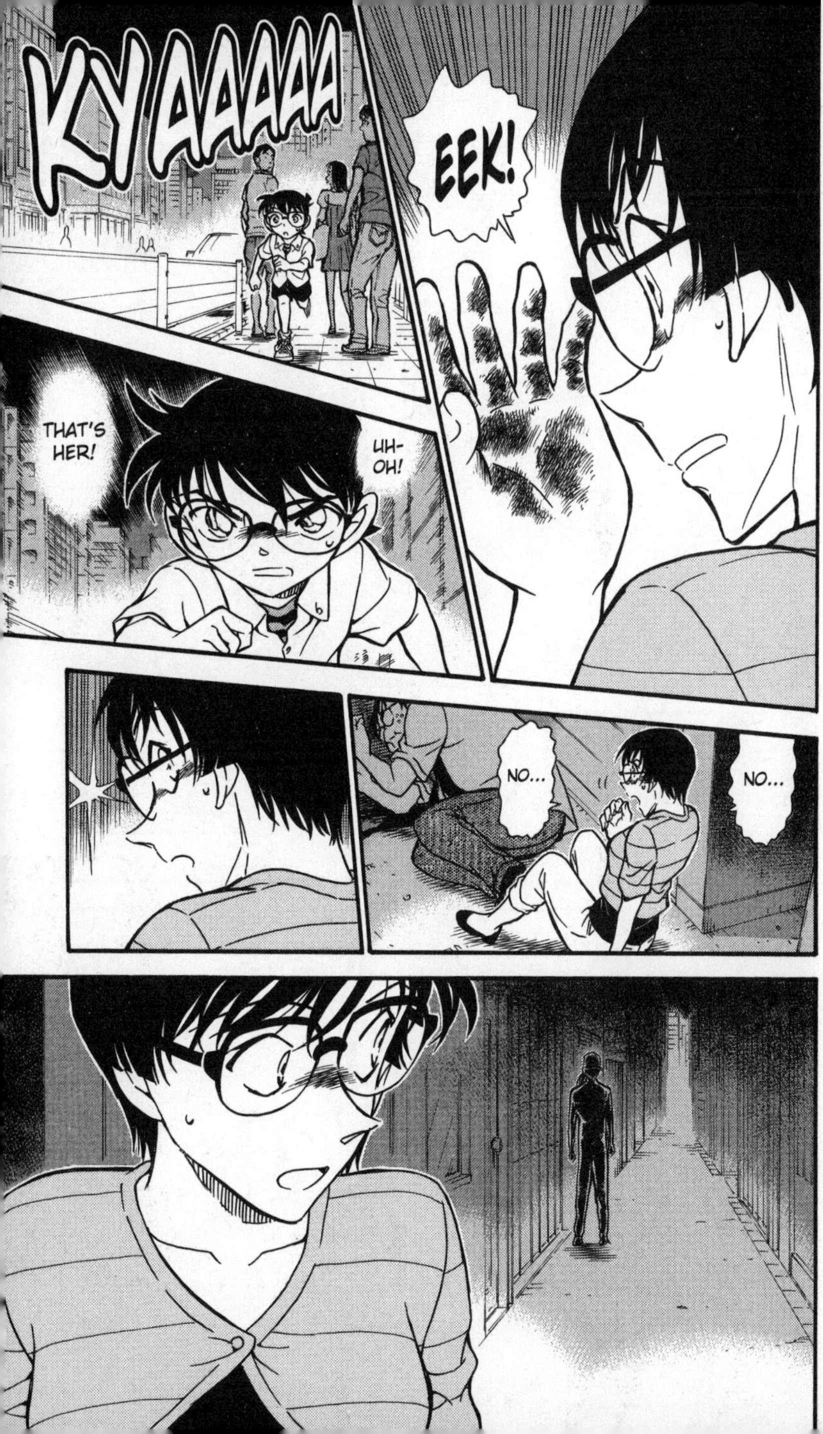
EEK!
KYAAAAA
UH-OH!
THAT'S HER!
NO...
NO...

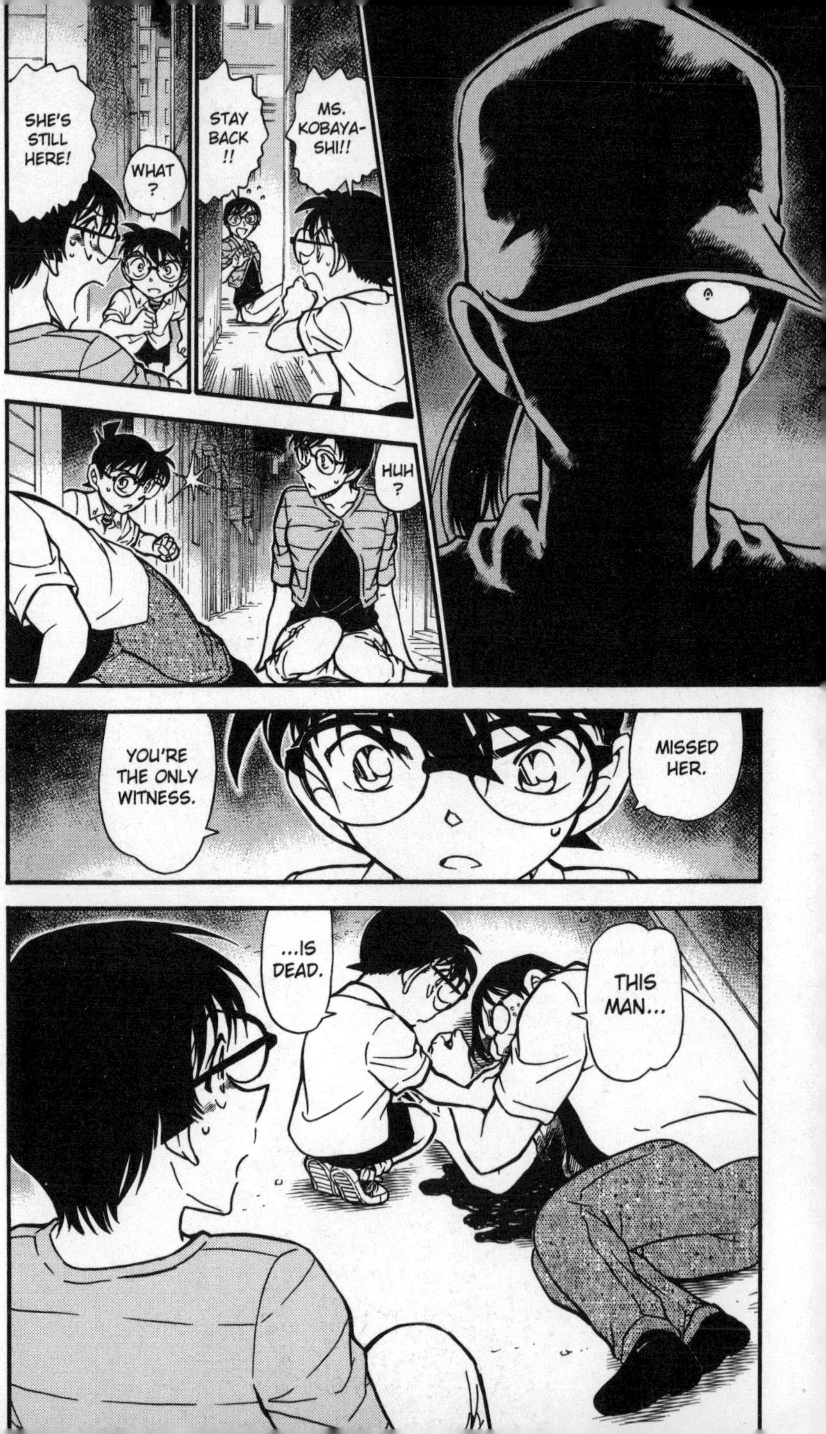
MS. KOBAYA-SHI!!
STAY BACK !!
SHE'S STILL HERE!
WHAT ?
HUH ?
MISSED HER.
YOU'RE THE ONLY WITNESS.
THIS MAN...
...IS DEAD.

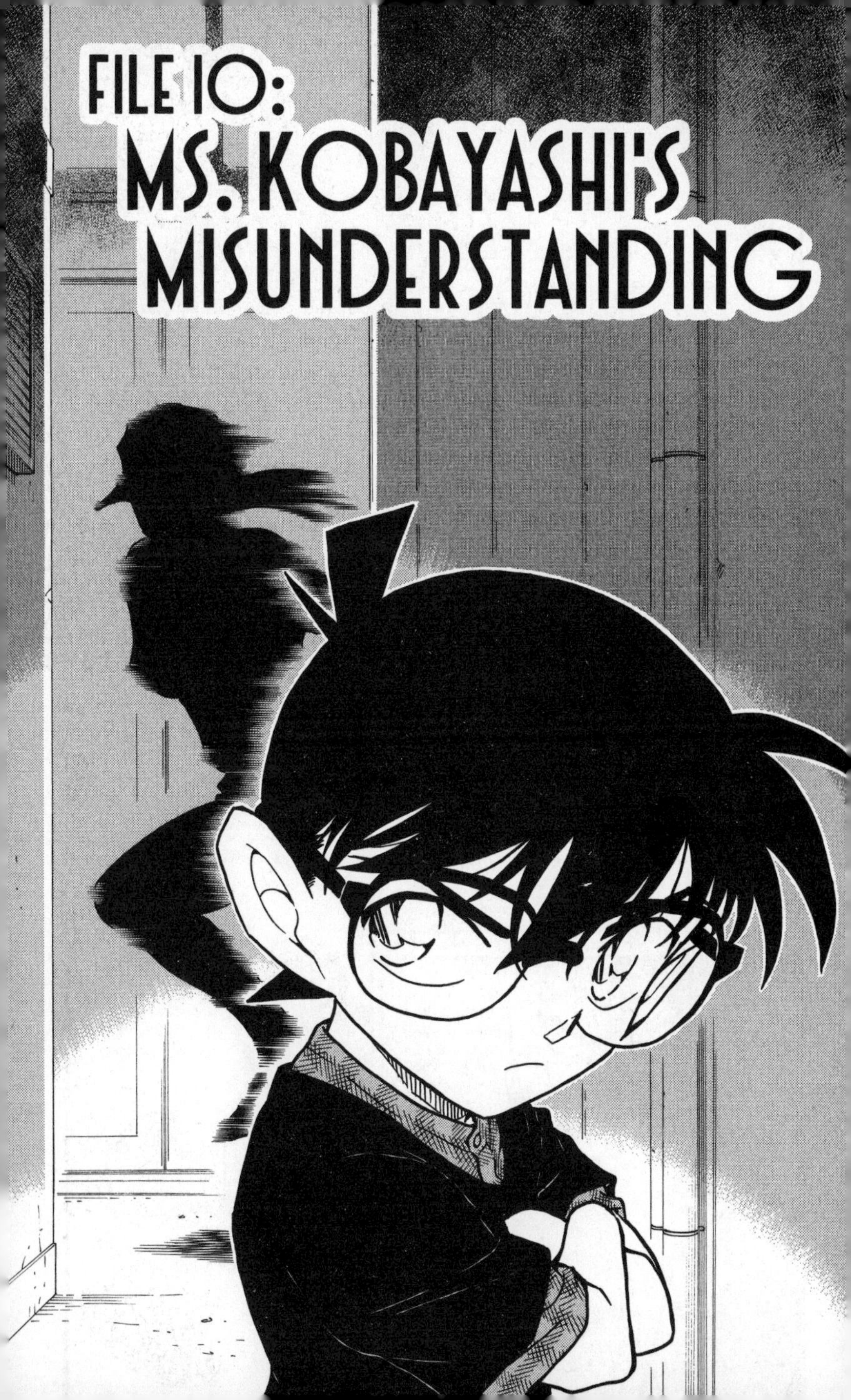
FILE 10:
MS. KOBAYASHI'S MISUNDERSTANDING

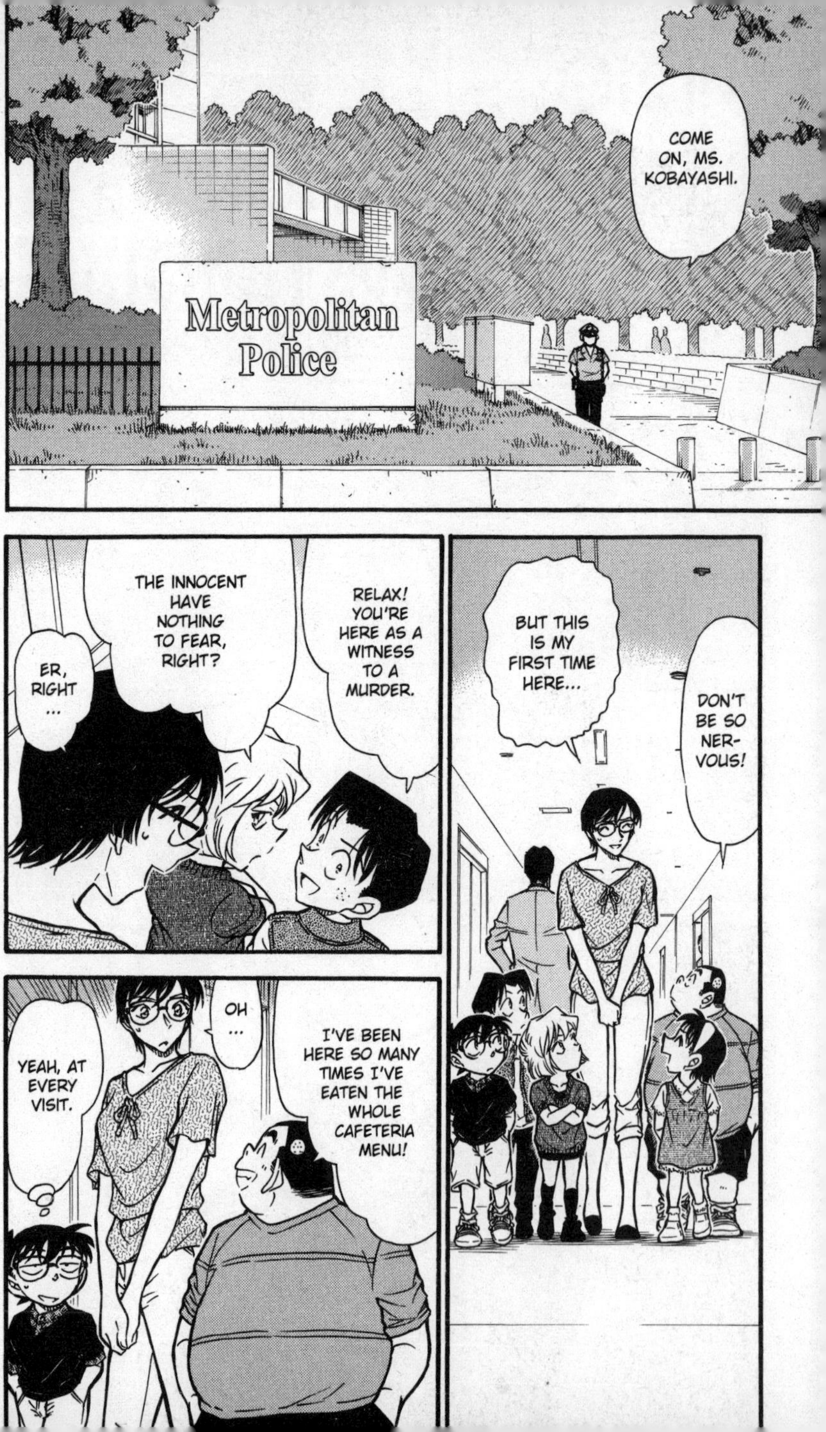
Metropolitan Police
COME ON, MS. KOBAYASHI.
BUT THIS IS MY FIRST TIME HERE...
DON'T BE SO NER-VOUS!
RELAX! YOU'RE HERE AS A WITNESS TO A MURDER.
THE INNOCENT HAVE NOTHING TO FEAR, RIGHT?
ER, RIGHT...
I'VE BEEN HERE SO MANY TIMES I'VE EATEN THE WHOLE CAFETERIA MENU!
OH...
YEAH, AT EVERY VISIT.

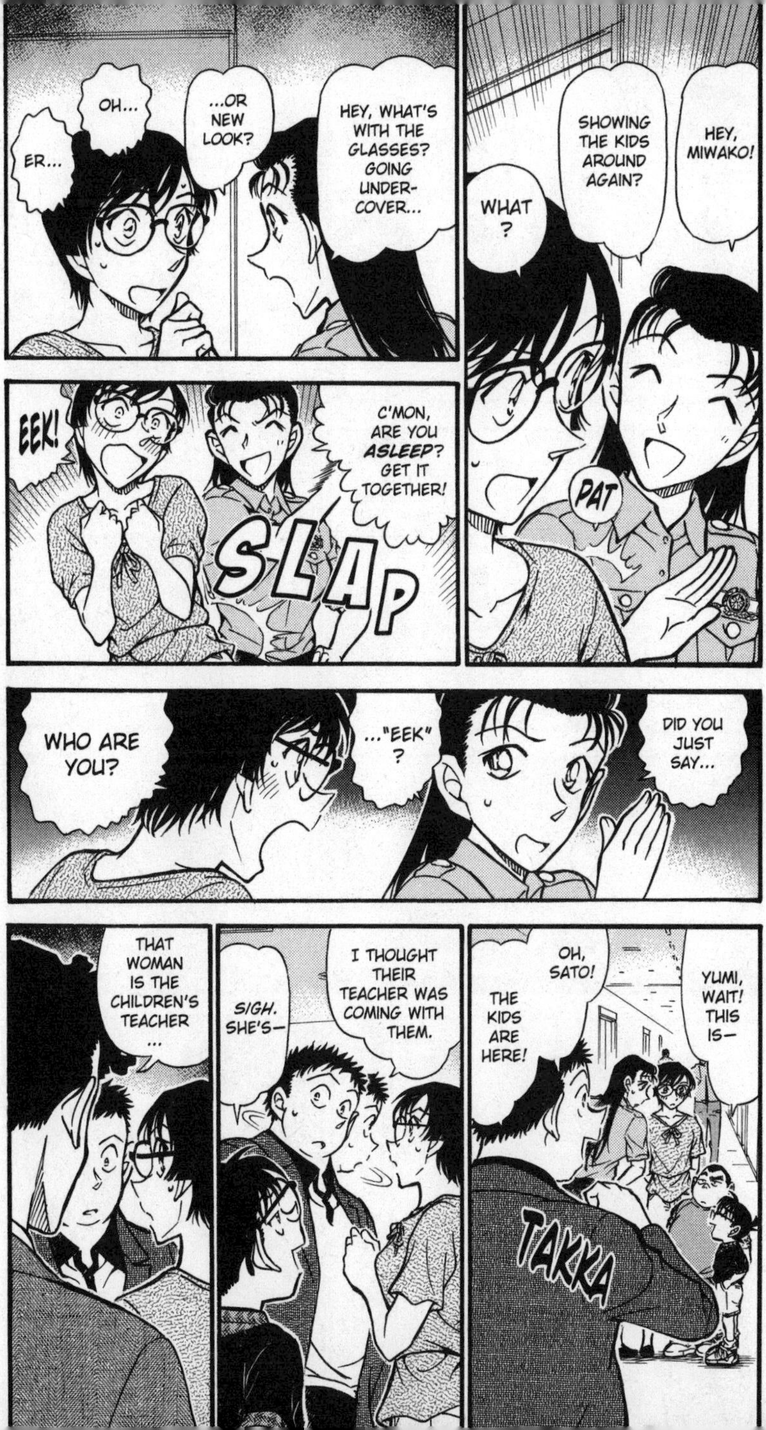
HEY, MIWAKO!
SHOWING THE KIDS AROUND AGAIN?
WHAT ?
PAT
HEY, WHAT'S WITH THE GLASSES? GOING UNDER-COVER...
...OR NEW LOOK?
OH...
ER...
C'MON, ARE YOU *ASLEEP*? GET IT TOGETHER!
SLAP
EEK!
DID YOU JUST SAY...
..."EEK" ?
WHO ARE YOU?
YUMI, WAIT! THIS IS—
OH, SATO!
THE KIDS ARE HERE!
TAKKA
I THOUGHT THEIR TEACHER WAS COMING WITH THEM.
SIGH. SHE'S—
THAT WOMAN IS THE CHILDREN'S TEACHER ...

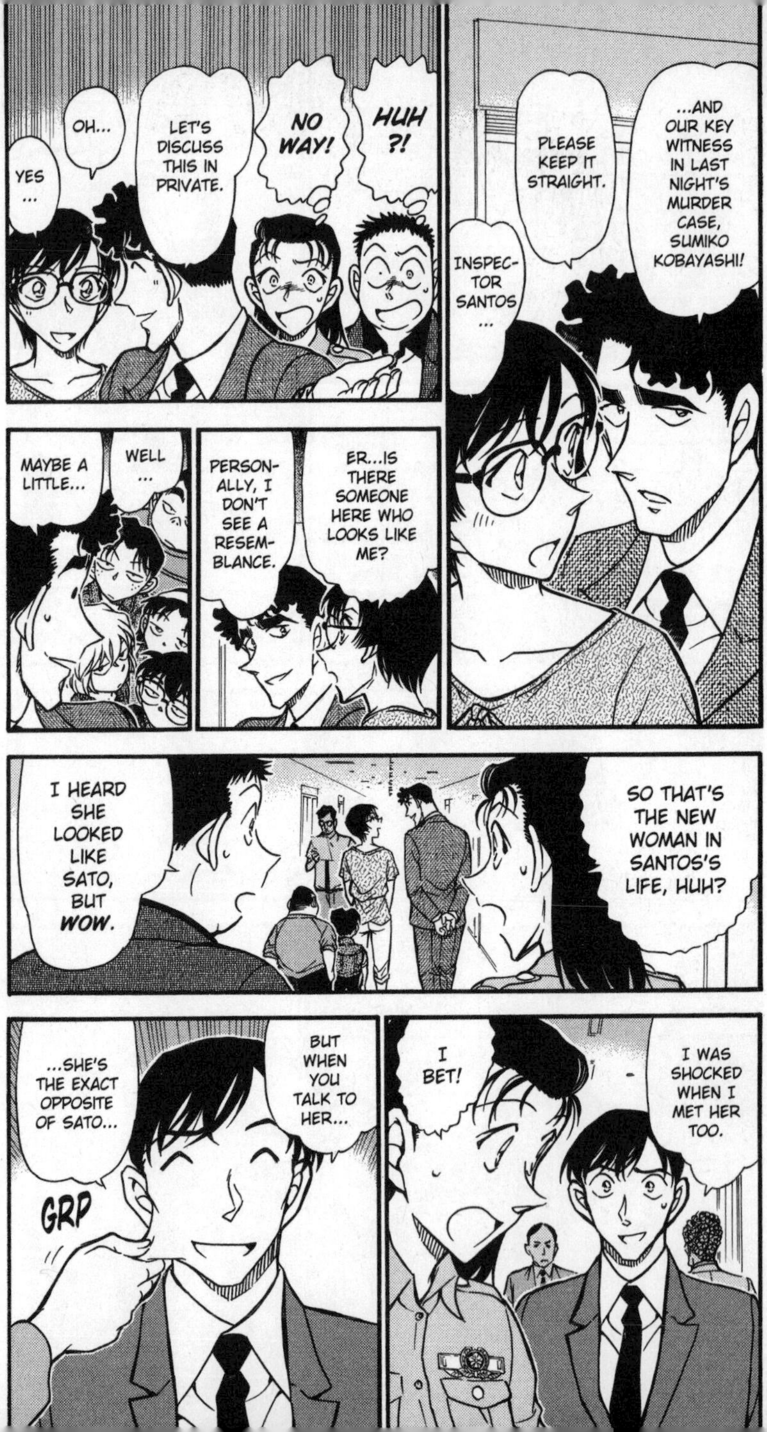

...AND OUR KEY WITNESS IN LAST NIGHT'S MURDER CASE, SUMIKO KOBAYASHI!
PLEASE KEEP IT STRAIGHT.
INSPECTOR SANTOS...
HUH?!
NO WAY!
LET'S DISCUSS THIS IN PRIVATE.
OH...
YES...
ER...IS THERE SOMEONE HERE WHO LOOKS LIKE ME?
PERSONALLY, I DON'T SEE A RESEMBLANCE.
WELL...
MAYBE A LITTLE...
SO THAT'S THE NEW WOMAN IN SANTOS'S LIFE, HUH?
I HEARD SHE LOOKED LIKE SATO, BUT WOW.
I WAS SHOCKED WHEN I MET HER TOO.
I BET!
BUT WHEN YOU TALK TO HER...
...SHE'S THE EXACT OPPOSITE OF SATO...
GRP

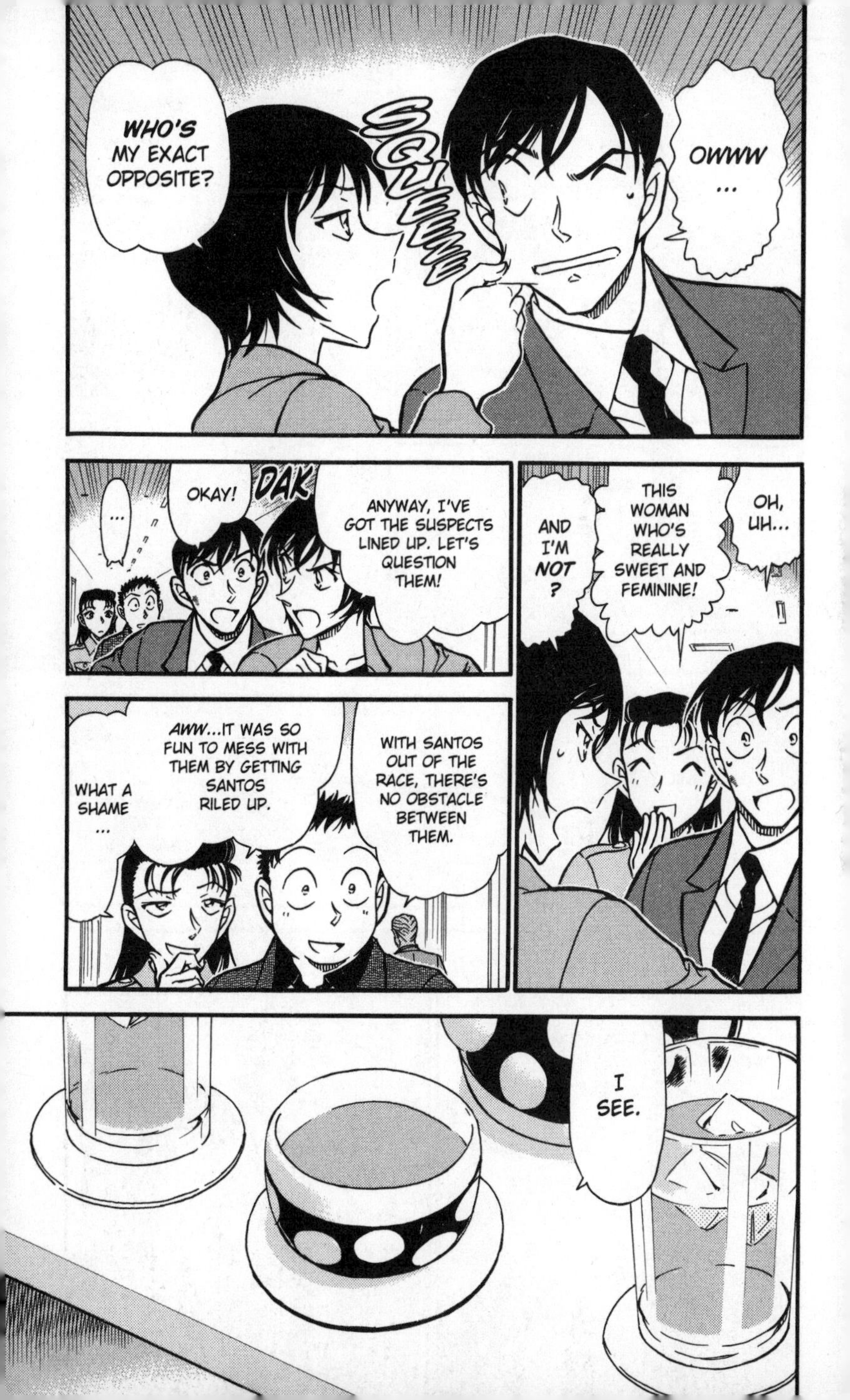
OWWW ...
WHO'S MY EXACT OPPOSITE?
OH, UH...
THIS WOMAN WHO'S REALLY SWEET AND FEMININE!
AND I'M NOT?
ANYWAY, I'VE GOT THE SUSPECTS LINED UP. LET'S QUESTION THEM!
DAK
OKAY!
...
WITH SANTOS OUT OF THE RACE, THERE'S NO OBSTACLE BETWEEN THEM.
AWW...IT WAS SO FUN TO MESS WITH THEM BY GETTING SANTOS RILED UP.
WHAT A SHAME ...
I SEE.

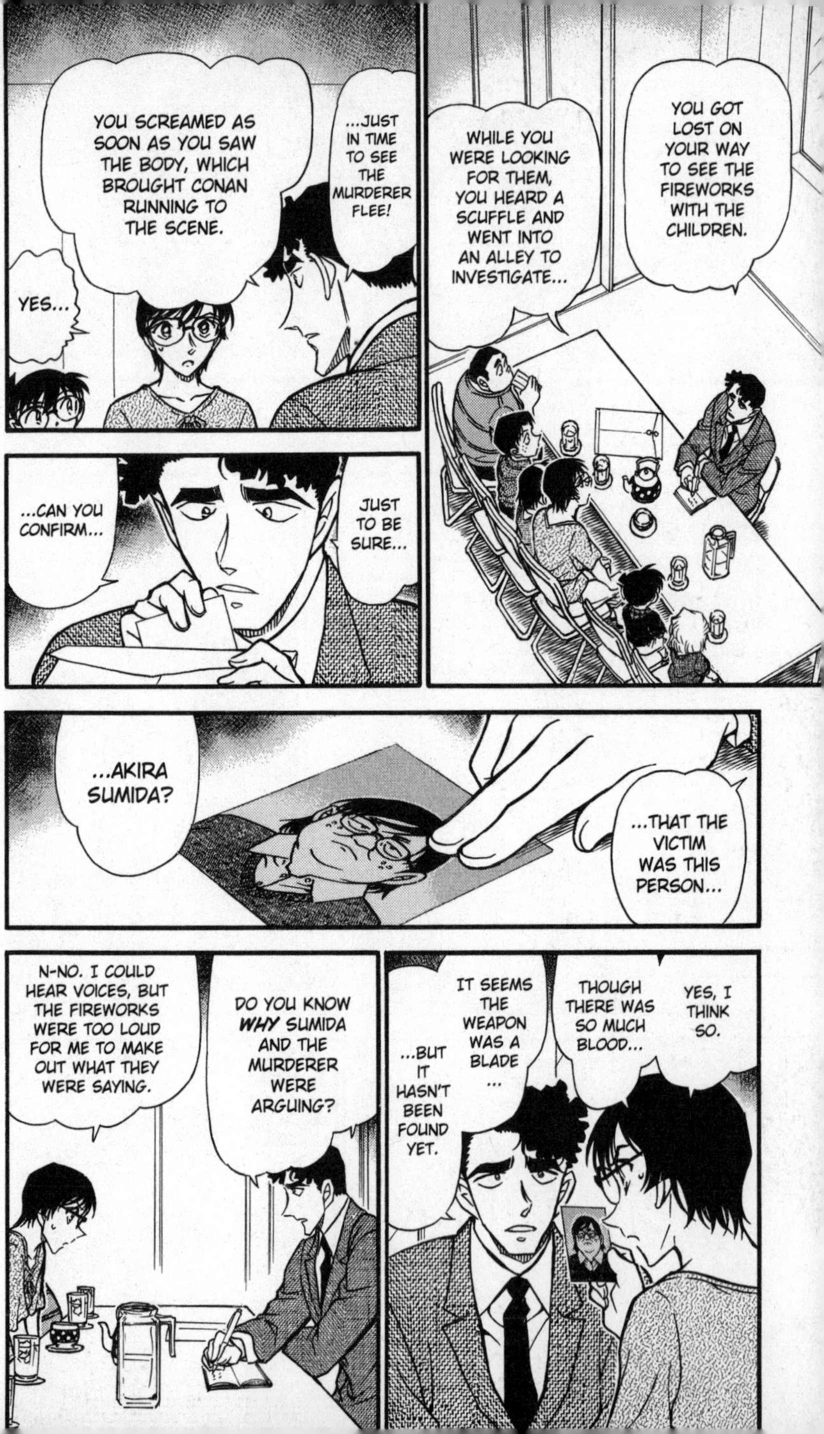
YOU GOT LOST ON YOUR WAY TO SEE THE FIREWORKS WITH THE CHILDREN.
WHILE YOU WERE LOOKING FOR THEM, YOU HEARD A SCUFFLE AND WENT INTO AN ALLEY TO INVESTIGATE...
...JUST IN TIME TO SEE THE MURDERER FLEE!
YOU SCREAMED AS SOON AS YOU SAW THE BODY, WHICH BROUGHT CONAN RUNNING TO THE SCENE.
YES...
JUST TO BE SURE...
...CAN YOU CONFIRM...
...THAT THE VICTIM WAS THIS PERSON...
...AKIRA SUMIDA?
YES, I THINK SO.
THOUGH THERE WAS SO MUCH BLOOD...
IT SEEMS THE WEAPON WAS A BLADE...
...BUT IT HASN'T BEEN FOUND YET.
DO YOU KNOW *WHY* SUMIDA AND THE MURDERER WERE ARGUING?
N-NO. I COULD HEAR VOICES, BUT THE FIREWORKS WERE TOO LOUD FOR ME TO MAKE OUT WHAT THEY WERE SAYING.

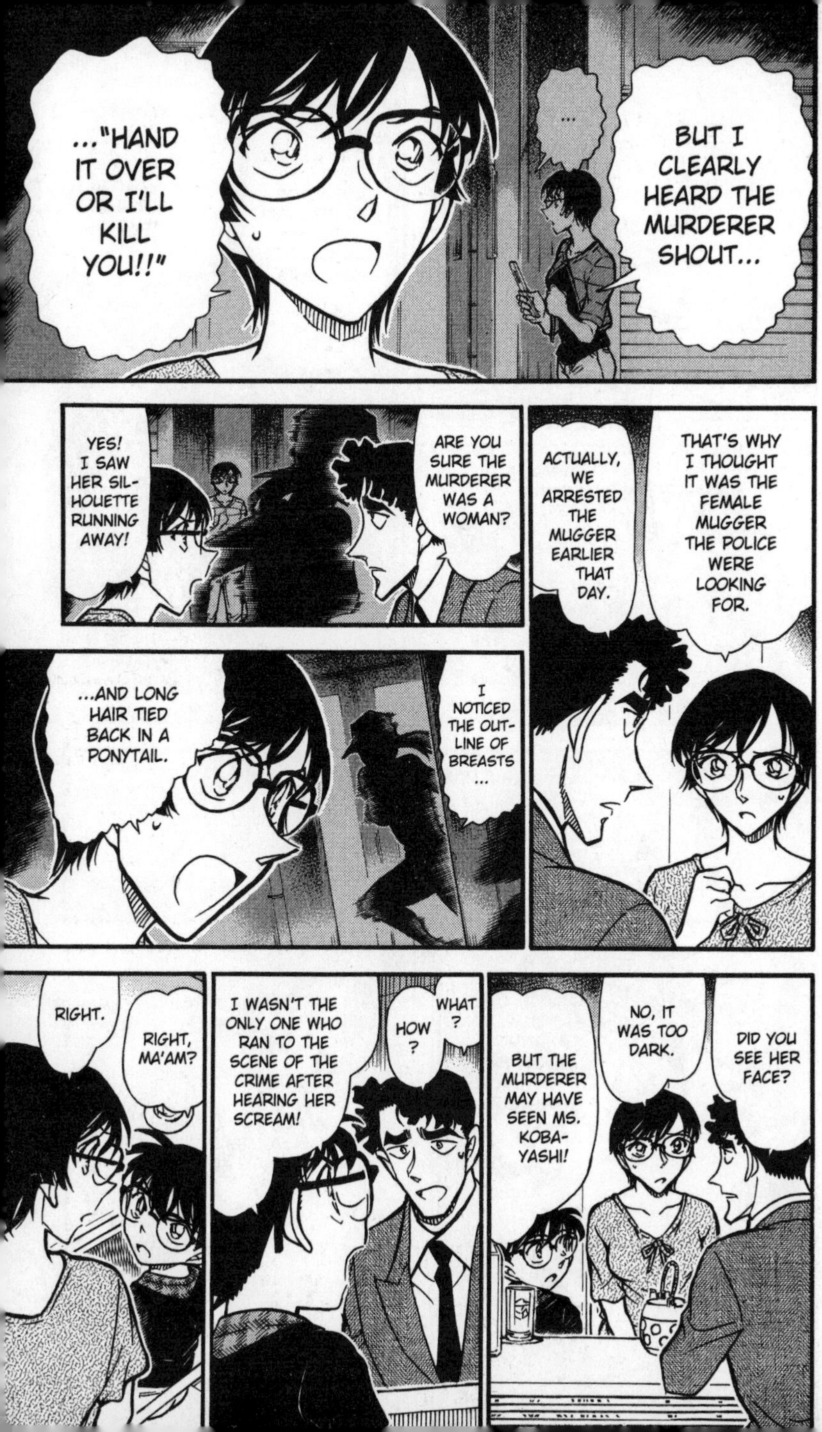

BUT I CLEARLY HEARD THE MURDERER SHOUT...
...
..."HAND IT OVER OR I'LL KILL YOU!!"
ARE YOU SURE THE MURDERER WAS A WOMAN?
YES! I SAW HER SIL-HOUETTE RUNNING AWAY!
I NOTICED THE OUT-LINE OF BREASTS...
...AND LONG HAIR TIED BACK IN A PONYTAIL.
THAT'S WHY I THOUGHT IT WAS THE FEMALE MUGGER THE POLICE WERE LOOKING FOR.
ACTUALLY, WE ARRESTED THE MUGGER EARLIER THAT DAY.
DID YOU SEE HER FACE?
NO, IT WAS TOO DARK.
BUT THE MURDERER MAY HAVE SEEN MS. KOBA-YASHI!
WHAT?
HOW?
I WASN'T THE ONLY ONE WHO RAN TO THE SCENE OF THE CRIME AFTER HEARING HER SCREAM!
RIGHT, MA'AM?
RIGHT.

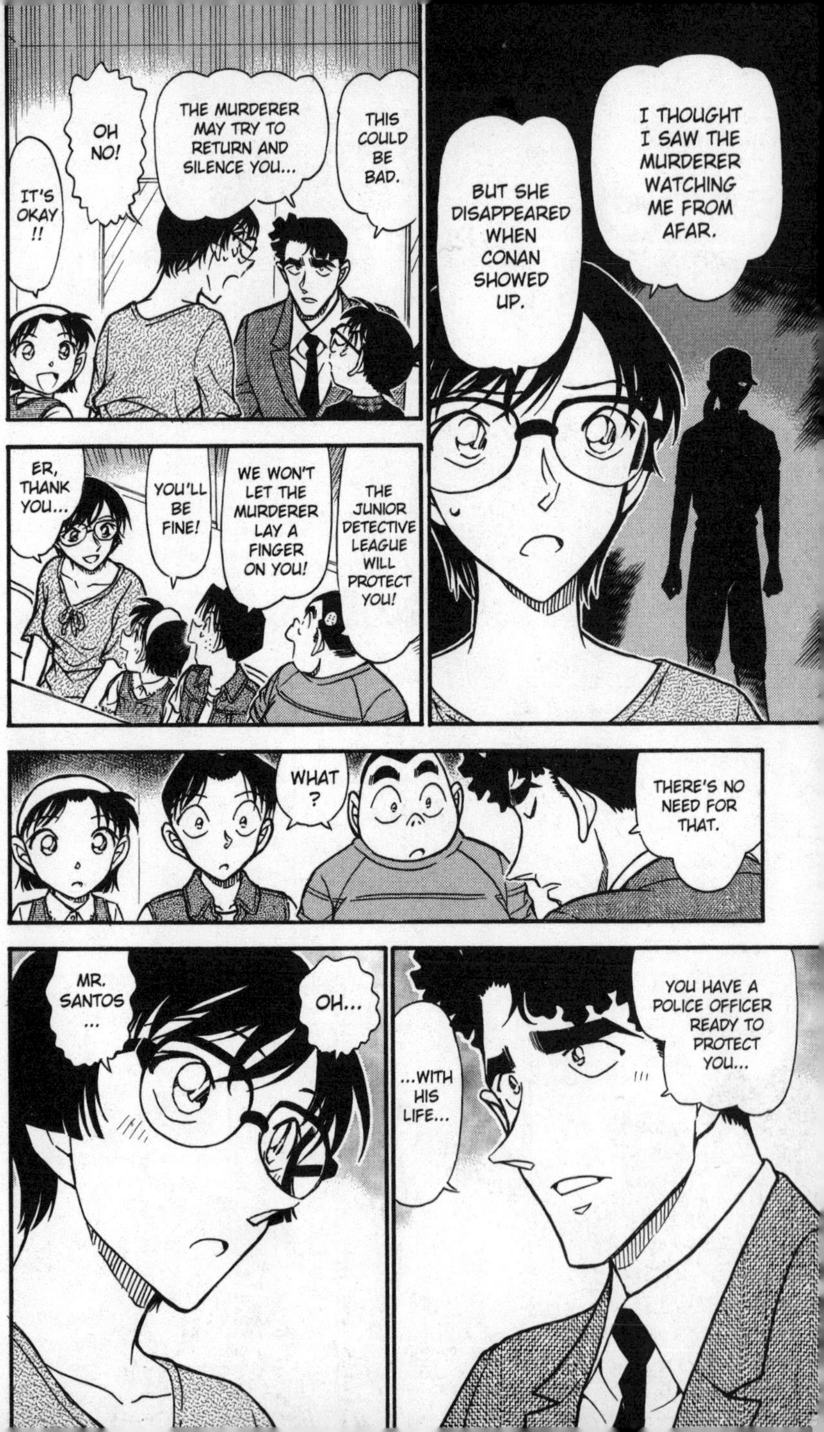
I THOUGHT I SAW THE MURDERER WATCHING ME FROM AFAR.
BUT SHE DISAPPEARED WHEN CONAN SHOWED UP.
THIS COULD BE BAD.
THE MURDERER MAY TRY TO RETURN AND SILENCE YOU...
OH NO!
IT'S OKAY !!
THE JUNIOR DETECTIVE LEAGUE WILL PROTECT YOU!
WE WON'T LET THE MURDERER LAY A FINGER ON YOU!
YOU'LL BE FINE!
ER, THANK YOU...
THERE'S NO NEED FOR THAT.
WHAT ?
YOU HAVE A POLICE OFFICER READY TO PROTECT YOU...
...WITH HIS LIFE...
OH...
MR. SANTOS ...

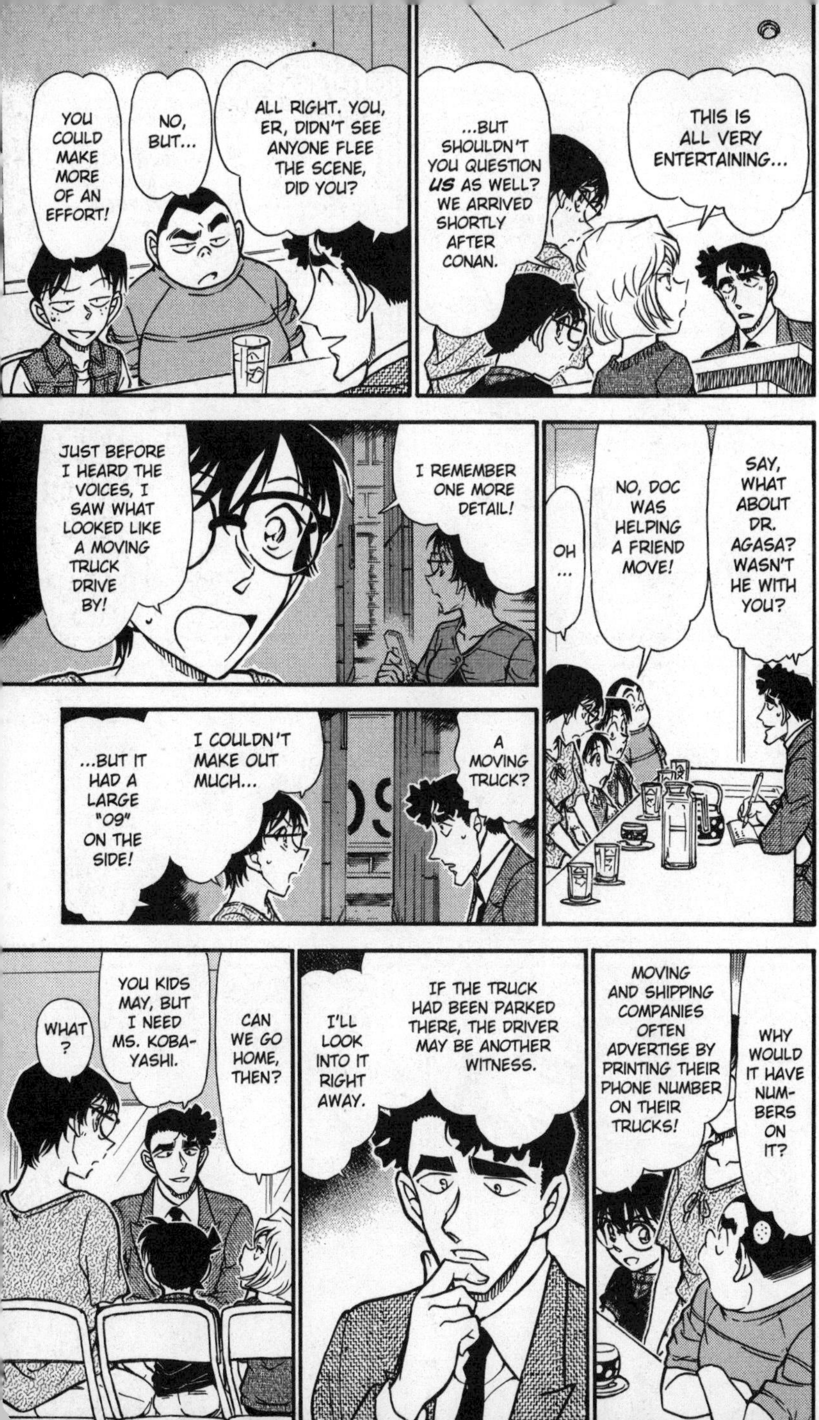
THIS IS ALL VERY ENTERTAINING...
...BUT SHOULDN'T YOU QUESTION *US* AS WELL? WE ARRIVED SHORTLY AFTER CONAN.
ALL RIGHT. YOU, ER, DIDN'T SEE ANYONE FLEE THE SCENE, DID YOU?
NO, BUT...
YOU COULD MAKE MORE OF AN EFFORT!
SAY, WHAT ABOUT DR. AGASA? WASN'T HE WITH YOU?
NO, DOC WAS HELPING A FRIEND MOVE!
OH...
I REMEMBER ONE MORE DETAIL!
JUST BEFORE I HEARD THE VOICES, I SAW WHAT LOOKED LIKE A MOVING TRUCK DRIVE BY!
A MOVING TRUCK?
I COULDN'T MAKE OUT MUCH...
...BUT IT HAD A LARGE "09" ON THE SIDE!
WHY WOULD IT HAVE NUMBERS ON IT?
MOVING AND SHIPPING COMPANIES OFTEN ADVERTISE BY PRINTING THEIR PHONE NUMBER ON THEIR TRUCKS!
IF THE TRUCK HAD BEEN PARKED THERE, THE DRIVER MAY BE ANOTHER WITNESS.
I'LL LOOK INTO IT RIGHT AWAY.
CAN WE GO HOME, THEN?
YOU KIDS MAY, BUT I NEED MS. KOBAYASHI.
WHAT?

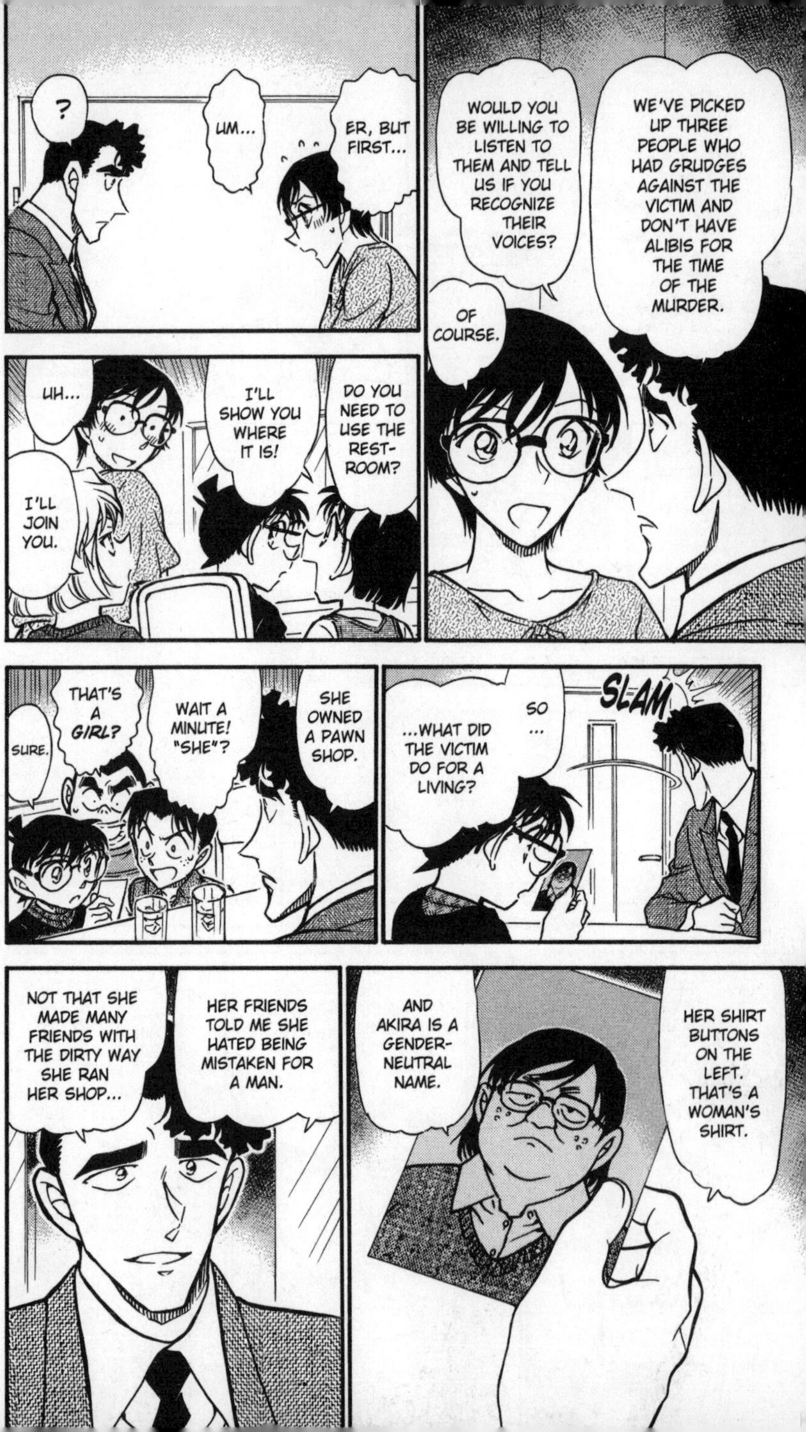
WE'VE PICKED UP THREE PEOPLE WHO HAD GRUDGES AGAINST THE VICTIM AND DON'T HAVE ALIBIS FOR THE TIME OF THE MURDER.
WOULD YOU BE WILLING TO LISTEN TO THEM AND TELL US IF YOU RECOGNIZE THEIR VOICES?
OF COURSE.
ER, BUT FIRST...
UM...
?
DO YOU NEED TO USE THE REST-ROOM?
I'LL SHOW YOU WHERE IT IS!
UH...
I'LL JOIN YOU.
SLAM
SO ...
...WHAT DID THE VICTIM DO FOR A LIVING?
SHE OWNED A PAWN SHOP.
WAIT A MINUTE! "SHE"?
THAT'S A *GIRL*?
SURE.
HER SHIRT BUTTONS ON THE LEFT. THAT'S A WOMAN'S SHIRT.
AND AKIRA IS A GENDER-NEUTRAL NAME.
HER FRIENDS TOLD ME SHE HATED BEING MISTAKEN FOR A MAN.
NOT THAT SHE MADE MANY FRIENDS WITH THE DIRTY WAY SHE RAN HER SHOP...

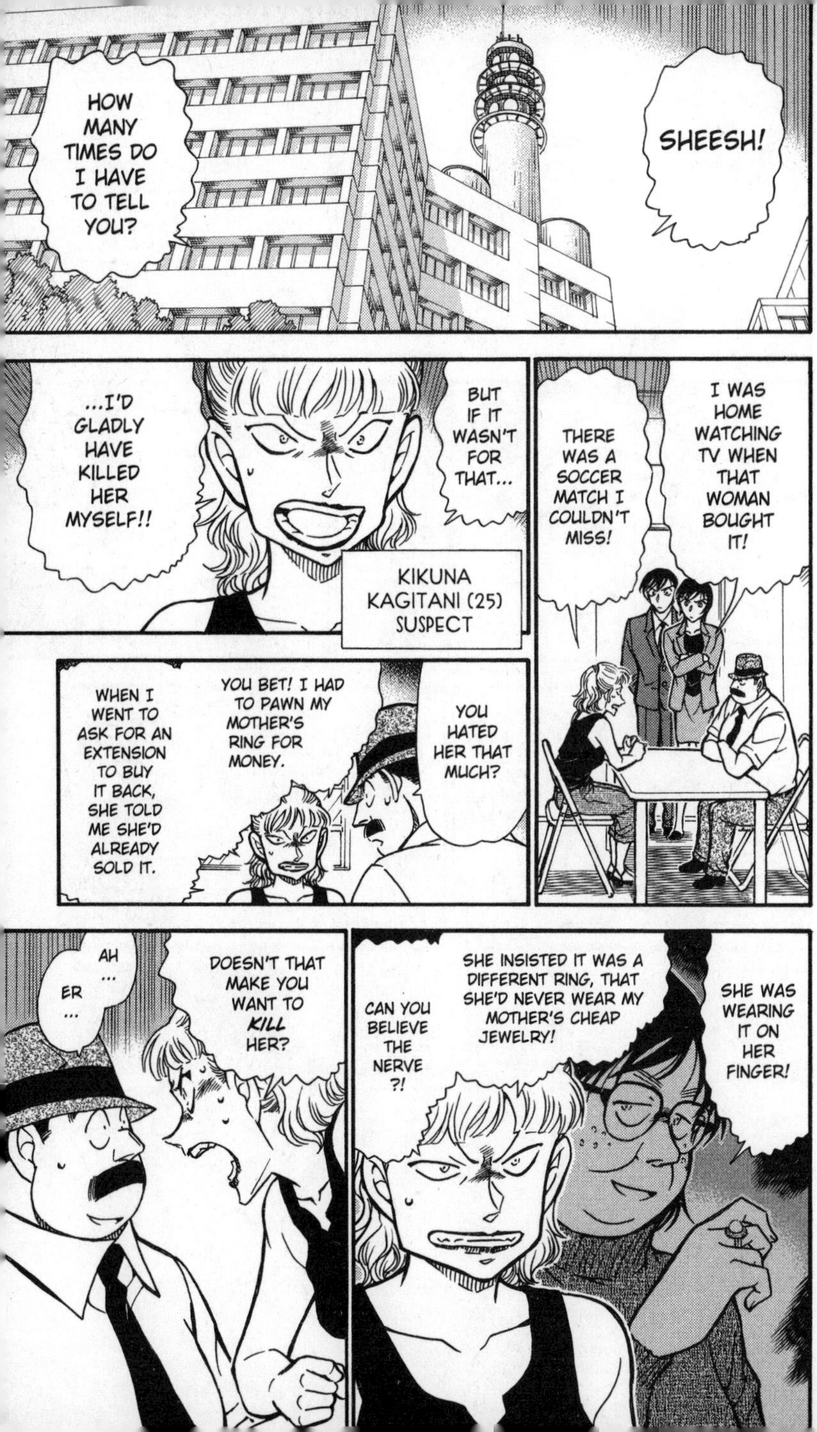
SHEESH!
HOW MANY TIMES DO I HAVE TO TELL YOU?
I WAS HOME WATCHING TV WHEN THAT WOMAN BOUGHT IT!
THERE WAS A SOCCER MATCH I COULDN'T MISS!
BUT IF IT WASN'T FOR THAT...
...I'D GLADLY HAVE KILLED HER MYSELF!!
KIKUNA KAGITANI (25) SUSPECT
YOU HATED HER THAT MUCH?
YOU BET! I HAD TO PAWN MY MOTHER'S RING FOR MONEY.
WHEN I WENT TO ASK FOR AN EXTENSION TO BUY IT BACK, SHE TOLD ME SHE'D ALREADY SOLD IT.
SHE WAS WEARING IT ON HER FINGER!
SHE INSISTED IT WAS A DIFFERENT RING, THAT SHE'D NEVER WEAR MY MOTHER'S CHEAP JEWELRY!
CAN YOU BELIEVE THE NERVE?!
DOESN'T THAT MAKE YOU WANT TO *KILL* HER?
AH ...
ER ...

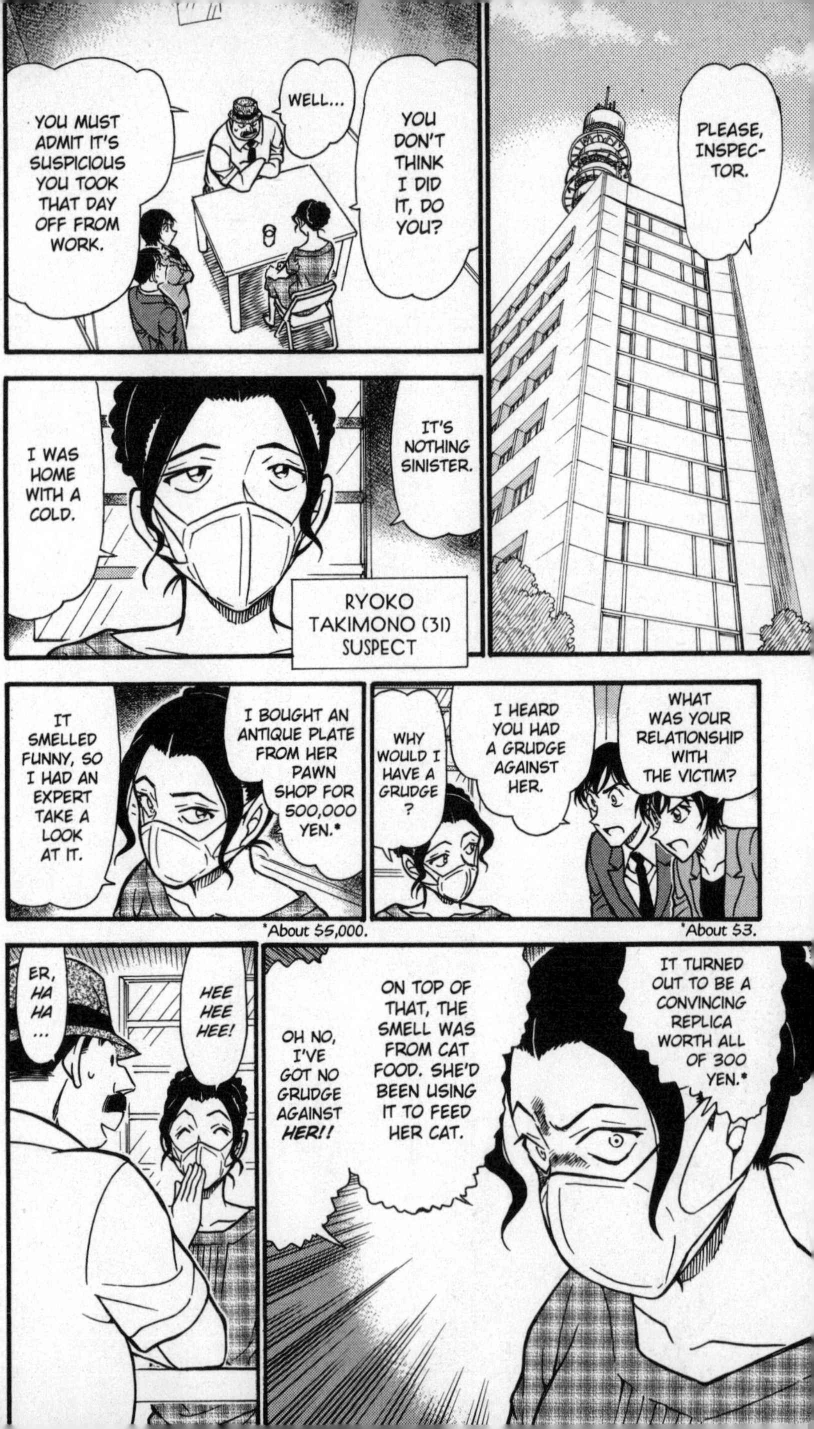
PLEASE, INSPECTOR.
YOU DON'T THINK I DID IT, DO YOU?
WELL...
YOU MUST ADMIT IT'S SUSPICIOUS YOU TOOK THAT DAY OFF FROM WORK.
IT'S NOTHING SINISTER.
I WAS HOME WITH A COLD.
RYOKO TAKIMONO (31) SUSPECT
WHAT WAS YOUR RELATIONSHIP WITH THE VICTIM?
I HEARD YOU HAD A GRUDGE AGAINST HER.
WHY WOULD I HAVE A GRUDGE?
I BOUGHT AN ANTIQUE PLATE FROM HER PAWN SHOP FOR 500,000 YEN.*
IT SMELLED FUNNY, SO I HAD AN EXPERT TAKE A LOOK AT IT.
IT TURNED OUT TO BE A CONVINCING REPLICA WORTH ALL OF 300 YEN.*
ON TOP OF THAT, THE SMELL WAS FROM CAT FOOD. SHE'D BEEN USING IT TO FEED HER CAT.
OH NO, I'VE GOT NO GRUDGE AGAINST *HER!!*
HEE HEE HEE!
ER, HA HA ...

*About $5,000.

*About $3.

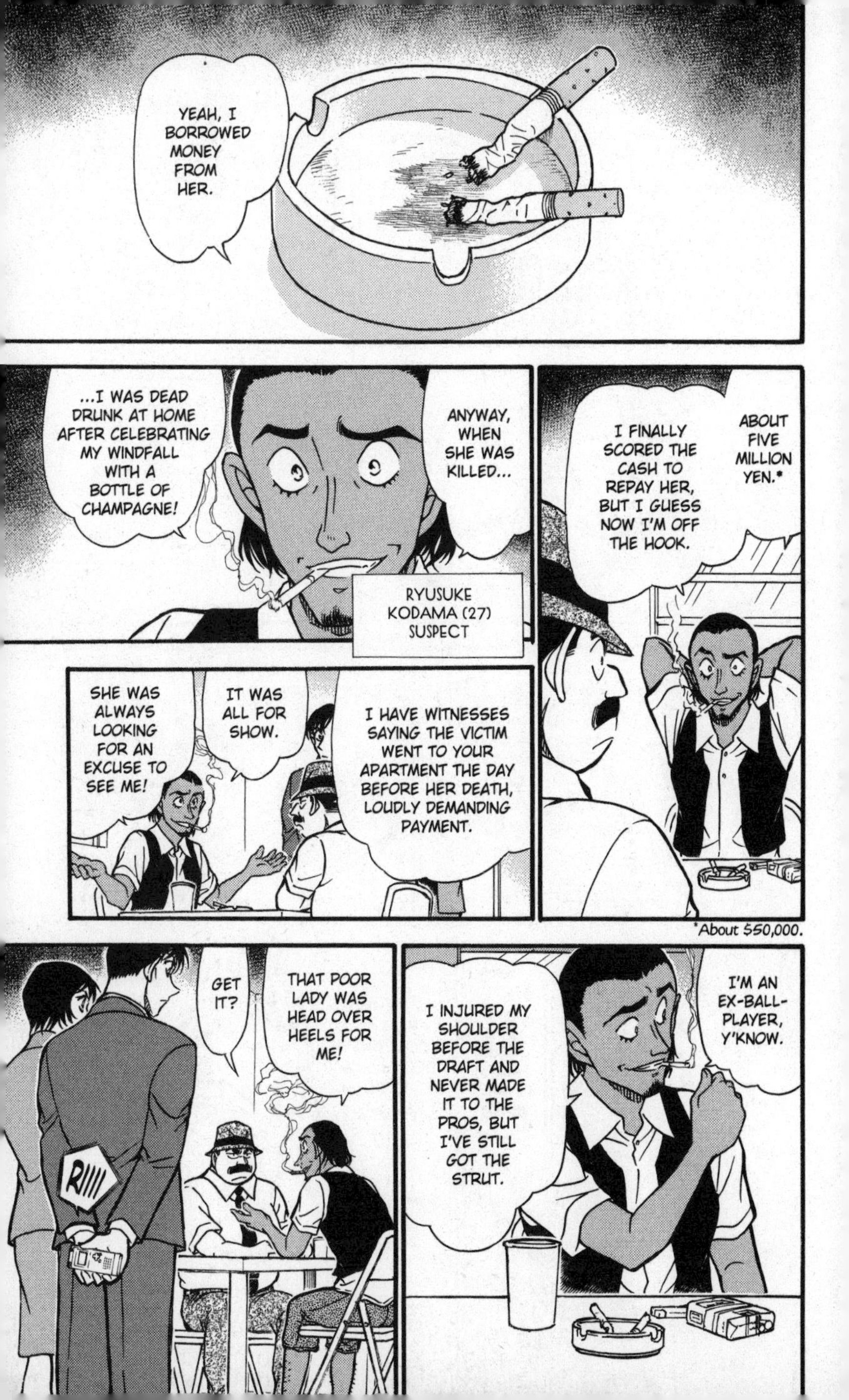
YEAH, I BORROWED MONEY FROM HER.
ABOUT FIVE MILLION YEN.*
I FINALLY SCORED THE CASH TO REPAY HER, BUT I GUESS NOW I'M OFF THE HOOK.
ANYWAY, WHEN SHE WAS KILLED...
...I WAS DEAD DRUNK AT HOME AFTER CELEBRATING MY WINDFALL WITH A BOTTLE OF CHAMPAGNE!
RYUSUKE KODAMA (27) SUSPECT
I HAVE WITNESSES SAYING THE VICTIM WENT TO YOUR APARTMENT THE DAY BEFORE HER DEATH, LOUDLY DEMANDING PAYMENT.
IT WAS ALL FOR SHOW.
SHE WAS ALWAYS LOOKING FOR AN EXCUSE TO SEE ME!
I'M AN EX-BALL-PLAYER, Y'KNOW.
I INJURED MY SHOULDER BEFORE THE DRAFT AND NEVER MADE IT TO THE PROS, BUT I'VE STILL GOT THE STRUT.
THAT POOR LADY WAS HEAD OVER HEELS FOR ME!
GET IT?
RI////

*About $50,000.

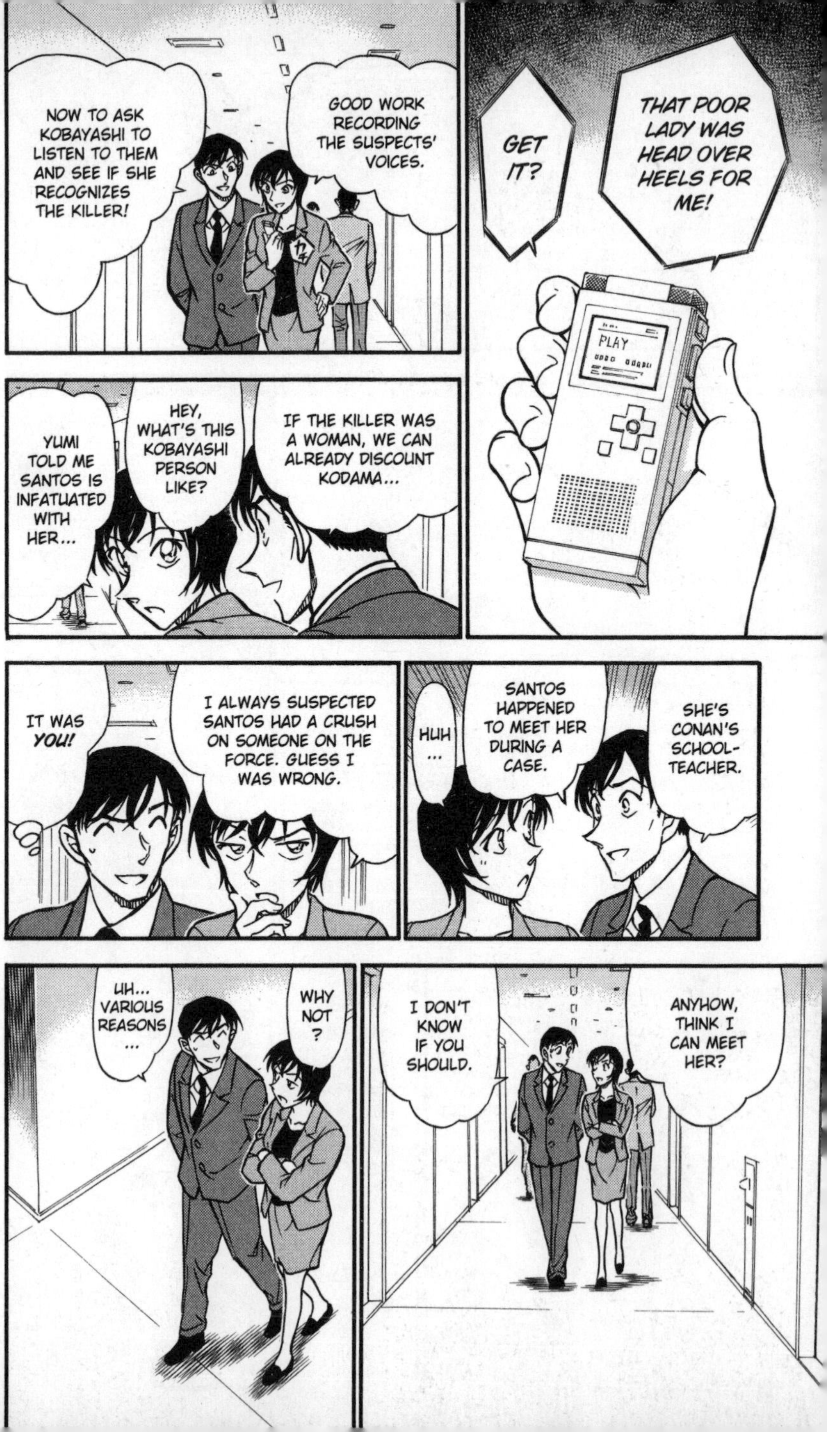
THAT POOR LADY WAS HEAD OVER HEELS FOR ME!
GET IT?
PLAY
GOOD WORK RECORDING THE SUSPECTS' VOICES.
NOW TO ASK KOBAYASHI TO LISTEN TO THEM AND SEE IF SHE RECOGNIZES THE KILLER!
IF THE KILLER WAS A WOMAN, WE CAN ALREADY DISCOUNT KODAMA...
HEY, WHAT'S THIS KOBAYASHI PERSON LIKE?
YUMI TOLD ME SANTOS IS INFATUATED WITH HER...
SHE'S CONAN'S SCHOOL-TEACHER.
SANTOS HAPPENED TO MEET HER DURING A CASE.
HUH...
I ALWAYS SUSPECTED SANTOS HAD A CRUSH ON SOMEONE ON THE FORCE. GUESS I WAS WRONG.
IT WAS *YOU!*
ANYHOW, THINK I CAN MEET HER?
I DON'T KNOW IF YOU SHOULD.
WHY NOT?
UH... VARIOUS REASONS...

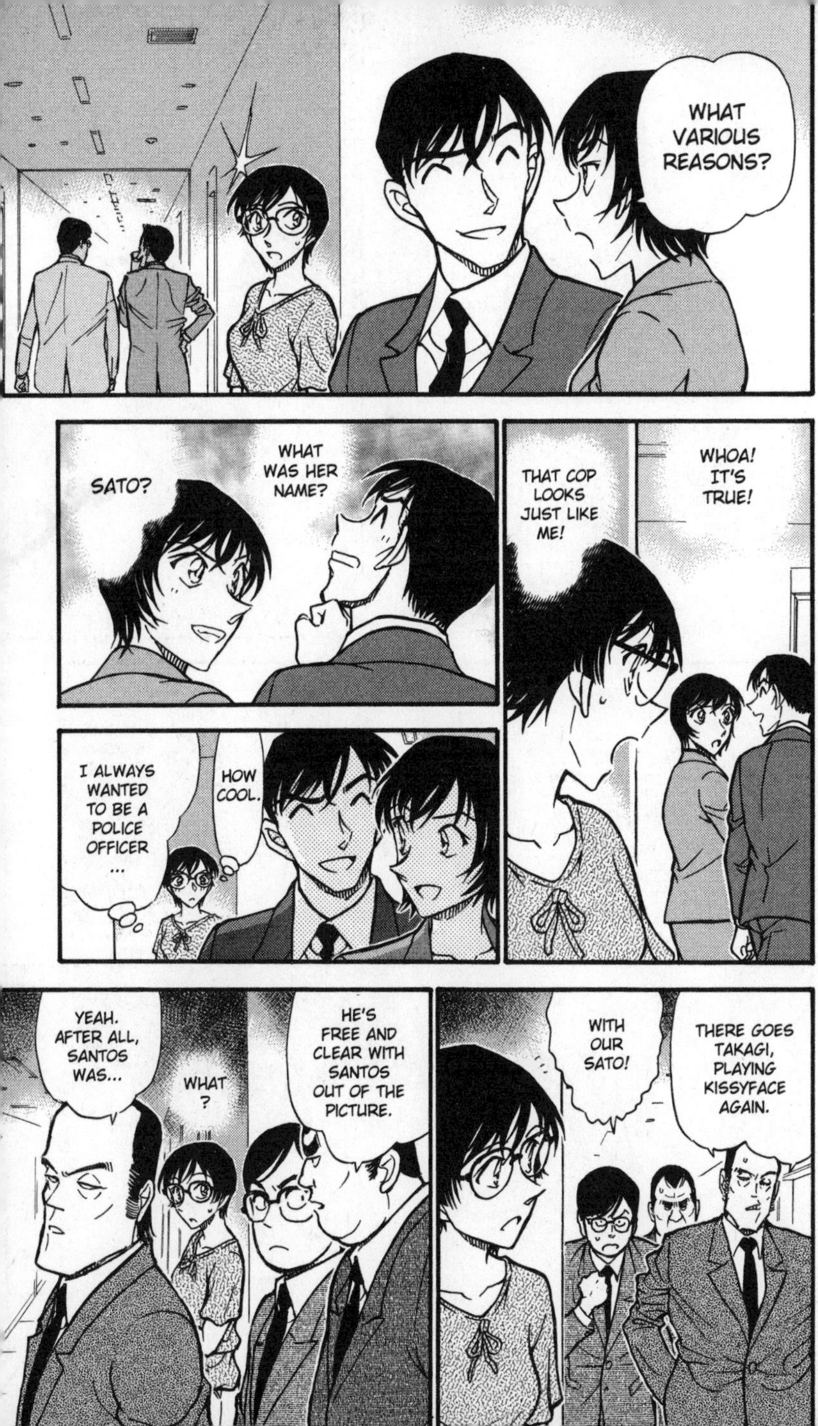
WHAT VARIOUS REASONS?
WHOA! IT'S TRUE!
THAT COP LOOKS JUST LIKE ME!
WHAT WAS HER NAME?
SATO?
HOW COOL.
I ALWAYS WANTED TO BE A POLICE OFFICER ...
THERE GOES TAKAGI, PLAYING KISSYFACE AGAIN.
WITH OUR SATO!
HE'S FREE AND CLEAR WITH SANTOS OUT OF THE PICTURE.
WHAT ?
YEAH. AFTER ALL, SANTOS WAS...

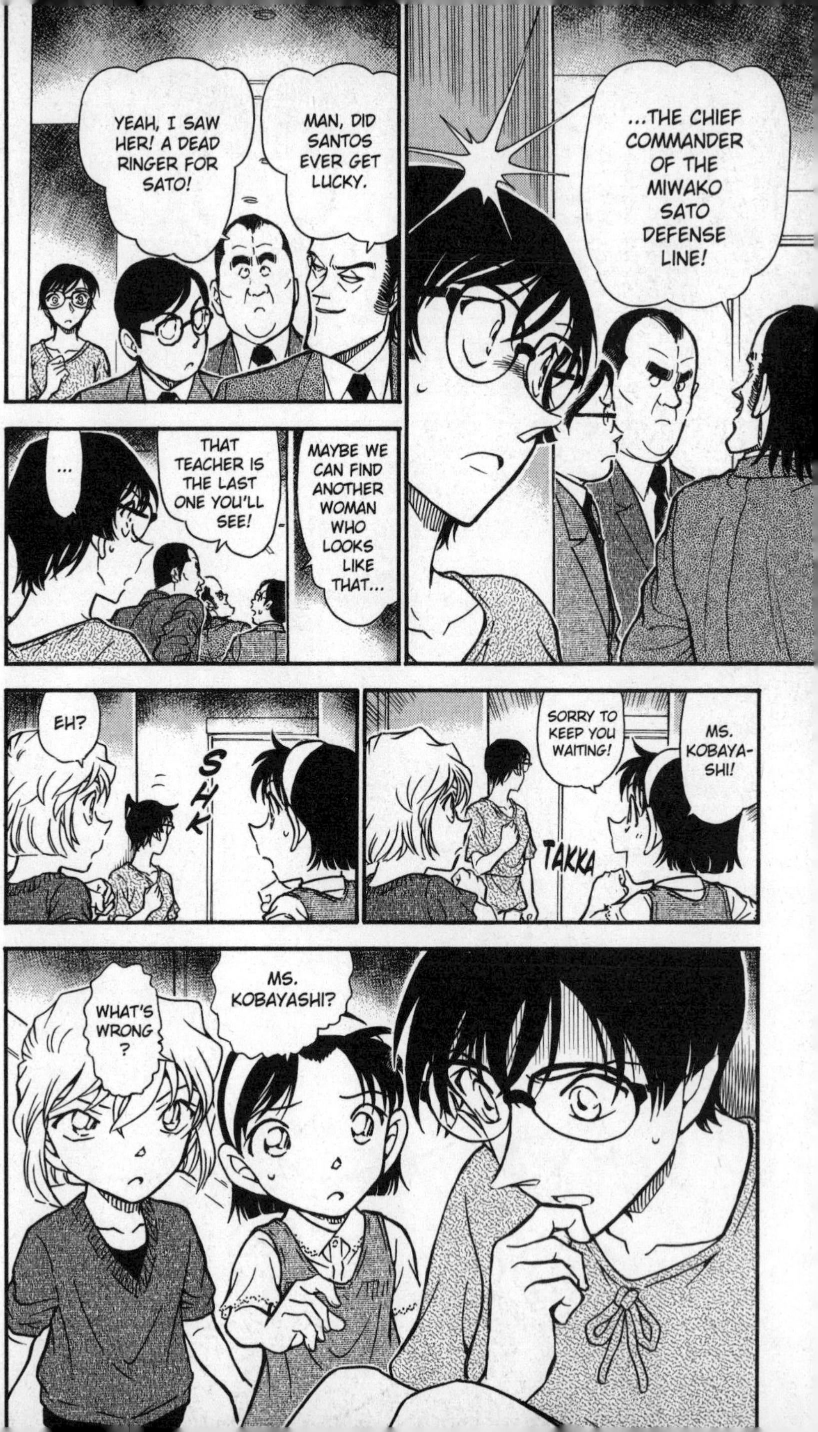
...THE CHIEF COMMANDER OF THE MIWAKO SATO DEFENSE LINE!
MAN, DID SANTOS EVER GET LUCKY.
YEAH, I SAW HER! A DEAD RINGER FOR SATO!
MAYBE WE CAN FIND ANOTHER WOMAN WHO LOOKS LIKE THAT...
THAT TEACHER IS THE LAST ONE YOU'LL SEE!
...
MS. KOBAYASHI!
SORRY TO KEEP YOU WAITING!
TAKKA
SHK
EH?
MS. KOBAYASHI?
WHAT'S WRONG?

FILE 11: CHERRY BLOSSOM GIRL

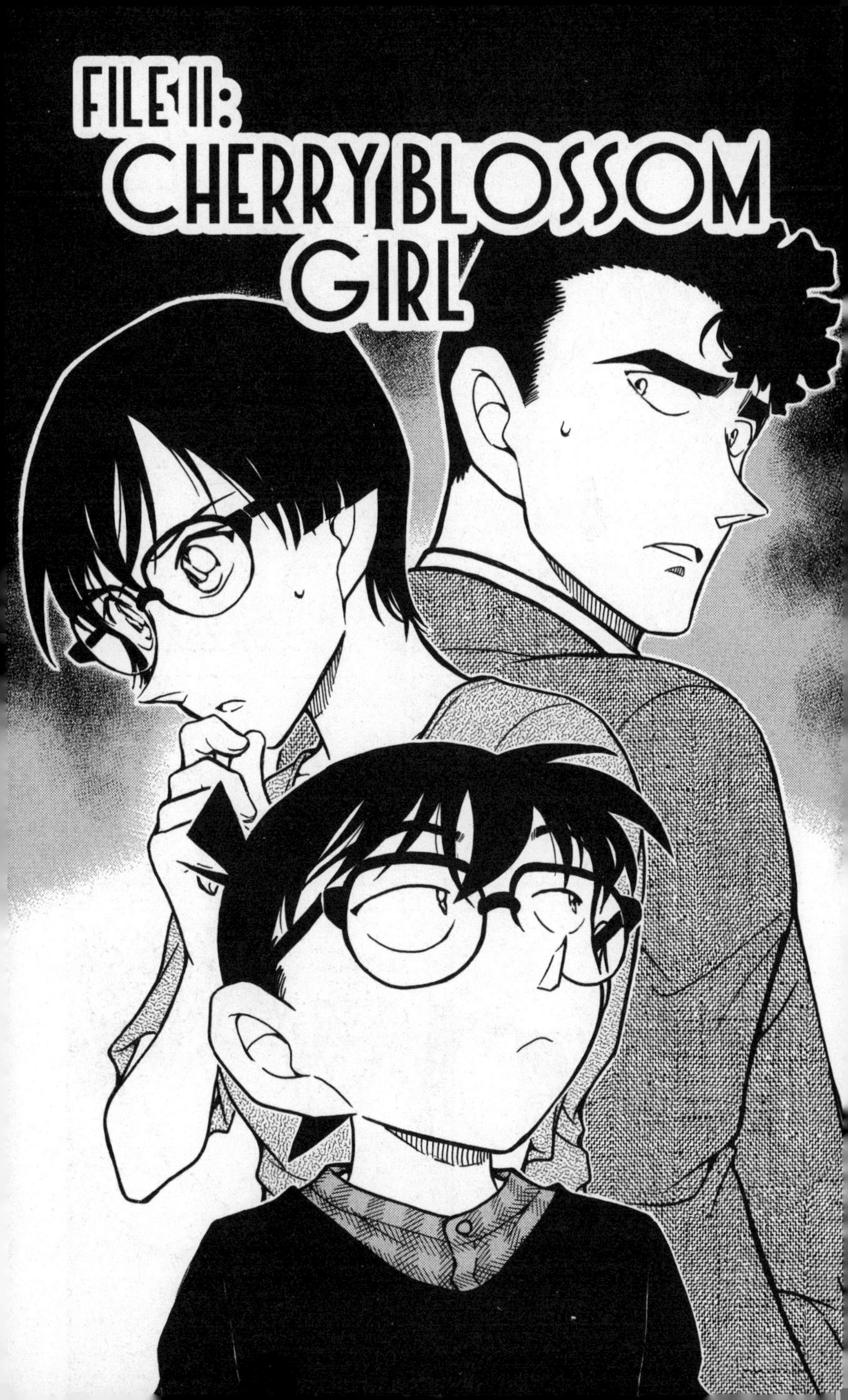

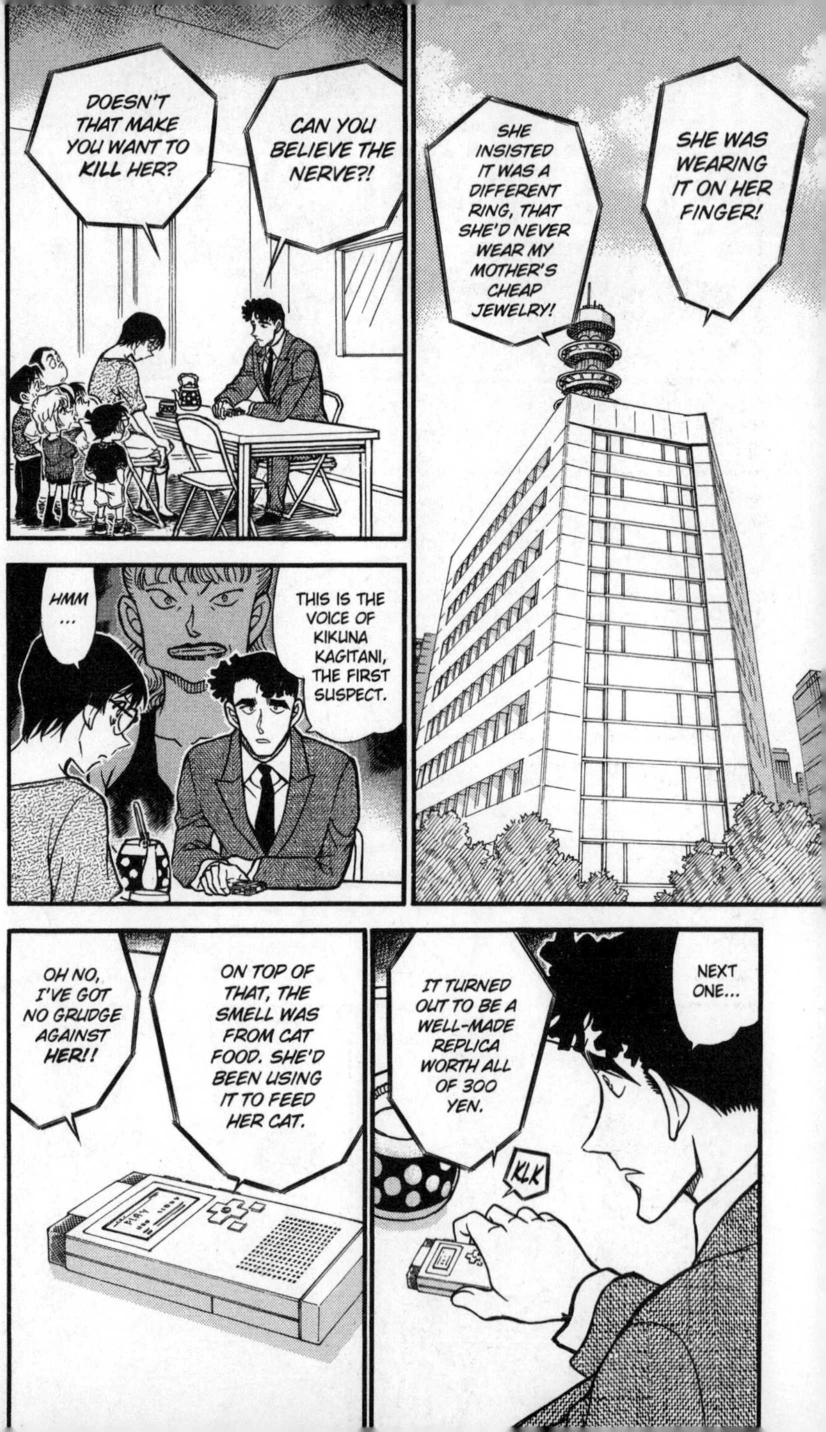
SHE WAS WEARING IT ON HER FINGER!
SHE INSISTED IT WAS A DIFFERENT RING, THAT SHE'D NEVER WEAR MY MOTHER'S CHEAP JEWELRY!
CAN YOU BELIEVE THE NERVE?!
DOESN'T THAT MAKE YOU WANT TO KILL HER?
THIS IS THE VOICE OF KIKUNA KAGITANI, THE FIRST SUSPECT.
HMM...
NEXT ONE...
IT TURNED OUT TO BE A WELL-MADE REPLICA WORTH ALL OF 300 YEN.
KLK
ON TOP OF THAT, THE SMELL WAS FROM CAT FOOD. SHE'D BEEN USING IT TO FEED HER CAT.
OH NO, I'VE GOT NO GRUDGE AGAINST HER!!

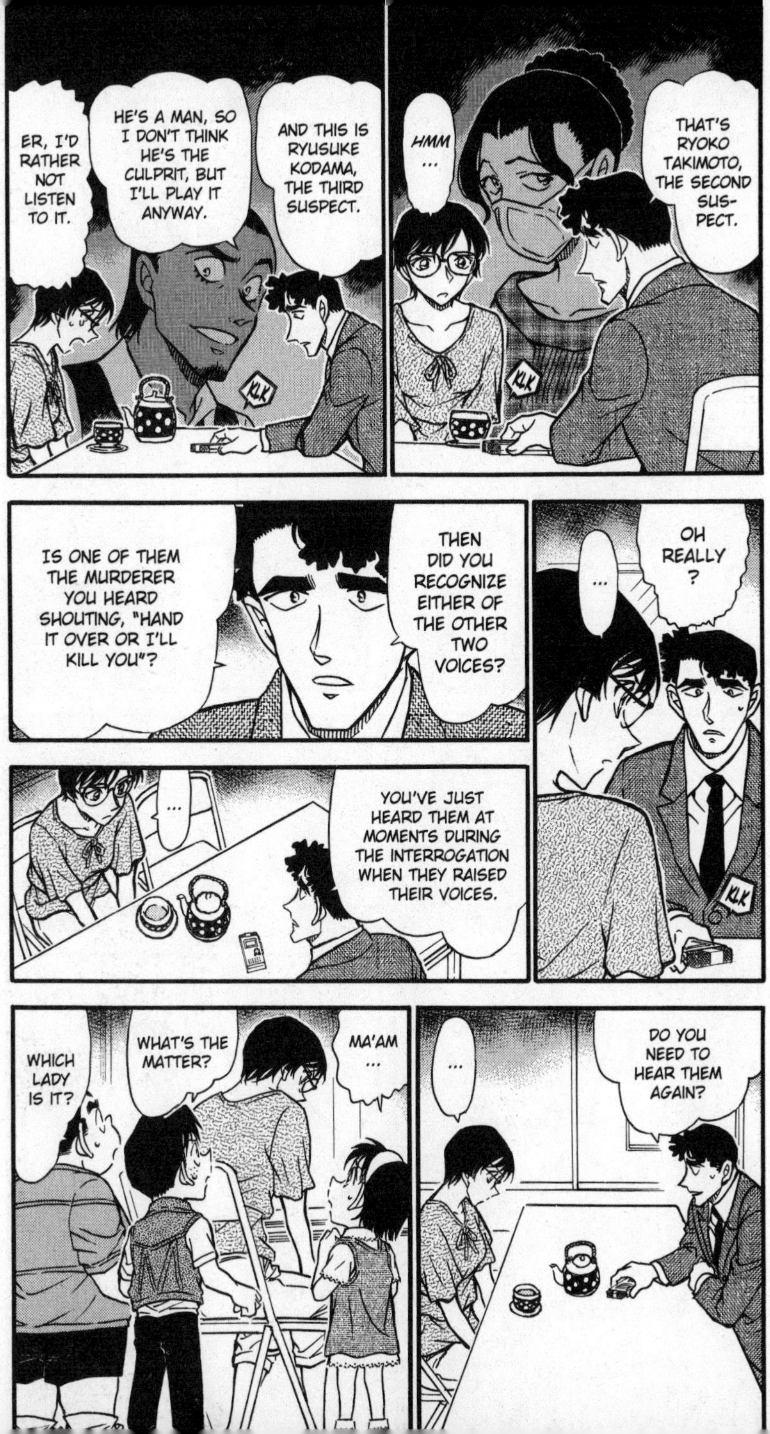
THAT'S RYOKO TAKIMOTO, THE SECOND SUS-PECT.
KLK
HMM ...
AND THIS IS RYUSUKE KODAMA, THE THIRD SUSPECT.
KLK
HE'S A MAN, SO I DON'T THINK HE'S THE CULPRIT, BUT I'LL PLAY IT ANYWAY.
ER, I'D RATHER NOT LISTEN TO IT.
OH REALLY?
...
KLK
THEN DID YOU RECOGNIZE EITHER OF THE OTHER TWO VOICES?
IS ONE OF THEM THE MURDERER YOU HEARD SHOUTING, "HAND IT OVER OR I'LL KILL YOU"?
YOU'VE JUST HEARD THEM AT MOMENTS DURING THE INTERROGATION WHEN THEY RAISED THEIR VOICES.
...
DO YOU NEED TO HEAR THEM AGAIN?
...
MA'AM ...
WHAT'S THE MATTER?
WHICH LADY IS IT?

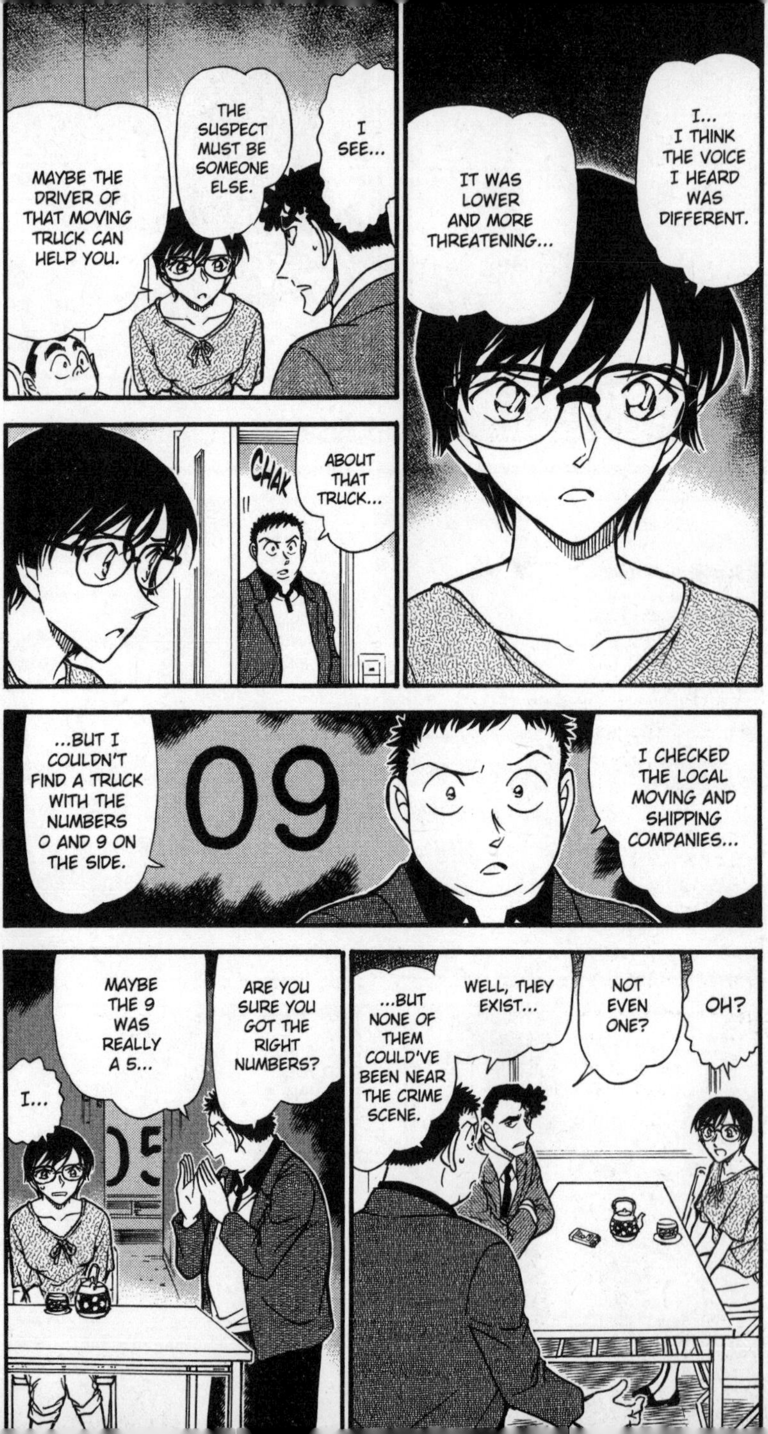
I... I THINK THE VOICE I HEARD WAS DIFFERENT.
IT WAS LOWER AND MORE THREATENING...
I SEE...
THE SUSPECT MUST BE SOMEONE ELSE.
MAYBE THE DRIVER OF THAT MOVING TRUCK CAN HELP YOU.
CHAK
ABOUT THAT TRUCK...
I CHECKED THE LOCAL MOVING AND SHIPPING COMPANIES...
09
...BUT I COULDN'T FIND A TRUCK WITH THE NUMBERS 0 AND 9 ON THE SIDE.
OH?
NOT EVEN ONE?
WELL, THEY EXIST...
...BUT NONE OF THEM COULD'VE BEEN NEAR THE CRIME SCENE.
ARE YOU SURE YOU GOT THE RIGHT NUMBERS?
MAYBE THE 9 WAS REALLY A 5...
05
I...

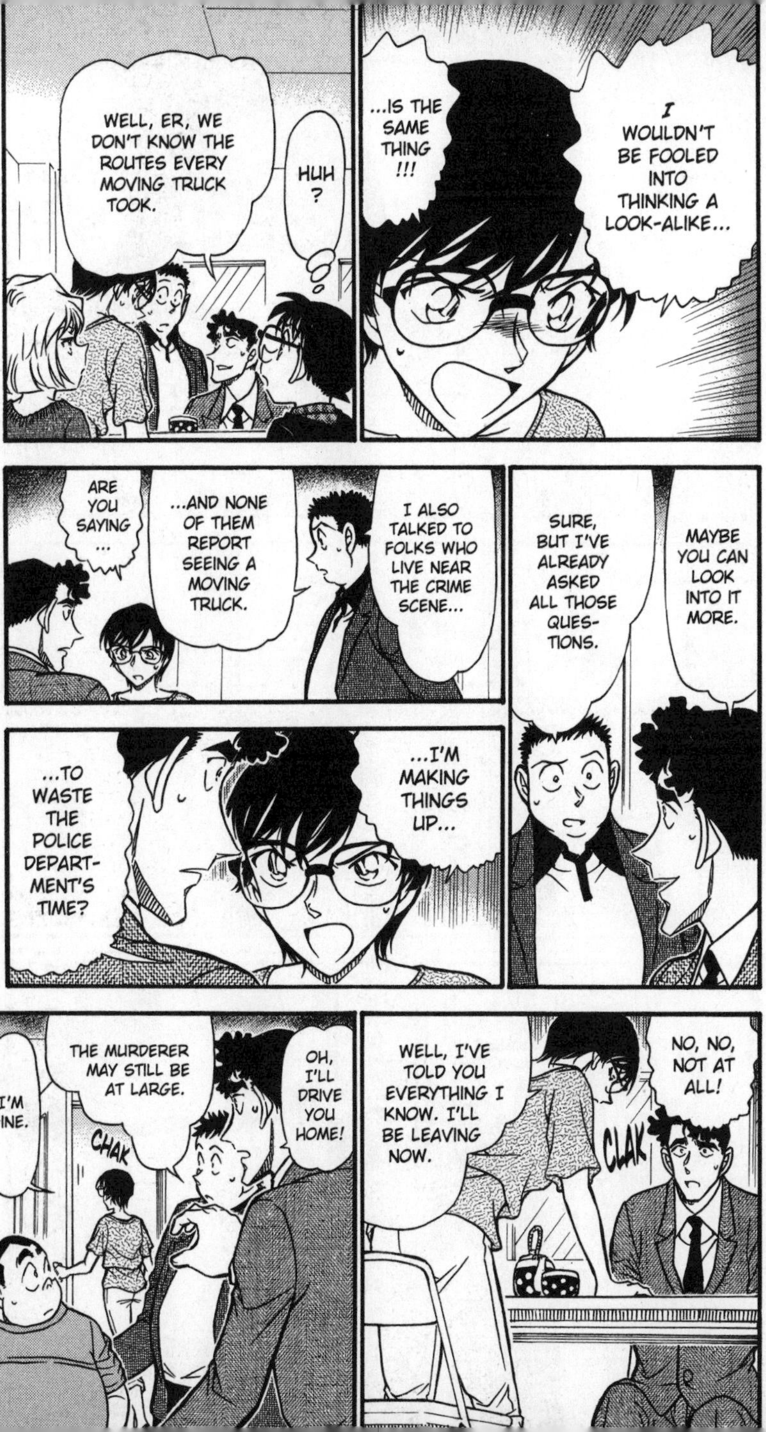
I WOULDN'T BE FOOLED INTO THINKING A LOOK-ALIKE...
...IS THE SAME THING!!!
WELL, ER, WE DON'T KNOW THE ROUTES EVERY MOVING TRUCK TOOK.
HUH?
MAYBE YOU CAN LOOK INTO IT MORE.
SURE, BUT I'VE ALREADY ASKED ALL THOSE QUES-TIONS.
I ALSO TALKED TO FOLKS WHO LIVE NEAR THE CRIME SCENE...
...AND NONE OF THEM REPORT SEEING A MOVING TRUCK.
ARE YOU SAYING...
...I'M MAKING THINGS UP...
...TO WASTE THE POLICE DEPART-MENT'S TIME?
NO, NO, NOT AT ALL!
WELL, I'VE TOLD YOU EVERYTHING I KNOW. I'LL BE LEAVING NOW.
CLAK
OH, I'LL DRIVE YOU HOME!
THE MURDERER MAY STILL BE AT LARGE.
CHAK
I'M FINE.

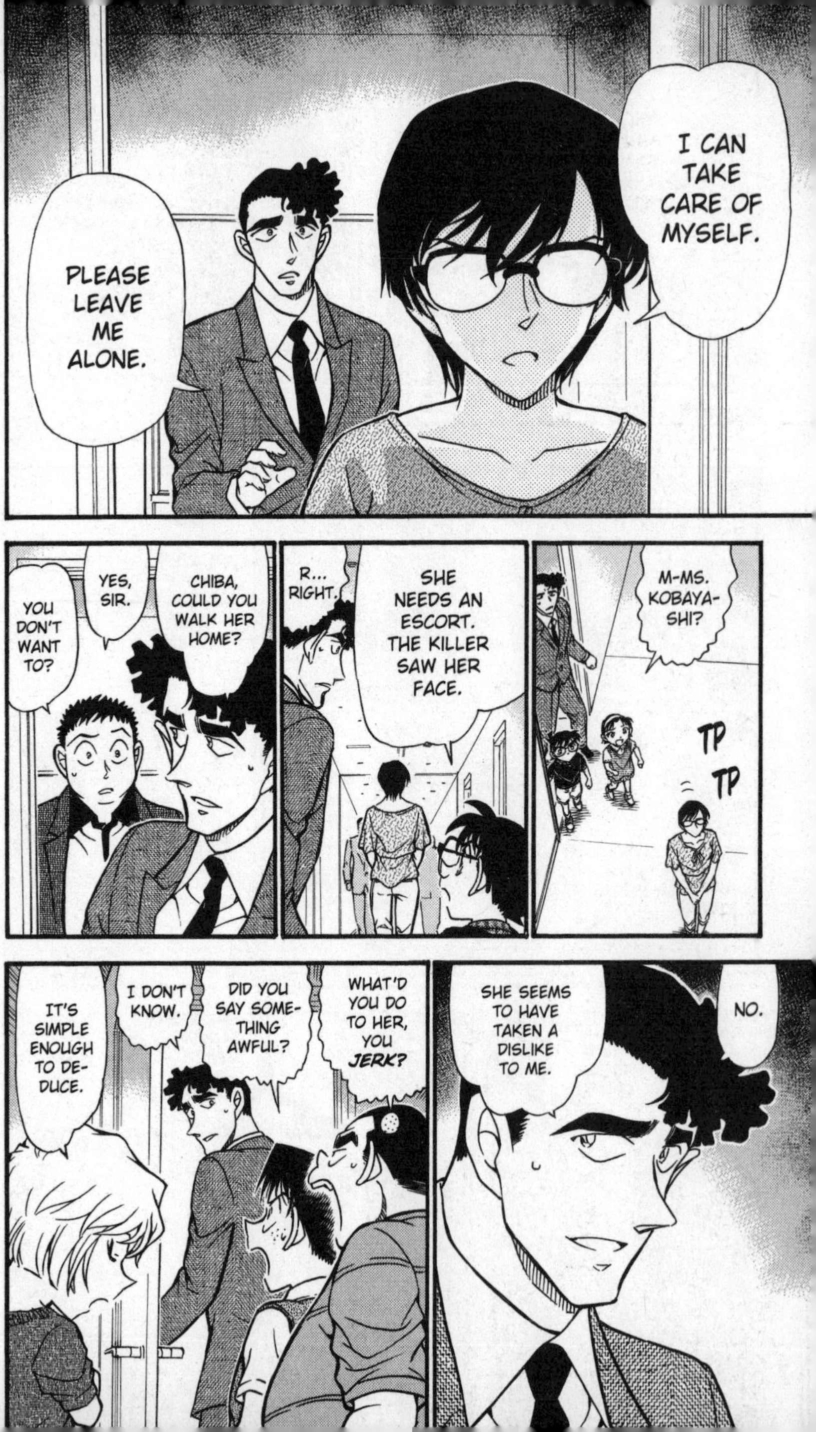
I CAN TAKE CARE OF MYSELF.
PLEASE LEAVE ME ALONE.
M-MS. KOBAYA-SHI?
TP
TP
SHE NEEDS AN ESCORT. THE KILLER SAW HER FACE.
R... RIGHT.
CHIBA, COULD YOU WALK HER HOME?
YES, SIR.
YOU DON'T WANT TO?
NO.
SHE SEEMS TO HAVE TAKEN A DISLIKE TO ME.
WHAT'D YOU DO TO HER, YOU *JERK?*
DID YOU SAY SOME-THING AWFUL?
I DON'T KNOW.
IT'S SIMPLE ENOUGH TO DE-DUCE.

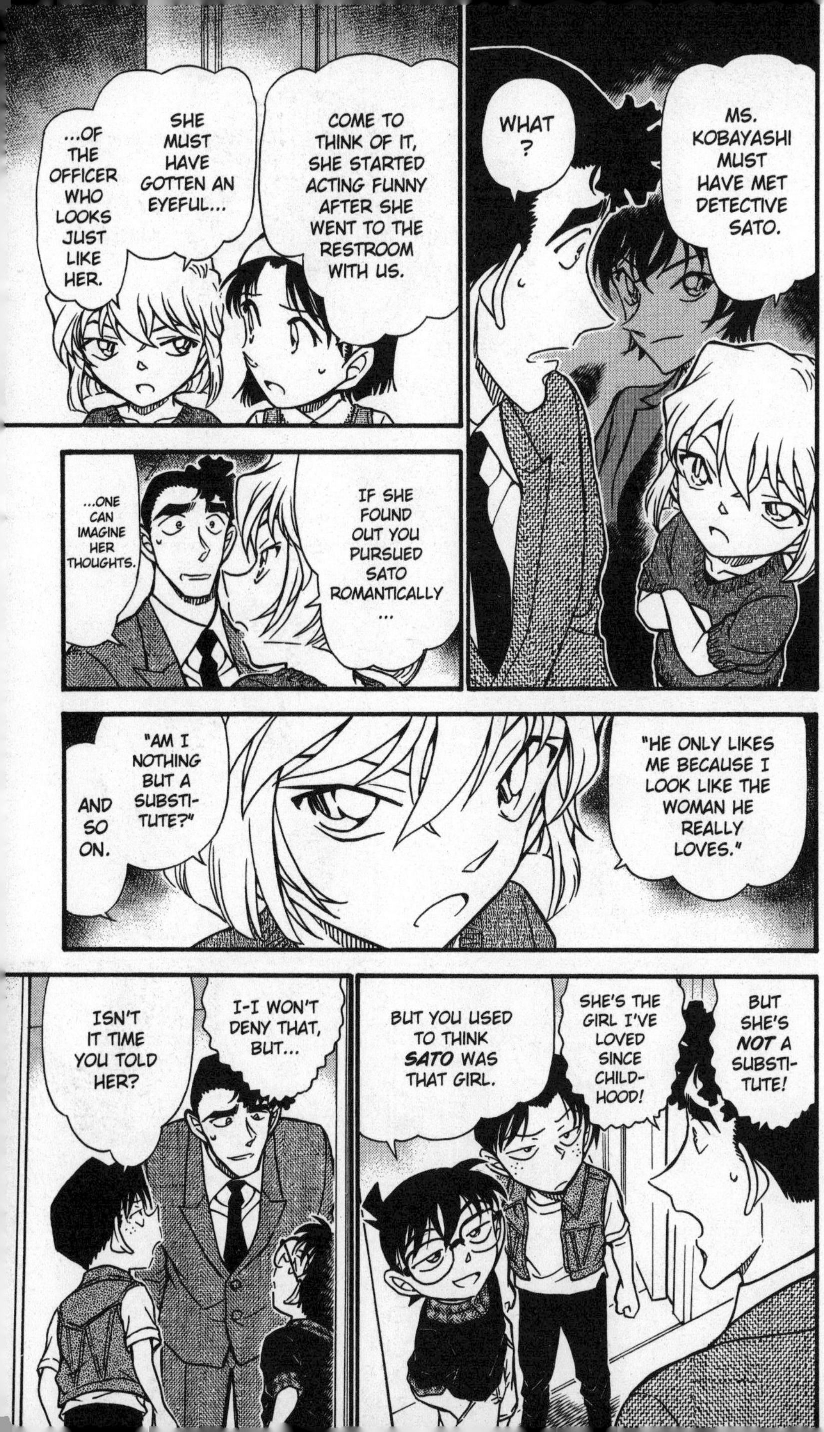
MS. KOBAYASHI MUST HAVE MET DETECTIVE SATO.
WHAT?
COME TO THINK OF IT, SHE STARTED ACTING FUNNY AFTER SHE WENT TO THE RESTROOM WITH US.
SHE MUST HAVE GOTTEN AN EYEFUL...
...OF THE OFFICER WHO LOOKS JUST LIKE HER.
IF SHE FOUND OUT YOU PURSUED SATO ROMANTICALLY ...
...ONE CAN IMAGINE HER THOUGHTS.
"HE ONLY LIKES ME BECAUSE I LOOK LIKE THE WOMAN HE REALLY LOVES."
"AM I NOTHING BUT A SUBSTITUTE?"
AND SO ON.
BUT SHE'S *NOT* A SUBSTITUTE!
SHE'S THE GIRL I'VE LOVED SINCE CHILDHOOD!
BUT YOU USED TO THINK ***SATO*** WAS THAT GIRL.
I-I WON'T DENY THAT, BUT...
ISN'T IT TIME YOU TOLD HER?

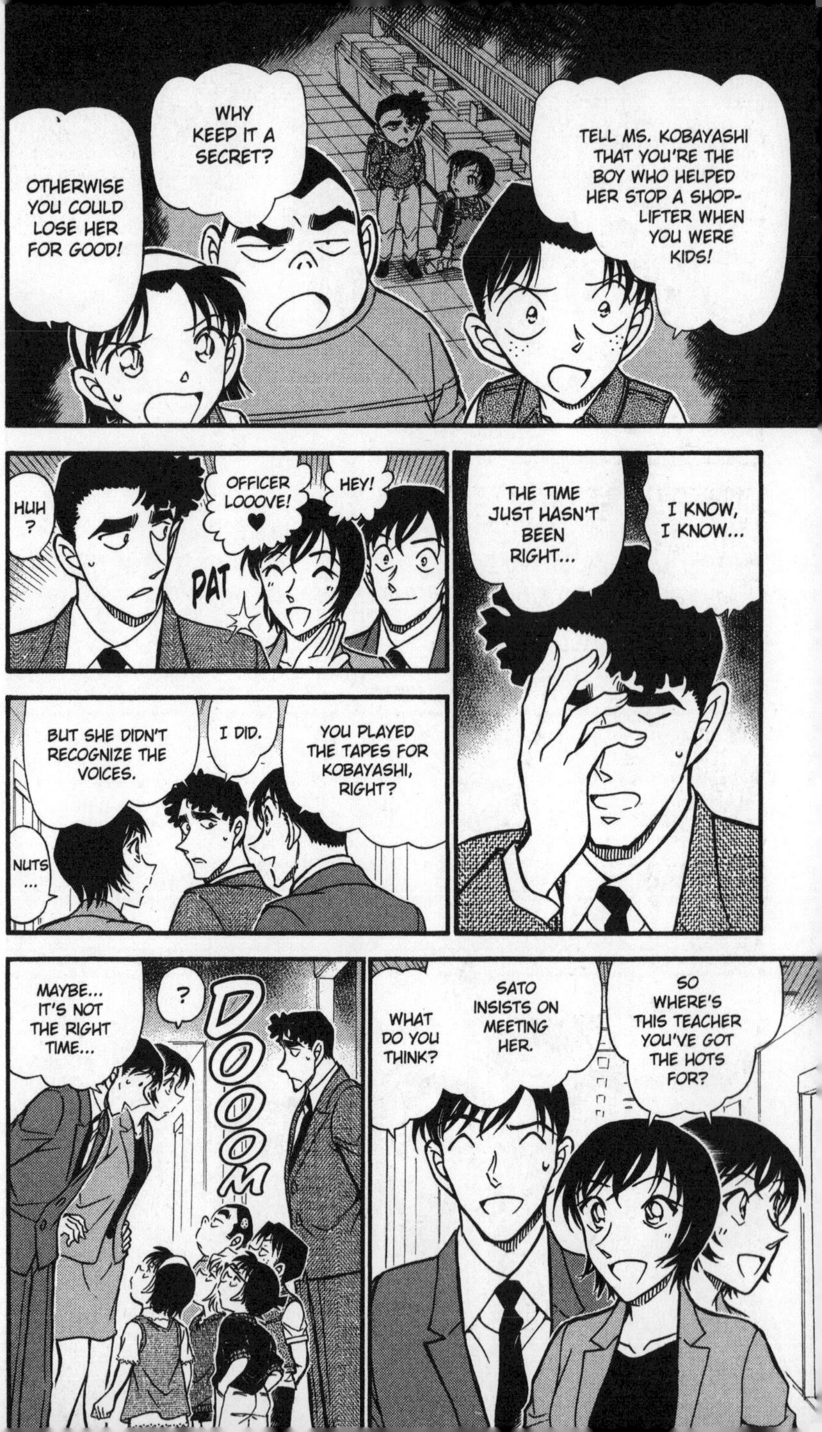
TELL MS. KOBAYASHI THAT YOU'RE THE BOY WHO HELPED HER STOP A SHOP-LIFTER WHEN YOU WERE KIDS!
WHY KEEP IT A SECRET?
OTHERWISE YOU COULD LOSE HER FOR GOOD!
I KNOW, I KNOW...
THE TIME JUST HASN'T BEEN RIGHT...
HEY!
OFFICER LOOOVE! ♥
PAT
HUH?
YOU PLAYED THE TAPES FOR KOBAYASHI, RIGHT?
I DID.
BUT SHE DIDN'T RECOGNIZE THE VOICES.
NUTS...
SO WHERE'S THIS TEACHER YOU'VE GOT THE HOTS FOR?
SATO INSISTS ON MEETING HER.
WHAT DO YOU THINK?
DOOOOM
?
MAYBE... IT'S NOT THE RIGHT TIME...

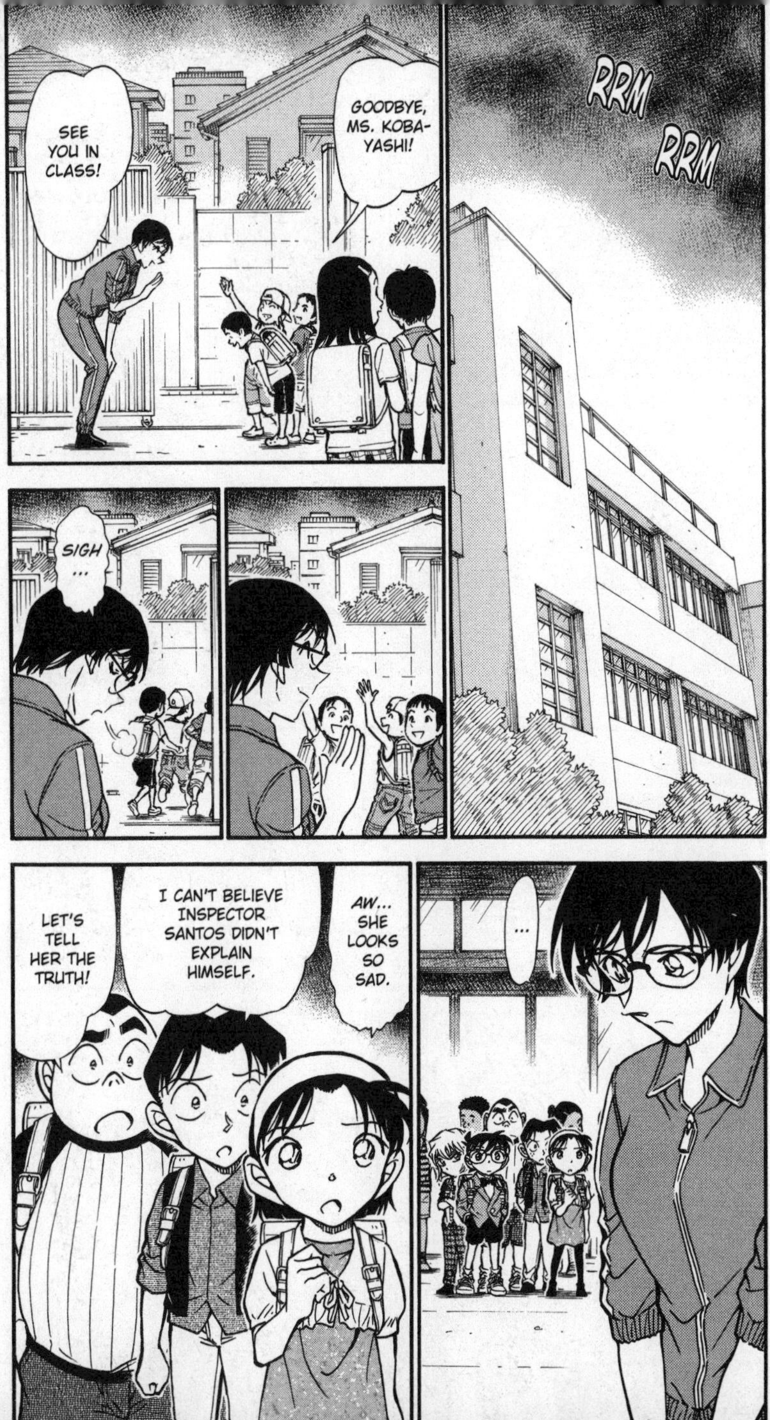
RRM
RRM
GOODBYE, MS. KOBA-YASHI!
SEE YOU IN CLASS!
SIGH ...
...
AW... SHE LOOKS SO SAD.
I CAN'T BELIEVE INSPECTOR SANTOS DIDN'T EXPLAIN HIMSELF.
LET'S TELL HER THE TRUTH!

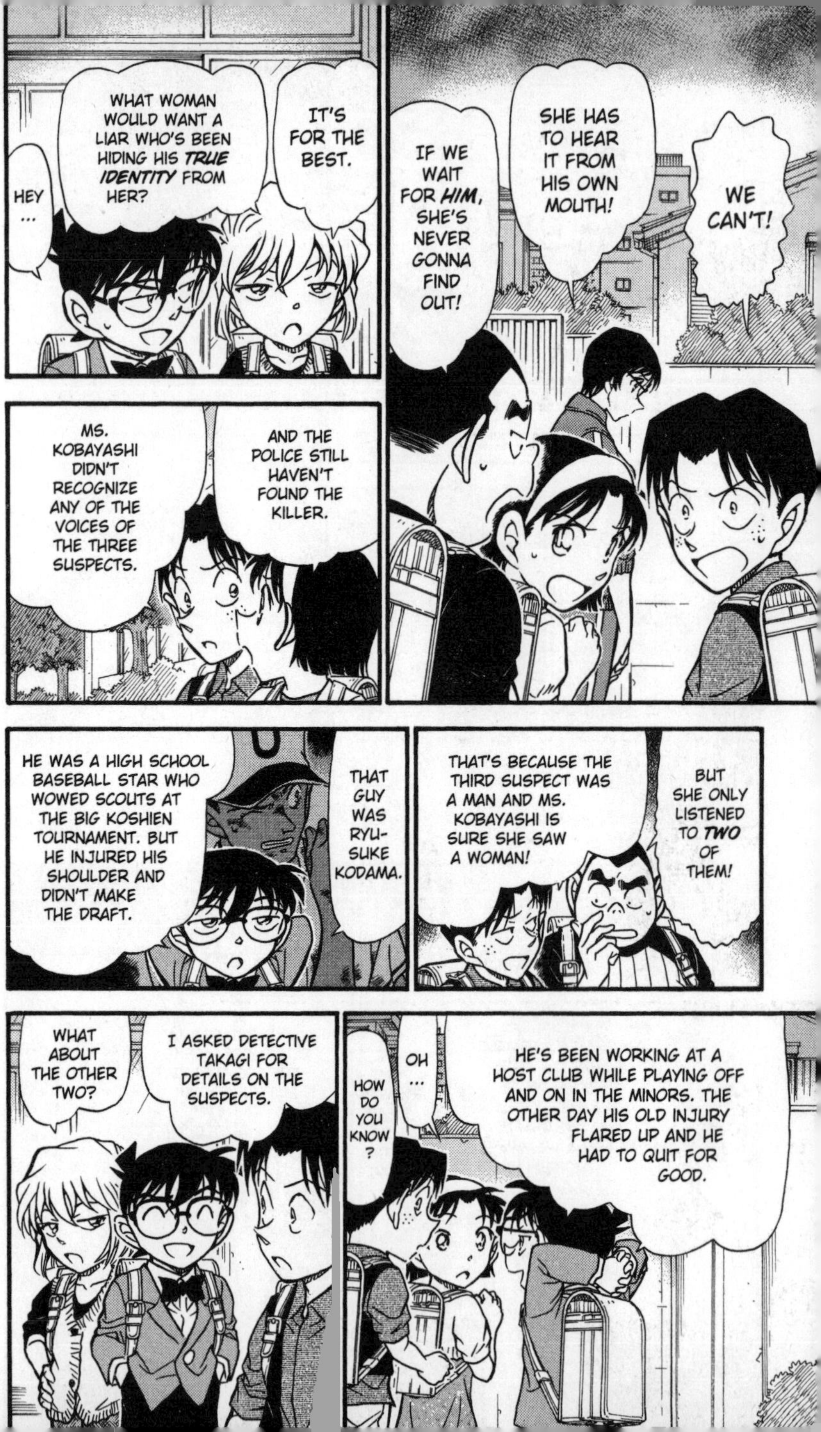
WE CAN'T!
SHE HAS TO HEAR IT FROM HIS OWN MOUTH!
IF WE WAIT FOR HIM, SHE'S NEVER GONNA FIND OUT!
IT'S FOR THE BEST.
WHAT WOMAN WOULD WANT A LIAR WHO'S BEEN HIDING HIS TRUE IDENTITY FROM HER?
HEY ...
AND THE POLICE STILL HAVEN'T FOUND THE KILLER.
MS. KOBAYASHI DIDN'T RECOGNIZE ANY OF THE VOICES OF THE THREE SUSPECTS.
BUT SHE ONLY LISTENED TO TWO OF THEM!
THAT'S BECAUSE THE THIRD SUSPECT WAS A MAN AND MS. KOBAYASHI IS SURE SHE SAW A WOMAN!
THAT GUY WAS RYU-SUKE KODAMA.
HE WAS A HIGH SCHOOL BASEBALL STAR WHO WOWED SCOUTS AT THE BIG KOSHIEN TOURNAMENT. BUT HE INJURED HIS SHOULDER AND DIDN'T MAKE THE DRAFT.
HE'S BEEN WORKING AT A HOST CLUB WHILE PLAYING OFF AND ON IN THE MINORS. THE OTHER DAY HIS OLD INJURY FLARED UP AND HE HAD TO QUIT FOR GOOD.
OH ...
HOW DO YOU KNOW ?
I ASKED DETECTIVE TAKAGI FOR DETAILS ON THE SUSPECTS.
WHAT ABOUT THE OTHER TWO?

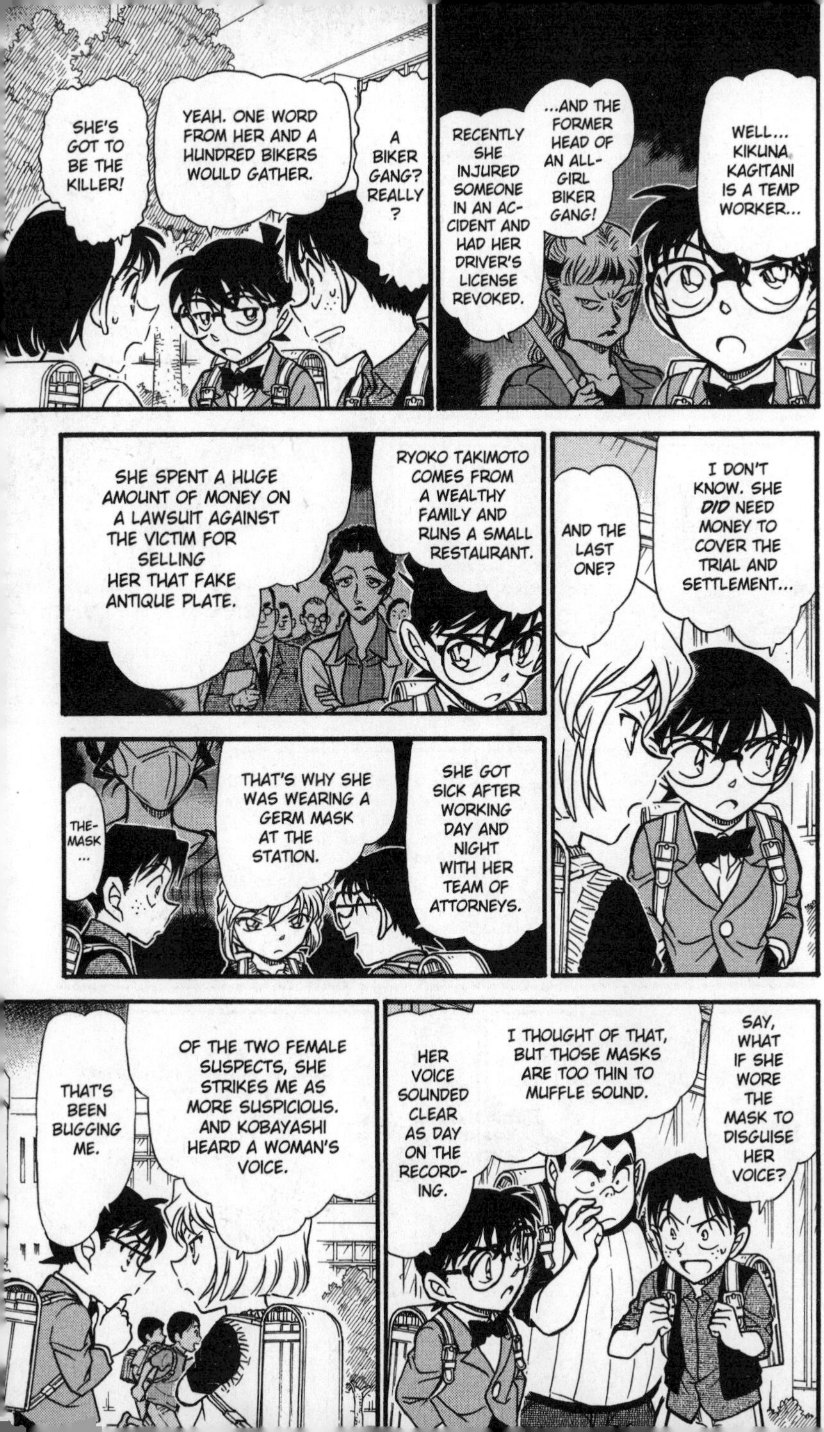
WELL... KIKUNA KAGITANI IS A TEMP WORKER...
...AND THE FORMER HEAD OF AN ALL-GIRL BIKER GANG!
RECENTLY SHE INJURED SOMEONE IN AN ACCIDENT AND HAD HER DRIVER'S LICENSE REVOKED.
A BIKER GANG? REALLY?
YEAH. ONE WORD FROM HER AND A HUNDRED BIKERS WOULD GATHER.
SHE'S GOT TO BE THE KILLER!
I DON'T KNOW. SHE *DID* NEED MONEY TO COVER THE TRIAL AND SETTLEMENT...
AND THE LAST ONE?
RYOKO TAKIMOTO COMES FROM A WEALTHY FAMILY AND RUNS A SMALL RESTAURANT.
SHE SPENT A HUGE AMOUNT OF MONEY ON A LAWSUIT AGAINST THE VICTIM FOR SELLING HER THAT FAKE ANTIQUE PLATE.
SHE GOT SICK AFTER WORKING DAY AND NIGHT WITH HER TEAM OF ATTORNEYS.
THAT'S WHY SHE WAS WEARING A GERM MASK AT THE STATION.
THE-MASK...
SAY, WHAT IF SHE WORE THE MASK TO DISGUISE HER VOICE?
I THOUGHT OF THAT, BUT THOSE MASKS ARE TOO THIN TO MUFFLE SOUND.
HER VOICE SOUNDED CLEAR AS DAY ON THE RECORDING.
OF THE TWO FEMALE SUSPECTS, SHE STRIKES ME AS MORE SUSPICIOUS. AND KOBAYASHI HEARD A WOMAN'S VOICE.
THAT'S BEEN BUGGING ME.

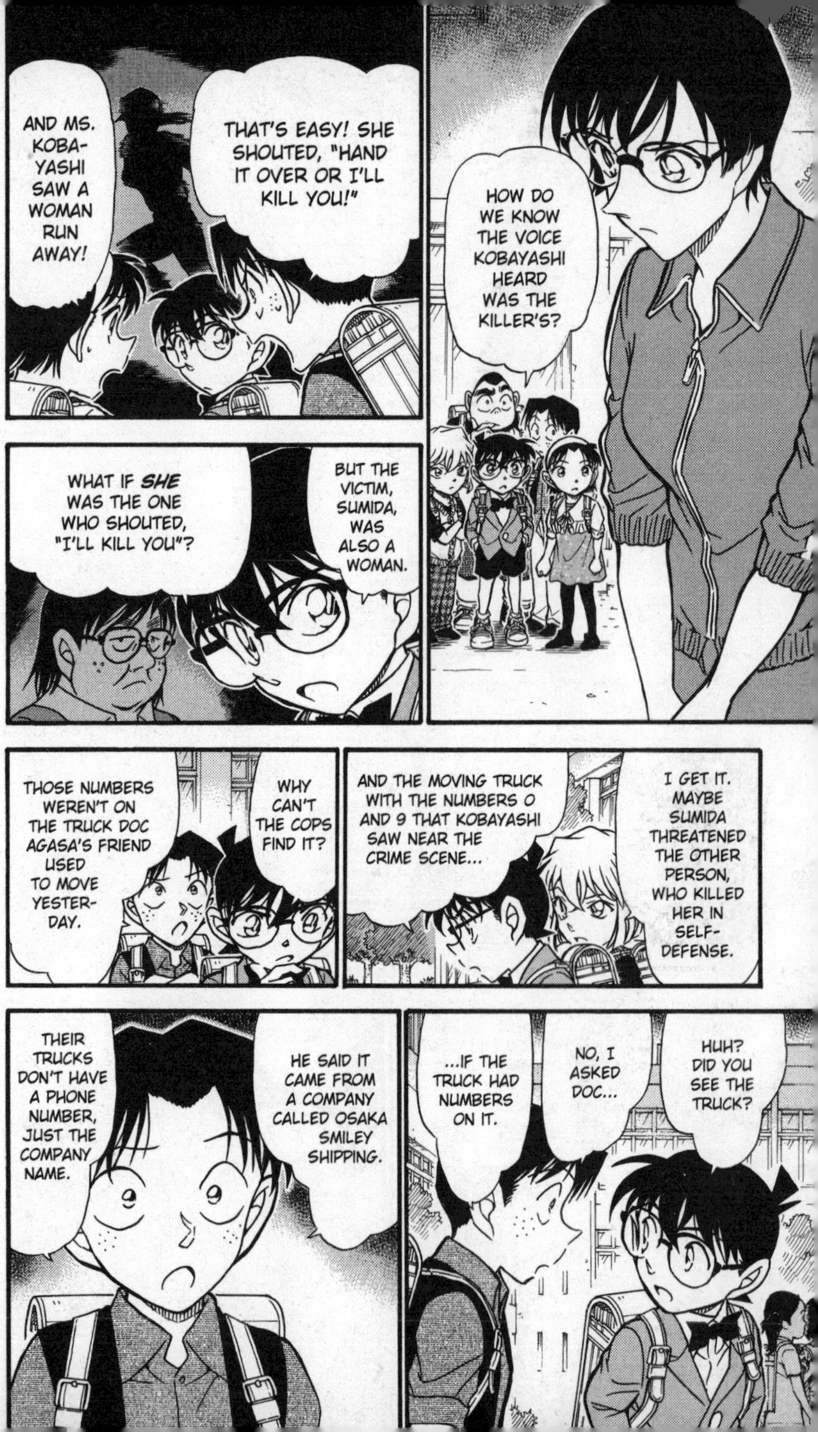
HOW DO WE KNOW THE VOICE KOBAYASHI HEARD WAS THE KILLER'S?
THAT'S EASY! SHE SHOUTED, "HAND IT OVER OR I'LL KILL YOU!"
AND MS. KOBA-YASHI SAW A WOMAN RUN AWAY!
BUT THE VICTIM, SUMIDA, WAS ALSO A WOMAN.
WHAT IF *SHE* WAS THE ONE WHO SHOUTED, "I'LL KILL YOU"?
I GET IT. MAYBE SUMIDA THREATENED THE OTHER PERSON, WHO KILLED HER IN SELF-DEFENSE.
AND THE MOVING TRUCK WITH THE NUMBERS 0 AND 9 THAT KOBAYASHI SAW NEAR THE CRIME SCENE...
WHY CAN'T THE COPS FIND IT?
THOSE NUMBERS WEREN'T ON THE TRUCK DOC AGASA'S FRIEND USED TO MOVE YESTER-DAY.
HUH? DID YOU SEE THE TRUCK?
NO, I ASKED DOC...
...IF THE TRUCK HAD NUMBERS ON IT.
HE SAID IT CAME FROM A COMPANY CALLED OSAKA SMILEY SHIPPING.
THEIR TRUCKS DON'T HAVE A PHONE NUMBER, JUST THE COMPANY NAME.

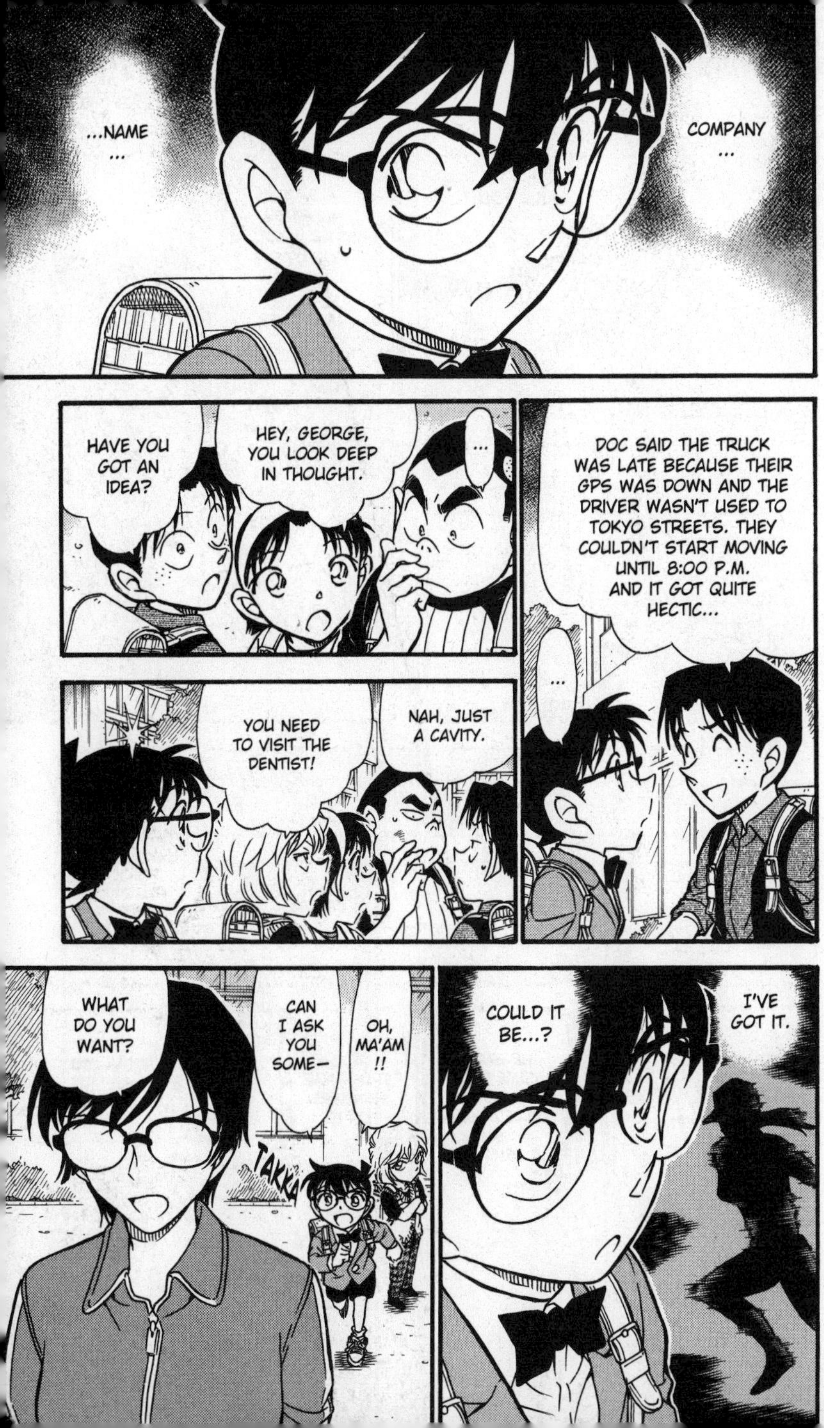
COMPANY ...
...NAME ...
DOC SAID THE TRUCK WAS LATE BECAUSE THEIR GPS WAS DOWN AND THE DRIVER WASN'T USED TO TOKYO STREETS. THEY COULDN'T START MOVING UNTIL 8:00 P.M. AND IT GOT QUITE HECTIC...
...
...
HEY, GEORGE, YOU LOOK DEEP IN THOUGHT.
HAVE YOU GOT AN IDEA?
NAH, JUST A CAVITY.
YOU NEED TO VISIT THE DENTIST!
I'VE GOT IT.
COULD IT BE...?
OH, MA'AM !!
CAN I ASK YOU SOME-
TAKKA
WHAT DO YOU WANT?

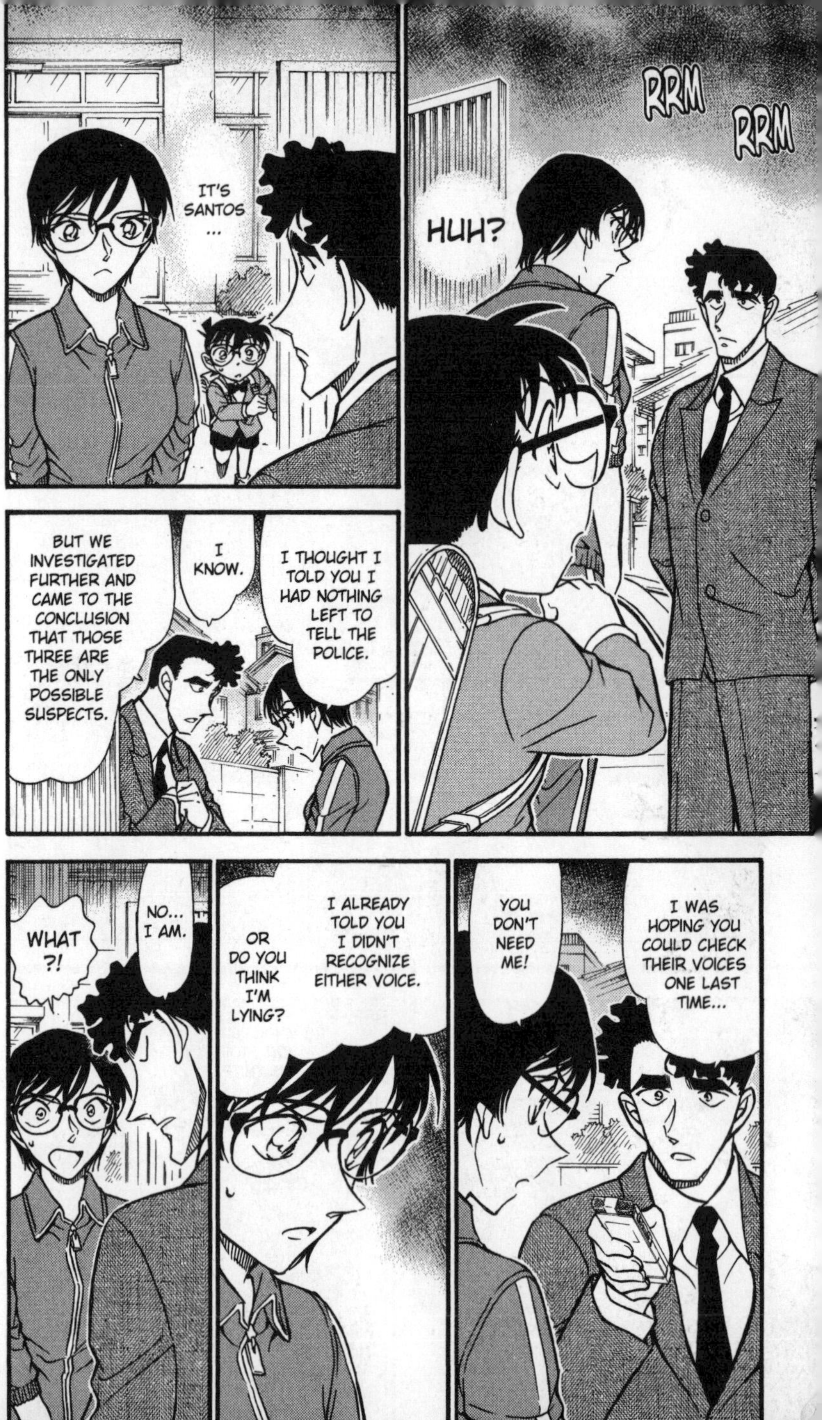
RRM
RRM
HUH?
IT'S SANTOS ...
I THOUGHT I TOLD YOU I HAD NOTHING LEFT TO TELL THE POLICE.
I KNOW.
BUT WE INVESTIGATED FURTHER AND CAME TO THE CONCLUSION THAT THOSE THREE ARE THE ONLY POSSIBLE SUSPECTS.
I WAS HOPING YOU COULD CHECK THEIR VOICES ONE LAST TIME...
YOU DON'T NEED ME!
I ALREADY TOLD YOU I DIDN'T RECOGNIZE EITHER VOICE.
OR DO YOU THINK I'M LYING?
NO... I AM.
WHAT ?!

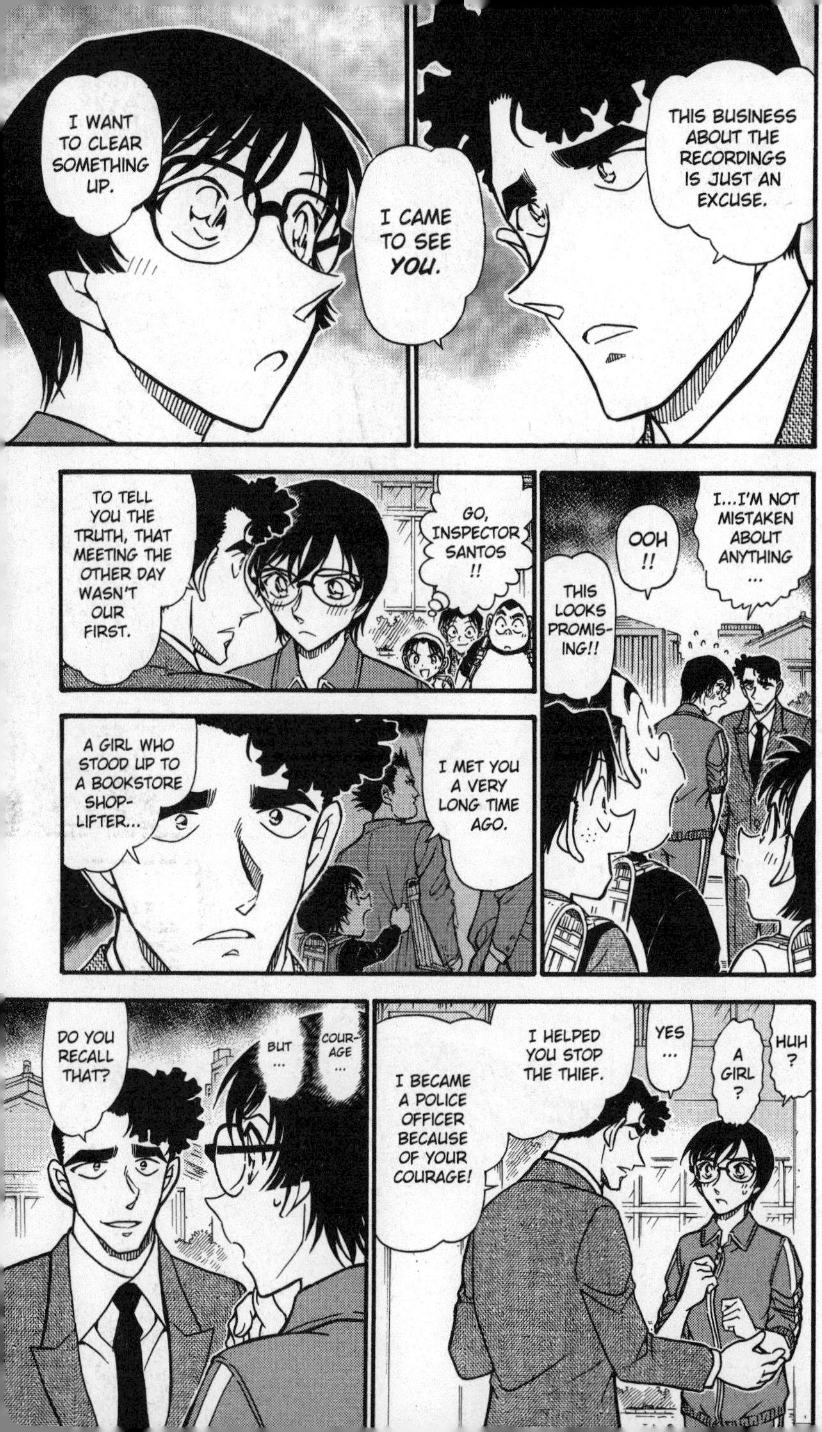
THIS BUSINESS ABOUT THE RECORDINGS IS JUST AN EXCUSE.
I CAME TO SEE *YOU*.
I WANT TO CLEAR SOMETHING UP.
I...I'M NOT MISTAKEN ABOUT ANYTHING...
OOH!!
THIS LOOKS PROMISING!!
GO, INSPECTOR SANTOS!!
TO TELL YOU THE TRUTH, THAT MEETING THE OTHER DAY WASN'T OUR FIRST.
I MET YOU A VERY LONG TIME AGO.
A GIRL WHO STOOD UP TO A BOOKSTORE SHOP-LIFTER...
HUH?
A GIRL?
YES...
I HELPED YOU STOP THE THIEF.
I BECAME A POLICE OFFICER BECAUSE OF YOUR COURAGE!
COURAGE...
BUT...
DO YOU RECALL THAT?

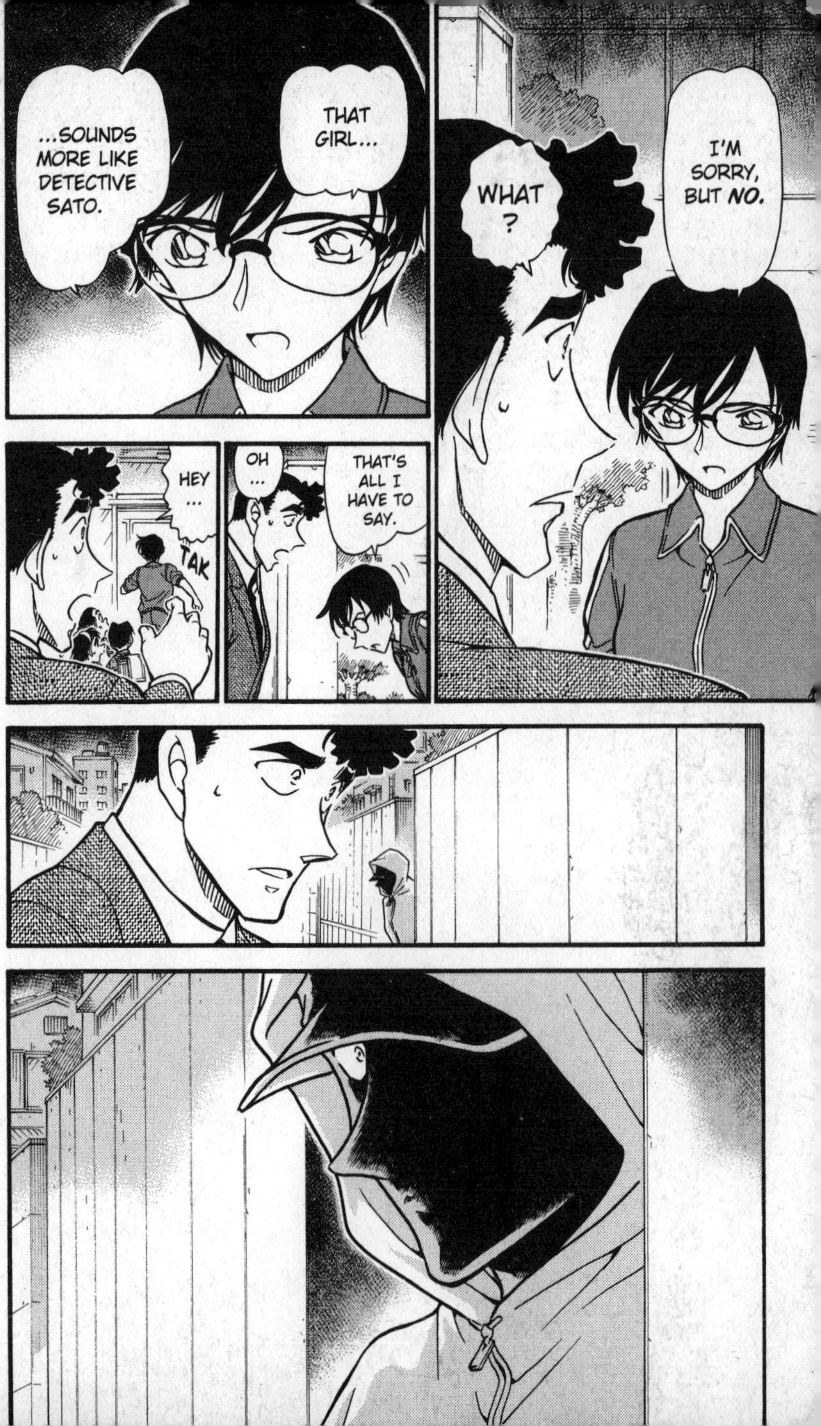
I'M SORRY, BUT NO.
WHAT?
THAT GIRL...
...SOUNDS MORE LIKE DETECTIVE SATO.
THAT'S ALL I HAVE TO SAY.
OH ...
HEY ...
TAK

Hello, Aoyama here.

2009 was the year of baseball! It started with Samurai Japan winning the 2nd World Baseball Classic tournament, followed by Ichiro setting up a record 200 hits for seven consecutive years and, last but not least, Matsui being chosen as MVP in the World Series!
It was truly the year when Japan proved its power in the world of baseball. (Plus my team, the Yomiuri Giants, won the Japan Series.♥) So this year I want to see Japanese soccer show its strength!

Gosho Aoyama's Mystery Library

67

KANKI IBARAGI

The denizens of the underground who can't rely on the police or government have only one sleuth they can turn to: Kanki Ibaragi, the outlaw detective! An obese man with unkempt hair, a bad leg and a crescent-shaped scar on his cheek, he lives in a shabby apartment in a backstreet in downtown Shinjuku. He's an unlicensed doctor who chugs *shochu* liquor. But when a mystery arises, he becomes an incredible sleuth who leaves the police in the dust. He uses his abundant knowledge of medicine and countless other subjects, as well as his insight into human nature, to solve the strangest cases. Deep down, he's a compassionate man who sides with the weak. At times he even lets a criminal escape.

The author, Futaro Yamada, is famous for historical fantasy novels like *Iga Ninpocho* and *Makai Tensho*. I'd like to work on something similar if I get the chance. Wait...I already drew a manga like that, *Yaiba*, before I started *Case Closed*. Heh...

I recommend *Tridecagonal Relationship*.

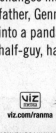

MAGI
The labyrinth of magic

Story & Art by
SHINOBU OHTAKA

A **fantasy adventure** inspired by
One Thousand and One Nights

Deep within the deserts lie the mysterious Dungeons, vast stores of riches there for the taking by anyone lucky enough to find them and brave enough to venture into the depths from where few have ever returned. Plucky young adventurer **Aladdin** means to find the Dungeons and their riches, but Aladdin may be just as mysterious as the treasures he seeks.